REBEL
WITH A CAUSE

REBEL
WITH A CAUSE

The Autobiography of

H. J. Eysenck, Ph.D., D.Sc.
Professor Emeritus, University of London

W H ALLEN

Set in Palatino by Phoenix Photosetting
Printed and bound in Great Britain by
Mackays of Chatham PLC, Chatham, Kent

for the Publishers, W.H. Allen & Co. Plc
Sekforde House, 175–179 St. John Street, London EC1V 4LL

ISBN 1–85227–162–0

PICTURE CREDITS

Sir Aubrey Lewis: reproduced by permission of Professor G.F.M. Russell, who received the picture from Professor M. Carstairs.

Professor Eysenck 'under attack at the London School of Economics': Express Newspapers plc.

Daily Express cartoon by Osbert Lancaster on page 217: John Murray (Publishers) Ltd.

For Sybil – whom else?

How many loved your moments of glad grace,
And loved your beauty with love false or true;
But one man loved the pilgrim soul in you,
And loved the sorrows of your changing face.

W. B. Yeats

CONTENTS

INTRODUCTION

My business is to teach my aspirations to conform
themselves to fact, not to try and make facts
harmonize with my aspirations.

T. H. Huxley.

Writing an autobiography is a serious undertaking; in offering the
history of your own life to the public, you are making implicit
assumptions about the importance of your existence, and giving
hostages to fortune, by opening your heart. Why do people write
autobiographies? Some do it because they have had important
adventures – they have conquered Mount Everest, reached the South
Pole, or pushed a peanut along the road, using nothing but their nose.
   Some have such refined sensibilities that they feel they must
communicate these refinements to those unfortunates who lack such
sensibility. Others can make even the *Diary of a Nobody* interesting by the
quality of their writing. Others yet feel that an *Apologia pro Vita Sua* may
be required in order to put the record straight. My own reasons are rather
more humble. Having no great explorations or other deeds of derring-do
to report, lacking the requisite aesthetic sensibilities to make my life a
work of art, and equally lacking the gift of the born writer to make
interesting anything he touches, I decided that a simple and truthful
account of the life of a supposedly well-known scientist might be of some
interest in throwing light on a number of puzzling psychological and
sociological questions. How does a scientist decide on the particular
discipline he wants to work in? What leads him to study one topic rather
than another? What are the most appropriate work habits that lead to
success rather than failure? How dependent is a scientist's reputation on
the *Zeitgeist*? How are new and original ideas received, and is there any
advice that can be given to scientists who wish to suggest new ways of
doing things without incurring the enmity of their colleagues? To what
extent does a scientist's life history impinge on his work, direct it in
certain ways rather than others, and determine what he shall and shall

[1]

not do – these and other questions will be dealt with in this book.

However, as P. M. Kendall points out in his *The Art of Biography*, even the most comprehensive and candid autobiographical works present serious problems to the historian who uses them as primary sources.

> Paradoxically, though the autobiographer enjoys a far more intimate knowledge of his subject than the biographer, he usually produces a life that is neither so rounded, so complete, nor so close to the actual life as a biographer's. Both aim at recapturing a person in his journey through time, but the biographer recreates a life out of evidences, whereas the autobiographer recreates it out of memory – and memory, unlike paper remains, is plastic, is itself created. The autobiography gives us a special truth: the life reshaped by recollections, with all of the recollection's conscious and unconscious omissions, distortions and illusions. Autobiography is not a true picture of a life; it is a true picture of what, at one moment of the life, the subject wishes, and is impelled, to reveal of that life. For this reason, of all the materials available to the biographer, autobiographical writings are the most dangerous, the most difficult, and the most exciting to handle.

The reader is warned!

I have tried to substantiate what might otherwise be subjective evaluations. I have quoted published and unpublished material from accounts written by former students and post-doctoral fellows. I have quoted figures from the Citation Index, which lists carefully all the times one's work has been cited by fellow scientists, to objectify what I perceived to be my own status, that of my department, and of the journals I started and edited in the general world of international psychology. I have quoted critics and enemies verbatim, to give them a chance to say what they had to say. Altogether, I think I probably have a more objective estimate of my own contribution than many scientists, if only because I could never consider it all that important. As a convinced Marxist, I applied a paraphrased version of Groucho's famous saying to myself: 'I could never take a scientific discipline seriously which would have me as a prominent figure!'

Somerset Maugham once observed that there wasn't a human being alive who wouldn't die of embarrassment if every detail of his private life was held up for public examination. True, but of course it is only some people whose private life – or sexual behaviour – is really relevant to their autobiography. I do not fall into that category. By Kinsey's standards, my life has been extremely average; nothing I have to say would bring a blush to the face of an octogenarian spinster in Bournemouth! I did, however, manage to marry for love, and remain in that state for some forty years now – a boring tale perhaps, but there is a lot to be said for such a state!

Though I have tried to be as accurate as possible, there may be some inaccuracies. Where records are missing, I have done the best I could to make my guesses reasonably close to the facts. Occasionally I have purposely changed situations, occasions and people from one year to another in order to preserve anonymity; in no case does this in any way alter the relevance of the narrative.

Writing an autobiography is a novel discipline for me, and while I enjoyed it, I also noted a number of problems. Modesty is one. We like our heroes to be modest, and we applaud John Stuart Mill, for instance, for saying at the beginning of his autobiography that he was not particularly bright, and owed it all to the teaching of his father. Modest, yes, but obviously nonsensical – we now know that genetic factors are primarily important in deciding a person's intelligence, and that Mill's father was lucky to have had a son whose genes made him receptive to such teaching as he received. A modern psychologist cannot adopt modest disclaimers of this kind; he is expected to tell the truth, as he sees it, and that may lead to claims and statements which appear immodest. Anyway, as Oscar Wilde said: 'Modesty is the worst kind of vanity.'

To return to the problems presented to the author of an autobiography. Another problem was predicted for me many years ago when I met Gordon Allport, the patron saint of psychologists interested in personality. He had transplanted the Heidegger and Windelband doctrine of idiographic study of personality (to wit, that there are no general laws or rules characterizing different personalities) to contrast it with the more usual statistical analysis of group data known as nomothetic personality study. He advocated a methodology which I had several times criticized as unscientific and useless. Allport was very kind and remarkably patient with my criticisms, and I still remember him telling me, at the end of our discussion: 'Eysenck, one day you will write your autobiography, and you will then see how right I was!' I had not considered such a possibility then, and I was unwilling to acknowledge his wisdom, but indeed he was right – in writing one's autobiography, one inevitably has to take the idiographic path of trying to see regularities in one's own life, look for behaviour patterns that repeat themselves, and try to discover variables that are important for oneself, even though they might not be of general interest.

Psychologists labour under another, rather severe handicap in writing an autobiography. Most people expect psychologists to have exceptional insight into their inner life, their emotions, motivations, and feelings. Some play up to this expectation, and claim insights for which there is no scientific justification whatever. My knowledge of psychology does not enable me to discover what is hidden in the depth of my soul – if indeed I should be found to have one! I will not try to psychologize and psychoanalyse myself or the people who will put in an appearance in the course of this book; where I try to make guesses about their motivation, these should be clearly understood to be guesses, no better because they are coming from a psychologist.

It will be seen that I have often had recourse to quotations. Emerson in his *Journals* said that he hated quotations; 'tell me what you know,' he urged. But if Montesquieu or Oscar Wilde, Lichtenberg or Montaigne said it so much better, it would be selfish and arrogant to put before the reader my own homespun bits of wisdom, and prevent him from enjoying the mature expressions of the masters. 'A fine quotation is a diamond on the finger of a man of wit, and a pebble in the hand of a fool.' Who said that? You will not find it in the *Oxford Dictionary of Quotations*, but I certainly could not myself have said it as elegantly.

So much for the prologomena. I have never pulled my punches, and I will not do so here. When I found a theory, an experiment, or a method of treatment, floccinaucinihilipilificationistic, I have always said so, and I will not depart from that habit. It does not make for popularity, but I think the scientist owes the public one thing above all, and that is honesty in telling the truth as he sees it. That I shall try to do; whether the truth is even approximately as I see it is of course another matter; that readers will have to judge for themselves. Many readers will already know that in many ways I am a rebel – this book will make it clear why I think I have a cause.

CHAPTER 1

I was Born in Interesting Times

Youth, what man's age is like to be doth show.
We may our ends by our beginnings know.

Sir John Denham

The Chinese are reputed to have a saying: 'Let me be born in uninteresting times.' I was not that lucky. I was born on 4 March 1916, in Berlin, in the middle of the First World War, lived through defeat in that war, inflation, unemployment, the Hitler regime, exile, the Second World War, and a variety of other events which no one could call 'uninteresting'. I was certainly lucky to survive all this; most of my class-mates at school died, or were severely injured, in Hitler's War.

I almost didn't make it. In his speech at the Drill Hall in Cambridge, on 9 December 1918, Sir Eric Geddes vowed: 'We will get everything out of her [Germany] that you can squeeze out of a lemon and a little bit more . . . I will squeeze her until you can hear the pips squeak.' I was one of the pips mentioned in this most Christian diatribe. In the armistice that followed the war, when the Allies continued to blockade Germany, I almost died of starvation. Having been blessed with a sound constitution, and a strong body, I managed to survive, but it was touch and go.

For reasons that will become obvious, I did not know my parents very well, but before they died they let me have official documents and brief written histories of their lives. I shall supplement them, where necessary, by my own experiences and memories.

My mother was born towards the end of the nineteenth century in Königshütte, a small town in Silesia; this is now Polish territory, and has been renamed Chorzew. Silesia had been made part of Prussia by Frederick the Great in the Seven Years War, and like the rest of Prussia

[5]

was fervently Protestant in its religion. Ruth Werner, my mother, although not very religious, was brought up in that faith. Her father was a doctor who was called to work in a hospital in Berlin when she was still · a little girl; he died of tuberculosis in his early thirties.

My mother was determined to study law, and I am sure she would have done exceptionally well as a lawyer because of her high intelligence, and her tremendous efficiency in all things practical. However, at that time it was almost impossible for women to study law, and the early death of her father left the family with very little income. She had always been exceptionally good-looking, and when she was fifteen years old a photographer took some excellent pictures of her which he thought might help her to get into films. My grandmother decided that she should obtain some serious training, and she went to the Rheinhardtschule, at the time probably the best training institution for actors and actresses in the country. My mother's first engagement was in Göttingen, where she fell in love with my father, also an actor, and married him. I was born a short time afterwards.

The marriage was not destined to last long. Working in different towns, my parents were hardly ever together, and after my birth my mother spent two years in Berlin looking after me while my father toured Germany, finally taking part in the war effort, leaving her destitute. My mother had no choice but to go back to the stage, and she, my grandmother and myself travelled all over Germany, going from one theatre to another. Finally my mother was offered roles in films, becoming a starlet and then a proper star with 'Bavaria' in Munich, and then with 'Terra Films' in Berlin in the twenties. My grandmother and I lived for five years in an old castle in Lichterfelde, a suburb of Berlin; it had a wonderful old park, and my first memories are of playing there, and living the life of Riley. In the holidays mother, grandmother and I would travel to the Baltic in the summer and to the Harz Mountains in the winter. It was at this time, too, that I became an actor – Germany's answer to Shirley Temple! I played my mother's son in a film in which she was divorcing her husband, and I brought them together again, although how I managed this I don't know – I was not allowed to see the film, which was for adults only. I do remember trundling my hoop through the Tiergarten, with the cameras turning and bypassers staring. My father was later on to press for me to enter the acting profession, but my mother firmly opposed it. But I never had any desire to act so the point did not really arise.

As my mother became more successful she assumed the name of Helga Molander for her screen roles and made some forty films. Most of these were of course silent, but I saw her in one or two speaking parts at the end of her career.

[6]

When the time came for me to enter school, my grandmother and I moved to a flat in West Berlin, not far from the Kurfürstendamm, in the Kaiserallee (now the Bundesallee). My mother says that I was '*Ein ausgezeichneter Schüler*', i.e., an outstanding pupil, but I have no memory of this. She also says, '*Er war ein bildhübsches Kind gewesen, mit langen blonden Locken.*' Whether I really was a beautiful child, with long blond locks, I cannot say; she also says that I was good-looking even in later years. She adds, rather unkindly: 'He seemed to know that, too. Uncalled-for modesty was never a fault of his.'

What can I say about my mother? She was exceptionally beautiful, highly intelligent, and fascinating to every male who came near her. I don't think she was a natural actress, but her combination of beauty and intelligence made up for what nature had failed to give her in talent. She certainly became well known enough to be called a star, although not an international one – at that time no German actor or actress managed to become known outside the confines of the homeland.

I don't think nature intended her to be a mother. I saw very little of her, except occasionally on holidays, and she never managed to treat me as a child, or show much interest in what I was doing. Conversation with her was always on strictly adult lines. She would talk to me about the theatre, plays, literature and poetry, and cultural topics of that kind, in self-defence I started reading through all the assorted German classics she kept in her library in our flat, and being a fast reader with a retentive memory, I was soon at home in this cultured atmosphere, and could hold my own in conversations. Indeed, I became genuinely interested in German literature, so perhaps her method of upbringing was not entirely mistaken.

My mother thought it important to be socially competent, and encouraged me to take up tennis, dancing and bridge. She herself taught me tennis, being quite good at it herself, and bridge; and for a while I earned some pocket-money going to the Kaufhaus des Westens, a large department store, which had set aside part of its coffee room for customers who wanted to play bridge. These, in the main, were old ladies who followed the then predominant bidding system of Culbertson, which is very precise in telling you exactly what to bid for each hand. I went along with a good friend and tennis partner, and we devised a system of anti-Culbertson, making our bids in such a way as to confuse the opposition completely. This paid off, and we nearly always won, which, in monetary terms, was quite important considering the paltry pocket-money I received!

For dancing lessons I went to the renowned *Salon* run by a former world championship pair of dancers, and while I enjoyed it and was quite good at it, I could never get rid of the idea that dancing was somewhat effeminate. I recognized this notion as absurd even then, but could not get it out of my mind. I fell in love with a beautiful assistant who danced with us, but when I found out that she supplemented her income by standing around the Kurfürstendamm at night trying to attract customers, I was deeply shocked and depressed – no prig like a young prig! (I was told later that her father had run away with a younger woman and her mother was dying of cancer; she was the only source of income for the family. I was beginning to learn not to judge other people and their actions in terms of a cosseted middle-class youngster born, if not with a golden, at least with a silver spoon in his mouth.)

My mother did one other good deed when she enrolled me in a kind of sports academy run by Hans Dietrich, a well-proportioned and sportingly outstanding man, who promised to take pounds of fat off his customers and turn it all into muscle. I went there twice a week, at the age of twelve or thirteen, to tone up my system and benefited a great deal in health and stamina. Dietrich was particularly keen on work with medicine balls, those large, very heavy leather balls with which many athletes work out. We were always working in twos; in one exercise one of the partners would lie prone on his back, the other holding his ankles. The one on his back would have his arms outstretched behind his head, holding the medicine ball; he would then convulsively engage the muscles of his stomach to raise himself up and throw the medicine ball as hard as he could at his partner who would release his ankles and catch the ball. This is hell on one's stomach muscles, and I remember slinking home on many an evening hardly able to walk. However, the next time somebody hits you in the stomach you are much better able to ride the blow!

Another favourite exercise was having two people standing a few feet away on either side of a line drawn on the floor with chalk. One would throw the ball as hard as he could, and the other would have to catch it and throw it back. Gradually the stronger would drive the other one away from the line, and against the wall; by the time he touched the wall, he had lost. There is a great deal more to throwing a medicine ball very hard than having strong muscles; just as a blow in boxing starts from the soles of the feet, and is really produced like a screwlike turning motion of the whole body, so is throwing of the medicine ball powered by the whole body. I eventually became quite good at this, and finally competed with Dietrich himself in demonstrations of how this should be done, although I must admit I never beat him. I mention these rather unimportant points because later in life I was quite unexpectedly to be involved again in a much more serious duel involving medicine balls – but of that more anon.

When my mother became a star for the Terra Film Company she soon became attracted by the best-known producer and director there, Dr Max Glass. They fell in love and lived together while his Catholic first wife refused him a divorce. When she died they married and lived happily together until his death some fifteen years before hers (she died at the age of ninety-four). While my grandmother and I lived in the flat in the Kaiserallee, Dr Glass and my mother lived in a large and opulent flat in the Uhlandstrasse also quite close to the Kurfürstendamm. He was a fascinating man, ugly but brilliant. He was short, fat and bald, but extremely vital. In his presence it was difficult to get a word in edgeways; he was constantly talking, but his conversation was so interesting, full of wit, humour, and novel ideas, that one could only listen in fascination. He was a typical middle-European Jew, or at least he was the way one imagines such a person to be. Born in Hungary, he had been a Professor of Aesthetics at the Sorbonne in Paris, had become rich as a director and then producer of films, had acquired a large estate near Linz, in Austria (on the banks of the Danube), had written novels, plays and books on politics, and seemed to know everybody who was anybody in the cultural life of Berlin. He could almost have served as a prototype of the extravert, and I liked him very much indeed.

Fortunately he returned that liking, for having been disappointed in his own two sons, he found in my somewhat introverted personality something that appealed to him, and we always got along famously. This of course made my mother happy. The fact that he was Jewish did not matter to me in the slightest, but when Hitler came to power it was necessary, inevitably, for him, and my mother, to emigrate to Paris.

But this is to anticipate events. I have said enough about my mother; how about my father? I have learned far more about the ancestry of Anton Eduard Eysenck, born on 28 March 1889 in Bergisch–Gladebach, and his ancestors, including his great-grandparents, than either I or the reader would ever wish to know. The reason of course is that when Hitler came to power my father, like most other Germans, had to prove his 'Aryan' ancestry, and accordingly he had this traced by some expert genealogist.

My father told me that in the course of the inquiries concerning his ancestry, it had been discovered that the family originated on the younger branch of a feudal baron who lived in a castle on the Rhine, hence Eisen-eck, or iron corner; the ending -eck also denotes a castle. The family then migrated down the Rhine, to Holland and Belgium, where the 'i' was turned into a 'y'.

My father also used to misquote the famous German revolutionary song:

> Der Gott der Eisen wachsen liess,
> Der wollte keine Knechte!

(God, who let iron sprout from the soil,
Never wanted slaves to be!)

Only he changed 'Eisen' to 'Eysenck', to let the song say, in effect, that God who let Eysenck grow wanted no slaves. In view of the fact that he later on joined the Nazi Party, I took the assertion with a good deal of salt!

My father's family was Catholic. They all lived in the Rhineland, and had solidly bourgeois occupations. One of my grandfathers was the owner of a restaurant, another a Customs Officer, and most of my other relatives were in business. Where my mother was the only child, my father was the youngest of three, having one brother (Ernst) and one sister (Elly). Like my mother, my father did not take religion very seriously, and I inherited this attitude. I could do nothing about having been christened in the Protestant faith, but when it came to being confirmed I had to be bribed by the gift of a bicycle to take part in the ceremony.

At my christening, I was given the name 'Hans Jürgen'. Does one's given name have any significance? In Plato's *Cratylus* Socrates argues that a man's name determines his nature – a rather odd notion that was later to inspire Sterne's *Tristram Shandy*. Hans Jürgen had the connotation of a simple, honest, none-too-bright youngster, reliable and trustworthy. Except for the bit about being none-too-bright, that was roughly how I saw myself – a large good-natured dog, always ready to be friendly, but possibly dangerous when kicked in the teeth. I was to receive many such kicks in the course of my life – but then I suppose most people do. Rebels are particularly exposed to such extremities, of course, and a rebel I was to become, more through force of circumstances than predilection.

I never had the slightest interest in religion, other than as a social and literary phenomenon. My grandmother, who brought me up, embraced the Catholic faith, and I know that it meant a great deal to her; it was to help her very much when, during the war, she was dragged off as a cripple to one of Hitler's Concentration Camps, where she died.

My disenchantment with the Christian religion began early on, when I found it impossible to reconcile the existence of evil with the omnipotence and essential goodness of God. St Augustine might get over this difficulty by saying: '*Credo quia impossibile!*' but I could see no sense in believing it because it was impossible. The Saint endeared himself to me when he said: '*Da mihi castitatem et continentiam, sed noli modo*', asking God to give him chastity and continency, but not quite yet. That seems a more reasonable and rational utterance than the one about belief.

The teacher who took us in religion tried to convince me that there was a common belief system underlying all the great religions, so I read the Koran, the Talmud, and some of the Buddhist and Hindi religious writings. I could see very little similarity between the Christian heaven, full of harp-playing angels, and the Mohammedan one, full of delicious Houris, out to fulfil the sexual needs of warriors fallen in the Jehad. Similarly, the proselytizing fervour of Catholics and Moslems alike contrasted strangely with its absence among Jews, and the Nirvana concept of the Buddhists seemed to me to be quite different from the ideals favoured by the other religions. My teacher was quite cross when I presented these arguments to him; typically he had not read any religious writings outside the Christian tradition!

My father began his working life in the German Navy, but then became an actor; he used to play the juvenile lead, being tall and very good-looking. (Several years later he was chosen as 'The best looking man on the Baltic' in a competition, though perhaps not a very serious one. He was inordinately proud of this title.) He was a great womanizer, and carried on with this habit through two marriages, right into old age. (His second wife stayed with him to the end.) He also appeared in operetta, playing Ruritanian princes in beautiful uniforms, although his singing left much to be desired. Indeed, my mother too played in operetta; I recall seeing a picture of her as one of the three young maids from school in *The Mikado*. Her voice, too, was tolerable but nothing to be remembered. Mine, unfortunately, was unbelievably bad, something I always regretted but could do nothing about.

As he became older, my father switched over to being a Conferencier, a kind of profession that does not really exist in England or the United States. A Conferencier is the anchor man in the large cabarets that used to be so popular in all the bigger towns in Germany. He introduces the acts, holds the show together, and has his own act, in which he tells jokes and stories, comments on politics and cultural affairs, and generally endeavours to be witty, clever and amusing. Nearly all the successful Conferenciers in Germany, at the time of the Weimar Republic, were Jewish. My father attributed this to the fact that most of the owners of cabarets were Jewish too, and favoured their own; he did not consider the alternative hypothesis that Jews are cleverer and wittier than non-Jews, an alternative for which there is much to be said. Perhaps both hypotheses are true, and may serve to complement each other.

In spite of the competition, my father was very successful, travelling from one month's engagement to another in his little Freia, the first car he ever owned, and later on in a larger but still pretty primitive Chevrolet. Finally he graduated to a Horch, an opulent and gigantic car which carried him around Germany in great style. As befits a Conferencier, he was a wonderful raconteur; he could tell stories, describe a play or a film, or the contents of a book so vividly that when you came across the real thing you were disappointed – his stories were so much better!

When Hitler came to power all the Jewish Conferenciers, who had been a thorn in the side of the Nazis because of their political comments, were dismissed, while my father, who had been pretty non-political in his talks, became even more firmly established. Goering apparently liked his act, and often invited my father to join his table. My own hatred of the Nazis had led me by this time to leave Germany, and my father's hobnobbing with these people did nothing to increase my love for him.

Typical perhaps of my father's method of upbringing is the occasion when he bought me a bicycle, and promised to teach me how to ride it. He took me to the top of a hill, told me that I had to sit on the saddle and pump the pedals and make the wheels go round. He then went off to release some balloons and shoot them down with the rifle he still had from the war, leaving me to learn how to ride all by myself. I got on it, started to pedal, and promptly fell off. But after an hour, and many similar discomfitures, I managed to wobble along. A good training in independence, but not perhaps the behaviour of a loving father.

Like my mother, he too did not know how to communicate with children, and when he talked to me it was about politics, which he was interested in, but did not take part in. As in the case of my mother, I had to fortify myself for these discussions, and I took to reading magazines such as the *Weltbühne* in its famous red cover and the *Tagebuch* in its equally famous green. These were similar to the *New Statesman* in its heyday under Kingsley Martin in England, or the *New Masses* in the United States; half political, half literary and cultural. Politically, the magazines were to the left of the SDP (the social-democrat party which was in power most of the time in the Weimar Republic), though definitely not Communist. Both later on favoured a united front against the Nazi menace, but the 'Eiserne Front' arrived too late to save Germany.

These two journals had a high literary quality, and my great hero was Kurt Tucholsky, whose writings I still admire. In so far as I have ever tried to imitate anybody's style, it was his – simple, ironic, witty, and always much to the point. He fled to Sweden after Hitler came to power, and finally committed suicide.

At that time I had an almost photographic memory, so by reading these two journals every week, I soon managed to argue successfully with my father, rather to his annoyance. All this was good practice for later on, when I had to argue with the many Nazi boys in my school, and with the Communists outside it. I think I rather overdid things; I began to feel personally responsible for all the evils of this world, wherever they might appear, and this is not a reasonable attitude to have, although it is fairly typical of young and idealistic people.

Much as I agreed with Tucholsky and the other writers in these two journals, I had been too much in contact with working-class people to share their almost pathetic belief in the virtues, the clear-sighted revolutionary attitude, and the political earnestness of the working class. He fell victim to what Paul Johnson has called: 'The great progressive fallacy: that certain categories of people are intrinsically moral, merely by virtue of their predicament.' The working classes of Germany had been treated abominably; this predicament, however, did not teach them political sagacity, moral values and Marxist zeal, but drove them straight into the arms of the Nazi Party! The fact that I, a schoolboy of fourteen, could see this, while these giant intellects, with all their knowledge and reading, could not, upset me greatly. This paradox still troubles me today.

When I was nine, my father remarried. His second wife, Tilly, was part of a dance group in a cabaret in which he appeared as a Conferencier; she was a pretty young girl, devoted to him, and travelled all over Germany with him, often acting with him on stage. I went by train to Munich to meet her; I remember her surprise at how tall I was – he had told her his son was just a little boy. This visit saw my introduction to opera – Wagner's *Flying Dutchman*, which bored me stiff, and began a life-long dislike of Wagnerian music. It also saw my introduction to sex. My father had borrowed the flat of a friend, who was away from Munich, and I was told to sleep on the sofa in the library. When I went to bed I decided to read for an hour or two, and the book that attracted my attention, lying open on the table, was Van der Velde's book on sex, one of the earliest of the many expositions of how to do it. I had always had my suspicions of adults, but this, I thought, really showed them up. I began to get amused when I read about cunnilingus, I guffawed when I read about fellatio, but when I got to soixante-neuf I laughed so much I fell out of bed! My father heard the noise, came in, tucked me up again and took the book away, but the damage was done. I could never take adults seriously again.

My feelings about Van der Velde's disclosures anticipated my later enjoyment of Lord Chesterfield's words about sexual intercourse: 'The pleasure is momentary, the position ridiculous and the expense damnable.' Perhaps he underrated the pleasure, not having read Van der Velde, and the expense can certainly be reduced by careful management. However, he was right about the ridiculous position, and this alone forever condemns hard-core pornography to be more ridiculous than exciting.

Like most parents, mine were not much help in sexual matters. My mother never mentioned such things. My father only gave advice on one occasion when he came to me rather nervously and said: 'Er . . . er, Hans Jürgen, I meant to tell you . . . er . . . when you . . . er . . . I mean . . . you don't have to marry the girl, you know.' This was the sum total of parental instruction in the practice and ethics of sexual behaviour. I learned a great deal more from Ilsemarie, my first girl-friend, than from my parents.

Ilsemarie was an innocent young girl, happy, extraverted and without any hangups. She was as innocent as I was, and our first kiss in the street outside the block of flats where she lived was a novelty for both of us. (I was fourteen at the time.) I remember walking home as if in a dream, my feet hardly touching the ground. Sweet innocence – absurd and ridiculous, but also with a charm of its own. After I left Germany Ilsemarie was to get married, have many children, including a pair of twins. Although we haven't met since then we still write to each other occasionally.

Even before meeting Ilsemarie, I had started smoking. When I told my grandmother I was going to buy some cigarettes, I fully expected her to forbid it, adding the stolen fruit thrill to the story. However, all she said was: 'If you like it, do it by all means.' I did try it, but didn't like it; I only smoked very occasionally, mostly to impress the girls. It was only during the war that I started smoking more seriously; in line with the theories I was to develop much later, I smoked in response to the stress of German bombing, and to relieve the boredom of endless nights spent firewatching. In 1955, when I noticed that smoking affected my stamina at tennis and other sports, I decided that sport was more important to me than smoking, threw away the pack and have never smoked another cigarette since. It was easy; I suffered no more stress, and I never got bored, so there was no need for cigarettes. Occasionally even now I feel like having a smoke, particularly after meals, but no thanks – once bitten, twice shy.

I have said a good deal about my father and my mother, but of course for me personally my grandmother was much more important, as it was she who was with me all the time, and who brought me up. She was one of these people who are born loving, kind and helpful; she never had a malicious thought in her mind, and surely deserved a better fate than the one the God she so firmly believed in dished out to her. She had been a beautiful and artistically gifted girl, musical and with an excellent voice. She attracted the attention of Max Rheinhardt, the great producer, and would probably have been a greater star than either of my parents but she fell and broke her leg. This was wrongly set, and she became a cripple; ever since I knew her she had to wear specially built-up shoes and had great trouble in walking. This was the first blow that fate dealt to her; her husband's early death was the second.

The third trouble was to have a daughter and a son-in-law who were both extremely egocentric and mean with money. Although my grandmother had the full responsibility of looking after me for nearly all my young life, and although both my parents were earning very good money, they only gave her a pittance, and she constantly had to worry about money.

If my parents were mean towards my grandmother, I felt they were equally mean towards me. I received very little pocket-money, and they seldom agreed to pay for what I considered reasonable expenses. When I was talent-spotted for the Blau-Weiss Tennis Club in the Grünewald, I was admitted without having to pay any fees, and balls were supplied free. However, I only had one racket, and often had difficulties in paying to have the strings repaired. When the Club had a large swimming-pool built, they charged for its use. I was keen to have a chance to use it, but my parents refused to pay the small amount necessary. All the other boys and girls in the youth section managed to persuade their parents to cough up; I was the only one who never used it. This has always rankled. When I won a national Club tournament, I had the opportunity to play in the German Junior Championships, in Hamburg, but my parents wouldn't pay for the trip. However, all this meanness had one positive side-effect: I knew that all the girls I was friendly with loved me for myself! It couldn't have been the non-existing money that might have attracted them – I could just about manage to invite them occasionally to go to the cinema with me, or to go dancing at one of those places where you paid one mark for a drink, and could stay the whole evening.

People like my grandmother who are intrinsically good are difficult to describe, and may even appear boring – villains are so much more intriguing than saints. With all that, however, I don't think that saints make good parents, and my grandmother was no exception. She lacked any notion of discipline, and with my father and mother hardly ever present, I grew up without the socializing influence of a good home. I did more or less what I wanted, with no one and nothing to restrain me, and if I didn't turn out a completely bad penny this must argue strongly for the quality of the genes I inherited from my parents. The environment certainly did little to fashion and constrain me in any way whatsoever. This, too, was a cross my grandmother had to bear, and I regret nothing more in my life than the fact that she was never to know that this particular bad penny, who gave her so much trouble, was to turn out reasonably successful in the long run!

Having introduced my family, I must try to go back to my own early life, and remember what I can of the events that might be thought in some way to typify my character.

The first conscious memory I have, other than my trundling my hoop in the Tiergarten when I was being filmed, is of a meeting with Dr Hugo Eckner, who at the time was a very famous and popular man, being the Commandant of the *Graf Zeppelin*, the great air ship that was becoming a symbol of national hopes and aspirations. I was five or six years old at the time, on holiday with my grandmother in Swinemünde, a well-known holiday resort on the Baltic, where we went quite often. There was a sandcastle competition in which I took part, and which Dr Eckner had been asked to judge. He walked around, talking to the various children, and finally came to my sandcastle – which, alas, was at best mediocre. However, he got talking to me, very animatedly, until he was prised away by his retinue. Before he left he said to my grandmother: 'This boy will one day be a great scientist.' I don't myself know what to make of this story. It is true, for although I might have misremembered it, my grandmother told me often enough about it, as did one or two other people who were there at the time. I can't say that I took it seriously at any stage, but it is an odd little story, and I like to think that Dr Eckner may have had some slight degree of precognition.

The next event occurred when I was still in primary school, so I must have been about eight years old. We had a new music teacher wished upon us, a Herr Meier, a fat and florid man who took himself very seriously. As an introduction, he wanted each of us to sing for him, and all the other pupils obliged happily. When it came to my turn, I stood up and said, very politely, that unfortunately I had no singing voice at all, and there would be no point in my trying to sing. He shouted that everyone could sing, and that I would be no exception, so would I please do as he said. I shrugged my shoulders and started to do the best I could, which of course was pretty awful. He stopped me very soon, shouting that I was obviously trying to take the mickey, and that he would tolerate no such insolence. He ordered me to go up to the dais where he was sitting, grabbed my right hand with his left, and threatened to hit me with the ruler he had in his right hand. When he brought it down I drew back my hand, and he hit the table, which seemed to infuriate him even more. He again grabbed my hand, holding it very tight, and lifted the ruler, to hit my hand really hard.

Without thinking I leaned forward and sank my teeth into the fleshy part of his hand, underneath the thumb. I have always been tall and strong, and I bit him very hard indeed. He dropped the ruler, blanched (I have never seen anybody's face go so white so quickly) and tried to withdraw his hand. I hung on like a bull terrier, and the class of course started erupting in a welter of shouts, screams and jumpings up and down. At that moment the headmaster was walking past, and, intrigued by the noise, he opened the door and imperiously asked what was going on. He must have been surprised by the sight that met his eyes – one of his teachers standing up on the dais, with a small boy dangling from his right hand, and the class in an uproar. He immediately came and tried to dislodge me, but without much success. Finally, with the help of several colleagues, poor Mr Meier was released and taken home in a taxi. He was away for a fortnight, and never returned to this particular class.

The headmaster clearly did not know what to do with me. Insubordination in the young was clearly not to be tolerated in the Prussian state, but on the other hand Mr Meier had violated the law in the Weimar constitution which forbade teachers to hit pupils. In the end, and rather wisely, he decided to do nothing, but while I was at primary school the children always referred to me as the boy who bit his teacher.

In many ways what I did then was prognostic of what I was to do later on, though in rather less physical fashion. You cannot let people get away with wrongdoing just because they are strong and powerful; whatever the cost, you have to stand up for yourself. It was not, alas, the kind of belief that would inspire the Weimar Republic to resist Hitler.

Another early incident I recall occurred somewhat later, during a biology lesson. The teacher was going to cut up a living frog, for no very obvious purpose – we could learn all we wanted to know about the inside of frogs from books. I demurred, saying this was barbarous, and I wanted no part of it. The teacher insisted, but finally allowed me to leave the room and express my disapproval that way. I know that vivisection is occasionally a necessary evil in medical research, but I also think that it is often used quite unnecessarily. Altogether I am soft-hearted to a degree that is perhaps excessive – I would run a mile to avoid seeing a film, or a play about Joan of Arc, because I cannot tolerate the final burning at the stake of the Maid of Orleans, and similarly I have avoided seeing *King Lear* because of the scene where Gloucester's eyes are put out. *Tosca* is bad enough, even though the torture scene is off-stage. My mind is too active and empathic in imagining the suffering of these people; in a similar vein I cannot tolerate seeing films, or reading books of the Nazi Concentration Camps, or the Russian Gulag.

I may have had some theatrical talent, because when I was about eight years old I won a major talent competition during one of our holidays in Swinemünde. My father had entered me for this competition, which required entrants to recite a poem; it was organized into age groups, and there was an overall prize for the best performer. I picked my own poem, a narrative about the German cruiser *Emden* which foundered during the First World War on the China coast in a typhoon. It is not a good poem in the literary sense, as I realize only too well now, but it had a strong nationalistic appeal, it portrayed a very eventful scene, and it ended on an elegiac strain which gave me a chance to vary the mode of presentation from loud to soft, from fast to slow.

My grandmother, who was very talented as a performer, undertook to train me, and I learned a great deal about presentation from her. I learned to vary the pitch of my voice in accordance with the content of the poetry; the value of pausing at the right moment and looking straight at the audience; how to make the rhyming scheme tell, without becoming too mechanical; to express bodily the emotions portrayed in the poem; and the value of stressing important words, without slurring over unimportant ones.

On the day I appeared dressed in a kind of sailor's uniform, as seemed appropriate to the spirit of the poem. The combination of boy, uniform and poem almost guaranteed a good reception in an audience that had only a few years before lost what to them was a patriotic war; the occasion reminded them of the heroism with which that war had been fought. When I finished there was a deathly silence, and then a wildly enthusiastic clapping and shouting. I won my section, and also the overall prize, against much older boys and girls, and I was asked to repeat the performance which I did, very proud of having won. I never forgot the tricks of the trade, and have always tried in my public lectures to embody an element of showmanship – a lecturer need not become less intellectual and scientific for also being entertaining!

This is about all I can recall before I entered secondary education at the Bismarck Gymnasium around 1925, where I spent several years. I was the youngest in the class, just as I had been the youngest in all the classes I went to later on. This can be a handicap, but I was well developed for my years, and always good at sport, so I could hold my own. The only exception was a big boy, who had failed to go up to a higher class several times because of his inability to learn; he must have been two or three years older than I was, and disliked me particularly, possibly because of the age difference, and possibly because I was rather bright and quick to learn. I had managed to avoid a fight with him several times, but one day I was swimming in the Halensee, a large lake at the top of the Kurfürstendamm where we used to go on hot days, when I saw him swimming towards me, his eyes gleaming with hatred. I couldn't get away, and when he got to me he pushed me down under the water, and kept me there. He might easily have drowned me, but I finally managed to grab him and use my knees to hit him hard in a most strategic place. He immediately let go of me, rolling up in a ball, and shouting fearsome oaths. I swam back to the shallow end, much relieved, and am glad to say that he treated me with more respect afterwards. He did, however, beat up one of the teachers, breaking his jaw, and was ignominiously thrown out of the school – in those far-off days beating up a teacher was still regarded as undesirable, and suitable for punishment.

I will spare the reader other instances of the kind of fighting that is so common in boys' schools, but it has to be mentioned at least once because there is a paradox involved, at least as far as I am concerned. With boys there is the firmly established principle of the pecking order, as definite as it is with chickens, monkeys and other animals. It is largely based on strength, fighting spirit and sporting ability, although intelligence may also play a part. From the beginning I felt I wanted to have nothing to do with this pecking order. It did not seem to me that fighting would ever settle who was right or wrong in a discussion, and I certainly did not believe that 'might is right'. I had no desire to fight anybody, to assert my superiority, or to lord it over the lower reaches of the pecking order.

Of course, life can be a misery for those who shun fighting, and literature gives many examples of boys who later became poets being driven almost to suicide by the cruelty of the 'alpha chickens' in their class. Thus I resolved very early that I would never seek out a fight, or force it on anyone weaker, but also that I would never shun one, and if forced into one would do my darnedest to win it.

Later, I would apply this principle to larger issues, such as peace and war. I was instinctively a pacifist, hating war and passionately believing in the peaceful settlement of all disputes. The utterly useless waste of lives during the First World War lay heavily on my mind, and I was certain that nothing could justify wars of that kind.

However, the advent of Hitler, self-chosen candidate for the 'alpha chicken' position in the world, changed all that. When there was only a choice between giving in to Hitler's insane ambitions, or standing up to him at the risk of war, I decided that pacifism was clearly the wrong policy. Thus I had to give up my cherished ideals, and agree with those like Churchill who demanded rearmament and argued for opposing dictators. It was a slow development, but it paralleled my attitude to classroom bullies.

To be successful in classroom politics, of course, you have to become pretty street-wise, and elaborate a series of tactics. Although I was big and strong, and was endowed by nature with long arms to keep my opponents away – and a really effective right hook to dissuade them from further argument – I realized from the beginning that there would always be someone who was stronger, a better fighter, and a more likely winner. Furthermore, I knew that however good you might be, you were helpless against a group of three or four boys out to get you. I managed to develop various tactics which served to overcome these difficulties, and in spite of the fact that I was almost the only non-Jewish boy in an almost entirely Nazi school who strongly and vocally dissented from this majority, I was never beaten up in my later schoolyears.

What are my tactics? The first of course is non-verbal communication – you must suggest by your bearing that you are not out for a fight, but if there is one, then your opponent, even if he might win, would have a Pyrrhic victory. This can be suggested by subtle ways of walking, holding yourself, looking at the other person – I didn't discover the psychology of non-verbal communication, but I certainly practised it at school.

Another important thing is to know how far you can go in verbal argument with a group of hostile boys around you. You have to watch carefully, be sensitive to their body language as well as to what they are saying, and be very careful to keep on the safe side of the line, and not to taunt them to such an extent that they feel duty bound to beat you up. But if you should cross that line, then another tactic becomes useful. You have got to shame the group into giving up the idea of a group attack; you must try to get them to choose their leader to engage in single combat, rather like David and Goliath. Better still, you can challenge one of them, whom you think you can beat, so that however reluctant, he feels obliged to take up the burden.

I elaborated these and many other tactics during my early years at school. Telling a story inevitably falsifies it, making the whole thing sound more rational than it was in actual fact. I did not reason out the tactics, or the whole notion of pecking order, pacifism, etc. in advance. I simply reacted in a way that came naturally to me, to a great variety of situations, and combined those reactions that turned out to be successful into a general strategy and attitude which in retrospect can be discussed rationally and analysed psychologically.

I should perhaps mention here that I had one other advantage in these battles – I was always good at sport. I was in the rowing team, in the handball team (handball in Germany is a game rather like football, but with the ball being passed from hand to hand; there is a large circle around each of the two goals which neither forwards nor defenders are allowed to enter, and the ball must be thrown at the goal from outside the circle); I played ice-hockey and field hockey; *Schlagball* (a rather rudimentary kind of baseball widely played in German schools); football, which of course on the Continent meant soccer; and indeed any game that had a ball in it. I was lucky in being born with the ability to hit, kick, throw, catch, bowl or field a ball – any ball, regardless of size or shape. Now it is a general principle that you don't beat up anyone who is an outstanding player in your team, and that helped a great deal in preventing aggression, however much I might annoy the others.

Even before I started to play football, I went regularly to watch games over the weekend. I supported Hertha B.S.C., the then (and now!) Berlin champions, and soon found out that I seemed to differ profoundly from all the other boys, in that I couldn't work up any degree of fanaticism for my chosen team. Where they called down the wrath of Jehovah on any unfortunate referee or linesman who penalized their chosen team, and attributed all sorts of unspeakable sexual delinquencies to him, doubting the details of his conception, and the moral habits of his parents, it seemed to me that the referee and the linesman were usually right in their judgement, and that if my team fouled the opposition, played badly, or generally misbehaved, then it was only reasonable to admit this. This attitude of relative objectivity was anathema to my friends, and they sadly shook their heads and decided that I was not a true follower of the Club. This attitude has persisted into old age. I have followed Chelsea, West Ham, Crystal Palace, and finally – at the insistence of my youngest son – Manchester United, but always without the emotional fervour and unqualified devotion that characterizes a true fan. After all, or so it seemed to me, facts are facts, and it's only a game.

It would be incorrect to pretend that I was a careful, mature, cautious youngster; if anything I was rather wild. On one occasion, for the sake of an example, I bet one of my cronies that I could go up to the roof of the gymnasium on the travelling rings and then jump off and land on my feet. Unfortunately some idiot had left some round iron bars lying about on the floor, and as it happened I jumped on to them, fell on my right arm and broke every available bone. The surgeon managed to set the ulna incorrectly, trapping a nerve, and had to break it again to set it right. This was the beginning of my distrust of all things medical.

Around the same time I almost lost my right eye. Some boys and I were playing in the street, shooting paper arrows at each other from rubber bands. One foolish boy used a metal staple, which hit me in the eye, the two sharp prongs embedded in it. The ophthalmologist managed to save the eye – just – but as I got older it weakened drastically, and after the age of sixty or so I was almost reduced to having only one useful eye. Spectacles strong enough to make my right eye functional would have to be so strong that the two images on the retina would not join. This has rather hampered my tennis in the last twenty years or so – with only one eye it is difficult to see the oncoming ball in the third dimension.

I have no illusion that in my youth I was a particularly nice person, or easy to get on with. However, those were wild times, and the meek certainly did not prosper. Political warfare was rife, and almost every day corpses of Nazis, Communists or even members of less extreme political parties were floating down the Spree. Even the innocent might get caught up in these quarrels; let me give an example.

I had been visiting my girl-friend Ilsemarie in her flat, and was just leaving when I was noticed by a group of young Communists drinking beer outside a pub near her house. I was wearing a brown *Affenjacke*, a short, military-style jacket which had no particular political significance. However, brown was the colour favoured by the SA, the brown-shirted storm-troopers, and Ilsemarie was known to be a Hitlermädchen; this was enough for these half-drunk yobbos to set up a hue and cry: 'There goes the Nazi!' I decided it might be wise to depart in the opposite direction, but about a dozen of the more athletic ones came running after me, and I thought that perhaps this was a good time to practise my 800-metres sprint. Being neither a smoker (except for the occasional cigarette) nor a drinker, and being in good physical shape, I easily managed to outrun this particular lot, but if they had caught me I might well have floated down the Spree the next day. It is this kind of insane politicization of everyday life which became more and more common in pre-Hitler days. If you didn't look out for yourself, no one else would, and the penalty might be severe.

There is another point. Having rejected the pecking order notion of society, it follows that I was always standing up to those who were in some sense above me, by virtue of strength, age or position; I simply couldn't snuggle under and pay obeisance to the powers that be. Mine was a non-conformist spirit, perhaps taking that attitude to an extreme that would normally not be justified.

There is also the other side of the coin. My position implied not only opposition to the strong, but also support for the weak. I have always had much sympathy for the underdog, and have tried to make it a practice to be particularly kind and helpful to those whom fate, society or accident have placed in a position of dependence. Again it should not be assumed that my attitude was the result of rational thinking; it just emerged quite naturally from the genetics of my personality.

As an example in the political field, I completely supported the workers and the principles of socialism in pre-Hitler Germany when power was almost completely on the side of the bosses, but I opposed the Trades Union supremacy of the 1970s which threatened to reduce Britain to a poverty-stricken Third World country because now power was on the workers' side, and the bosses were weak and ineffectual. This principle of limitation of power is I think a very important one politically, but it can be usefully extended to other fields, such as the relation between males and females.

My principle, I think, was sound; its application of course was never automatic, but needed careful thinking through. However that may be, certainly the Jews were powerless and persecuted, and this may have been part of the reason why so many of my friends have been among the Jews. At school this caused a certain amount of head-shaking, and I was called a 'white Jew', meaning the same as a 'nigger lover' in the Southern states of America during the early years of this century. I certainly found the notion of racism completely unacceptable, and argued against it vociferously whenever the occasion arose, extending my argument beyond the Jews to all the other groups hated by the Nazis – negroes, gipsies, and Japanese (these had not yet, as they were to later, become 'honorary Aryans').

One of the first and strongest social beliefs I acquired, apart from hatred for tyranny and the 'Führerprinzip' of Hitler, and a general belief in the aims, if not necessarily the methods, of Democratic Socialism, was a strong adherence to the principles of feminism, understanding this to mean the social and economic equality of women. I am not an advocate of the shrill lesbian overtones of some man-hating feminists, which seem to me counter-productive and fundamentally wrong, but rather the sane and rational feminism of John Stuart Mill, and his modern followers. The exploitation of women, both sexually and financially, was particularly obvious in the years of the Weimar Republic, and as my girl-friends were almost all working class, I heard a great deal about this exploitation from them and their friends. In addition, my father often took me to the cabarets where he performed, and there inevitably I met and talked to large numbers of 'hostesses', dancing girls and striptease artists, all of whom would have denied the appellation of *Hure* (whore) or *Nutte* (tart), but who were effectively prostitutes, though not always legally so designated. Their stories made a sad counterpoint to the self-satisfied tales of successful financial fraud and trickery of their often revoltingly fat *Freiern* (customers).

It is often said that anyone who isn't a socialist in his youth has no heart, and anyone who remains a socialist in his middle-age has no head. I think this slightly misrepresents the situation. The obvious injustices of any social system, including capitalism, are so transparent that they cry out for some form of readjustment, and the stress of socialism on social equality would seem to point in the right direction when one looks at the grotesque and obscene inequalities exemplified by a young girl selling her body to feed and educate her illegitimate baby, while some fantastically rich male spends tends of thousands of pounds or dollars on the throw of a couple of dice. The real problem that arises, once the aim is stated, is, of course, that of the means to be adopted in order to bring it about. It is here that many socialists and Communists advocate methods which would certainly not lead to the desired end of greater equality and higher standards of living, but rather to slavery and general poverty, as in the Soviet Union. As I grew older, I still agreed with the aims (or many of them) of socialists, but became more and more convinced that the means they advocated would be counter-productive.

Much the same may be said about feminism – no doubt many of the aims are completely justified, but the methods often used are not in the best interest of women themselves.

However that may be, in Germany, both pre- and post-Hitler, there was a strong attitude of male superiority, machismo, and *Kirche, Küche, und Kinder* for women. Church, kitchen and children as the appropriate sphere for women seemed unduly restrictive, but still infinitely preferable to male spheres restricted to war, politics and brothels! Art, culture, music and literature also formed part of the feminine sphere; as a man I was supposed to value aggression, machismo, strength and bodily endurance, courage and other 'male' values.

I tried to show my contempt for these allegedly male values in more ways than one. One day, when it was raining heavily, I borrowed my grandmother's umbrella and carried it proudly to school. Now German boys were supposed not to mind inclemencies of the weather, and certainly never carry an umbrella – this was something only done by girls. My arriving at school carrying an umbrella caused quite a sensation, and was talked about for weeks – it was rightly understood as a rejection of the accepted values of manliness to which practically everybody subscribed. I was only able to carry this off because no one could call me effeminate, or lacking in strength, vigour and stamina. Had I been small and weak, life would have been hell and all such protests completely ineffectual.

With all this, it seems a miracle that I was not more unpopular and disliked than I was. However, all the girls I knew were sad when I left in 1934, and so were my friends at school. Even the teachers, whom I had played up mercilessly, expressed what seemed sincere wishes for my future, and wanted me to keep in touch with them. I think possibly the reason for all this benevolence was the fact that I had, as a saving grace, a good sense of humour; the protests I made, however sincerely they were felt by me, seldom lacked a comical element – an indication that I didn't take myself too seriously, and even an indication of an ability to laugh at myself. All this served to make my arguments, if not acceptable, at least interesting enough to be listened to. I think for most of my peers I presented a puzzle and a paradox, rejecting my apparent birthright, always contrary and opposing the powers that be, and arguing for the rights of those who were rejected, debased and ostracized. Typically, when we read Homer, the hero of most members of the class was Achilles, mine Hector! This was an early indication that perhaps preferences in art could serve as a projection test for personality.

I also noted that in the Peloponnesian War, my classmates favoured Sparta, while I (and all the Jewish boys) wanted Athens to win. Now of course Sparta was the forerunner of totalitarian modern states, a precursor of Nazi Germany and Soviet Russia, with Spartan xenelasia antedating xenophobia, while Athens was free and openly welcomed all comers. Socrates, alas, came out on the side of the Fascists, as did Plato, his pupil; it was Aristotle, a generation later, who was to defend the democratic tradition so brilliantly started in Athens.

My interest in Greek and Roman history was aroused because I learned to love the stories and legends of these great countries. Homer's and Virgil's tales of Troy, of Ulysses, of Aenaes, of the founding of Rome; Jason and the Argonauts, Perseus and Medusa, Hercules and his twelve tasks – I read it all avidly, and it led me to an abiding interest in 'the glory that was Greece and the grandeur that was Rome'. Rome I respected, but Greece I loved.

I later tried to extend this principle to other forms of art, but with disappointing results. I prefer Puccini to Wagner, Mozart to Bach, Richard Strauss's *Don Quixote* to anything by Brahms, except his violin concerto, Beethoven to any of the moderns, Vivaldi to Schoenberg – but what does it all mean? When, later, I did my Ph.D. thesis on problems of experimental aesthetics, I hoped to get some answers – but without success.

My school career, first at the Bismarck Gymnasium, and later at the Prinz-Heinrichs-Gymnasium, was erratic. I found school boring, and that made me extremely lazy. I was, in fact, a textbook case of the usual difficulty that the exceptional child finds in an ordinary classroom. Actually, the classes I was in were quite highly selected; of my fellow-pupils who survived the war several became professors, one became German Consul in Sweden, and the others too did very well in one way or another. Only the most able went to a Gymnasium (rather like a British grammar school), so that a high degree of selection was already involved. Nevertheless, I found the teaching unbearably slow, and I soon discovered that I could easily do well without ever doing any work at all. When homework was absolutely unavoidable, I would do it at school, while apparently listening to some lecture, or watching some equally boring demonstration at chemistry or physics.

However, boredom and laziness were only part of my trouble. I was from the beginning a sceptic, disbelieving what I was told, and distrusting adults in general, and teachers in particular. Thus I argued with my teachers more than is advisable for a pupil, and although some took it quite well, others did not. The main causes of these differences were political. Through my reading of the *Weltbühne* and the *Tagebuch* I had developed strong socialist sympathies, and my observations of life in Germany at the time only served to strengthen these beliefs; politically I was half-way between the Social Democrats and the Communists. My teachers, on the other hand, were practically all right-wing nationalists, although before the advent of Hitler few favoured the Nazis. This led to many problems. Thus, when we were asked to write an essay on one of Germany's national heroes, I wrote a lengthy critique of Frederick the Great, whose rape of Silesia started the Seven Years War, a feat which seemed to meet with universal approval in Germany, or at least in Prussia. I ended my essay with the memorable words: 'Frederick the Great was a monster – a dictator in politics, a war-monger in international relations, and a poofter in his sexual habits. The fact that he is venerated as a "hero" in Germany is a devastating comment on German morality, sensibility and Christianity.' My teacher was ashen-faced with fury when he returned this to me; he did not give it a good mark! (I knew of course that there was more to Frederick the Great than that, but I was trying to make a point.) On other occasions I was equally scathing about Bismarck, Napoleon, and other idols of the militarists.

In a similar way, when we had to write an essay about the *Nibelungenlied*, Germany's national saga of Siegfried and his adventures, I wrote a persiflage of the story in terms of Freudian symbols and complexes. The vulnerable round bit of skin on Siegfried's heel on which a leaf had settled when he was bathing in the dragon's blood, thus making him vulnerable there, and Hagen's spear killing Siegfried by penetrating this vulnerable piece of skin, were tailor-made for Freudian symbolism. This too did not go down well with my teacher.

Mathematics was similar. We had a very good teacher, who once took me aside and said: 'Eysenck, you are the best student I ever had, but why can't you be content to use a formula I give you? Why do you have to try and work out your own?' The answer of course was exactly the same as before – once you have understood the reasoning underlying a formula, you want to get on and work out something original. Simply to apply it to hundreds of routine problems is extremely boring.

Physics and chemistry I found equally uninteresting. We were not allowed to do our own experiments, but at best watched the teacher at a distance performing experiments which often misfired, and which seemed to have little relevance to anything of general interest.

My boredom with the teaching level occasionally led me into truancy and other misdemeanours. I recall giving a particularly boring physics lesson a miss, and rolling down the Klixstrasse at the rear of the school on my bike, with a young lady elegantly draped over the handle-bars. I was just turning right at the bottom of the street, when out into the road stepped Dr Paetzel, our head teacher. I had no chance of stopping or avoiding him, and ran straight into his protruding stomach, shedding the young lady and burying his head in her skirt. When he emerged, furious and blushing, having disengaged himself from the young lady, I made matters worse by bursting out laughing – he was really cross. As a punishment I had to learn by heart Longfellow's *Psalm of Life*. It was worth it.

In spite of all my rebelliousness, I was offered the chance to jump a class (I think it was from the *Obersekunda* to the *Unterprima*). The move had one great advantage for it was made a condition that I would study with a private tutor the mathematics I would be missing because of the jump.

I had just discovered my real interest in life, by picking up a book by the famous physicist Max Born entitled *Umsturz im Weltbild der Physik* – i.e., revolution in the world picture of physics. In this book he described the new sub-atomic physics that followed Rutherford's investigations, and the beginnings of the Copenhagen School. I was entranced, and realized that natural science was what I wanted to do in my later life. Reading the book was a real revelation to me, and I started reading other books on physics and astronomy – chemistry did not seem to attract me particularly.

The private tutor who came to help me with my mathematics had a Ph.D. in physics and had studied with Einstein. Soon, instead of teaching me the dry-as-dust mathematics I should have learned, I got him to teach me about relativity theory and quantum mechanics; this was more interesting for him, and certainly much more so for me. I think I really got some elementary understanding of what the new physics was all about, and I was eagerly looking forward to the end of my schooldays, and the beginnings of a university career in the physics department of Berlin University, at that time perhaps the most outstanding one in the world.

A little while after I had fallen in love with science, and had promised to marry her, for better, for worse, I also met her ugly sister, philosophy. I was coming home from school when I passed a bookshop near our house. Arranging the books in the window was a beautiful girl – probably a little older than myself, but who was counting? I immediately asked myself how I could get to know her, and decided the best thing to do would be to go in and buy a book. Looking in the window I saw Kant's *Critique of Pure Reason*, offered at the price of 2.95 Marks, which seemed a snip for a book that might impress the young lady. I went in, bought the book and chatted her up. Alas, the story does not have a happy ending. When I returned at 5 o'clock to try and pick her up I saw her disappearing into the distance on the arm of a gigantic SS officer in full uniform! I decided an impecunious schoolboy could probably not compete successfully with such a knight in black armour, but I still had the book and resolved to read it. Fortunately it had an excellent and lengthy introduction, setting Kant's contribution in the context of

German idealism, English empiricism, and Humean cynicism, and with that help I think I understood what Kant was trying to do. I could feel the intellectual challenge, but concluded that philosophy was not for me. I needed the factual relevance of scientific theories, and did not feel at home in the rarefied atmosphere of philosophical speculation. I have had a love-hate relationship with philosophy ever since.

My cultural life developed slowly over the years, starting with poetry. I had always liked German poetry, particularly Goethe and the Romantics, but it was when I came across English poetry that I really began to feel those goose pimples which usually, at least for me, signal the height of aesthetic excitement. My favourites then were Shakespeare, Matthew Arnold, Byron, and the early Wordsworth, but above all I loved Milton's *Paradise Lost*. I read it several times in the original, and could quote large chunks of it by heart. Like all rebels, I was attracted immensely by the gigantic figure of Satan, and often speculated about what Milton really thought of him.

When later on I encountered French poetry, I was less impressed. It seemed to me that while the French language is exceptionally euphonious, it does not lend itself to poetry as well as does German, whilst English is the undoubted Queen.

My reaction to *Paradise Lost* suggested to me the possibility that perhaps preferences for certain poems and poets, composers and operas, paintings and sculptures might be linked with one's personality, one's motives and ideals. I had discovered the principle of modern 'projective tests', without of course having ever heard of the idea. I noted down the poems I liked most, and then tried to discover consistencies and trends. There certainly was a common thread running through *Paradise Lost*, Hardy's *Invictus*, Goethe's *Prometheus*, Villon's French poetry, Heine's *Schlesische Weber*, and many others – the rebellion of the underling against established authority.

Perhaps easier to decipher are my literary likes and dislikes, for whatever light they may throw projectively on my inner life. I have always preferred Flaubert's *Salambo* to his *Madame Bovary*; Tolstoy's *War and Peace* to his *Anna Karenina*; Goethe's *Götz von Berlichingen* to his *Werther*. My heroes were the Rassendyll of Ruritanian fame, the Beau Geste of the Foreign Legion; Hornblower and Ramage of Nelson's Navy; d'Artagnan and the unholy trinity of Athos, Portos and Aramis; Scaramouche and the Scarlet Pimpernel of the French Revolution; Karl May's Old Shattertand (a liking unfortunately shared with Hitler – black mark!); and finally the rather degenerate and down-market heroes of today, the Saint and James Bond. Maybe I should have become a secret agent rather than an intellectual – or maybe these are just emerging from my unconscious to show what I have repressed.

I think my appreciation of poetry was sharpened by my own efforts to write poetry, which I started at about fourteen – and continued over the years – in German, English and French! None of it was very original, or had any strong emotion behind it. It was really more a playing with language, reasonably well done as a kind of clever pastiche, but without much value as poetry. Writing verse, however, taught me a lot about techniques, technical difficulties and the achievements of the great poets, and to this day I can still feel the effects of great poetry on my autonomic nervous system.

It was in connection with poetry that I made my first excursions into psychological territory, although quite ignorant that there was such a terrain, or that what I was doing was a psychological experiment. Our German teacher was quoting Goethe:

> Und solang du das nicht hast,
> Dieses: Stirb und werde,
> Bist Du nur ein trüber Gast
> Auf der dunkler Erde.

> (But if you should lack in this,
> This 'die and rise again',
> You are but a gloomy guest,
> Here on this dark earth.)

This is what the poem says, but he quoted it wrongly, talking about *ein dunkler Gast* and *eine trübe Erde*. With that wonderful tact and diplomacy that characterized me from birth onwards, I spoke up and said: 'Surely that's the wrong way round – it must be *"ein trüber Gast,"* and it must be *die Erde* which is *dunkel.'*

As becomes an authoritarian, he told me in his most superior tones that I didn't know what I was talking about, but I said that no one who had any appreciation of language would call the earth gloomy, and the guest dark. He sent one of the other boys to fetch the Goethe volume from the library to check, and I was right. I had always assumed, as most people do, I suppose, that other people were similar to oneself, and to discover that a teacher of German could lack any fine appreciation of the language greatly surprised me. I followed this up, in a quite unsystematic manner, of course, taking brief quotations and changing a word the poet had used for another, less suitable one, and asking my friends which of the two was the correct one. I found that many of them lacked any appreciation of the finer nuances of language, and would pick the wrong word just as readily as the right. This was my first real lesson in individual differences, and it came as a shock to me. I did not have the knowledge or ability to create a real test, or try and use my examples systematically; it was simply a game for me, born from my interest in poetry, and an innate feeling for language.

Apart from poetry I very much enjoyed the theatre; I still remember seeing the second part of Goethe's *Faust*, with Gründgens as Mephisto and Kraus as Faust. Gründgens of course was born to play the devil, and anyone lucky enough to have seen the film *Mephisto* will know why; he rose high in the ranks of the Nazi Party and became a dictator in German theatrical circles. I remember coming away from this presentation of the play (the second part) with my head absolutely bulging with ideas, images, allusions, symbols and whatnot – it seemed to me the most tremendous three hours I had ever spent. It was a wonderful introduction to theatre, but unfortunately it never again quite lived up to the expectations then created.

I had one particularly cogent reason for not thinking very highly of my teachers, whom in retrospect I must say were excellent examples of their profession, compared with the average run of teachers. It was clear to me fairly early on that I was a good deal brighter than any of them, that intellectually I could run rings round them without any difficulty, and that even in their specialities I probably *knew* more than most of them. By the time I was fourteen or fifteen I had read through practically all the classics in my mother's library; that was certainly more than our German teacher had done. I was interested in history and read widely, particularly in world history – I simply couldn't get on with the emphasis on Prussian history, with lists of Brandenburg *Kurfürsten* to be learned by heart, and found the teaching singularly uninspired and ignorant of wider issues.

I had been in England three times before leaving school. The first time I spent the summer holidays in Folkestone, in a guesthouse, around 1929; the second time I spent a term in a small public school on the Isle of Wight around 1930; and the third time I spent a term at Exeter University (at that time still a college of the University of London) reading English language, history and literature around 1932. I certainly knew far more about the language than did our teacher, and predictably did not hesitate to tell him so; this did not add to my popularity. Having a certain gift for languages I also did quite well in French and Latin, but there the teaching was reasonable and I had no complaints.

During my schooldays on the Isle of Wight I not only learned some English, but learned to love England, and to play cricket. Unfortunately I could never manage to please the headmaster, who was training the cricket team. Batting in cricket requires one to hit the ball in a very artificial manner, and it was obvious to me that in the few months I had I would never learn this properly. On the other hand, particularly against the kind of bad bowling you encounter in school cricket, you can get away with cow-shots if you have good hand-coordination, and a strong arm. I soon perfected this shot, anathema to all real cricketers, and consistently headed the batting averages. The poor headmaster, who tried to teach his pupils the correct type of stroke, was furious, but at least I won a number of games for the team.

My term at the University of Exeter helped my English along very nicely; I attended lectures on English literature, history and language, and spent the rest of my time reading English poetry, and all the major classics. It was then I fell in love with English poetry, but unfortunately my spoken English was classical rather than idiomatic. We did have special courses on idiomatic expressions, going through them in alphabetical order, beginning, if I remember rightly, with 'Adam's ale' – i.e., water. Unfortunately few of the English students I talked to had ever heard of any of these idiomatic expressions, so that did not help very much.

I heard students talk about a girl they all seemed to know, called 'Fucky Nell'; possibly, I thought, a sister of Eskimo Nell, whose brave deeds I had heard about in sing-songs and at student parties. When I asked about her I never got much of a reply, other than hoots of laughter. Learning foreign languages is not as easy as it might seem at first.

Inevitably I came up against the typical Englishman's dislike and distrust of 'bloody foreigners'. I couldn't help playing up to the curious prejudices my fellow-students had, just to see them revealed in their full beauty. I remember coming back from playing Southampton University at tennis with our team, and being met outside the student hostel where I lived by the President of the hostel. 'And how did you get on?' he asked, meaning of course 'How did the team get on?' Just to tease him I answered: 'I won of course – both the singles and doubles!' All his prejudices apparently verified, he said patiently: 'I mean, how did the team get on?' 'Oh, they lost of course.' The interchange left both of us happy, having confirmed our mutual prejudices.

I think I may have said enough to make the reader realize that I was a sanctimonious prig ('conceited or didactic person'), who didn't suffer fools (or even ordinarily bright people) gladly; who objected vehemently to the tawdry values of his compatriots, and whose acidulous prose made his meaning quite clear. In retrospect this is not a pretty picture, and I regret the intolerance I showed at the time, even to quite well-meaning teachers. However, there was considerable provocation in the political atmosphere of the time, and I wish I had the pen of a poet to describe it. Lacking that, I must try and give a factual description of what was happening.

*   *   *

I have already mentioned my attitude to socialism of the left-wing variety. I emphasize the point, because Mussolini, and later on Hitler, preached a kind of socialism very different from that which I had embraced. It is not always remembered that the name of Hitler's party was the National *Socialist* German Workers Party – i.e., a unique and clever combination of nationalism with socialism. No matter that his socialism was bogus, many people, particularly among the working class, believed in it, and it was not until the 'night of the long knives', when Röhm and his friends in the leadership of the (working class) brown-shirted storm-troops were killed, that the socialist dreams of many of Hitler's followers were finally shattered.

I also made friends in the Communist Party, some of them reasonably high up in the Party, but I never joined; I could not accept the dependence on leadership from Moscow, which seemed to betray gross ignorance of the situation in Germany, and I found it difficult to regard Stalin as the great-hearted, kindly 'Uncle Joe' of his eulogists. The breaking-point came in 1930, when I returned from school on the Isle of Wight. This was the time of the Berlin tram drivers' strike, in which Communists and Nazis together challenged the Weimar constitution. Finding it impossible to understand the motive for this collaboration, I went to ask my Communist friends. Shaking their heads at my naivety, they told me that the first duty of socialists was to smash the Weimar state, and if they had to enlist the help of the Nazis to do that, then so be it. Once the state had been smashed, they would deal with the Nazis. I told them that the Weimar state was the only thing that stood between them and the overwhelming strength of the Nazis, aided and abetted by the police and the Army, and that in any trial of strength they would obviously be the losers. 'Ho, Ho,' they said, 'Are you pitting your dim little wits against the Great Stalin, who has sent us an explicit order to act in this fashion?' 'Yes,' I said, 'he obviously has no idea what conditions are like in Germany, and if you go on like that you'll end up dead.' Alas, I was proved only too right; all of them died bravely in the Nazi Concentration Camps. At the last minute they had tried to form the 'Eiserne Front' with the Social Democrats, against the Nazis, but it was too little and too late.

For the second time in my life I found that as an ignorant schoolboy I had seen much more clearly than these brave and clever people what the real situation was – simply because they wore rose-coloured glasses and wouldn't see what was so clearly before them. This, and the absurd veneration of working-class people by Tucholsky and his colleagues taught me that in the realm of politics and social attitudes, feelings and emotions may be much more powerful than intellect, an observation which I tried later on to turn into research projects during my work on

The Psychology of Politics. I also learned that pointing out the truth to fanatics was not regarded with any favour; having disagreed with Stalin's *Diktat*, I was from then on regarded as an enemy.

I was already strongly opposed to Hitler and the Nazi Party, and never ceased to argue the case whenever possible, at school and elsewhere. However, my opposition was rational, lacking strong emotional backing. This I acquired in abundance when, after Hitler had come to power, we were marched to the Tempelhofer Feld, to listen with hundreds of thousands of other pupils to the man himself. I had heard his insane rantings before, on the radio, but to see and hear him speak, in his ungrammatical, badly pronounced pseudo-German, gesticulating like a puppet jerked here and there by its master, made an indelible impression on me – an impression of naked evil, of original sin, if you like, of unimaginable viciousness and cruelty. I had never felt such a strong emotion in my life, and when he ended his rantings, and everybody raised their hands in salute, shouting, '*Sieg Heil*', I turned round and whistled *Land of Hope and Glory* as a puny and utterly ineffectual protest. I knew at that moment that war was inevitable, that Jews, gipsies, and all sorts of cripples, mental defectives and other '*Untermenschen*' would be tortured and killed – let alone my fellow-socialists and Communists. And of course in the inevitable war, all these children now shouting Hosanna would be both executioners and victims. I knew exactly how Cassandra must have felt – able to foresee the future, unable to change it. It was a traumatic moment in my life, and it convinced me once and for all of the uselessness of pacifism when confronted with absolute evil. It was a lesson I was never to forget.

The insistence of the Nazis that the Jews presented a problem, and would have to be expelled or exterminated, began to arouse my interest. As a youngster I had imbibed the usual kind of stupid and unthinking anti-Semitism, which in Germany included the belief that Jews were cowards – a belief which a reading of the Old Testament should have dispelled very quickly. I found this easy assumption severely tested when I was about twelve or so. I had an older school friend, Robert Lieban, the son of the well-known bass-baritone who was singing at the Berlin Opera. He was Jewish, although I never realized it until one day, when his cousin, who was also in our school, was attacked by the school bully who called him a 'dirty Jew'. This was unwise, as the young man in question was in the Bar Kochba boxing team, and proceeded to take him apart, scientifically and painfully. As the bully was big and strong, and Robert's cousin small and seemingly fragile, I found this difficult to reconcile with the picture of the cowardly Jew.

I pondered over this when on another occasion our teacher made some remark about 'cowardly Jews', and decided to look for a way of getting some objective data. I hit upon the idea of using the award of the Iron Cross during the First World War as a measure of bravery, and compared the percentage of Jews who had received the Iron Cross with the percentage of non-Jews, finding that the Jews had a rather higher percentage. I knew nothing about statistics at the time, and therefore couldn't test the difference for significance, but the data certainly seemed to disprove the notion that Jews were cowards, even if they might not prove that they were heroes. Needless to say the teacher in question was outraged when I told him.

Another notion that bit the dust was the idea that Jews look Jewish, in some way. When Hitler came to power he sent around so-called 'biologists' who would measure the degree of 'Aryanness' of all school pupils. When he came to our class, I remember, I came out the second most Aryan looking, which I supposed was fair enough, but the most Aryan looking of all was my good friend Fritz Nova, who could trace his Jewish ancestry over several centuries! My Nazi school-fellows did not let this upset their firm beliefs, dismissing it as just one of those things, but it stuck in my mind and suggested to me that perhaps the whole notion of Jews as a separate 'race' was erroneous. I think the evidence is now pretty strong that the one thing upon which Hitler and the Jews agreed, namely that Jews were a 'race', is in fact untrue; Jewishness is a religious faith, and now maybe a national entity, but it is not a race. Arthur Koestler, whom I got to know rather well later on, describes very cogently in his book *The Thirteenth Tribe* how an Aryan-speaking tribe, the Khazars, were poised on the north-eastern side of the Mediterranean, between Mohammedans on the southern side, and Byzantine Christians, on the western. Pressed to give up their indefinite multi-theistic religion their rulers feared being swallowed up by either of the two parties if they adopted one religion or the other, and decided instead to make the country adopt the Jewish religion.

When later on the Huns came out of the east and defeated the Khazars, these were driven west into what is now Hungary, Yugoslavia and particularly Russia; from there they spread to Austria, Germany and other European countries. Thus a majority of the Jews in Germany apparently come from a non-Jewish race!

I didn't know all this then, of course, but my disbelief in the notion of the Jewish 'race' was strengthened when one day I was looking down from the balcony of our flat in the Kaiserallee and saw a troop of brown-shirts marching along. A Jewish-looking man was walking in the opposite direction, and they broke step and started beating him up. Full of indignation I raced down, although what I could have done to help him I can't imagine. However, when I got there they had already marched on and he was lying on the ground in a pitiful condition. When

I talked to him, however, I found out that he was, in fact, an early member of the Nazi Party, having joined it in the 1920s – the notion that he was Jewish was entirely mistaken. This cooled my sense of compassion, and I left him complaining and shouting.

As an aside, I may perhaps mention that many years later one of my Ph.D. students carried out an experiment which strengthened my view that Jews and non-Jews do not look different on the average. She got together groups of ten young people, five Jewish and five non-Jewish in each case. These mingled at a kind of party, talking freely to each other, dancing with each other, and having fun for a couple of hours. They were forbidden to mention their names, or to discuss religion, but otherwise they were quite free to talk about anything they wanted. At the end each person was asked to say which of his or her fellows was Jewish, which non-Jewish. In all the groups she studied, my student failed to find anyone who could do this at a better than chance level. This is not to deny, of course, that there are some Jews who look 'Jewish', but apparently there is an equal proportion of non-Jews who look 'Jewish'. Similarly, among non-Jews there are some who look 'Jewish', others who do not. It is interesting that both Jews and non-Jews, when I recount this experiment, often say that they themselves would have done rather better, but I doubt it. It is rather like the 'Can you tell butter from margarine?' story – most people think they can, until properly tested!

Certainly at school and later on in life most of my friends were Jewish, as is my second wife. So were many of my colleagues at the Institute of Psychiatry. When it is remembered that only about one person in a hundred in England is Jewish, it is obvious that the Jews have an attractive quality for me, possibly related to their high intelligence, their wit, their culture and their love of education, which distinguishes them as a group. All this is quite independent of the horror of the Holocaust which should always be in the memory of anyone who feels like criticizing Jewish national aspirations. I am neither proud nor ashamed of being a German – after all, I had little to do with it – but I can never forget what my fellow-countrymen did to the Jews, and will always have a feeling that there is a huge debt that can never be repaid.

It would be easy to think of all Hitler's followers as evil, but I think that would be a great mistake. One cannot condemn a whole nation, and many, if not most, of the followers of Hitler were the victims of his rhetoric, completely ignorant of the real meaning of his satanic will. Take Ilsemarie as an example. When I was fourteen, sexual impulses having begun to stir a year or two earlier, I fell in love with this very pretty young girl, about the same age as myself. (I know of course that 'love' is not the correct term for this immature mixture of feelings and lust which characterizes one's earliest sexual adventures, but there were some strong feelings between us, and the language lacks a correct term to describe what we felt.) Ilsemarie was a bright girl, the daughter of a hospital sister whose husband had died in the First World War; she herself worked in a laundry, taking in and washing clothes. She had left school because she had to earn a living, and when I got to know her she was already a 'Hitlermädchen' – i.e., she had joined the organization headed by Baldur von Schirach, comprising large numbers of boys and girls, wearing uniform and pledged to follow Hitler to victory. I argued with her frequently, pointing out what Hitler really stood for, but she was so persuaded of the rhetoric of his promises, his slogan of 'Gemeinnutz geht vor Eigennutz' – i.e., the wellbeing of the many is more important than the wellbeing of oneself – that she simply could not see the dark side of his nature. She was a sweet, innocent child, well-meaning, and altruistic; she would have been utterly horrified had she known what the Nazis were going to do. Here was my third lesson in politics – the utter impotence of reason when faced with rhetorical and emotional hogwash. It was an important lesson, and it was reinforced when one of my schoolfriends, Mathias Steinberg, joined the storm-troops and came to school in his uniform.

He was a bright, sensible and moral boy, quite the opposite of what one imagines as a typical SS man; nevertheless he too proved impervious to any arguments that I might put to him. Most of the non-Jewish boys in my class had similar attitudes; they were pro-Nazi, without realizing just what that implied. Typically I think I was the only one who had read Mein Kampf; the others simply read the Nazi newspapers, looked at the cartoons showing Jews doing the most disgusting things, and generally expressed chauvinistic and anti-Semitic ideas without really intending to put these into practice. When our mathematics teacher, who was Jewish, was dismissed, the class protested to the headmaster, and asked for him to be reinstated – he was a good teacher, and popular, and for them 'Jewishness' was a completely theoretical concept, quite divorced from the reality of a person actually being Jewish.

All this is not intended as an excuse, but to differentiate between the average German who voted for Hitler without understanding what he stood for, and the degenerates who helped him in his programme of preparing for and carrying out the Holocaust. I am sure such people could be found in England, France, or the United States as well as in Germany; eternal vigilance is not only the price of freedom, but also of keeping out the degenerates.

(Incidentally in the last free election held in Germany before the Second World War, Hitler's party only gained 43.9 per cent of the votes; he was put in power by the senile Hindenburg, and made sure that he

[36]

would never have to put his popularity at risk again in a free election. It is thus not true that 'Germany voted Hitler into power' although the fact that 43.9 per cent voted for him reflects badly enough on the political sense of the nation!)

Some of the young Germans who most deserve our regard and indeed admiration started out by being followers of Hitler; it was only when they discovered where he was leading them that they began to oppose him and all his works. A good example are the members of the 'Weisse Rose' (White Rose), an opposition group of Munich students centred round the Scholl siblings. They distributed leaflets opposing Nazi policies on ethical-Christian grounds, crossed out swastikas by painting red slashes across them, and carried out other minor acts of sabotage. They were caught, of course, and after a very short trial decapitated by the hangman's axe – an indication of how seriously even the slightest opposition was regarded by the Nazi butchers. It still makes me see red when middle-class left-wingers call Mrs Thatcher's policies, or the British police, 'Fascist'; they insult the memory of the heroic people who dared to oppose a genuine Fascist state.

Life in general was not dull or unpleasant for me, having put sport and girls well ahead of school in importance, and having made certain that I wasn't in the lower reaches of the pecking order, but relatively independent of it. I remember a few moments of pure happiness and ecstasy. One occurred during the winter, when I went skating with Ilsemarie, and we danced to the tunes of a Strauss waltz. Afterwards we went out and ate some Wieners with the next step being a visit to her flat, her mother being conveniently working at the hospital. I still remember biting into the sausage with a feeling of pure happiness and contentment – alas, it was not to last.

I was still playing tennis regularly, and was soon among the best juniors in the country. On one occasion I even won an Open Tournament against top opposition (which of course did not include international players). My tennis club, Blau-Weiss is one of the largest and best clubs in Germany, second only to Rot-Weiss which was our great competitor. The annual tournament was arranged at several levels, top being the International level, then the National level, and then several lower ones for Juniors and other less experienced players. I entered at the National level, very much against the advice of our pro who said that I would probably go out in the first round. Given a certain inconsistency in my play, he was probably right, for, unlike all the others I never practised – I found practice boring – and I relied entirely on my natural hand-eye coordination and stamina. In the games we played against other clubs, I often won against strong opponents but lost against weak ones, because I couldn't be bothered to try hard against them. These vagaries of motivation infuriated everybody, but I was quite happy to enjoy myself without trying too hard. I was suffering severely from the English malady – it's only a game!

In the tournament, to my astonishment, I got right through to the final, which was played on our number one court right outside the club house. As the international part of the tournament had finished, there were quite a lot of spectators when my opponent and I turned up. I was about sixteen then, and he was twenty-two, just about to get into the German Davis Cup Team and one of the star players of our sworn enemy, the Rot-Weiss Club. He sported a large swastika, and made no secret of his contempt for Blau-Weiss in general, and me in particular. He was surrounded by several beautiful groupies, and told them in no uncertain terms how he would dispose of me very quickly.

I had been quite prepared to put up some resistance, but lose to an obviously much better player, without trying too hard. However, all this talk annoyed me, and the swastika he wore was like a red rag to a bull. I tried hard in the first set, but he won it 6–4 and then turned to his girls and said something insulting about the poor quality of the opposition. When we went on the court again I was determined to fight for the match. I chased every ball, hit everything as hard as I could, tried to aim for the lines and corners, smashed the ball with every ounce of my strength, and generally played as I have never played before – or since. The terrace was by now full of spectators who cheered me on and, to cut a long story short, I finally beat him and received congratulations from everybody. I did, however, realize one thing – if this kind of motivation was necessary for me to really try hard and win, then I would never get anywhere, because I simply could never care enough, except in unusual circumstances.

Typical perhaps of my attitude was an occasion when I was playing in a tournament and was entering for the mixed doubles. I had a choice of two partners. One was Louise, a very pretty girl whose tennis was at best mediocre, and the other Elizabeth, an unusually ugly girl who was the best female tennis player in the club. I was almost certain to win the tournament if I played with Elizabeth, but, typically, played with Louise, losing in the finals. We might have won if we had practised more together, but instead we went to the Grünewald, to while away the time on the grassy slopes of the Havel River or the Wannsee. Future champions don't act like that!

Actually the curtain came down soon afterwards anyway. When Hitler came to power, under his edict of 'Gleichschaltung' – i.e., the law making every smallest group, club or assembly politically responsible to some Nazi Führer, our club was forced to throw out its Jewish members. I should have resigned in protest, but hesitated for a few months. Then I decided I could not honourably be a member of a club that obeyed such racist commands and resigned. Rather unwisely I explained my reasons in a letter to the Head of our Junior Section; fortunately he tore it up rather than pass it on! That was the end of my tennis career.

The appointment of Hitler as Chancellor in 1933 caused many changes in my life. Because my stepfather Dr Glass was Jewish, he and my mother went to Paris, to make films there. Under pressure, my father joined the Nazi Party, as without that membership he would not have been allowed to continue his profession. I was increasingly in trouble with the school over one thing or another. Hitler had abolished the Monday morning prayer meeting, and instead we had an assembly at which we were supposed to sing the German National Anthem, and the *Horst Wessel Lied*. Horst Wessel of course was a pimp who had joined the Nazi movement and was killed by the Communists (or so it was said); this song, based on an inspiring old tune, became the official party song. I refused to sing either song, not only because I couldn't sing, but also because I couldn't stand the nationalism of the one, and the venom of the other. By now several teachers had been dismissed for liberalism or for being Jewish, and we had a number of Nazi teachers who turned up in uniform (as indeed did many of the pupils). One of them complained to the headmaster, and our head teacher, Dr Paetzel, was asked to tell me off. Dr Paetzel had tears in his eyes when he implored me to sing at least *Deutschland, Deutschland über Alles*, the national song. He added that he and most of the teachers could understand my objection to the *Horst Wessel Lied*, but surely I could sing the National Anthem? I had to tell him that I was an international socialist, that I thought nationalism was the root of all war, and that the nationalist sentiments of the song were quite offensive to me. There were many similar events, and I could see that my life in Germany would encounter grave problems.

I did, however, attempt to enrol in the faculty of physics at Berlin University. I was told I could do so if I was willing to join the SS, Hitler's elite army of storm-troopers, clad in their elegant black uniforms. This was not a general rule for all students, of course; I imagine that the university authorities had heard of my political attitudes and behaviour, and wanted to ensure that I would toe the line. My father told Goering about the situation, and Goering promised to let me start as an officer in the SS. I didn't have to make any kind of decision; I knew that I couldn't live in that uniform, and with those people, and that emigration was the only possibility for me. I did not make the decision lightly. German language, German literature, the German countryside and German culture made a deep impression on me that could never be forgotten. I was leaving behind what seemed an assured future, the study of the subject I loved most in the best university department in the world; I had to leave my beloved grandmother and a secure home, and go into a lonely and difficult exile. My brain could evaluate the alternatives, but my heart could see none. My hatred of Hitler and the Nazis, and all they stood for, was so overwhelming that no argument could counter it. I had tried to go into opposition, but that sounds easier than it was – one couldn't just go and join what was a secret underground group desperately trying to preserve its identity in a hostile environment. In any case, I was not *persona grata* with the Communists, who constituted the major part of the opposition, and in any case, why should they trust me? There was nothing I could do to avert the tragedy that was so clearly approaching, and at the age of eighteen I finally took a train to France. I would have preferred to have gone to England, but with Dr Glass and my mother in Paris, and both speaking fluent French, I thought I should at least give France a try, and I went to Dijon to study French language, literature and history. I was to return to Berlin several times to visit my grandmother and my father in the next few years, but that was on short holidays and for limited periods only; this was goodbye to one life, and hello to another.

Saying goodbye to my grandmother was a sad occasion; I realized how much I meant to her, and how much my absence would grieve her. I would have stayed if I could, but I remembered the old saying, so often parodied and ridiculed, but still a good guide for conduct: 'A man's got to do what a man's got to do!' This was something I had to do, and nothing could alter my resolve. In the spring of 1934 I got on the train which wound its way through Heidelberg, across the border to Dijon. A chapter of my life had closed; I was now a refugee (or a refusee?) without a country.

On the train to Dijon I reflected over the events of this first chapter in my autobiography. I did not yet realize what it means for one to go into exile, to lose one's country, one's friends, one's whole cultural background, only to be received with suspicion, lack of understanding, and dislike by people brought up in a different tradition, having a different culture, and neither knowing nor caring about yours. I was not to know that many German writers who went into exile couldn't bear it and committed suicide – like Hasenclever, Tucholsky, Toller, and Stefan Zweig. Equally, it was no fun to run away, having apparently lost – Hitler and his thugs had won all along the line, and there had been absolutely nothing I could do about it. I could foresee the future – internal persecution of all his enemies, leading up to the Second World War, and the picture was not a pretty one. I was rather less worried than I should perhaps have been about my own future – youthful optimism suggested that I would find a niche in science somehow, and that after all science was international! But on the whole my mood was dark and gloomy, and it would no doubt have continued in that way had I not met and chatted up a very pretty Viennese girl, improbably called Mitzie, who was also on her way to Dijon to learn French. My mood immediately improved, and I felt quite elated when I left the train and made my way to the house where I was to live for the next few months.

CHAPTER 2

Student Life in Exile

Dilexi justitiam et odi iniquitatem,
propterea morior in exilio.

Gregory VII

(I have loved justice and hated iniquity;
therefore I die in exile.)

I spent the spring and much of the summer of 1934 in Dijon. It was a busy time which I used to learn the language, become acquainted with the history of the country, and to read as much literature as I could. It was also a reasonably happy time, because Mitzie managed to obscure the realities of exile. We spent much of the time together, went for long walks in the countryside, went swimming in the small rivers that surround Dijon, and generally enjoyed ourselves. The French students at university found it difficult to understand how such a pretty girl could fail to be won over by their Gallic charm, and the many foreign students at the university also tried to tempt her away, but without success. As so often in life, I was lucky, although I had to work hard for my luck!

On one occasion, for example, I took Mitzie to a student dance, but playing football at lunchtime I twisted my ankle and wasn't able to dance. How could I prevent her from going off with one of the many male students swarming around her? I told her that I was an expert graphologist, able to read people's characters from their handwriting; this aroused her interest, and I proceeded to read her character, and those of her friends and acquaintances at the dance, from their handwriting. Of course I had neither knowledge of, nor belief in, graphology, but I thought I could produce character descriptions which would combine the universally acceptable: 'You have a good sense of humour', or 'You sometimes worry about what the future may hold', with what seemed apparent from the behaviour of the person in question. Almost everybody agreed that my readings were astonishingly correct, and Mitzie hardly moved from my side all evening! It was more exhausting and less amusing than dancing, but it served its purpose. I was later to do a series of studies in which professional graphologists had to match writings and character descriptions; they managed to do slightly better than chance, but not much. Graphology is one of the many pseudo-sciences I was to investigate, and in this first encounter I discovered one very important thing about it: the fact that people accept your character description doesn't mean that it has any scientific value.

My stay at Dijon came to an end all too soon. My mother had wanted me to continue my studies in France, but I preferred England instead, where I felt at home as I never did in France. I liked the English in a way that I never got to like the French; I enjoyed English poetry and writing much more than anything the French had to offer; and, last but not least, I felt safer with the Channel between Hitler and myself. So the decision was made for me to go to London and enrol at the University there – to study physics and astronomy, or so I thought.

I still recall the evening when Mitzie left for Vienna. We went to hear the Don Cossack Choir, holding hands in the dark; then she got on to the express train, leaned out of the window and waved, and was wafted out of my life. The realities of exile began to dawn on me, the loneliness and the lack of a true home. I went into a music shop where one could have records played over acoustic earphones for the price of a few sous, and I listened again and again to 'our tune' – *Le chaland qui passe*. Even now, when I hear that tune, it conjures up feelings of sadness and desolation. I listened to it twenty times or more, then decided this was an unmanly reaction, and concentrated on the future.

The immediate future (before I left for England) was a lengthy visit to Paris, where my mother lived with Dr Glass. The casting director of his film was on holiday, and I was allowed to live in his flat in the centre of Paris, in the Avenue Victor Hugo. I fell in love with Paris, not yet the old harridan it has become since, with its odious high-rise buildings and its *périphérique*, and I spent every day walking its streets, admiring its buildings, and steeping myself in its history. I also extended my love of the arts in two new directions.

I had always been very fond of poetry, which was my first love. Next came drama and then novels. Opera, after my first encounter with Wagner, I had rather discounted, but after I saw *La Bohème* at the Paris Opera, and felt goose pimples all over – I knew I was smitten! For weeks I couldn't get *che gelida manila* out of my mind, and the romantic nonsense of the story didn't seem as obviously nonsensical to me then as it does now. I went to the opera quite often and can remember particularly *Carmen* and *Tosca*; altogether, Italian and French composers like Puccini, Verdi and Bizet appealed to me vastly more than the preposterous Wagner.

I also went to the Louvre, and there began my deep appreciation of painting, particularly that of the Impressionists. Cézanne, Manet, Monet, Pissarro and their brethren appealed to me tremendously. I could also appreciate the Dutch School of landscape painting, and painters like Canaletto, but many famous paintings left me quite untouched – the Mona Lisa, for instance. I didn't know anything about painting, but I did know what I liked! I couldn't know then, of course, that much of my early work in psychology would be devoted to experimental aesthetics, particularly the aesthetics of visual arts; one's choice of a subject for scientific research can apparently be powerfully influenced by personal experiences.

One other event stands out in my memory – my mother, on the day of my arrival in Paris, taking me out for afternoon coffee, and ordering for me a gigantic slice of raspberry tart. I had often heard of the superb quality of French cooking, but this was an event in my life that I have remembered over fifty years! German cakes and tarts were excellent, but this was truly a masterpiece to be eaten with reverence, and to be remembered with awe. When I think of the rubbish that is often sold along this line in English and American cafés, I could cry. Puritanism truly has exerted a terrible price, and the inability of many English and American people to tell the difference between the sublime and the ridiculous in food is a constant source of amazement to me.

Alas, the time soon came to leave Paris, and I took a train again, this time for London. I went to Russell Square, near the University of London Senate House, and lodged at No 2 Hunter Street, completely destroyed during the war. This was an old-fashioned house, run by an irascible Scotsman and his English wife. There were about a dozen rooms, each inhabited by a student. Heating was by gas fires which had to be activated by depositing coins in a slot meter – a primitive method almost universal in such lodging houses, which had the great disadvantage that one always tended to run out of the right coins when the need for a fire was greatest. Baths, too, had to be paid for – with a sixpence in order to get the plug. When you didn't have sixpence, and I often did not, you might get your bath by sitting down in the empty tub, and putting your heel over the outlet, then gradually run in the water. But you had to be careful not to be caught by the owner, who naturally disapproved of such practices.

We were given breakfast and dinner but lunch was not included in the price of the room. I had very little money, sent by my mother, while my father supported my grandmother, and often it was a question of taking the bus to go to the theatre and going without lunch, or walking and having a slice of Hovis and some cheese. For breakfast we had a choice of porridge and cereal into which you could slice a small banana. Our Scottish landlord, true to the stereotype of his race, bought third-quality bananas, which always had black spots and other imperfections that had to be carefully removed. I longed for the day when I might be able to afford a large banana free of such imperfections, but this was not to be for many years. Dinner, too, was not the kind of thing an epicure might have looked forward to, and for much of the time I was hungry and unable to do anything about it.

Occasionally I tried to cook something for myself, usually with dire consequences. I recall buying a piece of liver, and attempting to wash it in the small sink in my room. It suddenly seemed to come alive, jumped out of the sink, and I had to chase it all round the room until finally it escaped under the bed! I decided to give up the unequal struggle.

To my disappointment, the University required me to pass an entrance matriculation examination, and accordingly I went to Pitman's in Southampton Row, to get some tuition. Pitman's gave tuition in shorthand, typing and other commercial arts; it also had classes in subjects preparing future students for the London University entrance examination, and I took English, mathematics, and a few other subjects, as well as shorthand and typing.

I had thought that my knowledge of mathematics was quite sufficient to pass the entrance examination without any coaching, but I was wrong. The English system appeared to be based on Euclid, and, in Germany, we had never gone through Euclid in the same way, so that I had to learn what might be called 'the English approach'. I found this mechanical and boring, but it had to be done. I quite enjoyed the shorthand and typing, which proved useful later on.

Pitman's had some quaint paternalistic rules. For instance, male students were not allowed to speak to female students on the premises or within fifty yards either side of the entrance, at pain of expulsion. I remember the boy sitting next to me in one of the classes being called to the Principal. When he came back I asked him what had happened. He said: 'I've been given the sack, for talking to a girl.' I couldn't see any sack (this was an idiom I hadn't come across before), but the meaning became only too clear when he cleaned out his desk and left the building. Curiously enough, soon afterwards I ran into a young lady who had been teaching us English when I was at Exeter University; she had transferred to Pitman's in the meantime. Naturally we talked for a few minutes, but this was overheard by one of the teachers, who reported me to the Principal. When I appeared before him, he gave me a long lecture on morals, telling me that I ought to be expelled. 'However,' he finally said, 'we know all about you lascivious foreigners and your evil ways. Because you didn't have the blessing of an English upbringing, I will forgive you this time, but be sure that it doesn't happen again!' I promised to do my best to suppress these lascivious longings, and managed to stay the course. When I left the building, I counted off fifty-one yards, and then waited for the young lady, to escort her home and talk about Exeter and other things. I don't know whether Pitman's still has these rules but it seemed to me to incorporate a great deal of the charm of English life.

In addition to preparing myself for the University, I decided that I had to learn as much as I could about the British. Rather like Vicky, the famous refugee cartoonist who went through a special course of British life and letters in order to ply his trade, I too followed the same route. I read several newspapers each day, and the weekly *New Statesman*, which took the place of the German weeklies I had read at home. Under Kingsley Martin's editorship, it really was an outstanding left-wing political and literary journal. Later on I added the *Tribune*, an even more left-wing journal, to my reading list, and during the war was an ardent reader of the books published by 'The Left Book Club'. I had no doubts at that time that socialism was the only acceptable philosophy politically, although I was sad when the Labour Party voted against rearmament, apparently not realizing the danger presented by Hitler and Mussolini.

When not occupied with my academic preparations I spent the days walking around London, exploring all its historic nooks and crannies. In the evenings I went to the Old Vic to watch Shakespeare plays, or to cinemas to admire the great personalities of the time – Gary Cooper, Jimmy Stewart, Fred Astaire and Ginger Rogers, Clark Gable, Myrna Loy, and all the rest. Cinema-going in those days was a much more organized and romantic affair, with cinema organs, huge cinemas and long queues, and the usual cuddling in the back rows. I missed out on concerts – a bit too expensive for me, and a love of classical music didn't develop until somewhat later.

When I sat the exams at the University of London buildings in South Kensington in the spring of 1935, I came out near the top on all the subjects I took. I then proudly presented myself for registration at University College, and received what then appeared a mortal blow to my ambitions. In Germany, once you are admitted to a university you have a great freedom of choice, taking any courses and exams you like. I was told that in England this was not so, and that the courses you can choose depend on the topics you have selected for your entrance examination. I had omitted to choose some of those required for physics and consequently was not eligible. In despair I asked what I should do. 'Well,' I was told, 'you could always come again next year, having done the right subjects.' I pointed out that I didn't have the money to do that. Wasn't there any subject on the science side which I could take, given the subjects I had passed in? 'Oh yes,' they said, 'there is always psychology.' 'What on earth is psychology?' I said, never having heard of the subject. I had some vague idea about psychoanalysis, but psychology as a science? However, I had no choice, and so I entered the University as a psychologist. Thus is one's fate decided by bureaucratic stupidity!

At the time I was furious, but in retrospect all may have been for the best in the best of all possible worlds. Competition in the hard sciences is much fiercer than in psychology, and the really successful practitioners are quite something. I have met and got to know about half a dozen Nobel Prize-winners, and they certainly are an impressive bunch. I have known many of the leading psychologists, from Spearman to Koehler, from Tolman to Guilford, from Luria to Kretschmer, from Skinner to Koffka, from Thurstone to Allport; but none impressed me half as much as did the leading physicists and astronomers. It turned out to be quite easy to be a big fish in a small pond; in the larger ocean of the physical sciences life would have been very much harder, and I might have failed altogether. Luck, as so often in life, had taken a hand and insisted that I do the right thing, taking up a subject for which my special abilities and personality were most suited.

At London University, at the time, the degree course took three years: the first year was spent on four or five subjects which might or might not be relevant to one's major; the next two years on the major subject and a minor subject which might be chosen from a small group. For the intermediate I did Latin, English, German, Economics and Ethics. For my major of course I had chosen psychology; as a minor I wanted to take physiology, but there were no vacancies and I chose sociology instead.

The University of London is merely an administrative unit; all teaching is done at separate colleges. I registered at University College, but some courses were at other schools. Sociology I took at the London School of Economics, and some of our psychology courses, such as animal psychology, were taken at King's College in the Strand. The teacher there was Dr Aveling, an unfrocked priest who, we were told, had married one of Marx's daughters; he was a bibulous character who seemed never to have done any actual research work with animals, but to have read it up instead.

We also had lectures on ancient and modern philosophy at King's College. The professor used to come in at the beginning of the hour, carrying a handwritten tome with him. He would sit down, open the tome and start reading his lecture. At the end of the hour he would snap the tome shut, get up and walk out. He read in such a monotonous tone that it was never clear whether he was quoting a given author or giving his own opinion. On one occasion he brought the wrong tome and started reading his notes on modern philosophy when it should have been ancient philosophy. I politely drew his attention to this error. He immediately closed the tome, walked out, went to his rooms, which were at the other end of the college, returned with the right tome, opened it and started reading, without saying a word of explanation or excuse. He never interacted with anybody, and never spoke a word to any of the students. It was an extraordinary performance.

Even worse was our lecturer in Latin history. He had a cleft palate, which made his speech unintelligible, but the rules of the University forced us to sign the attendance sheet, so we all turned up, and while this unfortunate man was trying to speak we would read our assignments for other courses, or do other types of work. University teaching was pretty poor, but these were the worst examples I came across.

While still preparing myself at Pitman's I voraciously read practically all the volumes in Benn's Library – a series of sixpenny paperbacks dealing with physics, chemistry, astronomy, biology, philosophy, and many other topics – and all the volumes in The Thinker's Library, which cost one shilling, and had proper covers, dealing with much the same topics. I found no difficulty in understanding and integrating all the bits I read. When I started at University College I found to my surprise that the courses were ridiculously easy for me and I collected Alphas in practically all the work I did. It very soon became clear that in my year there were three really outstandingly successful students. Apart from myself there was John Butler Parry, who had spent ten years in a bank getting bored stiff, finally settling for some early retirement scheme which gave him just enough money to allow him to fulfil his ambition to study philosophy; and Hans Hausmann, a Jewish German refugee who read English. John became a close friend; his study of philosophy included psychology, just as mine included philosophy, and during the war he became Head of the Psychology Department of the Air Force, and wrote a book – together with Philip Vernon who fulfilled a similar function for the Army – on the work of the psychologists in the Armed Services.

Economics was the subject that interested me most among those I took for the intermediate. It was supposed to be the most scientific of all the social sciences, but it seemed to me that it was based, exceptionally weakly, on psychology. It postulated people who buy in the cheapest market and sell in the dearest, and who behave in ways altogether different from those people I knew behaved. This was just a commonsense judgement, but as I got into psychology proper, I found that there was a flat contradiction between what psychology taught me about people's behaviour, and what economics assumed that behaviour to be. I was not surprised to find that economists have no predictive power, and that they keep contradicting each other.

Among my teachers in economics was Hugh Gaitskell, later to become leader of the Labour Party and only prevented from becoming Prime Minister by his untimely death. He was not a good lecturer, but I was so surprised to hear someone in authority freely being allowed to advocate socialism that I became quite attached to him. He was a good man, and might have saved Great Britain from the locust years under Macmillan and Wilson, the co-founders of our misery in the 1960s and 1970s.

When I finished my intermediate exams I joined forces with my new close friend John Parry to rent a flat, seeing that neither of us could afford to do so by himself. At first we lived in Mill Hill, but we later moved into a more centrally situated block of flats near Belsize Park, in Hampstead. I enjoyed having a highly intelligent and knowledgeable friend who studied the same subject, but from a rather different point of view, and we had many debates which clarified our views. By the time I left No 2 Hunter Street, however, I had met a young Canadian girl, Margaret Davies, who was working as a secretary, and we became friendly and finally married in 1938, when I received my final degree. John also married shortly afterwards, but during the war years we drifted apart. Just for the sake of argument I adopted a very hostile position towards philosophy, while his of course was very favourable.

In 1936 I started out on my training in psychology. Head of the Department was Professor Cyril Burt, later to be knighted for his services to education, and later still to be accused for falsifying data and expelled from the Temple of Academe. He was a pleasant, short, rotund, insignificant-looking person with owlish eyes and spectacles. His second in command was J. C. Flugel, who taught social psychology and psychoanalysis; he was a practising psychoanalyst who is well known for his books on the family, and also for a history of psychology.

A third member of the teaching team was S. J. F. Philpott, who taught psychophysical methods and experimental psychology. He was a tall, fat man who seemed to have little interest in the subject he was teaching, who could never seem to make his instruments work, and who seemed to believe in some of the more mystical ideas of Jung. Altogether the department was very psychoanalytically inclined, with Burt being one of the founding members of the British Psychoanalytical Society. The Freudian mythology states that psychological departments were all hostile to psychoanalysis, but this was certainly not true of University

College. The only criticism that Burt could find of psychoanalysis in his lectures was that they talked about unconscious ideas, which he asserted was a contradiction in terms. There are rather more serious criticisms than that of psychoanalysis.

During these years I used to go back to Berlin once a year, to visit my grandmother. Mostly I went alone, but on one occasion with Margaret and her parents, who had come over from Canada to visit her, and on one or two occasions with John Parry. Each time the situation seemed to get worse, and I was truly appalled at what I saw and heard. It is almost impossible for anyone who has not lived in a totalitarian society to imagine what life is like. To take but one example, on one occasion I went to consult the dentist who had looked after my teeth for many years, a Dr Sultan, who was Jewish. When I got there he was nowhere to be found, and the porter told me, rather curtly, that a few months before a group of storm-troopers had come to take him off to a Concentration Camp. He had jumped out of the window and killed himself, leaving a wife and several children to suffer whatever fate had in store for them. This sort of thing was a daily occurrence, and few things in life made me more furious than to hear English people returning from Germany saying that all the stories of Concentration Camps and atrocities against the Jews were vastly exaggerated, and that they hadn't come up against anything of the kind.

Life in Germany could be quite Kafkaesque. On one occasion, for instance, I went out with an old friend of mine, Egon Borgerhof, to paint the town red. We got back in the early hours of the morning, and I was going to drop him at his flat and go on to my grandmother's flat, where I was living at the time. We were just about to turn the corner into the street where he lived when two large trucks of storm-troopers drove up, stopped, and two dozen brownshirts descended and surrounded his house. Egon was a member of a small right-wing political group led by the Strasser brothers who had fallen foul of the Nazis – they had come to catch him and take him to a Concentration Camp. Had we been just sixty second earlier, we would both have been dragged off – my innocence would have made no difference to my fate. Guilt by association is enough in a dictatorship – to be friendly with someone who is considered an enemy of the State is to be an enemy of the State yourself. My guardian angel was fortunately awake at the time, and I got away with it. Egon of course could never go back to his flat. He went across the border on skis, crossing the Erzgebirge into Czechoslovakia, and finally made his home in Denmark. We wrote to each other, but letters ceased abruptly when the Germans marched into Denmark, and I have never heard of him since.

Eysenck, Hans J. (1990).
Rebel with a Cause:
The autobiography of Hans
Eysenck. London; with.
Allen

Another example of the unpredictability of life in a dictatorship occurred during my last visit to Berlin, in 1937. While I was there, visiting my grandmother, a law was passed stating that all male Germans of military age had to have a special permit before they were allowed to leave the country. Naturally, there was no way I could obtain such a permit – it would hardly impress the officers concerned if I said that I hated Hitler and militarism, and wanted to have nothing to do with the Army. I decided to try my luck, and boarded the train anyway; perhaps, when I got to the border, I might get some ideas as to how to get out of this sticky situation. If the worst came to the worst I thought I might have to follow Egon's example and cross the Erzgebirge on skis. However, this proved unnecessary. We got to the border somewhat earlier than I had thought, and suddenly a gigantic storm-trooper in his black death-head uniform appeared at the door of the compartment, shot out his arm and shouted 'Heil Hitler!'. As it happened, the compartment was full of English people who all had their passports ready and held them out for him to see. Mine was still in my luggage, and I got up to try and get it out. He looked at the assembled company contemptuously, said: 'Ach, Englander!', turned around and went on to the next compartment. I was through. My guardian angel had done his job again!

Not all my trips were so eventful. I had always wanted to learn to ski, and when I went home on one occasion for the Christmas holidays this became possible. I went off into the mountains, and became a member of a ski club. We had a first-class teacher, who coached the German Olympic Team. When he found that I had a natural aptitude for skiing – just as for tennis – we became friendly. Three days after putting on skis for the first time in my life I won a race. This was the men's section; the women's section was won by a beautiful young lady with whom I instantly fell in love. At the end of the day we had to go up the mountain in order to celebrate in one of the Bergherbergen where a band played, the Glühwein flowed, and Helga and I, as victors, had the first dance together. It was not to be the last, and I still remember that evening as one of the outstandingly happy times of my life. Having spent hours going up the mountain (all had to be done by muscle power in those days!), we now skied down to the little village where we lived, carrying blazing torches and making wonderful patterns in the snow. There is something to be said for youth, in spite of all the *Sturm und Drang*, and I still remember these days in the snow with great affection. In spite of my love for this sport, I never had another chance to ski again.

I took up boxing while an undergraduate and joined the boxing club to get some tuition. I was a 'middleweight', but sometimes had to fight in the cruiserweight, or once even in the heavyweight class. This last fight was wickedly arranged by the team captain, our heavyweight representative. I had just pinched his girl, and in revenge he pitted me against a man who turned out to be the university heavyweight champion! I lost on a technical K.O., and came home with two black eyes and a bloody nose.

I also learned that stereotypes are not always wrong. Our trainer said to me before one bout against a black chap: 'Don't hit him on the chin; these blacks (he didn't actually use the term "blacks") have very hard chins.' I thought: 'Oh, yes, typical prejudice!', and promptly hit my opponent on the chin. My metacarpals got all but broken, and I couldn't use that fist at all during the rest of the fight.

I found my work in psychology and in sociology excessively easy. Much of it seemed to me purely semantic and I noted a clear-cut difference between students in the hard sciences, who used to spend the day in the laboratory, and students in psychology and sociology, who spent the day drinking coffee and talking.

What I did was relatively simple, but perhaps not to be recommended to others. I got a dozen or so textbooks out of the library, quickly read through them, and thanks to my retentive memory, I could reproduce practically all I had read. After a few months I had learned so much about empirical psychology that other students were asking me to coach them. I attended lectures only when I had to, finding it much easier – as well as much quicker – to absorb information through reading. In the physical sciences anything of this kind would be quite impossible, but in psychology so few facts seemed to be known that one could get a good background in a short period of time. Much the same was true of sociology, where facts were even more scarce, and theories abounded.

In one way I was lucky in having chosen University College. British psychology at the time was split between the strictly experimental, conceived in a very narrow sense at Cambridge, and the psychometric and statistical approach of the London School, which emphasized individual differences in personality and intelligence. Frederick Bartlett was the Head of the Cambridge School, Cyril Burt the Head of the London School, having just taken over from Charles Spearman.

The two schools were at daggers drawn, and each tried as far as possible to disregard the contributions of the other. Thus I was later to teach students who had received a first-class degree at Cambridge, but couldn't even calculate a simple product-moment correlation! One student told me that they had only one hour's teaching of statistics in their training; this was deemed to be sufficient. Contrariwise, in Burt's department there was very little teaching about experimental psychology. In our whole course, conditioning and learning was summarily disposed of in one hour! L. J. Cronbach was later to talk about the two disciplines of scientific psychology in his famous American Psychological Association Presidential Address (as had William Stern already in 1911), but it was clear to me from the beginning that this feud was insane, and that psychology clearly needed both approaches. This view, which I advocated robustly, made me highly unpopular with both Bartlett and Burt, although no doubt there were many other causes of this unpopularity.

Cambridge and London (Oxford didn't have a psychology department at that time) were also divided along another line. Cambridge preached the gospel of 'pure' psychology, whereas London was more concerned with 'applied' psychology. This is the well known contrast between discovering abstract laws and applying these laws to practical problems. Burt had made his reputation in educational psychology, and in dealing with young criminals; in any case the study of personality and intelligence is obviously closely related to clinical and educational psychology, industrial selection and vocational guidance, the rehabilitation of criminals, etc. Bartlett did indeed found the Cambridge Applied Psychology Unit, but kept it strictly apart from the academic side. It has had a very successful career, particularly under the guidance of Don Broadbent, and he is perhaps the outstanding example of the application of experimental methods to practical affairs. On the other hand Burt made an important contribution to 'pure' psychology, particularly the theory of intelligence. The contrast, therefore, is not absolute, but it was there, nevertheless.

Altogether psychology at the time in England was parochial, small-scale, and exceedingly feudal. There were only a few departments in the country; these departments were very small, usually consisting of one professor and one or two assistants; and almost everyone carrying out academic work had come from Cambridge. When I obtained my Ph.D. and looked for academic work in England, it was obvious that my failure to have studied in Cambridge presented a fatal obstacle, and I only managed to get a Chair by creating my own department.

I have said that I was lucky in getting my training in psychology at University College, and the reason is not far to seek. Such abilities as I have in science lie largely on the quantitative side, in measurement, psychometrics and statistical analysis. This type of work brings one into contact with aspects of psychology which were intrinsically more interesting to me than the narrow experimentalism of the Cambridge School. In Cyril Burt I had an excellent teacher – one of the outstanding leaders in that field – and I owe a lot to him in this respect. We also had lectures on psychometrics from William Stephenson who came down from Oxford, where he was trying to organize a small institute of psychology. He and Burt were constantly arguing, particularly about priority in the rather esoteric field of the analysis of correlations between persons; oddly enough I was to be drawn into this when I was doing my Ph.D. thesis. I also went to lectures by Egon Pearson in the Statistics Department, and often listened to J. B. S. Haldane lecturing on genetics. His quantitative treatment impressed me greatly.

I soon became bored with the regular course of experimental work we had to do each week – the experimental methods in psychology seemed to me so obvious that I didn't require much teaching! Of course I had to do the course, and kept an accurate record, using my newly acquired skills in typewriting for the purpose. I had bought a second-hand machine which cost £3.00 at the time, and lasted me for many years; I was to type my first and second books, *Dimensions of Personality* and *The Scientific Study of Personality*, on it. Thereafter, fortunately, I was to have some secretarial help and that expedited things considerably.

Among the many aspects of psychology that interested me, hypnosis was one, and I was fortunate enough to make the acquaintance of an older student who was earning a living as a psychotherapist, although he never had any training for that role. He had some experience in hypnosis, and we decided, in 1937, to do some experiments in that field. I devised the methodology, and did the statistical treatment; he carried out the hypnotic induction. All this work, done while I was still an undergraduate, was later published under my name, my friend having no interest in publication. As might have been expected from someone of my temperament, the paper debunked many current views about the wonders of hypnosis, such as its producing hypersensitivity to various visual and auditory cues. We did, however, find that under deep hypnosis pain could be abolished for all practical purposes, and muscular endurance increased considerably. The paper is still occasionally cited after more than forty years, and I think its conclusions have not been challenged.

This publication brought me into conflict with the psychoanalysts for the first time. At the end of the paper I had argued that Pavlovian conditioning provided the only acceptable explanation of hypnotic phenomena, using the concept of verbal conditioning as an intermediary stage. When I took the paper to the editor of the *British Journal of Medical Psychology*, a confirmed psychoanalyst, he said he liked the experimental part, but he would prefer me to give a Freudian explanation! I was so surprised by this absurd suggestion that for once in my life I was almost speechless, though I did manage to say in a few words what I thought of his suggestion, and we finally compromised by leaving out all theoretical discussion of the causes of hypnotic phenomena.

Burt did not fulfil his duties as professor very well – he was a poor administrator and organiser – and didn't spend much time in the laboratory. Indeed, the whole department was suffering from neglect. There was a single hand-crank calculating machine in the department, itself a relic from the days when W.Yule was Professor of Statistics at University College, and few books or journals in the library. Flugel was too busy treating patients to spend much time with us, and Philpott was too poorly paid to throw up a chance of giving external university lectures, which took up a great deal of his time. It was a discouraging department in many ways. As I told Burt, on several occasions when we had a chance to talk together, I admired the clever way in which he used statistics to tease out different aspects of his empirical results, but I thought that the quality of the empirical studies themselves, and the results which they gave, were hardly worth the bother. To analyse in great detail the results of tests administered by largely untrained teachers, to unwilling pupils, in any old school that would allow the test to be done, did not, in my view, provide results that could be relied upon, however inspired the statistical treatment.

However that may be, Burt was impressed with my progress in statistics and psychometrics, and in my second year in the undergraduate course asked me to collaborate with him in the review of a monograph recently published by Leo Thurstone which had aroused a great deal of interest. Spearman had argued, on the basis of correlational studies of intelligence tests, that the body of inter-correlations could be explained in terms of a single general factor (g) of intelligence, and special factors specific to each of the tests used. Thurstone administered fifty-six tests to groups of university students, analysed them by means of factor analysis, and concluded that there was no general factor, but instead half a dozen or so primary factors of mental abilities which could explain all the observed data. Burt had been asked to review this monograph extensively in the *British Journal of Educational Psychology*, and he wanted me to re-analyse the huge matrix of inter-correlations that the Thurstones had presented, using a method of analysis Burt himself had developed. His view was that there was a general factor of intelligence, as Spearman had said, but also that there were group factors of intelligence, very much like those discovered by Thurstone. He thought the re-analysis of Thurstone's data would prove his point.

Obviously I was flattered by this invitation, and immediately accepted it. I hired a hand-crank machine (nothing else was available at that time of course), and spent countless hours doing the elaborate and detailed analyses that were required, coming up with the outcome that Burt had predicted. He had told me that he would write the text, which he showed me, and that the table of factor loadings that I had worked out would be published in the review, which would carry both of our names as authors. I read the text he had written, which seemed perfectly straightforward to me, and awaited with bated breath the final publication. When it appeared it had only my name on it, and the text had been extensively re-written, to be much more critical of Thurstone and much more laudatory of Cyril Burt. This seemed an odd way of behaving to me, but there was nothing I could do about it, the editor of the journal being a close friend of Burt's.

Many years later I was to give a talk at one of Thurstone's seminars in Chicago, and was greeted abruptly. He very much disliked Burt, thought him dishonest, and because of this review assumed that I was one of Burt's pets. The fact that I spoke at the seminar about my theory of criterion analysis, which cut across his notions of factor analysis, did not help. At the end of my talk several of the students, taking their cue as they thought from Leo, eagerly criticized my method, and so did Thelma Thurstone. Leo silenced them, saying they were talking nonsense, and Thelma quickly disappeared into the kitchen, saying she was going to make coffee for all of us. Thereafter we became very good friends, and I had a chance to explain to Leo my complex relationship with Burt, about which more anon.

Leo Thurstone, for my money, was one of the most outstanding psychologists of his age, and in addition a very intellectually honest person. (I had pointed out that part of the reason why in Thurstone's study there had been less evidence of a general factor than was usually found, was the limited range of ability of his population, which consisted entirely of advanced students. Leo and Thelma repeated the study with unselected schoolchildren, and found, very much as my analysis had suggested, that they needed both a general factor and group factors of ability.)

If Burt behaved somewhat oddly in this instance, he did so even more on another occasion. In connection with my thinking about experimental aesthetics (which was to be the material for my Ph.D. thesis), I had argued that if there is such a personal quality as artistic good taste, distributed variably across individuals, then it would follow that judgements about works of art of any kind should show some degree of similarity between individuals; so that if large numbers of individuals were to rank works of art in order of preference, these orders should correlate positively together on the whole. From this I deduced that if we correlated individuals together, the correlations might be quite low. If we then took random aggregates or groups of five individuals, correlating together the average rankings of these groups, the correlations should be a good deal higher. Taking larger and larger groups, the correlations should begin to approach unity. I worked out a formula which would predict exactly what should happen, collected large-scale data, and found that the formula fitted pretty well. I wrote all this up and showed it to Burt, who returned the draft to me without saying anything. It was only then that I stumbled across the awkward fact that the formula I had worked out was not in fact original; it was simply a version of the well-known Spearman-Brown Prophecy Formula, usually applied to correlations between tests, or test items, but in this case applied to persons.

In other words, I had re-invented the wheel, an achievement not usually treated with great enthusiasm by professional scientists. Had I published the paper as it stood, I would have exposed myself to eternal ridicule! Burt must have known this, but didn't warn me. The article, with all claims for originality removed, was accepted for publication by the *Journal of Experimental Psychology*, and was my first venture in the realms of statistical psychology.

In 1938, I obtained my Bachelor's Degree with First Class Honours; Burt told me later that it was the best set of examination papers he had ever read. (He also told me, on another occasion, that he only gave me a First because he knew the quality of my work, but that my handwriting was so bad that he hadn't been able to read anything I had written!) Actually, I expected to do well in the exam, having successfully predicted the questions that were going to be asked – a feat I was to repeat to help many other students whom I was coaching in the years to come. This coaching was one way of earning a little money for me; I also taught German in a language school, and gave lessons in statistics to students in the Statistics Department of the University. I had occasional difficulties in collecting my money; I recall one young lady who thought I might prefer the enjoyment of her body to the few pounds she owed me – a demonstration of her psychological incompetence! Altogether money was an awkward subject for me; as an alien I was not allowed to work, and the money Dr Glass and my mother were sending me was barely sufficient.

At the same time as getting my degree, I married Margaret Davies, whom I have already mentioned. She was a pretty, vivacious Canadian girl, several years older than myself, who earned a living as a secretary. She was highly intelligent, well organized and superbly efficient. In addition to carrying out her job over the next few years, she got interested in psychology, and decided to take a Master's Degree in that subject. Her first degree in Canada had been in mathematics, and she did her thesis on the topic of individual preferences for different types of olfactory stimuli – smells to the uninitiated. It said much for her drive and general ability that she was able to do this in record time in spite of having a full-time job, and looking after our household. We lived in a block of flats in Hampstead, where we stayed throughout the war. Our honeymoon was spent on the Scilly Isles, where we swam, sailed, and went for long walks. Inevitably our marriage was a rather drab affair, both of us being quite poor; also the coming war cast its shadow over everything.

Margaret was rather right-wing in her political attitudes, and was scandalized by my strong left-wing opinions. Altogether my views were unacceptable to the majority of English people I met. I was what was later called a 'premature anti-Fascist', and this was anathema at a time when appeasement was all the rage. I still remember the day when Hitler marched into the Rhineland, breaking all treaties and effectively starting the Second World War. I was in the flat of Edith, a girl-friend at the time, when the radio announced the event, and it became clear that the British and French Governments would do nothing about it. I was stunned, realizing that this was the last chance to get rid of Hitler and avoid the war, and that the democracies were throwing it away. Hitler obviously wasn't strong enough militarily to resist the democracies if they had insisted on his removing his troops, and as we now know, the German generals were planning, if that should happen, to depose Hitler. Whether the British and French leaders were too stupid to see this, or whether they were hoping, as I surmised, to enlist Germany in a war against Communist Russia, is difficult to ascertain now. What is certain is that the chance was lost, and that my anticipations were unfortunately borne out a few years later.

Similarly, when the Civil War broke out in Spain I was vehemently anti-Franco, while most of my friends seemed to think that he should be supported, as being an ally against Communism. I argued desperately against this view, but without much success. England at the time was steeped in political apathy, desperately trying to avoid conflict with Germany, and hostile to Russia; only Churchill expressed views which seemed to me rational and forward-looking, and he of course was far removed from the centres of power. Those who opposed the philosophy of appeasement were looked upon with disfavour, labelled 'Communists' and troublemakers, and regarded with considerable suspicion. It was an unhappy time, and it was not until the outbreak of the war that attitudes began to change slowly.

During the late thirties, I committed two crimes which at the time were punishable in Germany by the death penalty. One was treason: having refused to vote in the election called by Hitler, and refusing to return to Germany and fight for the Fatherland, I was committing treason, and had the war ended in Germany's favour I would have been shot (or hanged, more likely).

The other crime was more adventurous. My mother decided to smuggle our family fortune out of Germany, as Hitler had laid down rules that made it impossible for refugees to take any money or valuables out of the country. We cooked up a rather clever plan, which involved using the ferry from Germany to Gjedser, a small Danish port which was quite near. The ferry was used by holidaymakers who went across on a day-trip and came back a little later; for this you didn't need a passport. Nor was there any inspection of whatever bits of luggage one might carry along. We turned all our money into stamps and pearls and other valuables which didn't take up much space, and my mother booked a return trip on the ferry, while I booked a trip across to Gjedser and then by rail all the way to Copenhagen. We pretended not to know each other, the idea being that she would carry these valuables through to Gjedser, where we would meet; she would hand them over to me, and I would then take them on to Copenhagen where she would join me a few days later.

The plan worked beautifully, up to the point where she had to go though the control. For some reason the guards were more attentive than usual and searched the belongings of all passengers. She played her part beautifully, however; when she reached the guard she smiled at him with those beautiful eyes of hers, and got him talking – he forgot all about her handbag! The rest of the adventure went like clockwork, but had we been discovered we would have ended up in a Concentration Camp. In retrospect I still shudder to think what might have happened.

During this time I had developed certain views about psychology which have not changed since then, and which powerfully influenced me in designing and carrying out the kind of work I have been doing since. It appeared fairly obvious that two kinds of psychology existed, and that many problems were created by the constant failure to distinguish between the two. This view grew out of Eddington's famous story of the two tables, which formed the introduction of one of his popular books on modern physics. On the one hand, he pointed out, we have the table with which we are all familiar – solid, weighty, the thing that impinges on all our senses. On the other hand, however, we have the table as physics sees it – myriads of molecules flying about in space, each in turn made up of electrons and protons, cruising around planetary orbits and leaving much the greater part of the table as empty space. Physics started with reality as our senses perceived it, but it has gone well beyond that stage and introduced concepts completely alien to the layman.

Nevertheless, popular physics has much to be said for it. We become acquainted with it as we grow up, and we certainly become adept at adjusting our behaviour to its laws. The footballer who curls his shot into the corner of the net; the tennis player who serves accurately at a speed of 100 miles an hour into the corner of the service court; the high-jumper who clears a bar at a great height – these are all making use of an acquired knowledge of the laws of physics, including those applying to gravitational forces, without any knowledge whatsoever of experimental physics. The man in the street knows a great deal of practical physics, without having any knowledge of scientific principles.

In the same way we all have a considerable amount of knowledge about psychology – about drives and motivation, intelligence and personality, love and attraction; we simply couldn't exist without fairly accurate estimates of our own and other people's potentials, wishes, desires, and behaviours. All this is quite independent of scientific psychology – i.e., the factual information we have about intelligence, memory, habit formation, conditioning, etc. Thus, just as there are two kinds of physics, so there are two kinds of psychology.

It may be asked, if so many people know how to cope with psychological problems on the basis of simple observation and experience, why then is scientific psychology needed? The answer, of course, is that judgements are often guided by our wishes, and that may be very misleading; we need a more scientific approach in order to improve them. As a typical example, take the commonsensical notion that children in school would learn better if they were in smaller classes, an observation repeated daily by parents and teachers alike. Yet the evidence of numbers of carefully conducted studies, in many different countries, has shown that it makes very little difference whether children are in classes of twenty or forty or even more; the rate of learning is only affected favourably when classes are very, very small – i.e., in single numbers!

Similarly, psychiatric judgements are more frequently based on experience than on scientific knowledge, and the unedifying spectacle of opposing psychiatrists in court swearing that the accused is/is not a psychopath, or schizophrenic, or mad, or incapable of distinguishing between right and wrong is a clear indication that a more scientific approach is needed.

My first public debate arose from my challenging one such prejudice. Psychologists assumed that a suitable expert, or group of experts, can ascertain, by interview, which of several candidates is the most likely to be successful in a job. I was interested in this topic, and was curious to see if there was any such evidence for this view. I went through the literature systematically, and soon found out that the evidence against the success of the interview was overwhelming – different experts examining the same subjects came to widely different conclusions. Candidates who did well or poorly had their future performance predicted by interviewers at a level no better than chance. Interviewers *do* seem to be successful, but that is only because those who come before them have usually already been highly selected on the basis of examinations, performance, etc. I once gave a talk on this topic to a group of nursing sisters, and one of them, a highly intelligent woman, said that in her experience the interview was 92 per cent successful; in other words, they only picked 8 per cent of nursing candidates who did not work out. I told her that as she was working in one of the most prestigious teaching hospitals in London, only the best nurses would apply, and if she picked her team at random, or by tossing a coin, she would probably still have a failure rate of only 8 per cent. She agreed to try out the experiment, and for the next intake she accepted everyone who turned up. The failure rate turned out to be 6 per cent!

The public debate came about because Alec Rodger (later to become Professor of Industrial Psychology at Birkbeck College), famous for his 'Seven-point Plan for Interviewing', heard of my impudent assertion that interviewing didn't do much good and decided to contest it. As so often happens with people in the applied field, he relied in his talk entirely on experience, disregarding the published evidence, and as a consequence I think I won on points.

The failure of psychologists to have particular insight in matters of ordinary life is intriguing. The equivalent is quite obvious so far as physics is concerned – we would not expect Einstein or Newton to beat Lendl at tennis, to be better at soccer than Pele, or to beat Davies at snooker. Similarly, it would not be reasonable to expect psychologists or psychiatrists to be better 'practical' psychologists than salesmen, whores, policemen, or pimps; indeed, scientists are often excessively ignorant of practical affairs, credulous to an incredible degree, and lacking in quite elementary insight. During the war, War Office Selection Boards held three-day trials in which candidates were subjected to numerous interviews, tests, and leaderless group and other situations in which they could show their qualities. At the end a group discussion was held between ten or so selectors, including psychiatrists, psychologists, weapon specialists, officers, etc. Each had to give a rating to the various candidates before the discussion was opened, and at the end an agreed rating was made by the Board. A follow-up study, tracing the future careers of the candidates, showed that the psychiatrists, followed by the psychologists, made the worst predictions of all – they tended to be influenced by complex and highly speculative theories, paying too much attention to the candidates' unimportant quirks of behaviour, and neglecting important and obvious details.

This absence of what one might call commonsense – i.e., an alienation from ordinary life, can also be observed in many psychological and psychiatric textbooks. I read several books on the psychology of sex at the time, none of which even mentioned one of the most important differences between men and women, namely the fact that men are stronger, and that the man can beat up the woman. This is unfortunately a routine happening, and some 80 per cent of women have experienced at least one such event in their lives. Unpalatable as it may be, it obviously has profound effects on the behaviour and the psychology of men and women respectively. Yet very little attention has been paid by psychiatrists and psychologists to this elementary factor.

Or consider physical attractiveness. The man in the street knows full well how important this factor can be in the life of a man or a woman, but until quite recently psychologists and psychiatrists have shied away from the concept. It is only now that studies are being done in this field, demonstrating considerable agreement between judgements of the given person's physical attractiveness, and demonstrating how vitally important this is in life.

I recall a meeting of the University Board of Studies concerned with the approval of Ph.D. thesis titles. One unfortunate candidate had suggested that he was going to do an experimental study of 'happiness' – this was greeted with guffaws, and the application was turned down on the ground that this was not a proper psychological study. In recent years there has been some interest in happiness as a psychological construct, to be investigated and measured, but even now very little is known about it.

It used to be said that experimental psychologists studied in a very scientific manner topics which were of no conceivable interest or importance, while psychoanalysts looked in a very unscientific manner at issues that were of extreme importance. I decided to look at issues which were of interest to the man in the street in as scientific a manner as was possible.

So much for what I might call the strategy of my research endeavours. How about the tactics? My method of working had by now been fully developed. I have always been an exceedingly fast reader. I could glance down a page for a few seconds and take in most or all of the useful information on that page; once acquired, the information would stay in my memory for a long time. For many years I used to read something like three books a day, but of course when I say 'read' I mean something quite different from what most people would understand by that term. I am here talking about the intake of information pure and simple, and that follows quite different rules from, say, reading a novel, poem or play – which cannot be hurried. Really fast reading is only meaningful in the context of information acquisition; and has no place in what we might call enjoyable reading – although I would not like to be quoted as saying that the intake of information is not enjoyable!

Speed of reading, therefore, must always be coupled with what I call 'functional reading'. When I read a book on psychology, the author inevitably cites a great deal of information that as a professional reader I already know; he will quote authors, articles, facts and theories with which I am already familiar, and which I can therefore skip. Very few books have as much as 10 per cent of new information to contribute, and it is that of course which is of interest to me. Combining this functional reading with speed reading means that I can go through many books at the rate of about half an hour to an hour each. I am able to both extract the important bits and remember them.

Retention of material so learned, however, depends on a third variable which I think is also very important, certainly for me. We may perhaps call it 'crystallization' – i.e., the formation of definite shapes or mental constructs. It is very difficult to remember isolated fragments of information; if we have no hooks to hang them on, they tend to vanish very quickly. I would always try and develop schemata as early in my reading as possible, so that new information would be *meaningful*, supporting or disproving hypotheses and theories I had formed, and in a general sort of way relevant to what I already had in mind. This crystallization, of course, has its dangers – we may only admit to our mind facts which are in agreement with our views and theories, and reject and forget those which are not. This method of working – speedy reading, functional reading, and crystallization – was to be my main help in coping with the vast array of facts and figures which threatens to overwhelm the novice in any scientific field.

I have mentioned that I used to read some three books a day. One of the books would be on psychology proper – i.e., on learning theory, memory, motivation, personality, intelligence, and so on. Another would be on some related topic in sociology, anthropology, criminology, genetics, physiology, psychopharmacology, philosophy of science, history of science, or whatnot. Finally, a third volume would be on an unrelated topic in physics, astronomy, biochemistry or whatever attracted my attention, including very out-of-the-way topics like the meandering of rivers, or the art of the conductor of an orchestra! My method of working proved suitable to my needs and abilities, and particularly important when I started writing popular books.

Going from the general to the specific, I worked out five principles which I thought governed the study of psychology as a scientific discipline, and I have oriented myself very closely along these principles. They seemed to me little more than commonsense. Nevertheless, each of them has been savagely attacked by what was often a majority of psychologists, and each of them has led to large-scale theoretical battles. I will mention these principles briefly.

(1) It seemed quite clear to me that man was a *biosocial organism*, whose

conduct was determined equally by biological factors such as hunger, thirst, sexual appetite, etc., and by social constraints enforced by the government, through agencies such as schoolmasters and police, or by public approval and disapproval. Around the turn of the century there was a strong emphasis on *biological* causes, along the lines of social Darwinism. In the last fifty years there has been an overwhelming emphasis on *social* factors, often leading to a complete disregard of biological ones. Genetic causes, in particular, have been decried. The fact, for instance, that aggressive and sadistic youths have often been savagely beaten by their parents when they were young is almost inevitably interpreted in a causal way – i.e., the beatings *cause* the aggression. But it is equally possible that the genes which caused the parents to beat the children were inherited by the children and led them into their aggressive and sadistic behaviour; or that the unruly behaviour of the children forced the parents to resort to savage beatings. It is possible that all three causes were active in a particular case. Obvious as these remarks may be, psychologists publishing their results, and editors publishing them in their journals, have never paid any attention to these various possibilities of interpretation, and have plumped 100 per cent for the social interpretation. Thus apparently my first principle required a statement, even though it attracted a great deal of hostile reaction.

(2) My second principle states simply that we must reject the Cartesian notion of body and mind as separate 'substances', and instead plump for a mind-body continuum – very much as physicists have plumped for a space-time continuum, and left off regarding space and time as qualitatively different. Such a principle again is too obvious to require any supporting argument. It does, however, offend traditional behaviourists, from Watson to Skinner, who want to study behaviour in the abstract, and want to leave physiological and biochemical determinants out altogether.

(3) My third point has already been mentioned, namely, the need to reconcile the two major disciplines of scientific psychology, the correlational and the experimental. Cronbach's eloquent plea in that direction in 1957, in his APA Presidential Address, has often been quoted with approval, but had very little effect on protagonists of either camp. The two disciplines are still as firmly divided as ever, although I have never seen any rational argument for such a division. I am still firmly convinced that only by bringing these two groups of investigators together will psychology emerge as a true unified science.

(4) One reason for holding this view is closely associated with my next maxim, namely that the distinction between applied and pure science is particularly uninformative in psychology, and ought to be abandoned. My reason is this. In physics, to take this as a model of the hard sciences, the experimenter can isolate variables to his heart's content; the subject matter is, to put it in a rather old-fashioned way, almost infinitely sub-divisible (a-tomos). This is not so in applied physics: when we want to build a bridge, or an aeroplane, or a gas chamber, we must have some regard to the unit itself; we cannot sub-divide it indefinitely. I recall visiting the National Physical Laboratory on one occasion, and being shown a wind tunnel which had a model of a bridge in it. I asked why they tested this model in the wind tunnel, rather than deriving its wind resistance from a formula. This caused a good deal of merriment, because apparently even the best formula gives a solution which has an error of several hundred per cent! The complexity of the structure – i.e., its 'Gestalt' characteristics, make it impossible to treat a bridge as we would a molecule, or an atom.

Now by definition psychology deals with the behaviour of organisms, and organisms are indivisible in that sense. We may concentrate on a particular type of behaviour, such as pressing a button in response to a light stimulus, or even the patellar tendon reflex. But the pushing of the button, or the excursion of the leg following the hammer blow on the knee, cannot be completely isolated from the organism itself, the motivation of that organism, the degree of cortical arousal, the visceral reaction to the situation, the understanding of the instructions, and many other factors. Thus psychology, even studied as a science, inevitably resembles applied physics more than pure physics. Experimentalists often disregard this holistic quality of their subjects, and pay no attention to individual differences, but this merely means that they throw away a large proportion of the total variance, and are eternally plagued by very high error variances. These could be reduced tremendously by incorporating individual differences in personality and intelligence in their experiments.

Another reason why the distinction between pure and applied science is blurred in psychology is this. The physicist can do what he likes to his subject matter; he can expose it to temperatures near the absolute zero in cryogenic experiments, or he can heat it to unimaginable temperatures. The psychologist, in contrast, is extremely restricted. If we want to study real fear, we find immediately that ethical considerations make it impossible for us to produce such strong feelings in the laboratory. Our only justification for arousing such strong feelings would be in a therapeutic context; in other words, we may do it in order to cure a phobic or anxious patient, where the arousal of the emotion is part of the therapy, as in behaviour therapy. Thus our 'pure' research into the nature of emotion or motivation is immediately confined to 'applied' contexts. The same is true of industrial, educational and social phenomena; it is difficult to produce laboratory phenomena which are even approaching in strength those which can be observed under more realistic conditions. This does not rule out the experimental study of such phenomena, but it has definite limits, and suggests where possible the use of real-life settings.

(5) The last of my five principles, like the others, may seem so obvious that no discussion is necessary. I proposed very simply that for any assertion in psychology, there should be an attempt at proof. Such a proof would have to be empirical, and preferably experimental, but no assertion should be accepted without adequate proof. This might be considered the minimum requirement for differentiation between science and pseudo-science, and I would not expect any reader to disagree. Nevertheless, when I looked at the field as it was at the time of my obtaining my Bachelor's Degree, there were glaring and obvious exceptions to this rule. The most obvious one was the general acceptance of psychoanalytic claims that this Freudian type of treatment was successful in curing neurotic patients of their disorder, and was indeed the only treatment capable of doing this. As I will discuss in more detail later on, this assertion was almost universally accepted by psychiatrists and psychologists, although I could not discover any empirical basis for it whatsoever. Assertions of this kind were frequent, but proofs were lacking.

These five governing principles contributed, singly or in combination, to my becoming, to quote the title of a profile that was to appear in the *New Scientist*, 'The Psychologist They Most Love to Hate'. My insistence on the biosocial nature of man enraged all the 100 per cent environmentalists, at that time the vast majority of psychologists; my insistence on the interaction between mind and body infuriated the behaviourists, at that time the most influential group in psychology. My insistence that the two disciplines of science and psychology could not rationally exist and work apart from each other was greeted with disapproval by both sides, and my rejection of the applied versus pure dichotomy in psychology did not please either the 'applied' or the 'pure' psychologists. Last but not least, my insistence on proof annoyed all those who, like psychoanalysts, psychiatrists and clinical psychologists, wanted to earn their living in peace, without having to demonstrate empirically that what they were doing was socially useful. Add to all this the ideological and political factors I have already mentioned, and it will become clear that I was not to be psychology's favourite son!

By now of course the situation has changed considerably, and the views which were anathema fifty years ago are widely accepted. As Bertrand

Russell once pointed out, in England, if you have unorthodox opinions, you will be disregarded at first, persecuted if you persist, but finally, canonized if you live long enough. Having experienced the first two stages, I seem to be approaching the third, having just been given the 'Distinguished Scientist Award' of the American Psychological Association. Perhaps if I should live to be ninety . . . However that may be, until now academic life has been more of a struggle than I anticipated, for I naively supposed that scientists were calm, reasonable and objective. I had not then read what Max Planck, perhaps with Einstein the greatest theoretical physicist of the century and the author of modern Quantum Mechanics, had to say in his autobiography: 'The new scientific truth does not triumph by convincing its opponents and making them see the light, but rather because its opponents eventually die, and a new generation grows up that is familiar with it.' And I was equally unfamiliar with Machiavelli's warning that 'there is nothing more difficult to carry out, nor more dangerous to handle, than to initiate a new order of things. For the reformer has enemies in all those who profit by the old order, and only lukewarm defenders in all those who would profit by the new.' Perhaps it was just as well for my peace of mind that I was still ignorant (in 1938).

I now had to consider what I would be doing for my Ph.D. The University of London required a large-scale research project, written up as a thesis, under the supervision of a professor in the University. Unfortunately war was approaching, and University College, together with its Psychology Department, was moving to Aberystwyth. I could not follow as Margaret was working in London, and had no chance of getting a job in Aberystwyth. We were entirely dependent on her earnings. I obtained permission to carry out my research in London, without direct contact with my supervisor Cyril Burt. In many ways this arrangement suited me quite well; I didn't think I needed much supervision, and in fact would have disliked any interference with my plans. Burt, it turned out, was under the impression that I was doing something entirely different and left me completely in peace. I think he was rather upset by my refusal to fall in with one of his plans. He had been asked to standardize the Binet Test in England, and wished me to carry out this task for him, as my Ph.D. thesis. Although I appreciated the compliment, I felt it was a routine exercise with little scientific interest. I declined as gracefully as I could and decided instead to do some research in experimental aesthetics, combining two very important considerations.

The first of these was a genuine interest in art, which led me to ask questions which psychological experiment might be capable of answering. Second, and equally important, was the fact that with the absence of the psychological laboratory and all its equipment, I would have to work without any apparatus, and experiments in aesthetics, particularly visual aesthetics, lend themselves to this type of situation. It was easy to buy postcard reproductions of works of art, or to use coloured papers, polygonal figures, etc. in getting subjects to make preference judgements. In any case I thought I could make a go of it, and decided to spend the next two years on such projects.

The initial impetus for my studies came from a series of lectures given by Professor Susan Stebbing, a well-known British philosopher who had written an excellent book on the philosophical implications of the new physics, and who gave a course on the philosophy of aesthetics. I still recall her telling us about the fundamental law of aesthetics, which she declared to be: 'unity in diversity'. I also recall sitting in the Tube, going home that evening, and seeing an advertisement for Colman's mustard, showing, in glaring poster colours, a plate with a slice of bacon and two eggs on it, as well as some chips, a sausage, and of course some Colman's mustard. Here, I thought, was a wonderful example of unity in diversity – the unity being provided by food on a plate, the diversity by the various different types of food on the plate. But would anybody consider this advert a work of art? Clearly there was something wrong with these philosophical deliberations, and when the time for Susan Stebbing's next lecture came around, I put the question to her. She was an articulate woman, and spoke for ten minutes in answer to my question, but I gathered that she really didn't know the answer. This suggested to me that perhaps an experimental approach might be intriguing, and out of this grew my Ph.D. thesis.

Another factor was my dissatisfaction with a famous statement by Jeremy Bentham, the Utilitarian philosopher and founder of University College, where I was studying, and where his skeleton is still exhibited. He gave it as his opinion that 'push-pin was as good as poetry', and while I was not quite sure what push-pin might be (presumably a precursor of the games youngsters play in amusement arcades), I was convinced that poetry was superior in a meaningful sense. This early insistence on the relativity of values has recently been extended by whole-hogging egalitarians to comparisons of whole cultures, insisting on the equal value of European music, painting or sculpture and, say, African or Bushman or Red Indian art. This seemed to me nonsensical, and I cast around for a methodology that would support or refute my notion of artistic excellence.

In fact, Cyril Burt was also influential in my coming to this decision. Speaking about appreciation of visual stimuli, such as pictures, he asked the question: 'If we could brush aside all irrelevant associations, and take a completely detached view . . . would there be any solid grounds for preference left?' He and some of his earlier students had published studies in which individual subjects ranked or rated a number of pictures, and had shown that they tended to agree in their views; in other words, their rankings or ratings were positively correlated on the whole. Did this prove that there was some degree of objectivity to aesthetic judgements? The question of course has a long history, with commonsense giving typically different answers. On the one hand we say that '*De gustibus non est disputandum*' (There is no arguing about taste); on the other hand we value a Titian or a Van Gogh more highly than the scribblings of a child. Unfortunately the Burtian studies did not resolve the issue, because the pictures judged were subject to all sorts of outside influences which might affect the issue. One of these studies, for instance, included 'reproductions from classical masters, second-rate painters, every variety and type known to the crudest and most flashy birthday card'. It would be obvious to the judges which were the socially accepted pictures and painters, which would cost the most money, and which would be regarded by experts as superior; any or all of these influences might produce the agreement between them. Burt, though stating that all irrelevant associations should be eliminated, had in practice violated this rule.

Another criticism that occurred to me was that only one test was used. Visual appreciation should be defined as broadly as possible, and this could only be done by having a number of dissimilar tests, each consisting of different types of stimuli. Accordingly, I devised a two-stage procedure. In the first stage I collected eighteen sets of pictures of a variety of different types of material. For example: thirty-two reproductions of comparatively unknown portrait paintings by modern painters and old masters; thirty-two reproductions of modern statues, which would be unknown to my subjects; sixteen coloured photographs of vases from the British Museum; twenty reproductions of pencil drawings by Claude Lorrain; twelve coloured landscape paintings by Japanese artists; twelves curves of mathematical functions drawn in ink; and so forth. As far as possible each of these eighteen sets contained items such that judgements of preference could only be based on aesthetic merit, not on knowledge, reputation or any other outside factors. I did indeed find that there was agreement between my judges on the aesthetic merits of the items in each of the sets, which suggested that aesthetic judgements were objective to some degree.

My next step was to ask the question whether individuals differed with respect to their aesthetic judgements, some being better judges than others? In other words, given that there is such a thing as 'good taste', do some people have better taste than others? To answer this question I took each of the eighteen tests and scored the degree to which any individual agreed with the average order of the objects contained in each of the sets. Having given each individual a score for each of the eighteen tests, I then intercorrelated the scores of the individual judgements over the eighteen tests. If I was right in postulating the existence of individual differences in 'good taste', then these judgement scores should intercorrelate positively and, lo and behold, they did! The study thus seemed to show that there was some objectivity to aesthetic judgements, and that individuals differed in the degree to which they approximated this objective measure of 'good taste'.

I carried out another similar study to replicate these findings, and to extend them in another direction. In addition to universal agreement on the aesthetic excellence of my various test items, I thought I had discovered what in Burt's theory of intelligence would have been called 'group factors'; some people preferred modern paintings, others more old-fashioned paintings. In this second study I replicated the findings of the first, as far as the general factor was concerned, but I also found a second factor of the kind described. I went one step further and correlated the second factor with a test of extraversion and introversion, finding that extraverts – as expected – preferred modern, colourful pictures, whereas introverts preferred the more old-fashioned, less colourful type of pictures.

It had seemed to me from observation that extraverts paid more attention to colour, introverts to form, and I constructed a special test to measure this tendency. The subjects were required to rank in order of liking ten polygons and ten colours. They were then required to put in order of liking ten coloured polygons in which the colour and the form were combined in such a way that the best-liked colour was put with the worst-liked form, and vice-versa. Thus a conflict was set up within the individual, and the way in which this conflict was resolved indicated which of the two characteristics – colour or form – had more influence on the subject's aesthetic preference. As expected this test correlated with extraversion–introversion, and also with the dichotomy of modern versus old-fashioned painters.

I carried out a series of other studies. In one of these I looked at simple colour preferences, for there had been some argument about the existence of a general degree of agreement. Reviewing the literature, and carrying out a study of my own, I found a considerable amount of agreement between individuals, which extended to agreement between different countries and races. In other words, the situation was nothing like as chaotic as some authors had suggested. Quite generally, a preference for any colour varies inversely with the luminosity factor of that colour (i.e., the brightness at any wavelength relative to that at

5550 A.U. along the equal energy spectrum). What is more, I found that an individual's agreement with this colour ranking was correlated with his standing on the general factor of aesthetic sensitivity which I had discovered, and which thus can be shown to extend to relatively simple aesthetics judgements, like choice of colour.

In addition to my absorption in the aesthetics of colour vision, I was also interested in form. The famous American mathematician, G. D. Birkhoff, had published an influential book on the *Aesthetic Measure*, in which he suggested a general formula derived from his notion that pleasure in any work of art depended on two variables: one of Order (O), and one of Complexity (C) in the object. These combined in various ways for different classes of object, but all classes obeyed the general formula: M (the amount of pleasure derived) = O/C. Birkhoff had worked out his formula in detail for 90 polygonal figures, using such notions as vertical or horizontal symmetry, rotational symmetry, repetition, the complexity of the figure, re-entrant angles, angles close to 90°–180°, etc. to measure the order and complexity elements in question, and to attribute the value of M according to his formula to each of the 90 polygonal figures he published. However, as is typical of a mathematician, he never tested his formula on a group of subjects; had he done so, he would soon have found that their judgement of preference did not correlate at all with his formula!

I decided to do some experimental work in this field, starting out with an alteration of the theory. If there is any meaning attached to the phrase 'unity in diversity', then surely the formula should read: M = O × C – i.e., a work of art is 'better' to the extent that it contains a high degree of complexity as well as a high degree of order. The results bore this out; correlations between my formula and the observed rankings of the polygons were much higher than those obtained with Birkhoff's formula. Indeed, I was able to combine the various O and C elements used by Birkhoff in a general predictive formula which could be applied to polygons (many-sided figures), and which gave high correlations with observed data. People whose rankings correlated well with this formula also did well on the general test of aesthetic sensitivity. Factor analysis disclosed also a second factor, contrasting liking for complex with liking for simple figures, and it was later on found that artists tended towards a greater liking for simple, lay people towards a greater liking for complex figures – perhaps in line with another later finding that artists tended to be rather introverted.

In spite of their differences artists and controls did of course agree on the whole, the correlation being 0.67; agreement is very much stronger than disagreement. Those who feel that only artists and experts should be listened to in their likes and dislikes for works of art might take notice that on the whole there is considerable agreement between experts and lay people.

Readers unfamiliar with Birkhoff's polygons may like to see some examples, and accordingly I give here two figures (Fig. 2.1 and Fig. 2.2), the first showing the sixteen polygons having the highest 'Order' scores, and the second showing the sixteen polygons having the highest 'Complexity' scores.

A lot of additional work was done to discover the major factors determining liking and disliking of polygonal figures, such as rectangularity, simplicity, rotational symmetry, the presence of projections, etc., and also of geometrical designs and devices, but these studies are probably of less general interest.

In another study, carried out relatively recently, I attempted to provide a scientific test of aesthetic sensitivity. Several such tests exist, such as the Maitland Graves Design Judgement Test, and the Barron-Welsh Art Scale, but on the whole these have not been very successful. They usually contrast two drawings, one 'good' and the other 'bad', and the subject has to say which is which. The tests are empirically poor, for a variety of reasons; in the main, the drawings are artistically inferior, and tend to put artistically minded people off. What I was looking for in creating my own test was a genuine artist who could draw aesthetically pleasing figures, and who was sufficiently interested in the psychology of art to collaborate.

It might seem easy to find such a person, but in fact it proved surprisingly difficult. I had occasion several times to address interested audiences over the years, including painters, sculptors, art critics, and generally people interested in the visual arts; and found that the reactions to what I had to say about my experiments were curiously hostile. By that I do not mean that they were critical of the methods used, the results obtained, or any particular aspects of the research; they seemed to resent the very fact that research was being done into these 'intangibles', and tended to discourage the search for factual evidence in a realm which they thought was entirely subjective. Finally, I discovered Professor K. O. Gotz, perhaps the best-known non-representational painter in West Germany, who was keenly interested in the psychology of aesthetics, and offered to collaborate in the creation of such a test. We became friendly, and I often visited him in his beautiful house set in the middle of a large wooded part of rural Germany. He and his wife Rissa, also a well-known painter, created many paintings there, including the designs for our test.

There are several versions of this test differing in degree of difficulty and the numbers of pairs of items. In each pair, one drawing is 'right' and the other 'wrong'. Figure 2.3 shows three typical items, illustrating easy,

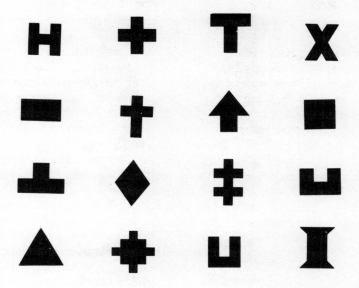

FIG. 2.1 *Simple polygons as stimuli for aesthetic evaluation.*

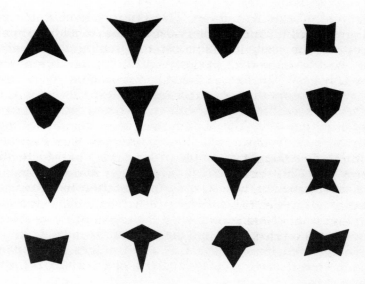

FIG. 2.2 *Complex polygons as stimuli for aesthetic evaluation.*

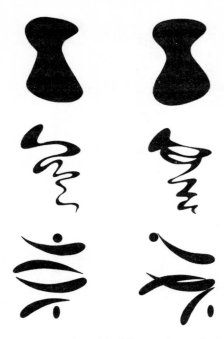

FIG. 2.3   *Three pairs of good-bad figures for aesthetic evaluation.*

middling and difficult item levels. The difficulty level of an item was judged in terms of the proportion of correct choices made by a random group of subjects, with 50 per cent constituting the chance level (impossibly difficult), and 100 per cent constituting the opposite extreme of impossibly easy. The item at the top is an example of an easy item, with an average proportion of correct answers at 95 per cent. The middle item constitutes a difficult item, with an average proportion of correct answers of 60 per cent. The bottom item is an example of middling difficulty, with an average proportion of correct answers of 79 per cent. These proportions are for a sample of 111 British university students without any special artistic training.

In the construction of the test, the artist first drew the 'good' picture, and then made certain alterations which intentionally incorporated faults in the design. Having completed the sets of pairs, he asked eight well-known painters to go through the test to make their choices. A pair was then accepted for the test if all eight judges gave unanimous agreement. Thus we have a professional criterion as a basis of the scoring procedure.

The instructions emphasized not so much the individual's preference for one item or the other, but rather the *quality* of the design. Instructions were as follows: 'You will be shown a series of pairs of designs; each pair consists of two rather similar designs. One of these is constructed to be more harmonious in its configuration than the other. Look carefully at the two designs, and you will see that the less harmonious design contains errors and faults; this assessment is based on the unanimous judgement of a group of experts, painters and graphic artists. Your task is to discover which of the two designs is the better one – i.e., more harmonious. Sometimes the "better" design will be on the right, sometimes on the left. Look carefully and take your time before coming to a decision. When you have made your decision, write "R" (for right) or "L" (for left) after the corresponding number of the design. Note that you are not asked to say which design you find more pleasant. Your task is to discover which design is the more harmonious one.' (There is, of course, high agreement between judgements of 'harmonious' and 'pleasant'.)

This test has now been widely used, and there are some interesting findings. In the first place, the *average* judgement of quite untutored audiences, including young schoolchildren, agrees 100 per cent in judging which is the 'better' or the 'worse' design in each case. This is an important point; there has been no specific training of the lay group, yet on the average they agree with the unanimous judgement of the experts.

It might be said that unintentionally the culture in which these people grew up determines their judgements. There are two reasons to doubt such an argument. Firstly, we did not find that training in drawing and painting and other artistic pursuits made any difference to the scores of our subjects. Secondly, we found that culturally diverse groups, such as Japanese students and pupils, made choices almost exactly resembling those of our English and other European samples. The test does seem to measure something approaching aesthetic sensitivity for visual stimuli, and although it correlates moderately with intelligence, this correlation is too low to account for the observed findings.

G. T. Fechner originally introduced experimental aesthetics into our culture, and contrasted aesthetics *'von oben'* (from above) and *'von unten'* (from below) – i.e., the theoretical, philosophical and speculative discussion of great works of art, while the empirical study of aesthetic judgements made of sometimes quite simple stimuli by untutored people was of course on the experimental side, looking at aesthetics *'von unten'*.

So much for the studies I did for my Ph.D., as well as the mention of some of the studies I did later on. I presented the outcome of my work at a meeting of the British Psychological Society in Reading, which I believe took place in 1940, where it was favourably received. The meetings were held over a period of days, concluding on the Sunday with a general meeting at which anyone could raise points arising from any of the papers that had been presented. This is usually a well-attended meeting, and on this particular occasion I noticed a group of people centred around a small and voluble man, holding court among his admirers. He turned out to be C. E. M. Joad, a lecturer in philosophy at Birkbeck College, who had done no original work of any kind, but had become fairly well-known through his popular writings. He was later to become famous as one of the members of the *Brains Trust* on the BBC programme which brought him together with Julian Huxley, the well-known scientist and biologist. There his talent for extempore speaking blossomed, and his speculations contrasted rather nicely with Huxley's trim factual answers. He had a reputation for being a dangerous debater, quick to think on his feet and able to express himself well.

I had never heard of him, and was rather surprised when he got up and attacked the paper I had read. Obviously I would have to reply, and as he went on speaking I noticed that he violated almost every one of the rules of debate which I had adhered to over the years. These rules are simple, but I recommend them to anyone who has occasion to engage in public arguments. Briefly, they are as follows: (1) Never argue about something about which you are fundamentally ignorant. (2) Do your homework, so that you really know everything there is to know about the topic in question. (3) Keep what you have to say short, because if you go on for any length of time the audience will forget the points you are making. (4) Concentrate on the most important points, and don't go hunting after those that matter less. (5) Having decided what are the most important points, force your opponent to answer these points, and don't let him escape by dragging in all sorts of irrelevant matters.

Joad, I was delighted to see, obviously knew nothing about experimental aesthetics; he hadn't even listened to my talk, and hence was wildly wrong in what he was saying. But he did speak well, and certainly engaged the interest of the audience. When I got up to answer him I pointed out that, as he hadn't heard my presentation, none of the points he raised was relevant to my argument. Next I showed that the findings of my study completely disproved his speculations, and asked him to state specifically how he would explain my results. Finally, sensing that he was innumerate, I asked him to state how on his premises he would explain the fact that the matrices of intercorrelations I had found had a low rank.

When I sat down, Joad didn't answer but walked out, with a rather red face. Psychologists are not generally fond of philosophers, perhaps conscious of the fact that only a little while ago psychology was regarded as part of philosophy, and the audience applauded wildly as he left. No doubt he had counted on his reputation and his expertise in thinking on his feet when he made his intervention, but even the most expert debater must stick by the rules, or he will undoubtedly lose the argument – unless his opponent is exceptionally weak. I find it curious how many people disregard these simple rules, and expose themselves to defeat and even ridicule. It is so much easier to stay silent, even though people may surmise that you are dumb, rather than speak up and prove that you are!

In addition to my work on visual aesthetics I was also interested in humour, and did a number of experiments rather similar to those I had done on aesthetics – i.e., getting people to rate or rank cartoons or jokes in order of preference. My main contribution was on the theoretical side, where I tried to unify all the existing theories in terms of a diagram (Fig. 2.4) showing how laughter and amusement in a joke or comic performance could be caused by any combination of three factors. The first class of theories stresses such cognitive elements as incongruity, contrast between ideas, deceived ideational expectation, and the like. Almost equally numerous is another group of writers who stress an orectic aspect of laughter, relating it to the satisfaction of the desire for superiority, or 'self-glory' as Hobbes has it. Last but not least, the affective aspect of laughter is stressed by those who have directed their attention more to the emotional components of laughter which is usually conceived to be pure joy, or else joy in combination with some other emotion. My theory recognizes that all three factors make an important

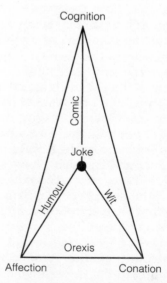

FIG. 2.4 *Theoretical conception of the theory of the comic.*

contribution, and that for different jokes, situations or behaviours, these three components can be joined in many different ways, emphasizing one or the other.

On the empirical side, I found different factors depending on the type of material used. For instance, there was a factor of 'sexual jokes' which correlated with extraversion as a personality trait.

I also found some evidence for two different types of 'sense of humour'. This may mean simply that a person likes many different types of humour, and indeed I found quite high correlations in that field. It may also mean that a person easily understands the meaning of jokes. I introduced into my cartoon test items where the cartoon was given a caption belonging to some other cartoon, and I found that some people appeared to quite like these nonsensical combinations. One cartoon, for instance, showed a witch riding, not on a broomstick, but on a Hoover. When asked to explain why this was funny, one psychology Ph.D. said: 'Well, the price tag on the Hoover says £10.50, and you would never get a Hoover for that!' Another cartoon showed a woman making up in front of a mirror, holding a telephone receiver with her right hand and apparently speaking into it. The caption said: 'Is that the Acme vanishing cream company?', and in the cartoon the woman had no face. Asked what was funny about this joke, a well-known psychiatrist said: 'Well, the wire connecting the receiver to the telephone shows that it isn't connected.' Indeed, the artist had simply put some squiggles in to indicate the connection, but that was hardly the point of the joke!

War finally broke out in 1939, and from being a premature anti-Fascist I was immediately transformed into an 'enemy alien', the official designation of refugees who had not been in England long enough to be naturalized. Soon after the outbreak of the war all Germans were interviewed by the Home Office, and classified into possible Nazis who were interned immediately, and anti-Nazis, who were left outside, but with a number of restrictions. There was a curfew, making it illegal for us to be away from home after midnight. As I soon found out, there were other limitations. I was eager to join the Royal Air Force, but was refused on the grounds that they couldn't possibly have enemy aliens flying their planes. The Army and the Navy proved equally recalcitrant, and in spite of all my eagerness to fight against the Nazi evil, I could find nothing to do to further the war effort. I was simply left alone to complete my Ph.D., not a task which seemed of the utmost importance at that time!

Worse was to follow. When France fell, and Quislings arose in Norway and other subjugated countries, the gutter press started a campaign against refugees, resulting in the Government interning the lot. Many were sent to Canada or Australia, including my friend Hans Hausmann, as well as other refugees I had come to know. After a year or so the Government saw the error of its ways, but it was a sad and stupid excess, rather like the internment of the Japanese in the United States after Pearl Harbor.

Actually I was lucky. The first time two detectives came to take me away I pleaded with them to allow me to finish my Ph.D., and they agreed. The second time round I was asked to go to the police station; I argued that the Government was just about to change its mind, and it would be rather silly to take me off to camp, only to release me immediately. The sergeant at the desk saw the sense in what I said, and let me go home; the day afterwards the Government did indeed proclaim its change of mind. But it was a narrow squeak.

I did not take this whole affair lightly. When I first came to England, I thought that democracy was the best form of government, and considered it near perfect. But I was gradually disillusioned. There was the refusal of England and France to oppose Hitler when he marched his army into the Rhineland, in defiance of the peace treaties; there was Chamberlain selling Czechoslovakia down the river in 1938, giving Hitler the gigantic Skoda arms works into the bargain; there was the refusal of the UK and the USA to do anything for the Jews on Hitler's hit-list, although millions could have been saved if only the will had been there, and less anti-Semitism in high places. Now there was this insane persecution of Hitler's victims, often interning them together with avid Nazis who used to run the camps! I concluded that democracy was the least bad form of government, but although that still leaves it ahead of others, my enthusiasm had decidedly waned. I remained convinced of the importance of freedom of speech, secret elections, and representative government, but I began to appreciate Mill's warning against the excesses of majority rule.

The churches too did not come out at all well from the Hitler challenge. The Protestant churches in Germany never opposed Hitler (except for one or two brave leaders) and they remained silent even after the infamous *Kristallnacht*. Pope Pius XI had planned to issue an encyclical containing a strong argument against racism, anti-Semitism and the persecution of the Jews in Germany, but this was side-tracked by Wladimir Ledochowski, a general of the Order of Jesuits, who saw Nazi Germany primarily as a barrier against the expansion of Soviet power. Pius XII shared Ledochowski's views, and declined to approve the encyclical. Had he done so, millions of lives might have been saved.

I finally did something for the war effort, although I cannot say it was of any great value. Living in the block of flats with Margaret and myself was a former member of the German Government in the days of Stresemann. He was working with the British Government to help in such things as propaganda, particularly with the broadcasts made from London to Europe. He asked me to listen to these, and report from the psychological point of view on how I thought they would strike listeners in Germany, a task I did to the best of my ability, but without much faith that it would contribute anything very important. The pay for this service was not excessive, but it helped to keep the wolf from the door – I was of course not receiving any more money from my parents. When the Germans broke through the Maginot Line, and France surrendered, the French police promptly interned all the refugee Germans in Concentration Camps, and my mother was one of them. She managed to escape, bribing the guards, and crossed the Pyrenees until she finally reached Spain, where she was reunited with Dr Glass who had been in Portugal on business. From there they went to Brazil, and stayed in São Paulo for a few years, my mother adding fluent Portuguese to her fluent French and not quite so fluent English. They finally went to New York, and returned to Paris at the end of the war, where Dr Glass resumed his business interests in producing and directing films.

I often thought of my grandmother, and very occasionally we could exchange letters through the Red Cross. Suddenly, near the end of the war, the letters ceased. I was to learn, after the war was over, what had happened. I received a letter from two Catholic Sisters who had hidden her, as a fellow Catholic, from the SS who were trying to put her in a Concentration Camp. About a year before the end of the war they finally found her, took her to a Concentration Camp, and there she died. The incredible courage of the two Sisters who could risk their own lives to shield her, and her own sufferings, gave rise to such a welter of emotion that I simply couldn't bear to think about it all. To this day I cannot look at pictures or films of Concentration Camp inmates, or even read about them. Repression as a mode of defence (using the term 'repression' in a non-Freudian sense, of course) is not my usual response to stress, but in this case I feel it may be the only appropriate one.

In their letter the Sisters also told me something that I had not known before. Assuming that the fact was well known to me, they stated that the Gestapo were interested in my grandmother's Jewish origin; apparently she came from a Jewish family in Silesia. It now became clear to me why my father had got Goering interested in me, and obtained a promise from him to get me into the SS – it was to protect me from persecution. Goering was well-known for his waywardness in racial matters; had he not promoted General Milch in his air force, in spite of the general's Jewish origin? When challenged, he declared: 'I decide who is a Jew!' I cannot say that this discovery affected me much; if Hitler won the war I would be hanged as a 'traitor' to the Third Reich anyway! But I could not escape the thought that in view of the disproportionately large number of Jews among Nobel Prize-winners and outstanding scientists generally, perhaps a little of that creative genius had touched my life!

The death of my grandmother crystallized feelings that had developed ever since I first heard Hitler speak. Before that I had been pretty happy-go-lucky, trusting and believing in the goodness of mankind. Hitler and the Nazi regime convinced me of the reality of the concept of original sin, of the existence of unredeemed wickedness, and of the weakness of the thin crust of culture and civilization overlying the bubbling cauldron of hatred, desire, cruelty, envy, rancour, malice, bitterness, spite, vengefulness, malignity, covetousness and sheer brutality that constituted the heart of man. This realization prevented me from accepting any purely cognitive view of human nature, although accepting of course the reality and importance of cognitive factors. It also separated me from do-gooders who only see the good in even the worst of us, without realizing the existence of the bad in even the best of us!

I made several attempts at getting a job, but this proved impossible: no-one was willing to employ an 'enemy alien', and the Law prevented anyone not British from accepting employment. The problem was finally solved when I was accepted into the ARP (Air Raid Precaution Service) shortly after I got my Ph.D. in 1940. This service was concerned with the after-effects of air raids, rescuing people from burning buildings, clearing sites of the dead, keeping people away from collapsing buildings, donning gas masks in case of gas warfare, shepherding people into Underground stations or other bomb-proof places, and so forth. I took up my station near the Angel in Islington, a very working-class area. The post was in what had been a school, now evacuated, and the personnel was rather odd. The brightest and best had been drafted into the Armed Services; what was left was a mixture of crooks, including one who had been serving a sentence for murder, men who had managed to persuade the Authorities that they were not fit enough to serve as soldiers; middle-aged merchants and stall-holders who spent most of their time selling a variety of goods from their barrows or shops; and a small number of pacifists and refugees, like myself. The average IQ of this group was not high, their mental age being around twelve years, and their behaviour like unruly and almost psychopathic schoolchildren. Law-abidingness was not one of their virtues; through the connivance of the people in charge they managed to steal blankets and other furnishings, and although supposed to be on the post for twenty-four hours, and off the post for twenty-four hours, they were absent on their own often nefarious activities most of the time.

I knew of course from my schooldays that there would be some kind of initiation ceremony, some way of trying to figure out where I would fit into the pecking order that had been established over the first few years of the war. As I had thought, this event was planned for the very first night I was to spend at the post. The men on duty slept in bunks, one above the other, each furnished with a pillow and a blanket. When I went up to the bunk that had been assigned to me, I found immediately that someone had swiped my blanket. The trial was on. Everyone was watching me surreptitiously to see what I would do. I knew that a great deal depended on my reaction to this particular situation. If I didn't manage to cope with it properly, I would for ever be the butt of similar stupid provocations, and life would be a misery. I pretended not to have noticed, but strolled aimlessly round the room till I saw someone lying in his bunk covered by two blankets. I wandered past his bed, then suddenly turned round, ripped off one of the blankets, and said politely: 'Oh, I think that one is mine.' I was standing near his head, daring him to get up. Had he done so I would have smashed my knee into his face, but he thought better of it and said rather ungraciously: 'Oh well, all right. Maybe.' I strolled off to my bunk, put the blanket on it and got into bed. I had passed my first examination.

A few days later came the second. The school contained a gymnasium, and the powers that be sent someone round to keep us amused and in good health by doing some gymnastics and throwing a medicine ball around. The first time we got on to the medicine ball we were throwing it more or less aimlessly at each other in a group, but I soon noticed that the chap who had pinched my blanket was organizing the rest to surround me and try to hit me with the ball. I pretended not to notice, thanking Dietrich from the bottom of my heart for the training he had given me in this game, and just threw the ball back politely and softly. Finally my opponent got to within a few feet of me, and threw the ball as hard as he could at me. I caught it as I had been taught to, bent my body around to absorb the shock, and then unwound, throwing it back at him with all my strength. Not expecting such a quick return he just stood there, and the ball caught him squarely between the head and the upper chest, throwing him back against the wall, where he collapsed on the floor. I leaned over him with a show of compassion, making sure that he wouldn't get up, but he had had enough. That was the end of persecution, but I was not really accepted until a week or two later, when the sun was shining on a beautiful early spring day and some of the more active of the men were playing cricket in the playground of the school.

I asked politely if I could have a go. They seemed surprised (enemy aliens don't play cricket!), but agreed. They had convinced themselves that having been born in Germany I must be a spy, although what I was to spy on in this miserable and decrepit place I couldn't imagine. Anyway, the game continued till I was called upon to bat, and having had some training in the game during my stay in the Isle of Wight school,

I hit the poor bowling all around the ground, including a lovely six across the road. This posed a severe problem for them. 'This man has a slight foreign accent and is a spy; such people can't play cricket. However, he obviously *can* play cricket.' They finally arrived at the solution. They decided I must be Welsh! The Welsh have a funny accent, but they do play cricket. From then on, whenever we played some other post at cricket, they introduced me as their Welshman. Sometimes they got quite nasty about this, saying: 'Taffy was a Welshman, Taffy was a thief', but maybe I was being too sensitive. Seeing that most of them were in fact thieves, perhaps they considered it a compliment. Anyway, from that time onwards I had no more trouble.

Up to that time my English had been more informed by Shakespeare and the BBC rather than by vernacular idiom. Here I had to accommodate to Cockney patterns of speech, rhyming slang and all. I had no idea what 'Khazi' was, or 'kip', or 'lettuce leaf' (thief) but, would you 'Adam & Eve' it, I soon learned!

During the period I spent at the Angel, there were no air raids, and the atmosphere was conducive to laziness – indeed, when I finally did find a job after about six months in ARP, I had at first some difficulty in getting back to real work. I did however learn a good deal about the great British working class, Trades Unions, and other aspects of real life which I had not encountered previously. We were all members of the Transport & General Workers' Union, but although there must have been over a hundred people at the post, Union meetings were attended for the most part by just two or three – the Secretary, who had to be there, of course; the Assistant Secretary, who should also have been there and myself! We made all the decisions for the rest of the group who couldn't have cared less. The Secretary was an elderly, intelligent and reasonable cobbler who had everybody's respect, so I don't suppose any harm came from all this, but it did illustrate the fact that small groups of militants could easily highjack a whole Trades Union because of the lack of interest of the majority.

It was during this period of *dolce far niente* that I started work on what was to be a major interest of mine for a long time to come, the statistical analysis of attitudes, and the psychology of politics in general. This exceeded my concern for experimental aesthetics, which was my first major area of interest and work. As with experimental aesthetics, studies then begun have continued to occupy me over the years, and are still going on; this makes it difficult to fit them into an autobiography.

I have always been interested in the question of why scientists undertake the particular studies and experiments they do, a question both in the philosophy and sociology of science. Usually there is a coming together of several different strands. Thus, for experimental aesthetics there was my general interest in painting and the arts generally, combined with the advent of war and the evacuation of the psychological laboratory, with all its apparatus, to Aberystwyth, making it necessary for me to carry out my research with easily available materials, such as picture postcards, coloured sheets of paper, etc. In the case of social attitudes and politics, there was again my strong interest deriving from my experiences in Germany, and as a 'premature anti-Fascist', but there was also an initiating event, in this case one that had many risible features. J. C. Flugel was one of my teachers, a devoted psychoanalyst who spoke fluent German, coming as he did from a German family background. He had done a large-scale study of social attitudes, in collaboration with Dr Pryns Hopkins, an American psychoanalyst who was at that time working at the department. Typically, the subjects of the experiments were members of odd organizations advocating certain changes in the mores and folkways of present-day society, such as the Sunbathing Society, the Eugenic Society, the Fabian Nursery Propaganda Group, the National Society of Non-smokers, etc. Equally, the attitudes measured related to a number of 'progressive' or 'unorthodox' issues, such as divorce reform, abortion, nudism, birth control, anarchism, Esperanto, etc. It had been planned to test some 5,000 members of these various organizations, but after no more than 700 replies had been received to the questionnaire a London evening paper learned about the investigation and came out with a headline accusing 'University Professors' of advocating 'communism'. This upset the Provost of University College, who told Flugel in no uncertain terms that he had to discontinue the research, and should burn the results. Although Flugel pointed out that burning books was rather more popular on the other side of the Channel, he finally had to compromise and promise that he would not analyse his data or publish them. Sticking by the letter of his promise, he came back to the department and asked me if I would analyse the data and perhaps publish the results – I was still an undergraduate, but had already acquired a certain amount of recognition as someone who knew about psychometrics and statistics.

I did carry out the analysis, and also read the literature very carefully; the results gave rise to my first paper on 'General Social Attitudes' which was published in 1944. Essentially, it showed that social attitudes are intercorrelated quite strongly, and that they give rise to two major independent factors, one of which is the usual one of conservatism as opposed to radicalism – i.e., the old right-wing – left-wing opposition. However, there also existed another factor which I called tough-mindedness as opposed to tender-mindedness, which divided both right-wing and left-wing proponents, and suggested that political opinions, and political parties, should be looked at not only from the point of view of conservatism-radicalism, but also from that of tough-mindedness – tender-mindedness.

I carried out many subsequent studies, using a better selection of attitudes to be sampled, and better samples of respondents, such as Conservative, Liberal and Labour party voters, or random samples of the population. All these studies verified the original hypothesis, and showed that Fascists on the Right, Communists on the Left, were tough-minded, Liberals were tender-minded, and intermediate between Right and Left, whereas Conservatives and Labour Party members were Right and Left respectively, but average with regard to tough-vs-tender-mindedness. Men were more tough-minded than women, and working-class people were more tough-minded than middle-class people in general; this we found true with each of these political groups – ie., working-class Communists more tough-minded than middle-class Communists, etc.

All this and much more was later on to form the substance of my book *The Psychology of Politics*, which in essence contains the at that time unpalatable warning that there was Fascism on the Left, as well as Fascism on the Right, and that tough-mindedness united Communists and Fascists in a common bond. Others, like Hayek and Shils, have since argued a similar point, but some may be surprised to have as a witness Adolf Hitler himself, who said this, in 1934: 'There is more that binds us to Bolshevism than separates us from it. There is, above all, genuine revolutionary feeling, which is alive everywhere in Russia, except where there are Jewish Marxists. I have made allowance for this circumstance and given orders that former Communists are to be admitted to the Party at once. The *petit bourgeois* Social Democrat and the Trade Union boss will never make a National Socialist, but a Communist always will.'

Among the many similarities we may note that Italian and German Fascism was not consistently right-wing in nature, and Soviet Communism not consistently left-wing. Fascism, to take but one example, introduced such policies as governmental control of private business, and Soviet Communism as official policy repressed national and religious minorities. Welfare legislation has sometimes been combined with political repression, while hostility to private property has been found together with racial and ethnic prejudice.

When I put all these ideas into *The Psychology of Politics*, and later on *The Psychological Basis of Ideology*, I encountered for the first time the hostility and hatred of the militant left. Hitherto I had always thought of myself as essentially Socialist in outlook. Suddenly, and without any change in my own views, I was cast in the role of a right-wing extremist, a Fascist, and an enemy of the working class. Severe criticisms of the book were made, particularly, by the London School of Economics (which was traditionally very left-wing), and in America by M. Rokeach and R. Christie.

In those days the picture of 'Uncle Joe' was still unsullied by the realization that he was responsible for even more cold-hearted murders than Hitler; the afterglow of having him as an ally against Hitler made people uncomfortable about the fact of left-wing Fascism. What annoyed critics particularly was a study done by Thelma Coulter, one of my Ph.D. students, on 'The Personality and Attitudes of Working-Class British Communists and Fascists'. To obtain her data she had to join both the Communist and the Fascist Parties of Great Britain, which presented a serious threat to her safety and perhaps even her life had anybody found out about this double allegiance! (The reason why she had to join both parties was simply that Fascists and Communists are highly secretive, and hesitate to speak to anyone or do a test for anyone not belonging to their respective parties.) She did manage to administer personality tests to her groups, and found not only a similarity in attitudes, but also in personality – both were dominant and aggressive in their attitudes and behaviour, as one might have expected. Unfortunately Thelma was killed in a car accident, so that her work, which was done in the early 1950s, was not published until 1972, when I wrote it up in article form.

It is interesting to compare the fate of my book on *The Psychology of Politics* with the much better known *Authoritarian Personality*, published around the same time. The major authors of this study were also refugees from Nazi Germany, combining neo-Marxism of the Frankfurt School with a rather old-fashioned type of psychoanalysis. They postulated, as I also had done, a kind of personality structure which determined people's attitudes, but they aligned this 'authoritarian-personality' with right-wing views. T. W. Adorno and his colleagues became popular in the USA, although it is now recognized that methodologically, theoretically and statistically their studies are weak. These conclusions were accepted because they fitted in comfortably with the *Zeitgeist*. My own conclusions, making tough-mindedness (or authoritarianism, if you like) independent of right- or left-wing attitudes, fell foul of the *Zeitgeist*, and hence, in spite of being methodologically and statistically much sounder, were hardly ever quoted in the American literature on social attitudes, other than in a critical manner. Yet my conclusions have been replicated many times, and today, even the major critics have come round to postulating very similar factors to those I discovered. Just as I had been penalized from the right-wing for my premature anti-Fascist beliefs, so I was now to be penalized from the left for having premature anti-left-wing Fascist attitudes.

In more recent years my interest in social attitudes has centred on the discovery, made by Lindon Eaves and myself, that heredity strongly determines our attitudes. Lindon Eaves is a brilliant behaviour geneticist, who originally obtained his degree in Birmingham, which at the time, and a few years afterwards, was perhaps the leading centre for behavioural genetics, under the guidance of first K. Mather, and then John Jinks.

What we found was rather sensational. Roughly half the causal factors in producing the variety of social attitudes we found to be of genetic origin, leaving the rest to environmental differences *within* families (i.e., accidental factors not common to kin or siblings) and in equal amount to environmental differences *between* families (i.e., influence of parents). These results were obtained first using the British Twin Register, which I had been busy keeping alive and enlarging at the Institute of Psychiatry, where it had been started by Dr Price, a psychiatrist interested in genetics, and later on using a much larger sample of twins in Australia, where the topic had been studied by N. Martin and R. Jardine. The discovery that prejudice, authoritarianism, religion, conservatism, and other social concepts require a very strong genetic component in their causation is one which is not easily acceptable to most social scientists who have taken for granted an entirely environmental mode of causation. Yet results are so similar in different studies, and the studies are based on such large numbers of twins, that they really are compelling, and future generations of social psychologists will have to reckon with the facts as described.

Indeed, the influence of genetics is even stronger than it would seem at first. The degree of assortative mating – i.e., like marrying like, is so high for attitudes that its genetic consequences could account for all the additional resemblances between twins that earlier analyses had ascribed to the family environment. When we allow for the joint effects of genes, cultural inheritance, and assortative mating in the model for family resemblance and conservatism, estimates of the cultural parameter (influence of environment) do not differ significantly from zero. Of all the novel facts produced by our research, this is one of the most surprising, and its political repercussions will be of long-lasting interest.

The beginning of my involvement with social attitudes and the psychology of politics marked the end of a period for me. Interesting as my work for ARP had been in getting to know the British working class better, it had also been frustrating because it kept me away from the experimental work I was keen to carry out in psychology generally. Fortunately, after six months at the Angel, an opportunity arose for me to get back into psychology, and again a stroke of luck was to alter decisively the course of my life. Having met, in Cyril Burt, the first rather extraordinary figure to influence my life, I was now to meet the second, Aubrey Lewis, the psychiatrist.

CHAPTER 3

Becoming a Professional

That which has been delivered by everyone, always
and everywhere, has every chance of being false.

Paul Valéry

I might have languished in my backwater as an ARP warden for a long
time had it not been for Philip Vernon, who was already an outstanding
psychologist, and was to become one of Britain's leading professionals.
He had been a student of Bartlett at Cambridge, but was more interested
in personality, intelligence and applied psychology than was compatible
with remaining there. He did his Ph.D. with Gordon Allport at Harvard,
and then spent some time in the Children's Department of the Maudsley
Hospital, learning about clinical psychology. Thereafter he went to the
Jordan Hill Training College at Glasgow, and during the war was the
psychological consultant to the Army, in charge of psychological
research. His outstanding work there was later published in book form
(authored jointly by him and John Butler Parry, who had a similar
position in the Royal Air Force), as I have already mentioned.

Philip was interested in experimental aesthetics, although his major
line of research was music – he played the French horn, and unlike
myself, was gifted musically. He was interested in my publications, and
visited me in London on occasion. We became good friends, having a
similar outlook on psychology as well as similar interests and likes and
dislikes. The major difference was his extreme degree of introversion;
although I, too, am somewhat introverted, compared with him, I always
felt like a raving extravert!

Philip had heard that Eric Trist, another Cambridge product who had
been engaged as research psychologist by Aubrey Lewis (an eminent
psychiatrist who worked as Director of Research at the Mill Hill

[88]

Emergency Hospital) had given up his post and gone into the Army to work as a psychologist at one of the newly set-up testing units for prospective officers, the so-called War Office Selection Boards (WOSBS). Aubrey Lewis consulted Philip Vernon about a replacement, and Philip Vernon suggested my name. Accordingly, Philip and I presented ourselves for afternoon tea at Oddeninos, at that time a large restaurant off Piccadilly Circus, to meet Aubrey Lewis in person. The meeting turned out to be a farce. I had come prepared to impress Aubrey Lewis with my psychological knowledge, and wanted to talk about research and theory. He, being a very experienced administrator, took Philip's word for it that I was a good and knowledgeable psychologist; however, he had his own theories about what kind of person he wanted, and that meant for him someone with a wide knowledge of history, literature, politics, painting, music, etc. – in other words, somebody who had a good cultural background. So we started to talk at cross purposes – I was trying to bring the conversation round to psychological topics, Aubrey Lewis to cultural ones. Fortunately I soon began to understand what Aubrey Lewis was after, and we settled down into a conversation I thoroughly enjoyed. He must have enjoyed it too, because he offered me the job, which I of course accepted without hesitation.

I could not know then, of course, that Aubrey Lewis had far-reaching plans in which I would play an important part. He was planning to found the Institute of Psychiatry, as part of the University of London; he wanted to get started a profession of clinical psychology (psychological knowledge applied to problems of neurosis, psychosis, and brain damage, both by way of diagnosis and treatment) which then did not exist in England; and he wanted to integrate psychology with psychiatry in this newly-formed Institute. He needed a psychologist who would combine a good background in psychology with sufficient worldly wisdom to help him in his endeavours, and while he might have had doubts about the latter, as far as I was concerned, he presumably decided he wouldn't find anyone better, and took me on for a trial period.

This may be the place to say something about the Maudsley Hospital, and Aubrey Lewis. The Maudsley Hospital had been founded at the instigation of Henry Maudsley, an eminent psychiatrist of late-Victorian England, who endowed the hospital which was to be named after him, and which was opened in 1923. The Maudsley soon became the centre point for British and indeed Commonwealth psychiatry, and a centre of excellence; most of the future professors of psychiatry went through its training course, and its renown soon became world-wide. At the beginning of the Second World War it was decided to disperse the staff to two major emergency hospitals for the care of psychiatric casualties, one at Mill Hill, the other at Sutton. Mill Hill itself was one of Britain's public schools. The school had a number of houses, which were to be used as wards for the patients, and one of them would contain a few rooms that were made available to me.

Aubrey Lewis, the guiding spirit of the Maudsley, and of Mill Hill Emergency Hospital, was born in the first year of the twentieth century, in South Australia, the only child of Jewish parents. His father had emigrated from London in the 1890s to earn a living in a small watchmaking repairing business, while his mother was a local teacher of elocution. Aubrey was an excellent pupil, but when he decided to take up psychology at university he was rejected and took up a medical career instead. He finally decided to specialize in psychiatry, and came to the Maudsley Hospital five years after it was declared open. His outstanding ability was soon recognized, and by the time the Second World War started he was already regarded as the leading British psychiatrist, knowledgeable in many different areas including biochemistry, psychology, genetics, and pharmacology, all of which contributed important information to psychiatry.

He did not achieve this distinction without worthy competition. At the outbreak of the war, the Maudsley contained a number of psychiatrists who were to achieve considerable renown, such as Elliot Slater, William Sargent, John Bowlby, Maxwell Jones and E. W. Anderson, as well as several distinguished German refugees, such as Willy Mayer-Gross, Harry Guttman, and Alfred Meyer.

When I started at Mill Hill I was sublimely ignorant of all this, or of the fact that the Maudsley had a great rival in the Tavistock Clinic, which was a private undertaking, given over entirely to psychoanalytic theory and treatment, and trying to extend its work into a number of different areas, such as industrial psychology. Fortunately Aubrey Lewis shared my developing feelings of antagonism and dislike for psychoanalytic speculations, although he never voiced them as openly as I was to do.

I assumed on starting at Mill Hill that Aubrey Lewis, as the Director of Research, would either tell me what to do, or would at least point out fruitful directions of research which I might follow. That, however, was not his way. He left me to swim entirely by myself, and I did what I had done when I started work in psychology – I got hold of a dozen textbooks and read them all through in a couple of weeks. I then got hold of a number of more specialized texts and spent the next two weeks reading through them. At the end of this month I had a great deal more theoretical knowledge of psychiatry than most of the psychiatrists at Mill Hill. I tried to remedy my lack of practical experience by assiduously attending case conferences, discussions, etc.; I was not impressed. It seemed to me that these so-called theories were purely semantic effusions leading to no testable consequences, that textbooks were full of assumptions without any foundations, that psychiatric methods of classification, diagnosis and treatment were haphazard and lacking in firm scientific foundations, and that altogether, if psychology was not the science, but the hope of a science, psychiatry didn't even have that hope.

I saw Aubrey Lewis once a week, for an hour, and I will never cease to be grateful to him for letting me find my feet, and sit peacefully on a bench in the parklands surrounding Mill Hill, trying to think out a research programme that would combine practical usefulness and scientific rectitude. We became good friends during that period, and remained so until very much later when an issue arose during our discussions, like a very small black cloud a long distance away. It was later to produce a struggle to the death between us. In discussing clinical psychology we agreed that clinical psychologists should not do psychotherapy, but for different reasons. Mine was that there was no evidence that it did any good, that there were no theoretical bases from which to derive proper methods, and that the training of therapists seemed to be completely random, giving rise to all sorts of unproven and esoteric methods. While Aubrey agreed with all this, his underlying motive seemed to be that therapy should be reserved for medical practitioners, which automatically excluded psychologists. I was already playing in my mind with the ideas that were later on to see the light under the name of 'behaviour therapy', but at that time these ideas were too vague and theoretical to deserve an airing.

At the beginning I obviously knew far too little about psychiatry and treatment to make any useful contribution. I did, however, have one shot at treatment, albeit quite against my intentions. I had started experimental work, and tested fairly large numbers of patients on a variety of psychological tests. I just wanted them as subjects, but they wished to discuss their problems with somebody, and apparently didn't get much of a chance to do so with their psychiatrists. I had no desire to hear about problems and complexes, but in the end I agreed to a compromise. I would test the patient for about half an hour, then talk to him for half an hour, and then resume testing. One patient told me that his major problem was an inability to consummate intercourse. I realized that this was very sad for him, but couldn't see what he expected me to do. However, I dutifully asked him how he went about things, and it appeared that he had never been told very much about sex, and tried to have intercourse with his girl-friend standing up, and without using his hands! I told him how to do it, and gave him a copy of *Fanny Hill*, which contained some fairly graphic descriptions. He was delighted, went off on a two-day pass to London to visit his girl-friend, and jubilantly told me the week after that he had finally succeeded. As this is my one and only case, I may say that I have a hundred per cent success rate in psychiatric treatment!

Several weeks later the psychoanalyst who was treating the poor chap used his case for presentation at a treatment conference, and discussed how a lengthy unravelling of the patient's Oedipus complex had finally led to a sudden improvement in his status, which he ascribed completely to the wonders of psychoanalysis – apparently the patient had never told him about my own intervention!

In settling down at Mill Hill, I became aware of its strong class structure: a definite hierarchy, with the medical doctors at the top, the nurses and secretaries in between, and the gardeners, handymen and labourers at the bottom. It was not quite clear where a research psychologist fitted in, and there were tempestuous discussions. Should psychologists eat with the doctors or with the nurses? I was consulted informally, and declared, with my usual exquisite tact, that I would much prefer to eat with the nurses, who were pretty, young and lively, but that in principle psychologists had an academic standing equal to that of the doctors, and that they should be recognized officially, even if it meant my having to eat with people with whom I had little in common. It was agreed that I should eat with the doctors, but of course I sloped off as often as I could and ate with the nurses.

Finally, I had to make some decisions about my research, decisions which were rather circumscribed by the position I was in. There was no laboratory, no apparatus of any kind, and no chance of buying any – all production had ceased during the war. Furthermore, there was no money; I had about £100 a year to spend on 'supplies', which meant paper and pencils (also difficult to get at that time), cigarettes, as reinforcers, and other bits and pieces. I had no secretary, but was allowed about half an hour a week with Aubrey Lewis's secretary. Tests were unobtainable, except Raven's Matrices, the IQ test most widely used in the Army at that time. These were the external determinants of my research programme and they were not to change when the war was over. Conditions could hardly have been less amenable to carrying out any useful work. I proceeded to act on the wise words of Lord Rutherford, of Cavendish fame: 'We have no money, so we will have to think!'

I decided that to begin with I would take a standard textbook psychiatric statement, and try to test it empirically. In view of my previous work on hypnosis I immediately thought of suggestibility, and took as my text the statement that hysterics are exceptionally suggestible. Using a number of standard tests of suggestibility, I then worked on fairly large groups of patients who had been diagnosed as 'hysterics', then contrasted them with patients who had been diagnosed as 'anxiety states', phobias, or 'obsessional/compulsives'. I analysed the data, and came to two major conclusions.

The first conclusion was that the tests which allegedly all measured 'suggestibility' actually fell into two groups, quite unconnected with each other. To begin with there was what I called 'primary suggestibility', measured by such tests as the 'Body Sway Test'. The subject stands with his back to the wall, with his eyes closed, and the experimenter repeats the words: 'You're falling, you're falling forward, you're falling forward now. You're falling, you're falling forward . . .', continuing for thirty seconds, or a minute. The amount of sway is measured, both forward and backward, and constitutes the score. Other methods would suggest raising or lowering the arm, or making other kinds of movement. I found that primary suggestibility was closely related to hypnotizability, but not to intelligence.

'Secondary suggestibility' was measured by tests originating with Binet. Thus the person might be shown a line of small boxes, asked to pick up the first and then the second, and say which was heavier. He would then compare the second and the third, going on in this way to the end. The first eight or nine times the second box would be heavier than the first, setting up a tendency in the subject's mind which would carry on to the last few boxes, all of which were of equal weight. Suggestibility is measured by the number of times a subject says 'heavier' when in fact the boxes are of equal weight. This type of test is not correlated with hypnotizability, but is correlated (negatively) with intelligence, very much as Binet had suggested.

The second finding – much more interesting to the psychiatrists – was that hysterics were no more suggestible than other types of neurotics. When I told Aubrey Lewis, he immediately requested to see all the patients I had tested, in order to discover whether the diagnoses had been accurate. He concurred in every case, and told me that he regarded this as a very important finding.

I reported my early work on suggestibility at a meeting of the British Psychological Society, and this in turn led to a meeting with Desmond Furneaux who was to become a personal friend, and an outstanding psychologist whose work on intelligence has had revolutionary consequences. He had been brought up as a physicist, but took courses in psychology at Birkbeck College. He was particularly interested in hypnosis, and during his free time would come to Mill Hill and work with me on testing patients. We replicated my earlier work on a larger sample and with more tests, arriving at similar results, as well as continuing the work of linking suggestibility and hypnosis.

I also did some work on the effects of drugs on suggestibility, together with Linford Rees, a young psychiatrist who became a firm friend. This was undertaken in order to discriminate between the *ability* to be hypnotized, and the *attitude* of the person towards being hypnotized. A person who did not have the ability could never be hypnotized, however favourable the attitude, but a person who had the ability might, with the wrong attitude, resist the suggestion. I had the idea that the injection of sodium amytal would not change the ability of the subject, but would change his attitudes, making him less able consciously to resist suggestions. We also used a control experiment in which a saline solution was injected instead of the drug. Thus, as anticipated, the narcoticizing action of the sodium amytal increased the response of the highly suggestible group, but not that of the non-suggestible group, demonstrating the differentiation between ability and attitudes.

The experiment may give some insight into the reasons why scientists choose one type of experiment rather than another. My choice of subject was dictated by rather unusual considerations. My marriage to Margaret turned out to be not very successful, and the presence of large numbers of pretty but unattached nurses in the hospital proved difficult to resist. I had a couple of rooms in one of the houses, to carry out my work, but neither contained a bed. Once a week all the staff were required to stay the night at the hospital, firewatching, keeping a look-out for incendiary bombs dropped by enemy planes. This was a nationwide practice, and it led to a great deal of extra-curricular sexual activity. My problem was the absence of a bed in my room, and the extreme vigilance of the matron, who happened to live in the same house, on the floor above. As I was thinking about the problem of getting a bed in my room, the idea of the experiment came to me, and it certainly did the trick, requiring the patient to lie down! In fact, the outcome of the experiment was quite an important one, and I am still quite proud of it – on purely scientific grounds, of course!

Aubrey Lewis was one of the most intelligent and widely read people I have ever known, but there were two weaknesses in his general make-up, as far as science is concerned. He was not a research man, and really did very little along those lines. I think the major reason why he did not was that he was a perfectionist. He couldn't bear the idea that anything he did was less than perfect, and of course that is an impossible attitude in a research worker. We all know that what we do can and will be criticized, that there are faults and errors which later work will correct, and that a perfect experiment can only be done when everything that needs to be known in that field is already known – in other words, when the experiment isn't required any more! But the notion of being criticized, of doing something less than perfect, was anathema to Aubrey Lewis.

His second weakness was that he was innumerate. Like many psychiatrists his abilities lay in the verbal field, and while he managed to understand elementary statistics, his understanding certainly did not extend to anything above Chi square, or simple correlation. I remember on one occasion, when we were both firewatching, he suggested playing a game he had just read about. Two players are given a number of matches, and the first player then puts down one, two or three. The other player does the same, and the player who manages to get rid of all his matches first wins. The game lends itself to being played by a statistical formula, which I quickly worked out in my head and used to play by. After a while Aubrey Lewis noticed that he didn't seem to be winning any of the games, and asked me why. I told him the formula and explained how I derived it. He was obviously impressed, but didn't seem to understand the formula, because he went on losing! Some time later, after the Institute had been founded, he asked me to give an ability test to all the incoming registrars; he wanted to follow them up and see how the tests would predict their achievements. I didn't think there was much possibility of doing that; achievement is so difficult to measure, being compounded of clinical excellence, political success, research ability, and many other factors. However, I did give the Thurstone Mental Abilities Test to the registrars, and was astounded to find that they had very high verbal ability scores, but incredibly low numerical ability scores – a difference vastly greater than any I have ever seen or read about in any other group. There are now a few psychiatrists who are distinctly numerate, but at that time I doubt if anybody, apart from Elliot Slater, who was interested in genetics, and Linford Rees whom I have already mentioned, could understand and follow a statistical discussion.

However, Aubrey Lewis knew what research workers needed in order to support their work, and inaugurated a large clinical data sheet which was filled in for every patient, and which contained a great deal of information on symptoms, diagnosis, age and sex, background, etc. These data seemed to me to be giving admirable information which could be used for quite important statistical calculations, and I decided to do two things. The first one was to look at the reliability of psychiatric diagnoses. At the time, there was no evidence available to show whether the diagnosis given by one psychiatrist might or might not be similar to that given by another. This is a problem of reliability; if you want to compare one clinical group, say 'hysterics', with another, say, 'obsessive/compulsives', it is essential that your classification should be accurate. This seemed a fundamental question, and accordingly I asked the Medical Superintendent to allow me to carry out this research. The Superintendent was an amiable man, quite elderly. He listened to what I had to say, namely that many of the patients had been seen by two different psychiatrists, each of whom had filled in their forms, so that it was possible to compare the two and arrive at some measure of reliability of diagnosis, symptoms, etc. He then said that this might be quite interesting, but surely I was not doubting the accuracy of the psychiatrists and their diagnosis. 'Dash it,' he said, 'they all have medical degrees!' I persisted, saying that it really was quite important to know the actual reliability of such judgements, until he finally rose to his full height and said: 'If you really want to carry on with this type of research, I suggest you do it somewhere else.'

I withdrew, but being rather stubborn did carry out the statistical analysis of the data and found a very poor reliability (around 0.20) of psychiatric diagnosis. There have of course since been many studies to demonstrate this fact, but mine would, I think, have been one of the first; unfortunately I wasn't allowed to publish it, and hence priority has gone elsewhere. The results did suggest to me, however, that one has to be very careful in comparing groups of patients on the basis of their psychiatric diagnosis, and so I decided that in future I would adopt a different approach.

The second use I made of the information sheet was based on the realization that diagnoses are highly complex cognitive processes, based on a variety of information, some of which can be interpreted on a subjective basis. The symptoms themselves, however, are fairly objective, and as the symptoms were recorded in detail on the form, I decided to look at the correlations between the symptoms and try out a factor analysis to see whether they might not give rise to superordinate concepts derived directly from the facts, rather than being filtered through some speculative set of assumptions. I did this, and found to my surprise that the results were perfectly intelligible, and indeed corresponded reasonably well with a theory Jung had advanced, most of which he stole from the French psychiatrist, P. Janet. (Freud indulged in the same habit, repeating Janet's important insights without giving him any credit. Janet is very much underrated by modern psychiatrists and psychologists, and it is time his value was better appreciated.) What Jung had asserted, in connection with his theory of extraversion-introversion, was that extraverted neurotics tended to have hysterical personalities and symptoms, introverted ones psychoasthenic ones. This is precisely the picture which emerged from my factor analysis of symptoms, but of course instead of dealing with categorically differentiated types, the solution suggested two dimensions, at right angles to each other – one to be labelled 'neuroticism', at one end, 'emotional stability' at the other, the other dimension one of 'extraversion-introversion'. Symptoms characteristic of hysterics were in the 'neurotic-extraverted' quadrant, those characteristic of psychoasthenics were in the 'neurotic-introverted' quadrant. Far from giving every person a categorical diagnosis, the results suggested giving everybody a position in a two-dimensional framework – so much extraversion or introversion, so much neuroticism or stability.

This problem was almost completely neglected in the literature on psychiatry, for, following the medical tradition, psychiatrists labelled patients in an either/or fashion – you are either a 'schizophrenic', or a 'hysteric', or a 'phobic', or a 'depressive', or whatever. This type of diagnosis might be appropriate for patients suffering from physical disorders, but the possibility seemed to suggest itself that in mental disorders the dimensional approach might be more useful – i.e., not labelling patients diagnostically, but rather assigning them a position on a number of different dimensions of which neuroticism and extraversion-introversion might be two of the more important ones.

The results also suggested the importance of personality theory, because clearly the two dimensions of N and E, as I was to refer to them, extended beyond the mentally abnormal field to perfectly normal persons. I went to the library to look at MacKinnon's chapter on 'The Structure of Personality' in the book on *Personality and the Behaviour Disorders* edited by McV. Hunt, which contains an excellent review of the evidence to date. His review suggested that many people had seen somewhat similar constellations to the one I had stumbled upon, but had never quite put the pieces together. I determined that I would do this, and thus try to demonstrate the importance of straighforward psychological principles and studies to a fundamental aspect of psychiatry. Much of the work that I have done within the ensuing forty years has been devoted to the pursuit of this apparition.

I was beginning, from that moment on, to study the relationship between the dimensions of N and E, on the one hand, and empirical tests of a variety of personality traits, on the other. I looked at the relevance of assessments and ratings, relations with physique and constitution, with ability and efficiency, suggestibility and hypnosis, appreciation and expression, and many other variables. Among the more interesting were level of aspiration, personal tempo, perseveration, persistence, aesthetic appreciation, colour-form attitudes, sense of humour, etc. Finally I was to combine all these studies into a book – my first – entitled *Dimensions of Personality*, which appeared in 1947, and showed conclusively that the major dimensions of personality were closely related to behaviours studied in special experimental situations – i.e., that far-reaching personality traits produced very different types of behaviour in different types of situations.

Dimensions of Personality was perhaps my most original work. It contained many suggestions which later investigations were to confirm, both theoretically and experimentally. I introduced a hierarchical model of personality, based on behaviour. At the bottom of the model are observations of what individual A does on a particular occasion O; say, he is late for an appointment. If we observe that this type of behaviour is repeated, we may postulate a habit of being late for appointments. If he is also unpunctual at classes, in getting to airports or stations, in finishing his work, etc., we may postulate a general trait of unpunctuality. And if we find that lack of punctuality correlates with other traits, such as sociability, liveliness, assertiveness, bodily activity, surgency, venturesomeness, carefulness and dominance, then we may talk about a type concept, namely that of extraversion. We are dealing with observable behaviour throughout, hence I labelled my theory 'behaviouristic', not realizing that behaviourists had little interest in individual differences of personality, and would turn up their noses at the idea.

Explicitly or implicitly, this notion of a hierarchical structure of behaviour constants anticipated much in the way of theoretical concepts now being debated – such as the difference between traits and states, the aggregation hypothesis, and many more. It also firmly established the relevance of traits and types in the description of individuals, at a time when these concepts were getting very unpopular. In addition there was always in the United States an unreasoning dislike of individual differences; the notion of 'equality', carried to irrational extremes as suggesting biological rather than social equality, created a *Zeitgeist* hostile to the study of traits and types. In spite of this, the book attracted a lot of attention; with its publication I had achieved a high degree of 'visibility', becoming identified with a definite theoretical stance which might not be popular, but which was recognized as having academic respectability.

Perhaps equally important to my theoretical conceptions and my psychometric analyses was the idea of testing predictions from the personality model in the laboratory. A few psychologists like E. Kretschmer, C. Spearman, J. P. Guilford, and, even earlier, G. Heymans had done the occasional experiment in relation to their particular theories of personality, but I think I was the first to do so systematically and on a large scale. American textbooks of personality hardly ever deal with the problems arising from this conception, or the pioneers I have mentioned; I have discussed their contributions in *The Structure of Human Personality*.

This, I believe, was a fundamental and path-breaking change in the way research into personality was conducted; it emphasized the importance of theoretical concepts of the nature of such factors as E and N, and the need for making testable deductions from these concepts, and actually testing them in the laboratory and in everyday life. Only in this way, I was convinced, could we get away from the inevitable subjectivity of factor analysis and other psychometric methods. If 'dimensions' did not go far enough in this direction, let it be remembered that we had no laboratory, no apparatus, and no money; we had to do the best we could by making use of whatever came to hand. Another obvious difficulty we had of course was the relative absence of adequate libraries. The University had gone to Aberystwyth, with its library; little else was available, and American material, such as journals and books, only arrived spasmodically, and was difficult to get hold of. Remember that I started out at Mill Hill with my mind a *tabula rasa* as far as psychiatry, clinical psychology, personality or individual differences were concerned, and it will be clear that research planning and theoretical works were not easy.

The book also contains an effort I had made to adapt a rather subjective but widely used test, the Rorschach, to a more objective format. The Rorschach, of course, is widely known, consisting of a number of ink blots, some coloured, some just black and white, to which the subject associates; these associations are then 'interpreted', usually in a 'dynamic' fashion, to give a picture of his personality. When I arrived at the Mill Hill Hospital, I met H. Halstead, a psychologist who was employed to give routine tests to the patients, either to clarify questions of intelligence and ability, or to assess their personality. He told me about the wonders which could be performed by the Rorschach, of which he was very fond, and offered to test me with it. Never having heard of it before, and being only too willing to learn, I took the test in a perfectly open-minded fashion, doing my best to comply with the instructions. Halstead then sent the replies off to one of the leading Rorschach experts in the country, who promptly returned a four-page description of my personality, based on the test.

I must admit I was rather surprised when I read it. Not only was I suffering from a very severe, full-blown schizophrenic illness, based on repressed sexual impulses of a homosexual kind; I was apparently unable to work, or use my above-average intelligence in a constructive manner. That, however, was only the beginning. The four pages were filled with symptoms, diagnoses and other psychiatric gobbledegook, all of which apparently characterized me personally. I decided that perhaps the Rorschach was not the perfect mirror of personality it had been portrayed!

It was becoming clear to me that the body of research I was envisaging could never be done by one person working by himself, and I started to attract a number of psychologists who might be able to help, and would be interested in the venture I was proposing. One of those who came to work with me on a voluntary basis was Desmond Furneaux.

Monte Shapiro was another such. Several other people who are listed in *Dimensions of Personality* also worked with me, but two are especially important because Aubrey Lewis managed to obtain money from the Rockefeller Foundation to employ them as my research assistants. The first of these was Hilde Himmelweit, who had come down from Cambridge with a First Class Degree, and who was looking for a job in London; I met her in the library of the National Institute of Industrial Psychology, and after getting to know her offered her the job. She had all the advantages and disadvantages of a Cambridge training – a good experimental background, together with an appreciation of theory, but a curious lack of knowledge in the psychometric field – in fact, when she joined me she couldn't even calculate a correlation! Being rather less tolerant then than I am now, I wrote a little poem which I dedicated to her. It goes like this:

> When the elephant has a baby,
> There's excitement at the Zoo.
> It takes so long to make one,
> It seems it can't be true.

The poem then goes on to say:

> But into utter nothingness
> Fades the elephant's big feat.
> Hilde has worked out a correlation,
> Incorrect and incomplete!

Needless to say it was not Hilde's fault that she had been so badly taught, and she soon caught up. In fact, she had an extremely successful career, carrying out much very important research, among other things on the effects of television on children, and becoming the first British Professor of Social Psychology, at the London School of Economics. She was my first Ph.D. student, and I was very proud of her achievements.

Much the same is true of my second research assistant, Senath Petrie. She came from a large Jewish family, many of whom became quite well known in Academia and politics, the Schonfelds. She had married Dr Petrie, and was keen to carry on her research activities. Like Hilde she was Jewish and also very good-looking; indeed, my department-to-be at the Maudsley and later at the Institute was destined to be filled with beautiful women, mostly Jewish, and good-looking men, mostly Communists. Among the women were Sybil Rostal, whom I was later to marry after my divorce from Margaret, and Irene Martin, the only non-Jewish girl. I mention the point about the outstanding good looks of these women, and others who joined us later on, because it has been suggested that I hired girls on the basis of their looks. Nothing could be further from the truth. All had extremely successful careers. I have already mentioned Hilde Himmelweit. Senath Petrie went to work in America, publishing a number of books and becoming internationally known for her conception of 'augmenters and reducers' (i.e., people who modulate stimulus intensity in opposite directions, a tendency closely related to extraversion-introversion). Sybil, as will be apparent later on, did a great deal of work on personality which was both novel and important, and achieved an outstandingly high publication and citation index status.

Irene Martin, together with Peter Venables, another Ph.D. student of mine, practically founded psychophysiology (the relation between behaviour and physiological events in the central nervous system of the brain) in Great Britain, edited and wrote textbooks on the topic, and carried out a great deal of highly original and valuable work on human conditioning.

Neither was I to choose the men who were to become my colleagues on the basis of their Communist beliefs. It just so happened that Monte Shapiro was quite a high-ranking member of the Communist Party, and this fact was later on to attract as Ph.D. students, and then as members of the department, other people of a similar political attitude. I was certainly by that time very disillusioned with Communism, and regarded it as being only marginally less obnoxious than Fascism, but I judged Monte Shapiro and all the others on the basis of their ability, their achievement, and the contribution they made to science; their political beliefs, which I didn't share, seemed to me irrelevant.

It has also been suggested that, being keen on tennis and trying desperately to have a game every day at lunchtime, I offered jobs in my department to people on the basis of their tennis-playing ability. Again it hardly needs saying that there is no truth in such a statement. None in fact played all that well when they came – they tended to improve while they were with me! Also, they all did very well academically – better on the average than those who did not play tennis!

But to talk about all this is to anticipate. The days I spent at the Mill Hill Emergency Hospital were some of the most interesting and fruitful of my life, and it was there that I laid the foundations for much of my future work. I was not only concentrating on personality; I also did some work on intelligence. John Raven, who had published the Matrices test which was widely used by the British Army, often visited the hospital as a consultant, and I got to know him quite well. I found Raven relatively innumerate but opinionated; he rejected the concept of the IQ for reasons I could never understand, and transformed scores on the matrices into percentiles instead, which is not a good way of doing business. He also made a number of decisions which seemed to me to contradict good psychometric practice, such as having a score distribution which was very skewed.

Working with him, however, gave me the idea that motivational factors might be important in carrying out the tests, and to study the influence of motivation I tested a number of patients as they came into the hospital, who were poorly motivated because of fatigue, because of their natural anxiety in encountering a completely new environment, and more than anything because many of them would want to get out of the Army, and might think that getting low scores on an IQ test might help them in achieving that end! I tested them again just before leaving the hospital, psychiatry having done whatever it could do for them. They were well rested, well fed, and highly motivated by the offer of a packet of cigarettes (difficult to get in wartime!) if they beat their previous score by a few points. On the whole there was no evidence of any improvement, thus motivation didn't seem to affect IQ to any marked extent.

Aubrey Lewis had invited me to join his group at the Maudsley, when they returned from Mill Hill and Sutton in 1945, and I was only too happy to accept, bringing with me Hilde Himmelweit, Senath Petrie, and Monte Shapiro. We were given a small number of rooms in the Maudsley Hospital building, which is located on Denmark Hill, a working-class district a few hundred yards from Camberwell Green. The hospital is really quite small, having about 250 beds; it also of course has a large outpatient population. Aubrey Lewis continued with his support and enthusiasm for psychological research; he was convinced that psychology was the most important of the sciences represented at the Maudsley, including biochemistry, neurophysiology, and various others. This view was not shared by the other psychiatrists, who had a much lower opinion of the possible contribution psychology could make. Indeed, they seemed to harbour the odd notion that they were themselves experts in psychology, a notion Aubrey Lewis never shared.

Another event that took place before we left Mill Hill was the birth of my first son, Michael William, later to become a well-known psychologist, and professor at the Royal Holloway and Bedford New College, one of the five major departments of psychology in the University of London. Margaret gave up her job and became a full-time mother, so that we were entirely dependent on my research money provided by the Rockefeller Foundation. This was a precarious situation, and I can't say that I liked it very much, but it gave me a chance to continue my research, and that was the most important thing for me at the time.

We continued research along much the same lines as before, and I put it all together in book form for my second book, *The Scientific Study of Personality*, which appeared in 1952, five years after *Dimensions of Personality*. *Dimensions* had been well received, and sufficed to make an international reputation for me; when I went to America for the first time in 1949 everyone seemed to have heard of it, and they received me very warmly. The second book inevitably attracted less attention.

When the original staff of the Maudsley moved back to the hospital from Sutton and Mill Hill at the end of the war, my contract and that of some of the people who were helping me was extended, and we continued with the work we had been doing previously. I also continued giving lectures to the registrars who were enrolling in courses for the DPM (Diploma in Psychological Medicine), a special psychiatric qualification which at that time could only be obtained at the Maudsley Hospital. I gave a lot of thought to the content of these lectures, as they constituted the initial contact of these budding psychiatrists with psychology, and would at the same time probably be the sum total of all the psychological knowledge they would absorb in the course of a lifetime! I decided that the contents should be relevant to the future work of the students, and thus concentrated on personality, and intelligence, learning and conditioning, memory, the practical applications of psychology in education, industry and psychiatry, hypnosis and suggestibility, and other similar topics. I also taught some statistics as I believe, without that, any reading of the research literature is impossible and meaningless. The contents of my course were soon to form the major part of my first popular book, *The Uses and Abuses of Psychology*.

The work done in the next year or two formed the essence of a number of research papers, and, as already mentioned, led to my second book, *The Scientific Study of Personality*, which introduced a third major dimension of personality, namely that of psychoticism – i.e., a continuum ranging from normality through schizoid and psychopathic behaviour to outright schizophrenia. I had been thinking seriously about some of the major debates in psychiatry, and had tried to devise some means of reducing them to an empirically testable form. One of the major debates was that between continuity or dimensionality, and categorical diagnostic schemes, as already mentioned. The medical model demanded categorical classifications, in psychiatry as in ordinary medicine, but some authors, like Kretschmer in Germany and Freud in Austria, suggested rather a continuity between normality and neurosis and psychosis, and this raised a second question.

Freud had suggested a continuum from normality, through neurosis, to psychosis; an alternative might be the postulation of two dimensions, one leading from normality to neurosis, another one to psychosis. I suggested a new method of statistical analysis, which I labelled 'criterion analysis', which would enable the investigator to see whether categorical or continuous categorization was more in line with the facts. The evidence seemed pretty conclusive that continuity was characteristic of the situation, both with respect to neuroticism and psychoticism, and the results also seemed quite clearly to suggest that two factors were required, rather than one. The nature of the three major factors involved in this continuous or dimensional analysis of personality are shown opposite, in diagrammatic form, and the traits, the correlations between which demand a postulation of these three factors of dimensions, are shown in some detail (Figs. 3.1, 3.2 and 3.3).

The notion of criterion analysis is probably the most original idea I ever had as far as statistics is concerned, but unfortunately it was misunderstood by the critics, and has been widely disregarded. I suspect this is because psychiatrists are medically trained and hence transfer the notion of categorical disease concepts automatically to the psychological field; and also because their training does not include much in the way of statistical knowledge, so that even if they were interested in the problem, they would not be able to follow the statistics. Clinical psychologists tend to take their concepts from psychiatrists, and would not be inclined to go too deeply into problems and solutions which might force them to adopt ideas different from current psychiatric wisdom. I may simply have been wrong in my estimation of the method, but I have not seen any criticisms of it that convince me that I was mistaken. However that may be, this book finalized my system of personality description in terms of three major dimensions, and a large amount of work done all over the world in this field suggests quite strongly that indeed these three dimensions embrace the major aspects of personality, although of course they do not constitute an exhaustive description.

Our flat had become too small with the addition of Michael William, as it consisted essentially of one room, with an alcove containing the bed, a small kitchen and an even smaller bathroom. Greatly daring I bought a house not too far from the Maudsley Hospital, but even further away from the centre of London. The house had quite a large garden, and overlooked a pleasant but small expanse of greenery on the other side of the road. Unfortunately, we occupied it in the late autumn of 1946, and the winter of that year was the most severe England had known in this century, with snow lying on the ground for something like three months – quite unheard of in a climate where normally there is hardly any snow.

All this would not have mattered so much had not the chimney of the house been so full of soot that it proved almost impossible to light a fire, and keep it going. Furthermore, the large copper container for the hot

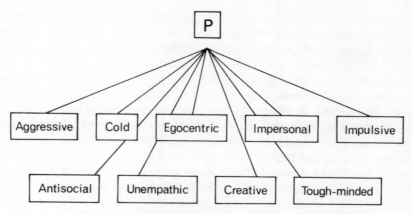

FIG. 3.1   *Psychoticism, and the traits whose intercorrelations give rise to it.*

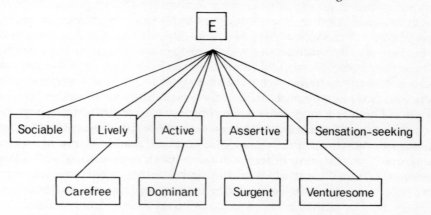

FIG. 3.2   *Extraversion, and the traits whose intercorrelations give rise to it.*

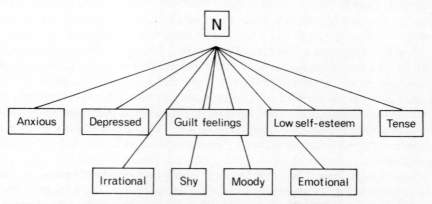

FIG. 3.3   *Neuroticism, and the traits whose intercorrelations give rise to it.*

water supply was leaking, and the man we got to fix it was mentally defective, unable to carry the job out satisfactorily, having to come again and again, disrupting the hot water supply, carrying the container away on his back, and refilling it with high hopes, only to find that these were dashed to the ground again! As if this was not enough misfortune to bear, Aubrey Lewis called me into his office in the spring of 1947 to tell me in his usual dry tones that the Rockefeller Foundation had discontinued its grant, and that consequently I was unemployed. He did not say that he was sorry, but he did suggest that I might be able to earn a few pennies by continuing to give my lectures. This was really catastrophic news: I had very little money, a heavy mortgage on the house I had just bought, a young child to bring up, and a wife who was not in a position to earn a living because she had to look after the baby.

For a while we existed on the money I earned for giving my lectures. I also continued giving courses in the Extra-Mural Department of the University of London. We managed to get by for a while but it was not a very happy period of my life. Above all, the unsatisfactory nature of my marriage was becoming more and more obvious. Margaret and I were, as the saying goes, 'incompatible', and our feelings for each other were not strong enough to make up for that. She was a very heavy smoker, I only smoked occasionally and disliked the smell. She liked staying up late, I didn't. There is a long list of such differences, and they added up.

Suddenly there was a complete change in the situation. Out of the blue I was offered the chairmanship of a large clinical department at Duke University in the United States; I had a letter from Godfrey Thomson, perhaps the leading mathematical psychometrist in the world, inviting me to the post of Senior Lecturer in his Department of Educational Psychology at Edinburgh; and, finally, Aubrey Lewis himself had advanced far enough in the preparations for getting the Institute of Psychiatry off the ground to suggest that he would like me to stay and become Reader (Associate Professor) in the Department of Psychiatry there.

Clearly, this was a critical point in my life. All three choices had advantages and disadvantages. The most prestigious was of course the Edinburgh job. Godfrey Thomson was the leading exponent of the application of statistics to psychology, an outstanding psychometrician who was widely regarded as the most rigorous and technically the most sophisticated of them all. His offer to me was a very welcome vote of confidence, and I had no doubt that I could have learned a great deal from him.

He was also a most likeable person. I had met him several times, and had a chance to get to know him well. In addition, Edinburgh was a beautiful city, which had many attractions. Yet I never seriously considered this offer. It would have meant concentrating on the technical side of psychometrics, rather than the substantive, and I did not feel that my abilities or my inclinations pointed that way. I would have become a much better psychometrist, but I would have lost out on the experimental and theoretical side, and I was unwilling to do that.

The offer from Duke also had certain obvious advantages, among them the salary – something like three times the Edinburgh or London salaries. It related to an established department, rather than to the hope of establishing a new one. Furthermore, psychology was much more highly developed in the United States than in England, and I would have gone to a country flourishing in the aftermath of the war, rather than staying in exhausted, tired and almost broke England.

However, here too I did not feel enthusiastic. Had I gone, I would have had to concentrate on clinical psychology, which was not my main interest. Furthermore, I would have had to forego the possibility of running an animal research section, a psychophysiology research section, a psychometric research section, and various other sections which I was envisaging, and which I considered essential for doing the kind of job in psychology I wanted to do. There was no guarantee that I could get all these things in London, but I was certain that they would not be obtainable in the clinical departments then existing in the psychiatric hospital in the United States, even though they were linked with the University.

Aubrey Lewis was a bit more forthcoming about his plans when I mentioned these alternative possibilities to him. At first, he thought, a sub-department of psychology under my direction would form part of the Department of Psychiatry in the newly-formed Institute. After a while the department would become independent, and he would suggest to the University that I should be its first Professor. He viewed psychology as an important science on which psychiatry would be based, others being biochemistry, neuroanatomy, genetics, etc. My main job would be to introduce clinical psychology as a profession, start a teaching section for that speciality within my department, direct the practice of clinical psychology at the Maudsley Hospital as an aid to psychiatrists, and generally take part in the work of the hospital. In addition, I was free to carry out any kind of research I wanted, have Ph.D. students to take part in that research, and run what would be essentially a postgraduate department within the University of London. He approved of my plans of incorporating animal research, psychophysiological research, and work on psychometrics and statistics within the newly-to-be-formed department, and promised me his wholehearted support for the carrying out of these plans.

The Institute of Psychiatry is rather special, its relations to the

Maudsley Hospital and the University of London unusual, and the whole conception alien to conditions obtaining elsewhere. The history of the Institute is rather convoluted, as from 1924 onwards, the Maudsley Hospital had already been recognized as part of the University of London as a medical school or institute, the only one in the country devoted wholly to postgraduate education and psychiatry. I tend to think of this mixture of hospital and central pathological laboratory as the Maudsley Hospital Medical School, and of the Institute in its later development as a separate part of the Postgraduate Medical Federation. The British Postgraduate Medical Federation (part of the University of London devoted to postgraduate medical studies) put forward the idea that the teaching of medical specialities like psychiatry should be conducted in institutes associated with specialized hospitals, so that the teaching, the research, and the treatment could be closely coordinated. For this purpose a number of specialized institutes were founded, of which the Institute of Psychiatry was to be one, located in close proximity to the Maudsley Hospital (and later associated with the Bethlem Royal Hospital, the former Bedlam).

Members of the Institute would be paid by the Department of Education, through the University; consultants and other members of the hospital would be paid by the National Health Service, but members of the Institute might have honorary positions in the hospital to enable them to work there. Thus, when I was appointed to the Institute, I was also given the honorary position of Psychologist to the Bethlem Royal and Maudsley Hospitals.

The main function of the Institute was research, and the teaching of psychiatry, psychology, biochemistry, etc. to postgraduate students. The Koch Institute in Berlin, the Lister Institute in London, and the Pasteur Institute in Paris, none of them dating back more than a hundred years or so, had set the pattern. Emil Kraepelin was particularly influential in suggesting the need of such an institute for psychiatry when he wrote in 1917: 'The nature of psychiatry . . . is such that questions which are constantly being formulated can be answered only on the basis of evidence supplied by a number of auxiliary disciplines; clinical observation must be supplemented by thorough examination of healthy and diseased brains, the study of heredity and degenerative diseases, the chemistry of metabolism, and serology. Only exceptionally well-trained specialists possess competency in each particular field . . . only a well-planned and comprehensive programme of research can bring us closer to the goal which we are striving to attain.'

It was Kraepelin's idea of a psychiatric hospital specializing in early treatment, research and teaching that inspired Henry Maudsley to make his original offer of £30,000 to the London County Council and persuaded Sir Frederick Mott to move his laboratories to the newly named Maudsley Hospital in 1933. The notion of an institute, however, was first advanced by Edward Mapother in 1935 when he approached the Rockefeller Foundation for financial assistance to set up what was, by the standards of the day, a large-scale project, namely an embryo institute, with a professional clinical director and six senior workers.

The grandeur of these plans, and the possibilities they held out for founding a true research department not concerned with undergraduate training (in which I was not particularly interested) combined to reassure me that the clinical duties involved would only form a small part of my work, and that I could concentrate on the research side. When Lewis told me that my grant had ended I was naturally upset and furious with him, but I soon realized that the fault lay with the Foundation, not with him, and that the impersonal way in which he communicated the decision was part of his personality, rather than indicating a lack of feeling – he was less given to demonstrating his feelings than anyone I have ever known. He was a man of integrity, and his statement that his plans for the Institute were making progress sufficed for me.

With money again becoming available, and the Institute on the horizon, I settled down again to proper research. So did Hilde Himmelweit, Senath Petrie, Monte Shapiro and one or two others who had come to join me, including a few Ph.D. research students who were assisting me in my research programme. I was not at that time a 'recognized teacher' of the University, and hence was not officially in a position to supervise research students. As a consequence we had to adopt a stratagem: the students were registered officially with Aubrey Lewis, or sometimes with Cyril Burt, but their real supervision would be carried out by me, and in future I will refer to them as 'my' students.

Among students registered for the Ph.D. was George Granger, who was to continue my early work on experimental aesthetics in an original and extremely interesting fashion. Around this time I also obtained the services of my first secretary, Shirley McIntosh. She had taken some of my extra-mural classes in psychology, courses of lectures arranged by the University of London in aid of adult education for people who had missed out on a university education. I was impressed with her written work, and her personality, and when I got the 'go ahead' for appointing a secretary I offered the job to her, and fortunately she accepted – she was the best secretary I ever had, and my productivity during those years owes much to her cooperation. She was to marry her childhood sweetheart later on, a medical student who became a successful doctor, and unfortunately (for me!) she left to bear children and lead a happily married life. I have had many secretaries whom I liked, and who contributed greatly to the work of the department, but Shirley's personality, modesty and competence set a standard difficult to follow!

Another event occurred around this time which was to have a very profound influence on my life. The students and I used to gather in the Outpatients Hall of the Maudsley Hospital for morning coffee around 10.30 a.m. or so, discussing research, politics, and anything else that might be of interest. There was little age difference between us – some of the students were in fact older than I was – so there was no formality on these occasions, or indeed generally. I have never believed that a leader should set himself apart in academic life, exploit his position, or insist on formalities of any kind. Aubrey Lewis and Cyril Burt were quite different in this respect; practically nobody, students or staff, would call them by their first names, and they in turn would meticulously address everybody by their titles and full names. I have always preferred the American system of dropping such formalities early on, and certainly by the time you got to know your students reasonably well. People should honour you for what you are, not for your position, and formalism can easily lead to ridicule. I recall writing a letter to 'Prof. Cyril Burt' when he was away in the department at Aberystwyth, and receiving a letter back expressing his annoyance at not being addressed as *'Professor* Cyril Burt'! This kind of standing on your dignity is quite alien to me, and I couldn't help laughing at this absurdity.

What happened on this happy occasion, with the sun brightly shining outside, was that the door opened and in came Monte Shapiro with a young lady in tow whose appearance immediately brightened up my day. This young lady, or perhaps girl – she was still a teenager! – was of medium height, had raven-black hair, the figure of Marilyn Monroe, and a degree of sex appeal I had never encountered before. In addition she was exceedingly pretty, and showed a great deal of dress-sense in the frock she was wearing. I have never believed in love at first sight, and still don't know whether it exists, but what I felt at that moment must have come pretty near to it.

The girl in question was Sybille Bianca Guiletta Rostal, the daughter of a famous violinist, Max Rostal. Her mother was Sela Trau, a well-known cello player. Sybil (to use the English spelling of her name) was an only child, like myself. Her parents were divorced, her father married again (and again!). Sybil had been born in Vienna, her parents had taken her to Berlin, but had then gone into exile in England when she was seven years old. After school she went to Imperial College to study mathematics and chemistry, but found these lacking in human interest. While socializing with members of the Communist Party, she met Monte Shapiro, who had quite a high position within the Party; he told her about psychology, and suggested that she might like to come to the Maudsley to work with our group. He introduced us, and I offered to take her on as unpaid research assistant, to carry out some of our testing, and recommended the extramural classes on psychology I was giving. I did not know then, although I had some presentiments, that she was to become my second wife, and stay with me for the rest of my life.

At the time I realized that I was not in a position to expect any such outcome. There is an equity theory of love and marriage, suggesting that advantages and disadvantages for both partners should be roughly equal if the partnership is to be successful. Sybil had so many advantages – she was young, pretty, vivacious and eminently desirable, and obviously had her choice of male partners; indeed, during the next year or two consultants and everybody else danced attendance on her. By contrast I must have seemed middle-aged, was in a relatively junior position, poverty-stricken and married. I decided to consign her to my dream world, and give no sign of the attraction I felt. This continued for a year or two, during which time she carried out a great deal of testing for me, showed considerable ingenuity, hard work and intelligence in doing so, and I became more and more enamoured of her.

Around this time the first International Conference of Experimental Psychology after the war was held in Edinburgh, and I arranged a symposium on the study of social attitudes, for participation in which I invited several of my students who had worked in that area. I was surprised to find that Bartlett was to be the Chairman, knowing that he had no interest in the topic, no knowledge of it, and indeed, felt hostile to the factor analytic and psychometric approach. We had been allocated twenty minutes each, and I was taken aback when before the meeting he addressed me in his Oxbridge drawl ('relaxed insufferability' it has been called) and told me that he had decided he would only give us ten minutes each, to have a longer discussion period. I told him that not one of the persons who was to speak, except for myself, had ever spoken at a conference, and had carefully prepared a twenty-minute paper, as I had instructed them. (I don't like speakers who exceed their time allocation.) I could not ask them to change their prepared paper now, with practically no warning. He insisted, with dictatorial insouciance, until I was forced to tell him that the meeting could go ahead without a chairman, but not without speakers, and that we would speak for twenty minutes each, no more and no less. Apparently, nobody had ever talked to him like that (after all he was the master of psychology in England), but we did speak for twenty minutes each, and he did remain in the Chair. After that, however, our relations were not as friendly as they should have been.

At the Maudsley I took part in ward rounds and clinical meetings, in order to understand better which problems in psychiatry psychologists could help with, and Hilde Himmelweit and Monte Shapiro, in particular, followed my example. My main interest, however, was in the research work done by the students. I was beginning to establish the principles according to which I would run my department. At that time the introduction of clinical psychology into the British framework was still in the future, and I concentrated on the organization of research. What I was intending to implement was what Don Marquis, in his 1948 Presidential Address to the American Psychological Association, was to call 'Program Research'. In this important paper, he defines 'Program Design' as the planning of an integrated series of research activities, focused on a central problem, and employing a number of scientists for several years. As he pointed out, if a particular research project cannot be clearly related to an existing body of rigorous concepts and theory – and this was the position of most of personality research – it becomes necessary to design and carry out a programme of research. Anything else is apt to join the company of incomplete and forgotten research.

Like Molière's M. Jourdain, who had been speaking prose without knowing it all his life, so I had been doing programme research all the time I was at Mill Hill, and I proposed to continue doing this in the future, following up the work I had described in *Dimensions of Personality*, and continued in *The Scientific Study of Personality*. However, I realized that not all students would be interested in working within this framework, and was quite happy to give them the opportunity of carrying out any other research as long as it was rigorous, meaningful and theory-based. There is not much point in forcing students into a kind of research they don't want; it strains personal relations, the work will not be done with enthusiasm, and the student will not learn as much as he would if he were working on a topic that interested him. Thus while there should be programme research in a department, there should also be opportunities for unrelated research.

The department attracted a lot of foreign students; indeed, I think there were far more foreign than English students over the next thirty years or so. They came from all over the world – India, Germany, Poland, the United States, Canada, Australia, New Zealand, Japan, South Africa, the Black African countries, Egypt, South America and elsewhere. Most were attracted by the research programmes I offered, but some were not.

Among those who preferred not to work within the programme was a South African student, Joe Sandler, who insisted on working on the Rorschach, my dislike of which I have already mentioned. He was quite a good psychometrist, and his thesis was sufficiently well planned and analysed to be acceptable. He already showed some psychoanalytic inclinations, which led him afterwards to work with Anna Freud, and finally, to become Editor of the *International Journal of Psychoanalysis*. He is one of many who may be quoted to contradict the notion that I tended to brainwash students and insisted on rigid adherence to certain theoretical schemes. That would be the way to start a 'school' like the psychoanalytic, Gestalt, behaviouristic and other schools in psychology.

I have always insisted that my students should remain critical of my own theories as well as of everybody else's, and one of my proudest boasts as a teacher has been that there is no Eysenckian school in the sense that there is a Skinnerian, or a Freudian, or a Gestalt school. Naturally, there are people who test my theories, but they usually do so in a critical manner, and some of my former students have been among the most voluble critics of my work. There are advantages in founding a school, but the disadvantages greatly outweigh the advantages, and I think, hopefully, of scientific psychology as a unified discipline ridding itself of such undesirable ideologies.

Another foreign visitor was Don Prell, who arrived from the United States and with whom I carried out my first empirical study into the genetics of personality. He showed the typical character traits one often associates with Americans – friendly, sociable, energetic, hard-working and practical. We designed an experiment involving identical and fraternal twins, children who were given a whole battery of tests relevant to the concept of neuroticism. I introduced what I think was an important element into the design of the experiment, as follows.

Supposing you use a single test, call it T. This test will measure not only neuroticism (if that is the particular personality trait you happen to be interested in), but also a number of other traits, such as introversion perhaps, impulsivity, rigidity, anxiety, etc. It will also measure something quite specific to that particular test, which it shares with no other test. If we now determine the heritability of the test, this will be a mixture of the heritabilities of all the various traits which have been measured. Hence we cannot say with any degree of certainty that what we have measured is the heritability of neuroticism itself. To do that, what we would have to do would be to have a whole battery of tests, all of which measure neuroticism, but each of which also measures a variable set of other traits and specific factors. Overall, these other traits and specific factors will average out, leaving as much the most important, if not the only, factor that of neuroticism. Thus I combined factor analysis and behavioural genetics in a unique design, a design which I think is undoubtedly superior to the designs usually adopted. Unfortunately few if any investigators have followed this idea which I still believe contains an important contribution to the methodology of behavioural genetics.

However that may be, we found that there was a strong genetic contribution to neuroticism, a discovery contrary to prevailing opinion, and very much opposed to the then current emphasis on environmental factors. As an example, consider for instance a quotation from a book by F. C. Redlich and D. Freedman, concerned with *The Theory and Practice of Psychiatry*, which appeared in 1966. This widely used textbook makes only one comment on the importance of genetic factors in mental disorders: 'The importance of inherited characteristics in neurosis and sociopathies is no longer asserted except by Hans J. Eysenck and D. T. Prell.' It would be quite untrue to maintain that no one else was working in the field at the same time. Elliot Slater, for instance, was carrying out his well-known studies of the genetics of different mental disorders using the Psychiatric Twin Register at the Maudsley Hospital, and one of his assistants, James Shields, was working along a similar line to mine on normal groups, including separated identical twins. But the general climate was certainly environmentalistic.

I followed up this study later on with two Canadian students, concentrating this time on extraversion, and arriving at similar results. Both these two major dimensions of personality had a strong hereditary basis, which explained over half of the total phenotypic variance. The method used was rather primitive, and the numbers of twins too small to carry out a more complete type of analysis; nevertheless, later work on much larger numbers, using better statistics, has borne out the essential conclusions of this early work. I will return to a discussion of the genetics of psychological traits later on.

I have already mentioned the Edinburgh meeting. Apart from my donnybrook with Professor (later Sir) Frederick Bartlett, there occurred a meeting with Professor Maurice Viteles, a well-known industrial psychologist from the University of Pennsylvania, at Philadelphia. He invited me to spend six months as a Visiting Professor at the University, and this seemed an appropriate time to go to the United States, as well as a very appropriate place. Aubrey Lewis wanted me to have a good look at clinical psychology in the United States, where it had become established after the First World War, and where it was widely practised. This visit would just precede my appointment as Reader in Aubrey Lewis's department, and as Head of the Psychology sub-section; thus I would have a chance to find out a great deal about clinical psychology as it was practised in its homeland.

Equally the place seemed to be an excellent choice because it was there that Lightner Witmer had started the first clinical psychology teaching department. It was suggested that I should go there in 1949–50, just after the Annual General Meeting of the American Psychological Society in Montreal, which I intended to visit.

*   *   *

On the personal side events were moving to a climax. I was going to read a paper at the Annual General Meeting of the British Psychological Society in Bristol, and Don Prell and his wife, Annie, suggested that they might drive myself and Sybil down there for the occasion. Don was a shrewd observer, and he must have noticed my feelings; perhaps he also noticed, which I had not been able to do, reciprocal feelings on Sybil's part. Anyway, that trip brought us together, and precipitated the final breakup of my marriage with Margaret. It was a sad ending and an even sadder goodbye from Michael, who was five years old at the time.

Why did our marriage break up? It is difficult for me to say – people often drift apart, without any obvious reason. I was still young and immature when we were married; it is well known that early marriages seldom last. As an enemy alien I had to make my career against great odds – I had to give all my time to research, writing and lecturing, to reading, thinking and testing. That left little time for marital togetherness. I cannot blame Margaret for getting fed up with me, particularly when conditions were hard in the war and its immediate aftermath. When I fell in love with Sybil the decision to end what had become a loveless marriage was inevitable; I knew that my whole happiness depended on it. Margaret was young and attractive enough to have many suitors. Leaving Michael behind was worst; we always had a good understanding. Human affairs are always messy and involved; I was truly sorry about doing what I was doing, but I could see no real alternative. Margaret was unwilling to agree to a divorce, but Sybil and I agreed to live together in a small flat in Hampstead, after a short and very happy 'honeymoon' in Brighton. My coming absence rather threw a shadow over our happiness, but after I had arrived in Montreal, after a week on the steamer which at that time was the only way of crossing the Atlantic, Sybil decided with my enthusiastic agreement that she would join me in New York, after the conference was over, and after I had visited Berkeley, one of the institutions on the West Coast. This she did, and from then on our lives have been inseparable.

However, these and other events will be taken up in the next chapter.

I will close this chapter, rather, with a brief description of the personalities of the two people who had so very strongly influenced my academic life up to this point, namely, Cyril Burt and Aubrey Lewis, both to be knighted shortly afterwards. There were both resemblances and differences between them, but the main characteristics they shared were a scintillating intelligence, high ambition, great literary ability, profound erudition, lack of human commitment to students or colleagues, great tactical ability in practical affairs, and a great deal of dominance and assertiveness.

Burt's personality, as well as his life history and his academic achievement, have been well described by L. S. Hearnshaw in his book *Cyril Burt, Psychologist*. Aubrey Lewis's personality and work have been described by Michael Shepherd, a former colleague of his at the Maudsley Hospital and the Institute of Psychiatry, in a monograph entitled: *A Representative Psychiatrist: the Career, Contributions and Legacies of Sir Aubrey Lewis*. Here we will concentrate rather on what I personally experienced in my dealings with these two men, although at times I will need to have recourse to the historical records.

Cyril Burt, for all the great intelligence and erudition he showed, was essentially not a scientist. He was concerned with theories, and the mathematical and statistical elaboration and testing of models, but he lacked the practically instinctive veneration for empirical facts and experimental results which characterizes the true scientist. He used his statistics on data which, as I pointed out to him incautiously, were collected without the care and attention that should be given to scientific data. He would analyse personality tests and ratings made without any control at all by teachers and others; he would correlate and factor analyse scores on IQ and other tests collected in classrooms by teachers without any specific training in psychology; in fact, how the data were collected did not seem to interest him much. This was a trait he was later to show again in the extraordinary fraud of which Hearnshaw and others have found him guilty. He would be quite happy to analyse imaginary data.

Aubrey Lewis also was not, in my view, cut out to be a scientist. He was too much of a perfectionist, as I have already mentioned, to expose himself to the possibility of criticism; he wanted to publish only perfect experiments, and in science perfect experiments do not exist. He also lacked the statistical acumen, and indeed the numeracy, which are essential in scientific research. However, he was a model of integrity; I don't think it would ever occur to him to invent or falsify data, and what he did observe and write about one could accept as reliable and honest observations.

Both men were aggressive, but in rather a different manner. Burt always adopted a friendly manner, and appeared to think highly of whomever he was talking to, and to share their views and opinions. He showed his aggressiveness and his dominance behind the backs of the people involved, never to their faces. He never said an unkind word to me in person, but his letters and comments to others were dripping with poison, as Hearnshaw makes clear. In public debates he had a dangerous technique of praising the contribution of his opponent, only to insert the stiletto at the last minute.

Aubrey Lewis, on the other hand, was feared by all his students and registrars because of his openly critical attitude to their work which often expressed itself in strong and rather wounding words. I have seen some of his victims come out from such a session with tears streaming down their faces; I doubt whether this is a good way of educating students. Furthermore, his criticism often seemed to be irrelevant; he would chastise registrars for not knowing some recondite German or French reference, the knowledge of which would really make very little difference to the diagnosis or disposal of a patient.

In the characteristic of wanting to show their intellectual superiority, both Burt and Lewis were similar. Burt would crowd his books and journal articles with footnotes which, while ostensibly attempting to clarify the text, were intended to show off his erudition. In his book on factor analysis, there were occasionally two lines of text, the rest of the page being made up entirely of footnotes. On one occasion, for instance, he tried to illustrate a two-dimensional figure showing the intersection of two factors, creating four quadrants, by reference to the way coats of arms are designed in heraldry! The good writer clarifies a recondite concept by reference to a better-known one; here Burt was trying to clarify a very simple concept, probably known to all of his readers, by reference to a very recondite one, probably unknown to all but one or two.

In a similar way Lewis seemed to drag into the conversation, and into his writing, the most recondite references he could find, preferably in foreign languages which would be unknown to his listeners and readers, even when they made little or no contribution to the particular issue involved.

Lewis soon found out that when, at our weekly meetings, he supported his case by quoting some to me unknown psychiatric reference, I would respond by translating the statement into some kind of statistical or mathematical formula, and then proceed to argue that this contradicted his point of view. As he could never understand the formulae, he soon gave up, and from then on we either talked about practical matters of one kind or another, or indulged his love of gossip, which was a rather unexpected aspect of his personality.

With Burt the matter was rather more difficult because his statistical erudition was much greater than mine, and equally he had read far more sources in statistics and psychometrics than I had. Here my stand was the history and philosophy of science, and scientific methodology; these were aspects on which he was weak, and his memory for experimental details in particular was almost non-existent. As these were absolutely vital in evaluating research, and as my memory was still almost photographic in retaining such details, he too soon gave up arguing with me. I admired the great knowledge and ability shown by both Burt and Lewis, but it seems to me that they applied these treasures less efficiently than they might have done.

Burt and Lewis both showed a considerable degree of contempt for their colleagues and students. To Burt, as to Pavlov, they were just pairs of hands, useful in carrying out his instructions, but having no minds or abilities of their own. If they showed any sign of outstanding ability, he became upset and hostile. Lewis reacted rather differently, and much more intelligently. He realized that to carry out his great project he needed able and if possible outstanding people to run the various departments of the Institute, and hence he was careful to seek them out and persuade them to take part in the great venture. He never relinquished his critical attitude; I recall that he gave qualified approval to my first book, *Dimensions of Personality*, but thereafter his only comment on subsequent books was: 'Not as good as your last one, is it?' Having a good deal of self-confidence, I took these comments as a joke, but others took such remarks more seriously, and I think he permanently disabled and crippled the research careers of many quite bright psychiatrists.

Where Burt disliked opposition, and tried to squash it, Lewis seemed to appreciate it, at least in my case. As many psychiatrists were to state, rather morosely, I was Lewis's blue-eyed boy, and could do no wrong. He certainly supported me in every way possible; without him the department could never have been founded, nor could it have flourished as it did. His contribution to British psychology, and particularly to clinical psychology, should never be forgotten. Although later we quarrelled about behaviour therapy, when I was trying to introduce it into British psychology, he was a good and faithful friend to me, and an important support for psychology when it was in a very weak and febrile state.

Burt was an ever-hostile power threatening to make academic life in England difficult or impossible for me. But curiously enough he was never a real danger to me, and in spite of his enmity he never succeeded in blocking any of the things I really wanted or needed. Lewis, on the other hand, in spite of all the support he had given me, became a more difficult opponent when we fell out over the question of behaviour therapy, and almost succeeded in destroying all that I had done to build up clinical psychology in England. In this quarrel he turned out to be just as devious as Burt, but much more dangerous. He lacked the obvious irrationality of Burt whose motivation was ultimately rumbled by most of the people he had to deal with, whether in committee or in person. On the issue of behaviour therapy Aubrey Lewis was equally irrational, as I hope to show, but he managed to hide this so well that he persuaded many people of the correctness of his position.

However, this was to become an issue in the distant future. At the time of this early spring of 1949 we were the best of friends, and he had a good deal of fun dealing with the long line of consultants lining up outside his door to complain about the young psychologist who had irritated them beyond measure by criticizing psychoanalysis, psychotherapy, and other aspects of the trade they held dear. Lewis would nod gravely, listen sympathetically, and finally affirm his belief in academic freedom, and reject their proposal that I should be sacked. He often told me that he was in agreement with all the criticisms I had to make of the current state of psychiatry, but when he expressed his own doubts he did so much more tactfully, and in much more carefully worded language, than I. I always felt like Luther, when haranguing the Reichstag in Worms: '*Hier stehe ich, ich kann nicht anders, Gott helfe mir, Amen!*' (Here I stand, I can do no other, God help me, Amen!) It is obviously much more sensible to be less outspoken, and to hide your meaning in a maquis of words. But then tact and diplomacy have never been my strong points. I always felt that a scientist owes the world only one thing, and that is the truth as he sees it. If the truth contradicts deeply held beliefs, that is too bad. Tact and diplomacy are fine in international relations, in politics, perhaps even in business; in science only one thing matters, and that is the facts. I know that even in science I am probably in a minority on this point, but I seem to have had this view implanted in me with my genes, and there is not an awful lot I can do about it!

CHAPTER 4

The Battle for Behaviour Therapy

Tout le progres de l'homme,
toute l'histoire des sciences est
l'histoire de la lutte de la
raison contre le *sacré*.

Roger Vailland

Older readers may remember the occasion when the cinematic technique called 'Cinerama' was first introduced. There were three gigantic screens, surrounding the audience, with three projectors and many loudspeakers creating the impression of an all-enveloping three-dimensional reality. The performance would begin with a very ordinary, small black-and-white film, in which a narrator would rather boringly tell the story of the development of photography and films. After a few minutes, with the audience half asleep he would then say something like: '. . . and then came Cinerama!' At that moment all three screens would light up with the beginnings of a roller coaster ride so realistic in presentation and sound effects that one really seemed to be sitting in the car screeching down the steep inclines and experiencing all the emotions and physiological effects of such a ride. This dramatic transition was most effective and indeed startling.

Something similar happened when Sybil and I encountered the New World in 1949. Remember that in those days Britain was still severely rationed, with each person receiving perhaps two eggs (in the form of egg powder) and one tiny bit of meat a week. Cars were unobtainable, but if you had one, you couldn't get new tyres, or any other replacements; petrol was still severely rationed, and cigarettes, sweets and other similar comforts were difficult and often impossible to get. The 'blackout' didn't exist any more, but there were few things in the shops, and the general standard of living was very low indeed. Life in England at that time resembled the black-and-white lecture at the beginning of the Cinerama film.

America, to Sybil and myself, meant changing this for the pulsating sound and colour effects of the Cinerama film. There was food in abundance, shops open all night, filled with anything the heart could desire, no problems about cars, tyres, or petrol – the contrast was so great that it was difficult to believe the two countries were part of the same world. I remember going into a delicatessen shop in Philadelphia with Sybil to buy some food – the owner threw his dog a piece of meat which in England would have had to last a family for a week! Similarly, when we went to buy some chops to cook for dinner, they were so huge we could hardly believe our eyes! Add to all this the change from a dutiful marriage to the romance of a deeply felt love affair, and you will get an idea of the change that was taking place for me.

Financially, too, I was earning a reasonable salary for the first time, and could afford some of the good things in life. Ownership of a car was still way beyond my means, but there was no problem in renting a large one-room apartment in Rittenhouse Square in Philadelphia, at that time one of the better quarters in that town. Lecturing duties at the universities were not heavy, as I was giving courses on personality and similar topics to small groups of advanced students. We had plenty of time for sightseeing, going out at night to dances, or to jazz concerts, or travelling around and getting to know the country. I was invited to lecture in many different departments, and found that these invitations usually had an ulterior motive. After the lecture Sybil and I would be invited to dinner with the higher-ranking members of the department, and afterwards the Head of the Department would take me aside for a well-rehearsed seduction speech, offering me a job in the department. *Dimensions of Personality* had made my name quite well known, and the lecture served as an introduction to my teaching abilities. I must have had at least a dozen offers of a job, many of them quite inviting. However, as I still felt under an obligation to Aubrey Lewis, I had to turn them all down. I have often wondered what would have happened if I had taken the opportunity to go to the United States.

In Philadelphia I took up jitterbugging, a type of dancing at which Sybil excelled. Later on, after returning to England, we also took up country dancing, which has a charm of its own, although far removed from the rhythmic vigour of jitterbugging. I am now a little too old for such energetic working out, but I sometimes look back with longing on those happy days.

While staying in our Rittenhouse Square flat, we were invited by our neighbours for a game of bridge. Sybil had never played bridge, so I quickly taught her some basic rules just before joining our neighbours. All through the evening we had incredibly good cards, and won hands down. As we were leaving I noticed some silver and gold cups on the mantelshelf, and looked more closely. It turned out that our hosts were championship players, and had won many a bridge tournament. I could now understand the rather sour looks they gave me when I explained at the end that Sybil was just a beginner!

I should at this stage say something about myself as a lecturer. I had always enjoyed addressing audiences, and was quite successful; I certainly received a good deal of support and recommendation. As in my writing, I tried to make my talks logical, well organized, interesting and concerned with matters which would be relevant to the experiences and expectations of the audience. It has often seemed odd to me that psychologists, who ought to be particularly concerned with keeping in mind the psychological needs of the audience, are among the worst lecturers I have ever known.

Among the many errors committed are having no central theme, concentrating too much on unimportant aspects rather than vital ones, giving too much detail, both in the presentation and in the slides and tables offered, over-estimating the background knowledge of the audience, failing to set the research in its proper background, and so forth *ad nauseam*. I consciously tried to avoid all these errors, and think of the particular audiences I was addressing, their needs, interests and requirements. In doing this I learned a lot from my father, whose profession after all was to interest and amuse his audience. He did not of course talk about scientific matters, but the technique is pretty much the same whatever your topic.

He taught me that it is very important indeed to have a particular high spot in your presentation, something which stands out and which will be remembered by the audience for a long time. I have tried to follow this rule through, and found it enormously useful. Let me give an example:

At the University of Pennsylvania I had to give a set of lectures on personality, and the first of these, being open to all university members, and not only psychologists, was of course the crucial one to decide whether I would be a success or a failure. I decided to talk about the difference between the nomothetic and the ideographic approach – i.e., the scientific point of view, which dealt with the measurement of abilities and traits, as opposed to the more philosophical point of view, which stresses the uniqueness of each person and the need to get away from more general concepts. How can you pinpoint the differences between the two approaches in a single, memorable sentence? Following my father's example, I decided to look around for some person or event that would be familiar to everyone in the audience. I fastened on Professor Fernberger, the oldest member of the teaching staff, who had been a student of Wundt in the far-off days of the Leipzig laboratory. Fernberger was a likeable person, but also a well-known eccentric. Built like a pear, he had huge glasses which made his eyes appear gigantic, and having been a member of the University for so long, he was known to everyone. The oddities of his behaviour were bywords.

I spent some time telling my audience – which was very large for the first of my lectures – about nomethetic and ideographic approaches, the philosophy of Windelband and Heidegger, and about Allport, the American apostle of the ideographic movement – and I also mentioned some of the objections to the doctrine of uniqueness as fundamental in personality research. I then continued: 'Of course everyone is unique. Professor Fernberger is unique' (titter in the audience). 'So is my old slipper!' (loud laughter). Written and read in cold blood, this is not particularly funny, but in the atmosphere of the lecture, with everyone knowing that Fernberger himself was present, it brought the house down. It also beautifully illustrated the point that I was trying to make, namely that everything in nature is unique, but that science, not only psychology but also physics, chemistry, astronomy and every other science, must look at regularities in nature. Even now, forty years later, I occasionally meet people who tell me that they were present at that lecture, and still remember this particular phrase!

On another occasion I had to tell a large group of educational psychologists about factor analysis, and introduce a large innumerate audience gently to the wonders of n-dimensional geometry. Having thought about it for a while, I brought along a little toy parasol belonging to my daughter, who was five at the time. At the beginning of my lecture I put this on the desk, in everybody's view – quite clearly they were wondering what on earth I was thinking of, bringing a toy parasol along with me on a cold and wintery day. Half-way through my lecture, when I got to the topic of multiple factor analysis, I picked up the parasol, opened it and explained that the central stick was the general factor, the spokes sticking out in different directions the group factors, and I demonstrated how these could be rotated in space by twirling the parasol around. I think it clarified the issue by making it visual, and also kept this particular audience awake!

When I started using this technique, in the early forties, it was much criticized by Cambridge experimental psychologists, including Sir Frederick Bartlett. Some of these criticisms appealed to the statistically naive, because they seemed to embody simple commonsense. What factor analysis does, essentially, is to take a table of correlations between, say, a number of traits, or a number of questionnaire items, measuring different traits, and then try to discern clusterings and other regularities in this table or matrix of correlations. These regularities would then be interpreted in terms of factors, or dimensions, or whatever. The method is no all-embracing solution or panacea for psychological problems; it can be and often is misapplied and misunderstood; and above all its conclusions are tentative and never final.

'Oh, oh, oh,' Sir Frederick would boom. 'You only get out of such an analysis what you put in!' And Oliver Zangwill would pipe up, saying: 'Statistics can never show the structure of psychological reality!' Well, of course, in one sense they were right – statistics can really only be used to test hypotheses and show them to be supported or not by the results, as the case might be. And, yes – you cannot get out of a factor analysis what you don't put in. However, the real problem of course is a very simple one, namely: Do we really know what we have put into the questionnaire, or the experiment, or the tests, or whatever? We often *assume* that we know, but this assumption has to be tested, and factor analysis often shows it to be quite false.

For example, J. P. Guilford published a scale which he assumed measured a unitary trait of 'social shyness'. I put forward an alternative hypothesis, namely that there are two reasons why people are shy and unsociable. One is that they may be *afraid* of other people; this might be a feature of neuroticism. Another possibility is that they might simply not *like* having to deal with other people; this might be related to introversion. As N and E are quite independent, this suggests that there may be two groups of items in this questionnaire, uncorrelated with each other, corresponding to these two types. I analysed the intercorrelations between all the items, and found indeed that there were two sets of items, unrelated to each other, one correlating with N, the other with E! In other words, Guilford had *assumed* that all he put into the questionnaire was one single factor of social shyness, but in actual fact he had put into it two quite independent ones. It is difficult to see how any other method of analysis could have demonstrated this fact.

There are other examples. One of my students tested a theory of Kretschmer's according to which a series of laboratory tests all measured a single personality trait, namely that of schizothymia-cyclothymia. When the tests were done, and the correlations calculated, there was no evidence of this unitary trait – there was in fact no factor at all! So here again the theorist was quite wrong, and factor analysis conclusively disproved the theory. Another example I have already mentioned, namely that of suggestibility. When we used a whole group of tests of suggestibility, and factor analysed the intercorrelations, we did not find, as most people had expected, a single factor, but two quite independent ones, namely primary and secondary suggestibility. Thus factor analysis is an indispensable tool for testing hypotheses about the content of questionnaires or experimental tests; it often demonstrates how wrong we were in our assumptions about the contents of these tests!

When I prepare for a lecture I never write down anything except the most cursory notes, usually just the actual nature of the slides I'm going to show. In that way you can change your presentation to suit the occasion, and in any case a talk given without notes is much more interesting than one laboriously read out from a written paper. How important this sort of adjustment can be is illustrated by the public debate I had with B. F. Skinner at the Montreal meeting of the American Psychological Association.

We had agreed in writing that I would be the first to speak, and I had more or less outlined in my mind a talk in which I would criticize Skinner's failure to give adequate acknowledgement to the importance of genetic factors, physiological and other biological determinants of behaviour, and in particular the relevance of personality and individual differences. Just before the Chairman rose to introduce us, however, Skinner leaned over and said: 'I think it would be better perhaps if I started!' Seeing that he was much the older, looked very infirm and was clearly regarded by the audience as the 'grand old man' of psychology, I agreed. When Skinner started talking, it appeared clear that he was keen to pre-empt any of the criticisms he realized I was going to make.

To the surprise, I imagine, of his followers, he specifically stressed the importance of genetic factors, biology and personality and individual differences, thus rather taking the wind out of my sails! I had to completely change my tack, and make up my talk as I went along, stressing rather the things that united us, such as the concern for scientific understanding, the control of behaviour, and the rejection of psychoanalytic and other types of speculation. I shudder to think what would have happened if I had had a written speech which I couldn't have changed on the spur of the moment!

Perhaps a neutral observer's views about my lecturing style will be more interesting than my own recollections. Here is what an American observer of the 1964 Annual General Meeting of the British Psychological Society had to say in the *American Psychologist*:

> At one very interesting session, Eysenck lectured upon, and discussed, some of the theorizing and evidence presented in his *Handbook of Abnormal Psychology* (Eysenck, 1961). Perhaps because Eysenck occupies a very special as well as controversial role in British psychology, the lecture hall was filled with an overflow crowd. The symposium sparked with controversy, unlike most of the other relatively sedate and polite sessions. A number of people

on the floor raised strong and apparently legitimate arguments against Eysenck's points, but invariably Eysenck's command of his subject matter, his brilliance, and his incisive wit absolutely demolished and vaporized his critics. I strongly urge any critic of Eysenck's work to confine his controversy to the printed scientific literature, as verbal confrontations at meetings and symposia will only inevitably lead to utter and traumatic humiliation.

Unfortunately such considerations have not succeeded in discouraging my critics!

On the personal side these few months in Philadelphia enabled Sybil and myself to really get to know each other. I was beginning to realize how lucky I had been in winning her. In addition to the Monroe-like exterior, she was highly intelligent, extraverted and sociable, and had a very happy disposition – for the next forty years or more the musical tinkle of her laughter would punctuate our lives. She also possessed virtues not normally associated with extraversion, like extreme punctuality, and very great efficiency. I consider myself efficient, but compared with Sybil's achievements, I feel that I could never have coped with all that she did. Apart from having a very successful academic career as a lecturer and later senior lecturer, running the home, having four children and bringing them up, she became a magistrate which took up several days a week, and did many other things, such as helping me edit *Personality and Individual Differences*. All of this was done with effortless superiority. In addition, she gained an almost intuitive understanding of my approach to personality, and was later on to make significant contributions to it – I don't think there is anyone in the world who understands it better, or who is anything like as much on the same wavelength.

It would be true to say that in all the years of our marriage we have never had a serious quarrel. It did of course take a little while for us to shake down together – an outstanding dancer, she was used to going out dancing, spending Saturday night at discos and other places of amusement, and gallivanting about, while I was used to staying at home, reading my three books a night, and following an introverted style of life.

The only points on which we disagreed were really quite unimportant. I like sweet wines, like Barsac, Entre deux Mers or Sauternes, while she liked dry wines. We usually compromised on a fruity middling dry wine from the Mosel. I liked the room warm, she preferred it cool, so again we compromised on a middling temperature. Nothing worse should ever come between us! Altogether, my time in Philadelphia was the happiest period of my life.

*   *   *

But of course I could not forget the reason for my trip, and I conscientiously tried to find out about clinical psychology in the United States. I read widely, discussed the problems with many different people, and came to certain very definite conclusions. It seemed that clinical psychology in the United States had three major characteristics. Firstly, clinical psychologists played second fiddle to psychiatrists and psychoanalysts, adopting their theories, their methods of treatment and their diagnostic criteria. They were simply ancillaries whose actions were prescribed by others, merely helping hands to whom occasionally less important duties could be entrusted. The model they were forced to work on was a medical model, and medical people played all the leading roles.

Secondly, the major contributions clinical psychologists made were in the use of psychotherapy in relation to neurotic patients, the methods used being based mainly on psychoanalytic principles. Here again they were regarded as a second-hand, second-rate group of practitioners, whom the medically trained psychoanalysts would be reluctant to trust, in spite of Freud's own declaration that psychoanalysis was not a medical speciality.

Thirdly, methods of diagnosis were largely psychiatric tests of the projective kind, like the Rorschach 'ink blot' test. Rorschach experts had a high reputation, and were among the best paid of all the clinical psychologists I met. I was advised that this was the best of all clinical services in the world, and that I could do no better than take it back with me to the United Kingdom.

I decided that if this was the face of clinical psychology, I would have none of it – for psychology to be subservient to psychiatry was an inversion of the true role these two disciplines should play. Psychology is a fundamental scientific discipline which alone was able to discover the laws of nature according to which behaviour could be controlled; psychiatry was merely an applied discipline making use, at best, of the discoveries of psychology. The notion that psychiatry should rule the roost, and command the activities of clinical psychologists, was anathema to me. If there was going to be a clinical psychology in the United Kingdom, it would be independent and of equal status with psychiatry.

I looked at the published evidence concerning the efficacy of psychotherapy and psychoanalysis as methods of treatment, and came to the conclusion that there was nothing to suggest that it did any better than a placebo treatment or no treatment at all. Comparing all the studies which had been done I found that neurosis was a self-terminating kind of disorder, rather like the common cold; even without any formal kind of psychiatric treatment, most sufferers from neurotic disorders would often get better over time. This 'spontaneous remission' effect was very strong; after two years, some 70 per cent of severe neurotics would have recovered, or be much improved, without any treatment. Compared with that, neurotics who had treatment didn't seem to do any better. This did not suggest that psychotherapy would be one of the things we would teach our students!

I have already mentioned my opposition to the Rorschach test, and what I read and saw in the United States did not improve my opinion of it, or other projective techniques. I made friends with Joe Zubin, who in 1965 published a book together with Len Eron and Flo Schumer, *An Experimental Approach to Projective Techniques*; they came to pretty much the same conclusions as I had done.

I wrote a number of papers in the early fifties, in which I rejected the claims of projective techniques to be reliable and valid measures of personality for mental illness; and the idea that clinical psychologists should do psychotherapy. I advocated the view that psychologists should be independent administratively and in every other way from psychiatrists.

The only one of these opinions which attracted much attention was related to the effects of psychotherapy. I was not alone in questioning the efficacy of psychotherapy, or indeed the first. Denker, Hebb, Landis, Salter, Wilder and Zubin were writing along similar lines around the same time. Why was it then that, as Kazdin states in his *History of Behaviour Modification*, 'the most influential critical evaluation of psychotherapy appeared in Hans Eysenck's article, "The Effects of Psychotherapy".'? I think the major reason was that mine was the only paper which not only gave the evidence, but also explicitly formulated the conclusion that the emperor had no clothes! I discussed the whole question with Joe Zubin at the New York Psychiatric Institute, where he was working at the time. We were delighted that we completely agreed in our views about psychotherapy, but when I told him what I was going to write he visibly blanched and said: 'But you can't do that! We've got to work with psychiatrists and psychoanalysts, and the thing to do is win them over. A challenge like that is only going to antagonize them.' I told him that if the facts pointed to a certain conclusion, it was the duty of the scientist to state clearly what that conclusion was. Playing politics was for administrators and politicians, not for scientists. Furthermore if he and the others pulled their punches, then the powers that be would simply disregard what they had to say, and it would have no effect whatsoever. We agreed to disagree, but the future was to bear me out.

In writing my paper on psychotherapy, I took great care not to go beyond the evidence. The studies that had been done were clearly methodologically poor and inadequate; they could not be used to conclude that psychotherapy and psychoanalysis had no effect. This would be much too strong a conclusion; however, I was able to say that the evidence did not enable us to conclude that psychoanalysis and psychotherapy had a *measurable* effect. This was true beyond any doubt, because if the studies were judged to be too weak to be paid much attention, then there was nothing left whatsoever to support any positive conclusion about the efficacy of psychotherapy!

As Matthew Arnold once said:

> Nor bring, to see me cease to live,
> Some doctor full of phrase and fame,
> To shake his sapient head and give
> The ill he cannot cure a name.

As one might have expected, the outspokenness of my conclusions produced an outburst of hostility that was wondrous to behold. At least a dozen psychiatrists and psychologists wrote articles critical of my conclusion, in a variety of journals. Interestingly, their criticisms were based on the erroneous assumption that I had concluded that psychotherapy was useless; this of course I had quite intentionally avoided saying. I had merely said there was no evidence to show that it was useful, which is a much weaker, but perfectly true statement. The critics adopted the usual stance of any stigma being good enough to beat a dogma with, and criticized with great vigour a conclusion I had not drawn myself. This gave me a chance to reply, and of course enlarge the effects of my original paper a hundredfold. It finally took a Philosopher of Science, writing in the *American Psychologist*, to point out the logical error of my critics.

I reviewed the evidence several times later on, with similar results; the number of studies surveyed was of course much larger, but the quality did not seem to have improved very much! I finally got tired of the whole issue, and encouraged Jack Rachman to take over, and he produced *The Effects of Psychotherapy* in 1971, and later on in 1980 together with G. T. Wilson, *The Effects of Psychological Therapy*. These are still the best and most honest estimates of the effects of psychotherapy. Their conclusions were very similar to mine. Other methods of psychotherapy were criticized equally trenchantly, and only behaviour therapy, of which more anon, escaped with some credit.

My disillusion with the problem was essentially connected with the way the evidence was treated by psychotherapists eager to rescue their discipline from any criticism. In doing this they produced a confectionery made up in equal parts of *suggestio falsi* and *suppressio veri*; also there was a good deal of *argumentum ad hominem*, the *homo* in question usually being myself! Bergin and Luborsky, in particular, made summaries of their literature which excluded many studies that didn't support their case, and included many which were irrelevant. This is not my idea of a proper scientific debate. Even with the customary methods of being economical with the truth, the defendants of psychotherapy did actually give the game away. Thus Luborsky argued that 'everyone has won, and all must have prizes' – a statement intended to say that all the different methods of psychotherapy were equally successful, but only succeeding in reminding the reader of the Alice in Wonderland atmosphere pervading this whole field.

Let us consider Luborsky's claim logically. The original suggestion of Freud was that psychoanalytic therapy, call it T_1, was superior to all other techniques of therapy because it alone contains the vital ingredient H_1 (hypothesis on which psychoanalytic treatment is based). Jung would argue that his type of treatment (T_2) was superior to all others because it contained the essential ingredient H_2. Adler would advocate T_3, because it contained H_3, and so on for all the hundreds of different treatments available nowadays. Now if all are equally successful, then clearly all these claims are immediately discounted, because they depend essentially on the superiority of H_1, H_2, H_3 . . . H_n; if T_1, T_2, T_3 . . . T_n do not differ in effectiveness, then clearly what would be effective, if anything at all, must be something that is in common to all of them, not something that is specific to any one of them. But as this was the original claim made by the people who produced these theories, Luborsky's finding, if accepted, would prove them all wrong! This obvious fact does not seem to have occurred to Luborsky or those who accepted his summary as supporting the value of psychotherapy.

What is the latest evidence about the value of psychotherapy? Smith, Glass and Miller have published a book on *The Benefits of Psychotherapy*, which is often quoted as presenting the final word in this debate. Having analysed most of the existing studies, they come to the following conclusions:

(1) Psychotherapy is beneficial, consistently so and in many different ways. Its benefits are on a par with other expensive and ambitious interventions, such as schooling and medicine. The benefits of psychotherapy are not permanent, but then little is.

(2) Different types of psychotherapy (verbal or behavioural; psychodynamic, client-centred, or systematic desensitization) do not produce different types or degrees of benefit.

Altogether, they claim that:

the evidence overwhelmingly supports the efficacy of psychotherapy . . . psychotherapy benefits people of all ages as reliably as schooling educates them, medicine cures them, or business turns a profit . . . we are suggesting no less than that psychotherapists have a legitimate, though not exclusive, claim, substantiated by controlled research, on those roles in society, whether privately or publicly endowed, whose responsibility is to restore to health the sick, the suffering, the alienated, and the disaffected . . . the parity of psychotherapy with other institutions of human improvement is ensured not only by its research record of consistent benefits but also by its unique contribution . . . Psychotherapy is *primus inter pares* for the benefits it bestows upon the inner life of its clients . . . the consistent demonstration of the efficacy of psychotherapy under controlled conditions commends the study of psychotherapeutic processes to scientists of many types.

But is all this really true? Note first of all the statement that all psychotherapies do equally well, thus effectively destroying the theoretical claims made by psychotherapists of different schools. But more important, let us look at the table in which they compare the effectiveness of eighteen different types of psychotherapy. In standard terms the effectiveness of psychodynamic therapy is 0.69, that of systematic desensitization (a form of behaviour therapy) is 1.05, and that of cognitive behavioural therapy 1.13 – there does seem to be a difference favouring the methods of behaviour therapy, and indeed Smith, Glass and Miller show that behavioural therapies are reliably more effective than verbal therapies. This effectively disproves their notion of equality of effectiveness.

But even more interesting is the therapy they list as No 18. This is called 'Placebo Treatment', and its effectiveness is 0.56 – i.e., almost identical with that of psychodynamic therapy! Now placebo treatment is designed specifically to have no specific effect, no active ingredient that would be relevant to the disorder that is being treated. If placebo and psychodynamic therapy are for all practical purposes equally effective, then that suggests very strongly that psychodynamic therapy is a simple placebo treatment! This would agree well with the 'All have won, and all must have prizes' philosophy of Luborsky and the authors of this book. It certainly does not suggest that the panegyrics to psychotherapy we have quoted from their book are justified.

But worse is to come. Psychotherapy is generally considered by its practitioners from Freud onwards as a type of treatment which requires a lengthy period of training for the therapist, and a lengthy period of treatment for the patient. Smith, Glass and Miller find, however, that there is no relationship whatsoever between the success of the treatment and the duration of training of the therapist, or the duration of treatment. In other words, one hour's treatment by someone who has practically no training at all is as effective as several years of treatment by a psychoanalyst with many years of training behind him. As the Duke of Wellington said when, walking down the Mall in his Commander-in-Chief's uniform, he was addressed by somebody who said: 'Mr Smith, I believe?'; 'If you believe that, you'll believe anything!'

Clearly we have left the world of reality behind, and are entering 'cloud cuckoo' land in which placebo is a method of therapy, in which the shortest possible training and the shortest possible duration of treatment are as effective as the most lengthy training and treatment, and in which we can heap outrageous praise on methods of treatment for which there exists in truth no evidence of effectiveness whatsoever! No wonder I got disenchanted with the whole field, and prefer now to leave it to others to carry on the battle.

The reader who has followed my thinking up to this point will have discovered what I was not going to include in my training programme for clinical psychologists, but might very reasonably ask what should be included. Having rejected all the matters that made up the usual course in clinical psychology in the United States, what was left over? Here we come to a rather complex argument whose historical routes go back to the early years of the war, and my accidental meeting with Alexander Herzberg, a German psychiatrist of Jewish origin who left Berlin, where he had his practice, to come to London in the early thirties; he settled in the Swiss Cottage district, near Hampstead, where many refugees congregated. He was not quite forty when he emigrated, and he died at the early age of fifty; he is known mainly for his book on *Active Psychotherapy*, which was published in 1945. Herzberg was a small man, married to a rather larger wife who produced continental tea and *Guggelhupf* cake at our meetings. He had a dynamic personality, sparkled with intelligence, had a genuinely scientific outlook on psychiatry, and soon became the centre of a group of psychiatrists, mostly refugees, who used to meet in his house and discuss the theory and practice of psychiatry; gradually Herzberg made these informal gatherings into a forum for the discussion of his new methods of 'active psychotherapy' and the use of graduated tasks. I had just received my Ph.D., and was very glad to accept an invitation to attend these meetings; my interest was more in experimental psychology than in the abnormal field, but with the University gone to Aberystwyth there was little intellectual stimulation to be found, and any serious discussion of psychological problems was better than nothing. Herzberg, as he makes clear in his book, considered himself a psychoanalyst, and a follower of Freud; most of the people who came to these meetings had similar leanings, although some held rather more esoteric views. My own ideas had not yet had time to fall into place. The climate at University College had been rather favourable to psychoanalysis, with Professor Cyril Burt a founder-member of the British Psychoanalytical Society, J. C. Flugel, an internationally known psychoanalyst, as his assistant, and S. Philpott, a firm believer in Jung, as their main support; also active was Pryns Hopkins, another well-known psychoanalyst and writer. I had not exactly been impressed, but was willing to listen; these discussions of detailed case histories were exactly what I needed to gain some insight into just what was happening in therapy, and how the patients improved (or not, as the case might be).

As his book makes clear, Herzberg put forward many views which marked a departure from orthodoxy, and which may be considered to be precursors of theories associated with behaviour therapy; I doubt if he quite realized how incompatible these views were with psychoanalysis as taught at that time. Consider simply his statement of the aims of psychotherapy – 'to make the patient free of symptoms; . . . to make him safe from relapse.' This is not a Freudian statement; psychoanalysts tend to disregard the symptom and talk almost exclusively of hypothetical background factors and unconscious complexes, the elimination of which they regard as their prime concern. Herzberg's statement is a clear adumbration of the view that neuroses are essentially nothing but the set of 'symptoms' shown by the patient, so that the elimination of the symptoms eliminates the neurosis. In discussion I frequently pointed out to him that he was a more radical innovator than he was prepared to admit, but he always smilingly refused to agree, and insisted that he was merely trying to speed up the unduly slow process of therapy which orthodox treatment consisted of; he never considered himself anything but a true follower of Freud.

In his theory of neurosis, too, he clearly anticipates the application of Miller's doctrine of approach and avoidance gradients, and his method of treatment is based on a detailed consideration of these gradients. Nor was he ignorant of the facts of spontaneous remission: 'neuroses sometimes fade out without any treatment'. This fact too was not easily admitted by orthodox analysts, and it is difficult to reconcile with Freudian theory; Herzberg simply stated it as a fact of his clinical experience, without realizing the implications this might have for the theory he nominally subscribed to. Such intellectual schizophrenia is not infrequent in innovators, even in highly intelligent ones; they cling to orthodoxy in their formal statements, while rejecting it in their actual working and theorizing. Herzberg is an interesting case in point, and his book would repay an extended critical treatment by someone more expert in Freudian mythology than myself.

The main contribution Herzberg made to behaviour therapy, however, was of course his *method of graduated tasks*. Experience had shown him clearly that orthodox Freudian treatment took far too long to be practicable (or advisable) with the great majority of patients; he also found that it was not always (or even usually) successful. (J. Wolpe later progressed along exactly the same path, although he of course succeeded in taking the important step of cutting the umbilical cord!) Hence Herzberg's call for more 'active' therapy; the very term of course is opposed in essence to all that psychoanalysis stands for. The patient must be made to work, and work successfully, to overcome his symptoms: 'There is one psychotherapeutic agent by which we can attack a neurosis . . .; this is the achievements which we demand from the patient. Achievement is fulfilment of a task by an activity directed to that purpose.'

Herzberg insisted that the tasks which he set his patients must be 'graduated'; a term he defines as 'arranged according to their difficulty'. There is no explicit statement regarding relaxation in Herzberg's paper, but in fact the clinical sessions preceding and following the activities prescribed were used to discuss the events and feelings during the contrived situations, and reassurance and calming talk took the place of relaxation. The *de facto* similarities are probably closer than might appear from reading Herzberg's theoretical views, which are somewhat confused; here if ever seems to be a case of 'Do as I do, not as I say!'

Does 'active psychotherapy' work? It is difficult to form an accurate impression from the data given by Herzberg, particularly as there is no proper control group; furthermore, there seems to have been an unusually large number of patients who broke off treatment (possibly because Herzberg was much less selective in his choice of patients than is usual in psychoanalytic circles). However, when we look at the cases successfully treated it would be difficult to deny that Herzberg is right when he says 'that a treatment by practical tasks will probably be short in comparison with purely analytical treatment or, in other words, that tasks will considerably shorten even analytical treatment.' The shortening of treatment produced by the introduction of graduated tasks is a notable achievement, and one which one might have anticipated would have had a considerable impact on psychiatry. Why in fact was there no such impact?

The first reason that comes to mind is probably the simple one that Herzberg had no official position, was not connected with any university, and thus had no pupils who might have carried on his tradition, taught others, and extended his research. This is a terrible handicap, made worse by the fact that he was a refugee who had to reconstruct his professional life from the shambles produced by Hitler's thugs. He might of course have succeeded in time, had it not been for his untimely death which cut short any influence he might have had, and left his doctrine in an unfinished state, open to theoretical criticism, and virtually unsupported by factual and experimental material. Rebels to be successful must live long; and Herzberg's early death terminated his direct influence.

A second reason, perhaps, was the fact that he worked in England. The rapid adoption of new ideas has never been a characteristic of English establishments, and the insistence on efficiency and success shown in Herzberg's writings received almost as chilling a reception as my own views were to receive a few years later. Finally, he wrote in the middle of the war, and few psychologists or psychiatrists really had time or patience to bother with new ideas or methods; they hardly had time to read at all, even if they had the inclination. And when the war was over, Herzberg was dead. *Exoriare aliquis nostris ex ossibus ultor!*

Yet in another sense it may be said that Herzberg's views have not only survived, but triumphed. My own ideas of behaviour therapy were certainly very much influenced by what I heard and learned from him. We did, indeed, disagree on one vital point; he regarded 'graduated tasks' as merely an adjunct to psychoanalysis, which was supposed to carry the main burden, while I suggested to him that theoretically at least this notion could not be derived from the facts. 'Let P stand for psychoanalysis,' I said, 'and let T stand for "graduated tasks"; S for "spontaneous remission". You assume that P is greater than S, but you admit that there is really no evidence for this. You state that T + P is greater than S, and although there is no formal evidence for this, I agree that this is a tenable position. But from these equations one could also deduce the possibility that T is greater than P – i.e., that the treatment by tasks, without psychoanalysis, might be superior to psychoanalysis, so that we could dispense with the psychoanalytic part of the equation altogether and write: T is greater than S.' He agreed theoretically that such a possibility existed, but would not agree that it justified an experimental study of the effects of T in isolation, nor would he consider a clinical trial comparing T with P, with P + T, and with S.

Herzberg was always kind and considerate; although much older and wiser than I was, as well as very experienced in his field, he always talked to me as an equal, and never resented my continued questioning of what he regarded as his basic beliefs. I took all this for granted at the time; is this not the way scientists are supposed to behave? I was to find out later on how exceptional this attitude towards criticism was in a psychiatrist, or indeed in any kind of scientist. Herzberg was imperturbable; he never lost his temper, never showed any emotion, never resented criticism. He also completely lacked any sense of humour; he could never see the point of a joke, or understand the humour in a film comedy. He did not feel at ease outside the cognitive, intellectual field, or within an organized, circumscribed social situation. Also, he had to confess that he usually failed to understand what was happening in films! His social perceptions were thus seriously circumscribed. He was a nice person, as well as a creative one, and I shall always regret that he did not live to see the flourishing of present-day behaviour therapy. I think he would have approved.

I put together what I had learned from Herzberg with what I had read in the literature about the Watson and Rayner experiment with Little Albert (in which they had succeeded in implanting a neurotic phobia in an eleventh-month-old boy by banging a metal bar behind his head whenever he played with some white mice. He was not afraid of the mice, but was afraid of the noise; by pairing the two Watson made him afraid of the mice, as well as of many other furry objects). Watson had suggested that neuroses are essentially produced by Pavlovian conditioning along these lines, and one of his students, Mary Cover Jones, followed his suggestions of possible treatments through extinction in a series of treatments very successfully given to children suffering from neurotic disorders of various kinds.

By looking at these early suggestions of Watson and Mary Cover Jones, the work of Alexander Herzberg, the writings of the early learning theorists like Hobart Mowrer and Neil Miller, I came up with my first rudimentary idea of behaviour therapy – i.e., a method of treatment for neurotic disorders which would regard them as conditioned emotional responses, to be extinguished through well-known processes described in all the textbooks of learning and conditioning. I never thought I would have a chance to develop the theory, or try it out, but I spent a good deal of time thinking about it. Let me state here and now that I am merely intending to describe my line of reasoning as it historically developed. I have no wish to make any claims of priority; usually many people contribute in various ways to achieve a certain object or discovery, which should not be arbitrarily attributed to any one person. We might of course, as I have said, start with Watson and Mary Cover Jones, but Professor Bringmann has suggested that a good case might be made for Johann Wolfgang von Goethe, who not only used methods of behaviour therapy, but also stated the basic premise on which these are based in a quite explicit fashion. Here is a passage taken from Book IX of his autobiography, *Dichtung und Wahrheit*. This passage deals with his famous stay at the University of Strassburg as a twenty-year-old law student fom April 1770 to August 1771:

I found myself in a state of health which furthered me sufficiently in all that I would and should undertake; only there was a certain irritability left behind, which did not always let me be in equilibrium. A loud sound was disagreeable to me, diseased objects awakened in me loathing and horror. But I was especially troubled by giddyness which came over me every time that I looked down from a height. All these infirmities I tried to remedy, and, indeed, as I wished to lose no time, in a somewhat violent way. In the evening, when they beat the tattoo, I went near the multitude of drums, the powerful rolling and beating of which might have made one's heart burst in one's bosom. All alone I ascended to the highest pinnacle of the minster spire, and sat in what is called the neck, under the nob or crown, for a quarter of an hour, before I would venture to step out again in the open air, where, standing upon a platform scarce an ell square, without any particular holding, one sees a boundless prospect before, while the nearest objects and ornaments conceal the church, and everything upon and above which one stands. It is exactly as if one saw oneself carried up into the air in a balloon. Such troublesome and painful sensations I repeated until the impressions became quite indifferent to me, and I have since then derived great advantage from this training, in mountain travels and geological studies, and on great buildings, where I have vied with the carpenters in running over the bare beams and the cornices of the edifice, and even in Rome, where one must run similar risks to obtain a nearer view of important works of art. Anatomy, also, was of double value to me, as it taught me to tolerate the most repulsive sights, while I satisfied my thirst for knowledge. And thus I attended, also, the clinical course of the elder Doctor Ehrmann, as well as the lectures of his son on obstetrics, with the double view of becoming acquainted with all conditions and of freeing myself from all apprehensions as to repulsive things. And I have actually succeeded so far, that nothing of this kind could ever put me out of my self-possession. But I sought to steel myself not only against these impressions on the senses, but also against the infections of the imagination. The awful and shuddering impressions of the darkness in churchyards, solitary places, churches and chapels by night, and whatever may be connected with them, I contrived to render likewise indifferent; and in this, also, I went so far that day and night, and every locality were quite the same to me; so that even when, in later times, a desire came over me once more to feel in such scenes the pleasing shudder of youth, I could scarcely force this, in any degree, by the strangest and most fearful images which I called up.

The treatment procedures used by Goethe are currently known as 'reciprocal inhibition' and 'flooding with response prevention'. In the latter, the therapist has the patient imagine an experience of intense anxiety-arousing scenes with the therapist present; since this aroused anxiety is not being reinforced by unconditional stimulation it is expected to gradually extinguish, and indeed does so. Goethe used this technique to rid himself of his aversion to loud noises, heights, and dark places. The method of reciprocal inhibition was applied by Goethe to the control of his fear of 'diseased organisms'. In this method, fear and anxiety are put in opposition to positive emotions, intellectual curiosity in the case of Goethe, and these then displace the response of anxiety. The methods are certainly successful, and Goethe, in his novel *Wilhelm Meister*, expounded the rationale of his treatment for psychological disorders, justifying the advantages of action over insight-oriented therapies, saying, 'To heal psychic ailments, that we have contracted through misfortunes or faults of our own, the understanding avails nothing, reasoning little, time much, but resolute action everything.'

But we have even older theories going back some 2,000 years. These ancient theories were Greek in origin, but were voiced in their most convincing form by Marcus Tullius Cicero, in his *Tuscularum Disputationum*. In the first place he points out that '*Ab earum rerum est absentium metus, quarum est aegritudo*': in neurotic disorders, anxiety is felt of things not present, the presence of which causes grief, or distress. This suggests immediately a learning process by means of which the distress properly associated with the 'thing present' (the unconditioned stimulus, in modern parlance) is evoked when the 'thing' is not present; that is, through a conditioned stimulus. Now if we can remove the distress reaction, then the neurotic anxiety also will be taken away: '*Sublata igitur aegritudine sublatus est metus.*' This of course suggests a method of extinction, whether through 'desensitization', or 'flooding', or 'modelling'.

Cicero finally caps his account by appealing to individual differences: '*At qui in quem cadit aegritudo, in eundem timor; quarum enim rerum praesentia sumus in aegritudine, eadem impendentes et venientes timemus.*' Translated freely, this states that the man who is easily distressed is also an easy prey to anxiety and fear. For when stimuli cause distress by their presence, we are also afraid of the menace of their approach. In other words, people who have strong fear reactions to actual dangers and stressful situations also show strong learned anxieties in the absence of these stimuli. We cannot follow Cicero into the details of his discussion, but the elements of our modern way of looking at neurosis are certainly contained in his account.

Many others could be named as early advocates of some form of behaviour therapy; it would be pointless to go on. My own version, while thought out around the early 1940s, was never publicly expounded until 1958, when I gave a lecture on the topic to the Royal Medico-Psychological Association, which was published in 1959. For the purposes of establishing priority, of course, my early recollections can play no part; historians rightly rely on publication dates rather than on unverifiable reminiscences. The reasons why it took almost twenty years for my early theorizing to be translated into a published paper are of interest, and they are certainly crucially important for my life history.

In my early days at Mill Hill, and later on at the Maudsley, I found that Aubrey Lewis was as keenly opposed to psychotherapy being done by non-medical psychologists as were his colleagues, whether psychoanalytically inclined or not. The climate thus being very hostile, and my own interest in psychotherapy less than keen, I agreed in my American writings that it was inappropriate for psychologists to do psychotherapy, basing myself on the fact that psychotherapy had no proper theoretical underpinning in psychological theory, and had not been shown to be more successful than no treatment at all, or placebo treatment. I did seriously consider, however, the possibility of carrying out some pioneering research into behaviour therapy, which I contrasted in my mind with psychotherapy as being based on proper theoretical foundations, namely modern learning theory, and the principles of conditioning, and which I considered to be entirely different from psychotherapy as currently practised. This would be a prominent aspect of clinical psychology as I conceived of it but clearly it was premature to say so, for two reasons. In the first place behaviour therapy at that time was purely an idea in my mind, and there was little evidence that it would be decisively superior to psychotherapy. In the second place it was obvious that I would have to introduce it *sub rosa*, because of the hostility of psychiatrists to giving clinical psychologists any therapeutic function, and the fact that at that time I was still dependent on Aubrey Lewis.

The outcome of my deliberations was two-fold. When I came back to England I started a course on clinical psychology which would lay the basis of a professional training; this was concerned largely with training in intelligence testing, diagnostic testing, and a general area related to the assessment of brain damage and all the other contributions that could be made by tests at that time. I also encouraged my colleagues to undertake treatment of patients by means of behaviour therapy, using the methods pioneered by Mary Cover Jones, Herzberg, and others, and to think constructively along theoretical lines pioneered by the great figures in learning theory and conditioning. Among these early contributors were Gwynne Jones, R. W. Payne, Aubrey Yates, Jimmy Inglis, Vic Meyer, Monte Shapiro, Irene Martin, and many others. In these early single case studies there were many novel procedures which have since been widely used, such as biofeedback, desensitization, reciprocal inhibition, and others which at that time didn't have any names. All this work had to be done secretively, on patients sent by friendly psychiatrists, like Linford Rees, who appreciated our theoretical and practical efforts, and as independent consultants to the Maudsley Hospital had little to fear from the wrath of Aubrey Lewis if he should discover what was happening.

Thus I shifted the major centre of the conception of clinical psychology from diagnostic testing to behaviour therapy, but without openly 'coming out' and stating the position. This would have to wait until I was established enough to fight my corner and defeat any attempts to make us abandon our methods. I clearly foresaw the struggle that was to ensue when I first openly discussed my conceptions of behaviour therapy at the RMPA Meeting in 1958. However this is to anticipate events. In 1950 I returned from America with all these ideas in my mind, and was appointed Reader in the sub-Department of Psychology, which formed part of the Department of Psychiatry under Aubrey Lewis as the professor.

Sybil and I returned to London on the *Queen Mary* early in 1950. We now had to consider our financial position as alimony was taking a good proportion of my salary. We rented a large apartment in a block of flats near the Maudsley, but didn't have enough money to pay for much in the way of furniture – for a while we just had a bed, a table and two chairs! The Courts, in their wisdom, had decided that I would have to pay a third of my income to Margaret, and this I was to do for the next forty years, although as Michael grew up she soon took a job as a psychologist and earned a reasonable living. We did decide, however, that we would buy a cheap secondhand car, and finally plunged for a gigantic Renault, a rather rare specimen as only eight of its type had ever been built. The 'Lizzie', as we called it, took us on a continental honeymoon through France, Germany, Austria, Italy, France again and then home. It was a wonderful trip, although I had only just learned to drive, and knew very little about cars.

When we came back I had to think carefully about the shape of the department I was to build, and my role in it. The department of psychology having started out as a sub-section of the Psychiatry Department, I had to press for it to become independent, with myself as professor; and this was to happen in 1955, as I came back from another tour as a Visiting Professor in the United States, this time at Berkeley, California. I had very definite aspirations for such a department, which would mark it out from all other British or indeed European departments.

Firstly, the department would be postgraduate: we would not take any undergraduate students, but only students studying either for the Ph.D., by doing a research programme, or for the M.Phil., by doing a training programme in clinical psychology. It would only take people who had a first-class degree, or at worst, an upper second in psychology, or its equivalent from a non-British university.

Secondly, the department would be divided into an experimental section, and a clinical section, whose duties respectively would be the preparation of students for the Ph.D., or the M.Phil. The clinical department would of course be cooperating with the Hospital and the consultants there. The arrangement was a rather complicated one, the Hospital, through the Department of Health, paying for the services rendered by clinical psychologists, sending the money to the Education Department, which in turn would pay the psychologists directly. (I made this arrangement because I was worried that if the Hospital and its consultants were in charge of the clinical psychologists working there, they would choose psychoanalytically-minded Rorschach people whom I was determined to keep out.) The arrangement worked well.

On the experimental side I was determined to have a section of physiological psychology, with its necessary apparatus; a section of animal psychology, with the necessary animal colonies and laboratories; and a section of psychometrics, with the latest calculating machines and, later, computers. This was an ambitious programme, because at the time there was no physiological psychology in any of the departments in the country, nor any animal laboratories, and little by way of psychometrics after Burt's and Thomson's retirement. Gradually I managed to get all these established, and we did a lot of pioneering work.

My major problem was what to do about clinical psychology. I could have devoted my time equally to the experimental and the clinical sides, running both as best I could, but I felt that if I had to devote a lot of time to the clinical side, including perhaps actual treatment of cases, I would not be able to do the experimental work I planned. In the end I decided to delegate the day-to-day running of the clinical side, while still retaining overall responsibility. This raised the important question of to whom I should entrust this role. There were two people in the department senior enough and able enough to carry out the job – Monte Shapiro and Hilde Himmelweit. Neither Monte nor Hilde had had much experience in clinical work, but I was sure they could pick it up quickly enough. They were both excellent candidates but I finally chose Monte, primarily because I could foresee violent storms ahead, and I thought he was more likely to stand up to opposition. Hilde left shortly afterwards to start the Department of Social Psychology at the London School of Economics, where she soon became professor and head of the department.

[141]

I had not anticipated all the difficulties that would arise in starting a new profession. The obvious major problem is that before you can teach anyone, you must have teachers, and as the profession itself did not exist in England, the teachers did not exist. It was a case of hauling oneself up by one's bootstraps, and it took quite a long time to do this. Our first students became our next generation teachers, and gradually as our ranks of teachers filled up, the students departed to other universities and started training courses in clinical psychology there. Now there are thousands of clinical psychologists all over Great Britain, and the profession is well established.

Another problem which psychologists nowadays may find difficult to even imagine arose from the predominance of psychoanalytic thinking among the psychiatrists we had to work with. Let me give just one example. Dr Cameron was head of the children's department, and as a very enthusiastic psychoanalyst he used Freudian methods in dealing with such very elementary problems as nocturnal enuresis – or bed-wetting. Analysts have all sorts of rather odd theories about the origins of enuresis. Some believe that it is a substitute form of gratification of repressed genital sexuality – if I can't sleep with my mother, then I'll use my penis this way. Others regarded enuresis as a direct manifestation of deep-seated anxieties and fears. Yet others interpreted it as a disguised form of hostility towards parents or parent substitutes which the victim does not dare to express openly – if I can't attack my father because he is stronger, then I'll annoy him this way! All these theories insist on the primacy of some psychological 'complex', and the secondary nature of the 'symptom'. Concern is with the former, not the latter. Consequently, treatment is long-drawn-out, involves a searching examination of the patient's unconscious, through dream interpretation, word association, and other complex methods and takes into consideration many aspects of the child's personality apparently irrelevant to the simple act of bed-wetting.

According to this view of enuresis as 'a symptom of a deeper underlying disorder', the clinician attaches fundamental causal importance to the deep-seated patterns of child-parent relationships which are 'moulded from birth due to the complex interplay of unconscious forces from both sides'. Some of the specific theories embraced by analysts take the form of highly speculative interpretations based on psychoanalytical symbolism. For one analyst, for example, enuresis was an attempt to escape a masochistic situation and to expel outwards the destructive tendencies: the urine is seen as a corrosive fluid and the penis as a dangerous weapon. Another therapist suggested that usually enuresis expresses a demand for love, and might be a form of 'weeping through the bladder'.

As opposed to all this nonsense, behaviourists have a much simpler form of treatment. Normally the enlargement of the bladder leads to the child waking up and going to the toilet. This process of conditioning has failed in some children, and the way to produce the needed connection is by way of the bell-and-blanket method. The child is made to sleep on a blanket which separates two porous metal plates. These plates are connected in series with a battery and a bell. The dry blanket acts as an insulator; once the child begins to wet the blanket, the saline urine begins to act as an electrolyte, and a connection is made between the metal plates. This completes the circuit and the bell rings and wakes up the child – and causes him reflexively to inhibit the act of urination. This method was developed by Hobart Mowrer and found to be extremely efficacious in all cases where there was no physical reason for the enuresis, such as a virus infection of the urinary tract. Psychotherapy and psychoanalysis, on the other hand, have never shown the slightest effect; enuresis tends to disappear as the child gets older in any case, without treatment, and treatment does not hasten this process in any way.

I tried to get Cameron interested in this new method, and suggested we might try it out on a small group of children. He was highly indignant, and shouted that he would not allow anyone to give electric shocks to the penises of his children! I tried in vain to explain that electric shocks were not involved in any case, but he was clearly beyond reason. We had to wait until he died a few years later, when his successor was open to persuasion, and introduced the method which has since been used all over the country with considerable success. I doubt if anyone would now be found using psychoanalysis for the treatment of enuresis.

Psychoanalysts had suggested that the obvious anxiety and depression of the enuretic child were the *cause* of his disorder. Behaviourists suggest, on the other hand, that it is the enuresis that makes the child anxious and depressed, because obviously the enuresis produces many problems in his relation with his parents and peers. Psychoanalysts also suggest that curing the 'symptom' does not help in any way, because the child would develop substitute symptoms. Many investigations have failed to show any such substitute symptoms, and once the enuresis has cleared up, the child's anxiety and depression are much reduced or banished altogether.

It will be clear now what constitutes our problem. How can a clinical psychologist cooperate with psychoanalysts who hold absurd theoretical views? There was simply no common ground, and it was one of our tasks to create this common ground.

One way of doing this was through teaching. Aubrey Lewis suggested using the DPM (Diploma in Psychological Medicine), which at that time was the major psychiatric qualification in the country, and was much sought after by aspiring students. He made psychology an important part of the examination, and for many years I gave the lectures on psychology which the students had to attend. That gave me a chance to explain to them the psychological principles related to psychiatric disorders, and to acquaint them with the criticisms of Freudian doctrine which their clinical tutors would not have told them about. I must have taught most of the people who later became professors of psychiatry in Great Britain, and started them off with a better understanding of what psychology was all about, and how it could best be used. This process took many years, and at the beginning we had a pretty rough time in trying to coordinate our efforts with those of the psychiatrists, almost all of them strongly influenced by psychoanalytic thinking.

Gradually things came together, and when I returned from my visiting professorship in Berkeley (which I shared with Donald Hebb whom I got to like very much), I was made professor. My department was now independent of psychiatry, and I could concentrate wholeheartedly on the building up of behaviour therapy with the help of some of the outstanding students who had come through our course. Three years after my return I felt the time had come to come out of the closet, and to proclaim the virtues of this new discipline of behaviour therapy, which was to become the major part of our clinical psychology curriculum.

Up to this moment Aubrey Lewis had been a good friend and a staunch supporter. He saw to it that as the department grew, money was available to finance the new places, and he defended us against the sometimes vicious attacks of medical consultants and others who were unhappy with our general outlook. They would come and tell the clinical psychologists: 'Go and test so-and-so; I want you to give him a Rorschach and tell me about his repressions and other dynamics.' We would train our psychologists to say: 'I'm sorry, but I can't do that. If you will tell me what the problem is, I will try and find an answer for you as best I can, but the choice of instrument and so forth must be left to us.' Consultants are not used to having anyone talk back at them, and they would flood Lewis's office with complaints. He would tell them I was responsible for the Psychological Section, and that they should address their complaints to me. I took great pleasure in explaining to them at length the proper relationship between psychology and psychiatry, as I saw it! Without Aubrey Lewis we could not have started the department, we could never have established clinical psychology in this country, and we could not have withstood the onslaught of the psychoanalysts. For all this I will be eternally grateful to him, and I think British psychology as a whole owes him a great debt.

Arrangements were being worked out to integrate clinical psychology into the National Health Service. The two-year training we gave to our M.Phil. students was regarded as a proper entry into the National Health Service, and a career structure was being worked out to accommodate the new discipline. By the time my great battle about behaviour therapy began, I had carried out my bargain with Lewis about establishing clinical psychology as a profession in this country.

In 1958 I was invited by the RMPA, then the major psychiatric association in Great Britain, to give a talk at one of their meetings. I had already, usually at Aubrey Lewis's invitation, given several addresses to the Association; this time I chose the topic of 'Behaviour Therapy', and I asked Gwynne Jones to come with me and complement my theoretical account with a description of several cases he had treated using the principles of behaviour therapy. I had chosen my timing carefully; I knew that there would be a storm of protest, which I thought I could ride, although I must confess I had not expected it to be quite as vehement as it turned out to be. Above all, I had expected Aubrey Lewis to react more rationally than he did. But then I have never claimed to be a good psychologist in the layman's sense – i.e., a person who has an intuitive understanding of other people's reactions, and can predict what they will do.

The hall was spilling over with psychiatrists; it was as if they anticipated what was to happen. Sybil and some of my colleagues were sitting at the back of the hall; next to me on the podium were Gwynne Jones, on my left, and the Chairman, a Scottish psychoanalyst, on the right. This was the first time the term 'behaviour therapy' had been used in Great Britain, and it meant nothing to the audience. I explained the major differences between behaviour therapy and psychotherapy, discussing the underlying theories and hypotheses, the fact that behaviour therapy was founded on the secure foundations of experimental work on conditioning and learning, while psychotherapy had no such secure basis. I went on to tell them about the lack of proven efficacy of psychotherapy, and mentioned some of the successes of behaviour therapy. I made the talk as factual as I could, trying to avoid any provocative statements.

While I was speaking I noticed a growing irritation on the faces of many of my listeners, which soon turned to animosity, disgust, and finally, hatred. When I finished there was not even a pretence at polite handclapping; the audience seemed to erupt, jumping up and down, yelling, screaming imprecations, and waving their fists in the air. The Chairman tried to quell the uproar, imploring the audience to show some politeness to their guest, and gradually the uproar died down and Gwynne Jones was allowed to make his contribution. They didn't like him any more than they liked me, and at the end there were a lot of 'questions', which were rather speeches denouncing our methods. Sybil and the others in the back row were afraid that we might be attacked, but the thought never struck me. What did strike me was that this behaviour was a *reductio ad absurdum* of the claims made by psychoanalysts that training in psychoanalysis made people more rational, and less neurotic, by eliminating their infantile complexes. I have seldom seen an audience behave in a more infantile manner!

The Dean had been at the meeting, and hurried back to tell Aubrey Lewis about it. Then Hell began to break loose. Lewis tried to nip in the bud this apparent insurrection of the downtrodden. As he never discussed the issue with me, and never wrote about it or tried to reach a rational agreement, I find it difficult to guess what passed through his mind, or, indeed, exactly what he tried to do. I have to rely for reports on other people who attended the various committees where he tried to cut us down to size and block our work on behaviour therapy. Thus he got the Committee of Management of the Institute of Psychiatry and the Hospital to pass a rule that psychologists should not be allowed to carry out treatment. At the meetings of the Heads of Departments, he tried to reduce the size of the department, or even shut it down altogether, acting through the Dean and the Institute Secretary, both of whom were of course in his pocket. As representative of Psychiatry on the Medical Research Council, he blocked any efforts we made to get some money to carry out research into behaviour therapy and the principles of conditioning. From a friend he had become an implacable enemy, although still preserving a friendly exterior.

Psychiatric friends who were aware of much of the conflict advised me to give in. They reminded me, rightly, that Lewis was much better placed than myself when it came to waging war, and had more experience of political in-fighting. He was the representative of Psychiatry on the Management Committee, and the undisputed Head of the Institute, although not formally so designated. Everyone admired him, and everyone was afraid of him. I was never asked by the Committee of Management to present our case, nor by anyone else. 'You are bound to lose,' I was told. 'Why don't you chuck in your hand and abandon this attempt to get psychologists to carry out behaviour therapy?'

My answer was simple. Behaviour therapy had been put together as a treatment by psychologists, on the basis of psychological principles arrived at in psychological laboratories. All the work had been done by psychologists, who, unlike the psychiatrists, were the only ones with the background and the training to serve the patient in this manner. To add another couple of years to psychiatrists' very lengthy training in order to make them expert at learning theory and the other principles involved was plainly absurd. Thus in the interests of the patients, which had to come first, it was manifestly better for the treatment to be carried out by psychologists than any other group. What we were doing and advocating was the right thing, and in the long run that was more important to me than any Machiavellian intrigues.

I pointed out that I had never pulled out of a fight before, and was not going to pull out of this one. After all, I also had some weapons, and I would not hesitate to use them.

The main weapon was publicity. I made it quite clear that if the cabal continued, and in any way interfered with the functioning of my department, I would complain to the Postgraduate Medical Federation, of which we were a constituent part; I would get in touch with the Senate of the University of London to tell them what was happening; I would write to the Vice-Chancellor of the University, asking for help and advice; I would even go to the Chancellor, who happened to be the Queen Mother at the time, to ask her to intercede. I was going to air the whole issue in *The Times,* the *British Medical Journal,* and *The Lancet,* so that it would become a topic of discussion everywhere. I also managed to get the Medical Committee on my side – not so much because they liked *me,* but because they disliked Aubrey Lewis even more, because of his dictatorial and autocratic behaviour towards them.

Contrary to all the prognostications, I won. The department was not eliminated or reduced in size; we carried on with our investigations of behaviour therapy; we made it the central piece in the two-year M.Phil. course; and we got more and more psychiatrists to send us their patients for treatment. This they did, not because of any theoretical convictions, but because they found that patients they failed to cure prospered and improved under our treatment; this they found more convincing than any arguments. Aubrey Lewis of course remained stubborn to the end.

Aubrey Lewis once asked me: 'I imagine you think that I am behaving in this like a dog in the manger?' I told him frankly that yes, I did think that, expecting him to carry on to explain his position, to argue the case, and to discuss the whole question. But he simply gave a rather sad and pained smile, and went on to talk about something else. He never once discussed the problem with me.

It might be thought that I was over the moon, having won my battle. I could never bring myself to feel that way. Aubrey Lewis and I had been good friends for many years, and he had done an enormous service to psychology, as well as helping me to create what was to be one of the biggest psychology departments in Europe, and I think one of the best – at least if we can judge by the evidence of the Citation Index, as I shall try to show presently. He had forced this battle on me, but winning it did not make me happy. Browning's poem *The Lost Leader* encapsulates my feelings:

Just for a handful of silver he left us,
Just for a riband to stick in his coat.

I had gladly acknowledged Lewis's leadership in trying to make psychiatry and clinical psychology more scientific, more useful, more helpful to the patients; now he was throwing it all away for the sake of a cheap triumph for the medical profession over outsiders like psychologists and others. This, to me, did not seem worthy of him. To quote another poem:

It was because you were my friend
I fought you like the devils fight;
Because you dared lay down your crown,
And be a man like other men.

We still talked together regularly, and preserved the outward forms of politeness, and even jocularity, but 'it was never glad confident morning again', to continue with the *Lost Leader* poem.

To this day I regret the necessity of having to defend our position in this way, but I think it was necessary. In 1972, the Trethowan Committee, set up by the Department of Health and Social Security, to look at the problems of the psychologist in the mental health service, acknowledged the value of behaviour therapy as a treatment for neurotic disorders, and also accepted that psychologists should administer this treatment. Thus fifteen years after I had raised the banner, the psychiatric profession agreed with the major points I had made. Of course the Trethowan Report did not mark the end of hostilities; isolated skirmishes still went on.

The scientific and clinical development of behaviour therapy can be followed in books like Kazdin's *History of Behaviour Modification*, or Angela Schorr's *Die Verhaltenstherapie*. I will here only mention the major aspects which concern me, or in which I have taken a part. Having nailed the flag to the mast in the paper I read at the RMPA, which was published soon afterwards in the *Journal of Mental Science*, I decided that the time had come to flesh out the meaning of behaviour therapy to a greater extent, and I edited two books, one entitled *Behaviour Therapy and the Neuroses*, the other *Experiments in Behaviour Therapy*, in both of which were printed articles from the literature, in many cases originating from my collaborators, which exemplified the many different methods used by behaviour therapists. These illustrated the types of neurotic disorder to which they were appropriate, and gave some idea of the effectiveness of these methods. I also published, together with Dr S. Rachman, *The Causes and Cures of Neuroses: an Introduction to Modern*

Behaviour Therapy Based on Learning Theory and the Principles of Conditioning.

This was the first textbook of behaviour therapy, and together these three volumes formed the first introduction to behaviour therapy for many clinical psychologists who later on became well-known exponents in their discipline.

Jack Rachman had come to me as a Ph.D. student recommended by Joe Wolpe. Wolpe was a South African psychiatrist whose early leanings towards psychoanalysis, and use of 'dynamic' methods, had led him to a negative evaluation of these theories and methods. He began to read Pavlov, Watson and Mary Cover Jones, and developed theories and practices very similar to those with which we were experimenting at the Maudsley. He too had a hard time, of course, in the psychoanalytic climate prevailing in South Africa, but he did attract some able helpers of whom Jack Rachman, with a background in psychology, was perhaps the best. Jack wrote an excellent Ph.D. thesis for me, and very much against Monte Shapiro's wishes I got him on to the clinical staff. Monte was becoming quite hostile towards behaviour therapy, preferring the so-called 'client-centred therapies' of Carl Rogers. He probably perceived Jack, with his background in Wolpe-type behaviour therapy, as a threat, and not unreasonably so. Jack was an invaluable help in training students (and staff!) in behaviour therapy, and later succeeded Monte as Head of the Clinical Department, and became its first professor. We worked together on the book, which I think launched behaviour therapy as an independent discipline, and at the same time defined its content.

In the early years of the 1960s I decided that the time had come for a journal of behaviour therapy to help define the area, and to print relevant articles of outstanding quality. It is always difficult to get a journal started, particularly if it is unconnected with a society or an association. I decided to go and see Robert Maxwell, the originator and head of Pergamon Press, which was publishing many scientific journals. Jack accompanied me, and we explained briefly the nature of the enterprise, and the need for such a journal. He asked some decisive questions, and then nodded agreement; yes, he would do it. This was the beginning of *Behaviour Research and Therapy*, BRAT for short, and the journal has gone on for over twenty-five years now with outstanding success. I functioned as editor-in-chief until 1978, handing over thereafter to Jack Rachman. He had been assistant editor until then, but played a greater and greater part in the editing of the journal, so that much of the success it has had is due to his hard work, enthusiasm and wisdom.

Within seven years of the publication of the first issue, the journal had risen to ninth place out of seventy-seven psychological journals, as measured by the impact of its articles. With a Citation/Article Index of 1.184 ('an index of the importance of a given journal's articles on psychology' – *American Psychologist*, 1976, p. 674), *Behaviour Research and Therapy* was placed higher than the APA journals of overlapping content – the *Journal of Abnormal Psychology* and the *Journal of Consulting and Clinical Psychology*. Having regard to the advantages that journals published by large associations like the APA enjoy, this is a very gratifying record. Kazdin, the historian of behaviour therapy, observed that this first journal of its kind 'provided an identity to individuals working with distinct behavioural techniques, problems, and settings'.

About 1962 I entered into another contract with Robert Maxwell dealing with a project that was dear to my heart. I undertook to assume the editorship of an 'International Series of Monographs in Experimental Psychology' (see pages 289–90 for full list) on the basis that monographs constituted an important method of publishing extended research reports which could not be constrained into article form, but which would be too specialized to be acceptable for ordinary publication in book form. Some of these titles (for example, Nos. 1, 7, 8, 11, 12 and 15) have become quite well known.

My own major interest has been the development of theories underlying behaviour therapy. I drew attention to the need for distinguishing between Pavlovian A-type and B-type conditioning, as defined by D. A. Grant, and developed from this distinction the incubation theory of fear/anxiety, which I believe obviates many of the difficulties encountered by Watson and Mowrer. I also emphasized the importance of genetic factors in neurosis, and the relevance of personality differences to treatment. But most of all I have always insisted on the importance of learning theory as underlying any scientific explanation of the origins of neurosis, and any attempts to treat neurosis by behavioural methods. This has often been misunderstood to mean the defence of early versions of learning theory, such as the very primitive theories advanced by Watson, or later on by Hull. This is of course quite incorrect. Modern learning theory embraces cognitive factors in a crucial manner, and the distinction made by some cognitive behaviour therapists between conditioning and cognition is purely arte-factual and has no real meaning. All these issues are discussed at some length in a book I edited, together with Irene Martin, entitled *Theoretical Foundations of Behaviour Therapy*.

I have always agreed with Monte Shapiro that each patient constitutes a scientific problem of its own, and that the skill of the clinical psychologist consists in solving this unique problem in terms of the general principles offered by academic psychology. To illustrate these methods I edited a book of *Case Histories in Behaviour Therapy*. The principle, of course, is well established, having been enunciated by Claud Bernard in the middle of the nineteenth century.

In another book, written with D. K. B. Nias, I tried to extend the principles of behaviour therapy to a rather different field, namely television. Entitled *Sex Violence and the Media*, the book was perhaps the first to argue, as the basis of a wide range of empirical studies, that portrayals of sex and violence on the screen *do* have an effect on viewers; at the time the usual liberals were arguing the opposite, in spite of all the contrary evidence already existing. We added a theoretical underpinning to the argument; we not only demonstrated that there *was* an effect, but we showed that psychological theory *predicted* such an effect. Alas, the book had little effect against the *Zeitgeist*; now it is fairly universally admitted that we were right, but at the time we got more kicks than ha'pence!

Once the profession of clinical psychology had been established, with behaviour therapy as the central part, the British Association for Behavioural Psychotherapy was formed, and the *Journal of Behavioural Psychotherapy* was published, as the official organ of the BABP.

In America, too, a behaviour therapy association was formed, the American Association for the Advancement of Behavior Therapy, which produced a journal entitled *Behavior Therapy* edited by Cyril M. Franks, another of my earlier Ph.D. students. Other similar associations were formed, as in Germany where Hans Brengelmann, yet another of my former students, played a most active role.

A few words should be said about the way I tried to motivate my students and colleagues to collaborate in the 'vision' ('*Phantombild*', as Angela Schorr calls it in her history of behaviour therapy) which I had of a scientific approach to treatment. For many years Sybil and I would hold open house once a fortnight for any members of the staff, and any students who wanted to come to have a buffet dinner and talk about developments in behaviour therapy. It seemed to me that having laid out the general plan of what I thought was desirable, actual individual participation, discussion and, if possible, experimentation and treatment would provide the strongest motivation for people to continue working in this field, and make a genuine contribution. Many of those who took part have become important figures of their own in the development of behaviour therapy – Gwynne Jones, Vic Meyer, Bob Payne, Irene Martin, Jimmy Inglis, Cyril Franks, Hans Brengelmann, Monte Shapiro, Jack Rachman, Gordon Claridge, Aubrey Yates, and many, many others. These discussions and debates forged a general approach to the problem of treatment which became recognized as the 'Maudsley approach'. It was a psychological ploy on my part to get people interested and enthused, and it worked.

The other important ingredient of my approach was the determination to encourage individuals to think critically, even if their criticisms took my own theories as their objective! Cyril Franks put it well in one of his articles when he said that: 'The guiding role model, then as now, was that of the friendly but critical student rather than the unquestioning disciple. Inquiry always took precedence over ideology.'

These Thursday evening social meetings also gave me a chance to put into practice some of the ideas I had had concerning teaching. It had always seemed to me that there were two kinds of students, and consequently two kinds of teaching. There were the undergraduates, who knew nothing about psychology, and who had to be given factual information and practice in experimental methods. This could best be done in terms of lectures and reading, as well as practice with selected experiments. This was the kind of teaching I was doing with the registrars in the DPM course, but of course as far as the psychologists were concerned, we didn't run an undergraduate course, and consequently something else seemed appropriate.

There were also the postgraduates. Our task here was to make them good research workers or good clinicians – preferably a combination of the two. This raised the question of whether you can teach research methodology. Courses of lectures were quite inappropriate for the purpose; what was needed was for the student to work closely with an established scientist, to observe what he was doing and how he was doing it, and by interaction to learn the 'whys' and 'wherefores' of scientific research. But something more was required. How can you strongly motivate your students and collaborators, and in particular how can you get them to think for themselves?

I based my teachings on the methods used by E. C. Tolman, whom I had got to know quite well when I was Visiting Professor at Berkeley. He is often reproached by historians of science because he did not found a school, because he did not indoctrinate his students, so that instead of always spouting his words, they became independent scientists and sometimes even criticized him! The way I adapted his methods was as follows.

I was always available to students for a discussion of their problems and difficulties, whether theoretical or experimental, but I never forced myself on them. They would come with a problem, or a question, such as: 'Just what is your view of cortical arousal, and how would you define it?' Like Socrates, I would decline to give an answer, but try to draw them out. 'On the basis of your reading, and your thinking, how would you yourself define it, and what kind of a conception do you have of cortical arousal?' I would say. Having heard what they had to say, I would then point out theoretical or experimental difficulties with their particular definition, and ask them to go on and improve it.

With father and stepmother Tilly.

With Ilsemarie, aged 14.

Father and stepmother on stage.

Maternal grandmother.

Mother as
film star.

Margaret Davies.

Captain of the
college tennis team.

On holiday in the Scilly Isles, 1938.

Newly married – Hans and Sybil.

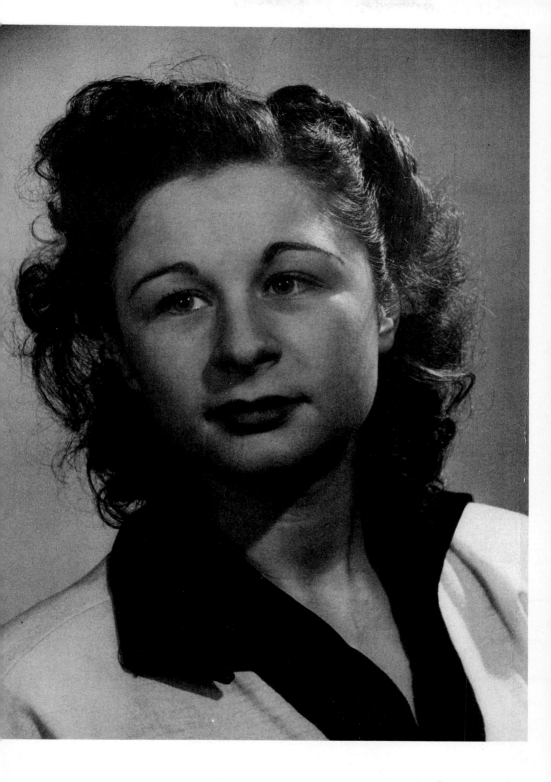

Max Rostal, father-in-law.

Sela Trau, mother-in-law.

Sir Cyril Burt

Sir Aubrey Lewis.

Oxymorons to end all oxymorons: Birmingham University.

Under attack at the London School of Economics.

Daubing by courtesy of the Animal Liberation Front.

Didier and Connie.

Kevin, Gilly and Damien.

Gary and Lilly.

Darrin.

Michael and HJE.

On the
Maudsley
tennis court.

With Michel and
Francoise Gauquelin.

Hilde Himmelweit.

Asenath Petrie.

Jeff Gray.

Jack Rachman.

HJE and Sybil with Desmond and Barbara Furneaux.

With the Prime Minister of Singapore, Lee Kuan Yew.

Ronald Grossarth-Maticek.

Arthur Jensen.

Gwynne Jones.

Lindon Eaves.

Irene Martin and Sybil.

Peter Broadhurst.

Richard Lynn.

Gisli Gudjonsson.

Given that we only accepted first-rate students, the method worked surprisingly well. It provided strong motivation, it led to independent thinking, and many of the students, even after they left, went on working in the fields related to their original research. Obviously it doesn't work with everybody, and some people need more specific guidance and interaction, but on the whole it succeeded in teaching my students independence, and enthusiasm, and at the same time a usable research methodology. The method was certainly successful in the worldly sense – one in three of my Ph.D. students became a full university professor, about fifteen in England alone, which is well above the average, and may indeed be something of a record. Remember that prior to my getting the Chair at the Institute, practically all professors in the United Kingdom had come from Cambridge!

I tried to do exactly the same sort of thing with the clinicians and students who came to the Thursday evening meetings. I could of course have tried to 'sell' them my idea of behaviour therapy, but it seemed much more Socratic to allow them to discover these things for themselves, through discussion, and through trial and error inspired through those discussions. It worked like a charm; people were really fired-up, devoured the books and writings of Hull, Tolman, Mowrer, Miller, Guthrie, Pavlov and the other learning theorists, and received a great deal of positive reinforcement when they tried out the methods suggested on their patients, and found they actually worked.

Arthur Jensen, who spent two years with me as a post-doc, has given a description of his experiences in my department. A brief section of this may be worth quoting:

> Eysenck ran a lively shop. Almost everyone in his department – the professional staff, postdoctoral fellows, and graduate students – was working on some facet of Eysenck's theory of extraversion–introversion. From Eysenck and all the others, I quickly learned what was going on and began to think about how I could become actively involved in their program of research. Because Eysenck was an incredibly productive researcher and writer, I was warned long before arriving in London, by persons who only surmised what it was like in Eysenck's department, that he would probably be very inaccessible to students and postdoctoral fellows. As it turned out, nothing could have been further from the truth. He was easily the most accessible professor I have ever known, either before or since then. He was always there and one only had to knock on his door. It seemed he was glad to discuss any problem at any time. He was always 'all business' and when the 'business' part of any discussion was over, that was that. He never engaged in social pleasantries or

idle chitchat. Nearly every dealing with him was in some way intellectually rewarding. In his discussions he brought to bear an exceptionally quick, incisive intelligence, a greater verbal and ideational fluency than I'd seen in anyone else, and a vast erudition, seemingly always at his fingertips. He was clearly a great professor and I felt lucky to be at the Maudsley.

His staff, too, was a stimulating group of workers. We all talked shop and little else every day at morning coffee, at lunch, and at afternoon tea. Rarely have I encountered a group of researchers more involved and excited in what they were doing. Eysenck's own powerful commitment to his research, I felt, had a lot to do with it.

So much for the research side. On the clinical side, Irene Martin has given a somewhat more detailed account of what happened at our 'At Homes':

It was during the late 1950s that some of the most interesting discussions took place at the At Homes. Among the network of factors which made these times so lively was Hans' confident and provocative leadership, and the variety of themes being floated: developments in personality theory, in particular links with inhibition and conditioning, inhibition and neurosis, and the role of these in behaviour therapy. It was an energetic mixture of events, enlivened by a number of able participants. The participants were clinical psychologists who were themselves engaged in research as well as research workers and Ph.D. students. Gwynne Jones emerged as one of the most skilled contributors, and Bob Payne as the most guilelessly provocative. The trio – Hans, Gwynne and Bob, with able interventions from Jimmy Inglis, Dougal Campbell, Russ Willett and others – debated week after week. Debate may not be an accurate description. There was something gladiatorial about these events. Hans was not much taken with the idea of entering into a real dialogue. His thinking was done in private, and if any discussant produced a good idea he was more likely to accommodate it into his subsequent thinking than to interact on the spot. Many approached the At Homes nervously having prepared some tempting tit-bit to engage Hans' attention.

At one of the symposia in the 1988 World Congress of Behaviour Therapy in Edinburgh someone asked me if I remembered the red leather chair. Like Proust's tea and madeleines it opened the gates of memory. It was the chair occupied by Hans at the At Homes. These took place in the Eysencks' home, a Hansel and Gretel sugar house of red and pink and yellow on the outside and a mix of brilliant

[154]

colours and patterns within. While Hans presided over the intellectual jousting, Sybil's hostess role included warm welcomes and generous catering. Much baking and preparation went into the open sandwiches and pastries, unstoppably passed round with coffee. Not that evidence of such devoted domesticity was apparent in Sybil's uniquely extravert style of dress – the leopard-skin cat suit, the exotic shoes, the extravagant scattering of sequins and jewellery.

Hans' theoretical preoccupations emerged in his talks and publications, a continuous 'casting of bread upon the waters'. After a spell of absence for maternity leave I returned to find that the conditioning theory of neurosis had been born in the short time I was away. This was presented provocatively, a scientific approach to be contrasted with the mish-mash and wishy-washy futility of Freudianism. Advance was always allied to attack. The matter of sober, analytical debate bothered Hans very little. The rightness of his position and the error of others, in particular psychoanalysts and psychiatrists, was obvious. The goal was to win, and his words waged wars. And that essential element – danger – was present. Hans made sure the opponents were unambiguously identified: psychoanalysts, dangerous through their wealth and influence, psychiatrists through their dominance, unscientific psychologists.

What made the challenge the more exciting within the immediate environs was the presence and aura of Sir Aubrey Lewis, whose intellectual rigour was virtually unsurpassable. Hans could and did accuse psychiatry of ignoring scientific evidence, of ignoring theoretical contributions. The Professorial Unit, nonetheless, was highly esteemed for its clarity of thought and criticism. No one there got by with shoddy presentations of case materials. Aubrey Lewis had been instrumental in appointing Hans to the Chair in psychology and hence was an ally. Concerning the issue of treatment by psychologists he remained an unmovable opponent.

Hans went gleefully into battle. If behaviour therapy based on theory was to dominate, then Freudians had to be demoted and psychiatrists put in their proper place. If his personality theory was to rise, others had to fall. If psychology was to be hauled out of the slough, then science and proper statistical analysis of data had to prevail. His comments were not always endearing and led to many a spicy confrontation.

We felt we stood behind an unconquerable leader, determined that psychologists should never become 'pale copies of psychiatrists'. He challenged everyone and enjoyed the fact that few would accept the invitation to compete. He well knew the strategies of fair and unfair debate!

The atmosphere created by Hans and enjoyed by the participants of the At Homes was one of defiance and rejection of the 'establishment'. Not that in those days the establishment was particularly well organized, but it was the case that psychiatrists controlled all therapy, and psychology within the UK could be criticized (Hans felt) as being either unscientific or confined to a restrictive clique. Not wanting to join them he defied them. Hence there was a sense of embarking upon an adventure, a crusade for a scientific theory of personality, a fight for psychologists' rights, a daring launching of behaviour therapy. Hans wanted to do this alone: he neither invited nor wanted allies outside the small circle who worked with him.

If you chose to join him, you were readily accepted. The participants of the At Homes, indeed the members of the Psychology Department, came from an extraordinarily wide range of backgrounds and countries. Hans imposed little or no selection on applicants in the Department, although there was self-selection by those who were attracted to what seemed a novel and exciting Department with who knew what prospects and developments. It is a policy he has steadfastly kept to: no detailed examination of one's past or history of achievements. What mattered was what you did with current opportunities.

The participants of the At Homes typically involved a nucleus of a dozen or so people, rarely more than twenty, and for some time discussion was spontaneous, often started by one of Hans' or a group member's current preoccupations or discoveries. The major influence at that time in the Behaviour Therapy movement was Hans, with Gwynne Jones as the right-hand man, diplomatic, genial, astute. Monte Shapiro, although not often attending the At Homes, provided a strong research orientation within the clinical section. These were pre-Jack Rachman days; as is well known, Jack subsequently continued and developed the research orientation of the Department's clinical section.

Eventually the impetus weakened, and the At Homes took a different form. Specific speakers would be invited to present their ideas for discussion, visitors would be invited or themes would be introduced by more peripheral researchers. The venue changed, and a rota was established in group members' homes. The peak period was over.

There were many factors determining the excitement of this era. Most significant were Hans' determination and uncompromising stance, backed up by a wide-ranging knowledge, statistical expertise and enormous verbal flair. Not that he was particularly talkative, but he could marshal an argument instantly. The strategy was to defeat, and the tactics employed were quite specific, frequently taking the form of counteracting the other's proposals by pointing out that they had ignored evidence presented on such and such a page in Journal X, or that their logic was faulty. This form of engagement was used with friend and foe alike, and no doubt contributed to a distance around him and an unease in attempting an interactive dialogue with him.

He was, however, unstinting in his support of those who worked with him. Equipment requests were generously met, Hans from the beginning being aware of the essential need to attract research money. He supported us in other less tangible ways. When he planned the first *Handbook of Abnormal Psychology*, published by Pitman in 1961, it was not outside 'experts' but his immediate staff and students whom he invited to contribute. By these means the Department flourished.

There were the people present – a mixed bunch but many willing to share in the promotional zeal. There was Sybil – lively and sociable, impossible to match with the conventional image of a dowdy professorial wife. The overall numbers within the Department at the time were large in comparison with other Institute Departments but small by any other standard and we all knew one another, had coffee together, organized and shared parties, the most successful of which included a brilliant transvestite striptease act.

All of this of course cannot be used to *prove* that research methodology and clinical methods can be taught, but I think the results were encouraging enough to suggest that perhaps the method has merit. What was particularly rewarding for me was the enthusiasm generated; these people really *cared* about developing a scientific psychology and applying it to practical problems, and they carried this enthusiasm back with them to many other departments and countries. Motivation, enthusiasm, call it what you will – this is a quality that is difficult to kindle in university departments, but all of those who came to our meetings attested to the vital part they played in their development. Maybe Socrates deserves our admiration not only as a philosopher, but also as a psychologist!

Of those who took part in these meetings, only Monte Shapiro developed an opposition to the principles of behaviour therapy. He did make an important contribution by recommending direct measurement of clinically relevant behaviour (i.e., the patient's symptoms) so that any behaviour change effect with treatment could be accurately assessed, as opposed to routine personality testing. He also favoured the intensive study of the single case, believing that the demands of a given patient could not await the findings from group studies. These are interesting and important points, but they do not constitute the essence of behaviour therapy.

In retrospect, could it be said that my venture into the field of behaviour therapy was a success or a failure? As usual, the answer must be that there are both successes and failures. Firstly, I did manage to get clinical psychology and behaviour therapy set up as professional activities in the United Kingdom, with a defined career and salary structure, with specific training schemes laid down by the Directorate of Health and Social Services in conjunction with the British Psychological Society, and this now constitutes practically the only branch of psychology which is crying out for recruits, and where vacancies outnumber available candidates.

Secondly, I think it may be said that the methods of behaviour therapy which I advocated have proved extremely successful. At the Maudsley and Bethlem Royal Hospital, for instance, more and more cases suffering from neurotic disorders are being referred for treatment to the Psychology Department; we are treating more than a thousand each year. This contrasts very much with the occasional case sent over to us in great secrecy when Aubrey Lewis was still opposing the notion of any form of treatment being carried out by psychologists.

Thirdly, there is no doubt that psychiatrists have come to terms with the profession of clinical psychology, and find psychologists extremely useful. Hardly a year goes by without some psychiatric group (children, forensic, geriatric, mental defective, etc.) asking for a psychologist to be appointed specifically to work with them, and the tail is very much wagging the dog – at the moment there are some fifty clinical psychologists in the department, as compared with only three or four on the experimental side. Were more money available, undoubtedly many more clinical psychologists would be employed.

Internationally, too, behaviour therapy has made great advances, although there are still countries like France, or the South American Republics which are still steeped in medieval Freudianism. But even there the revolution is beginning, and worldwide I think it may be said that behaviour therapy is universally accepted as a useful set of techniques, and a valuable set of theories.

So much for the success side. How about the failures? It seems to me that most behaviour therapists have adopted a policy of eclecticism, which is anti-theoretical and reduces the discipline to a kind of cookbook mentality in which more or less arbitrarily the therapist chooses desensitization, or modelling, or some other method of treatment regardless of theoretical considerations. This is not what I intended behaviour therapy to be. Behaviour therapy has also become a bandwagon, with many people trying to cash in on the scientific status of the discipline without having had the necessary training; this is surely most undesirable. There is little quality control, and too much dollar-hunting in the field to make anyone happy.

Altogether, few behaviour therapists are interested in the theoretical underpinnings of what they are doing, or the constant developments and improvements in learning theory which ought to be taken into account in devising methods of treatment. There has arisen a whole school of 'cognitive behaviour therapy' which argues against the importance of learning theory principles, criticizing the principles of learning theory as if there had been no change in the last fifty years.

Another point. Behaviour therapists consistently ignore two influences on behaviour which for me form an important part of behaviour therapy. One is the genetic contribution, which has been clearly demonstrated in twin studies and adoption studies. The other is the importance of personality variables. I will come back to these topics later on; here let me merely note that this part of my teaching has been consistently disregarded by behaviour therapists, and, in so far, this must constitute a failure.

In the book *Hans Eysenck: Consensus and Controversy*, Christopher Barbrack and Cyril Franks have written an excellent chapter entitled 'Contemporary Behaviour Therapy and the Unique Contribution of H. J. Eysenck: anachronistic or visionary?' They conclude that, very much as I pointed out above, there are successes and failures of my programme and they go on to say:

> Whether one considers Eysenck a gadfly or guardian angel, it is unwise to dismiss him too casually. Still, when all is told, the conclusion that Eysenck's influence on behaviour therapy is a fraction of what it could be is unavoidable. The reason may be, in part, related to the following: (1) he writes so clearly and specifically that others understand his position and dismiss it for the sake of something they like better even if it is not understood nearly as well; (2) his manner of expression is dogmatic; (3) the material he presents is too technical and demands much effort to read; (4) his approach demands that treatment plans be formulated on the basis of psychological knowledge, that predictions be made about treatment effectiveness and that treatment be assessed against this standard – and it is much easier to 'fly by the seat of your pants' and 'shoot the breeze' in therapy sessions; (5) behaviour therapists may find data gathering and treatment evaluation tedious and even aversive; and (6) some behaviour therapists may not understand or appreciate the practical value of theory.

> We believe that these and other barriers to Eysenck's influence will fall as the knowledge base of behaviour therapy expands. For influence already exerted in behaviour therapy, Eysenck has earned our gratitude. As behaviour therapy continues to evolve, one day Eysenck will receive the full measure of appreciation his unique contribution deserves.

I hope that they may be right, and that behaviour therapy as practised will develop in the direction I would like it to go.

Fundamentally the question is whether the clinician–scientist model originally proposed at the Boulder Conference of the American Psychological Association is appropriate – i.e., the ideal that the clinician will retain one foot in the academic camp, carrying out some research and reading the literature on recent developments. This certainly was my ideal, and also that of Aubrey Lewis. He himself thought that he was giving an example of what the model meant in psychiatry, trying to keep up with research in psychology, biochemistry, neurophysiology, genetics and so forth. He was revered as a polymath by most of the registrars, but he is probably the living proof that such a model may not be appropriate, or possible to approximate.

Lewis certainly knew more psychology than most biochemists, more neurophysiology than most geneticists, and more biochemistry than most psychologists. However, when it came down to specific subjects, his knowledge was at best superficial. He knew most of the 'buzz' words in psychology, but knew little about the experimental studies or theoretical concepts behind them. To say this is not to blame him in any way; what he was advocating is simply impossible, considering the speed of advance of modern science, and the gigantic volume of journals and books that keeps appearing. No-one could have done better, and his failure indicates that the ideal may be nothing but a chimera. Given that clinicians are probably too busy to do any experimental work, or much reading, I have suggested that we might take a leaf out of the book of modern physics. There is a gap between theoreticians and experimental workers which has become so wide that the former do not know or understand what the latter are doing, and the latter find the products of the theoretician too complex and difficult to understand. What has happened is that we have an intermediate group which explains the theories of the one group to the other, and tells the theoreticians what the experimentalists are doing, and why. Perhaps we too should have such an intermediate group, interpreting modern advances in theory and experimental practice to the clinicians in relatively simple terms, and informing the learning theorists and experimentalists about the problems encountered by the clinicians. I don't know whether this is a reasonable proposal to ensure that the future of behaviour therapy will be more science-oriented than in the past. Human organisms have a tendency to solve their problems in the long run, and I am sure these problems too will find a solution. Of one thing I am certain; as Kurt Lewin used to say: 'There is nothing as practical as a good theory!'

CHAPTER 5

The Battle of the Cigarettes

Convictions are more dangerous
enemies of truth than lies.

F. Nietzsche

The 1960s saw more than the battle of behaviour therapy. On the personal side, Sybil and I settled down in married life and bought a lovely house, with a large garden, not far from the Maudsley Hospital. A twenty minutes' walk through Ruskin Park, a small but delightful park with plenty of flower beds, and a small lake, took me from home to work every day, and back in the evening. This of course was greatly preferable to joining the rush of commuters, either by car or train, which is so characteristic of London. Not only did I get some exercise each morning and evening, but I also had a chance to think about what I would be doing that day as I walked to work, and a chance to consider what I had done on the way back! At noon I usually played tennis, a habit that was to continue until I retired, and well beyond that. Our bodies were made for walking and running, not for sitting on chairs all day, and I am sure it is this habit of physical activity that has kept me healthy, and (reasonably!) slim.

It was during this time, too, that we started our family. Gary is the oldest; there was a gap then before Connie was born, followed shortly by Kevin, and then finally Darrin. Sybil had no problems in giving birth and indeed enjoyed the experience, believing as she did (and does!) in natural birth, and rejecting medical advice. She never used drugs and other artificial means.

Sybil also got her first degree in psychology as an external student, and then her Ph.D.; I still remember her sitting up in bed, the evening before Gary was born, working out a complicated discriminant function analysis for her thesis on one of the departmental calculating machines.

My main work at the time was concerned with perfecting my theory of personality, linking it with abnormal psychology, with learning and conditioning theory, and with genetics. In those years I published *The Dynamics of Anxiety and Hysteria*, which was my first effort to produce a causal theory of the factors underlying the major dimensions of personality; I edited *Experiments in Personality*, a book which detailed the experimental studies we were doing at the time; I wrote *Crime and Personality*, in which I showed that certain personality types were causally linked with criminal behaviour, and elaborated a conditioning theory of anti-social conduct and criminality. I also edited the *Handbook of Abnormal Psychology*, which tried to demonstrate the experimental foundations of abnormal psychology. All of these books were quite successful in their own way, and the *Handbook* in particular was widely read in the United States.

The *Handbook* ran into a second and entirely revised edition in 1972, and I hope that someone will take up the burden of producing a third edition – a very big job in view of all the work that has been done in the last fifteen years. I also wrote a historical study on *The Structure of Human Personality* which ran into three editions, the last one in 1970.

All these books were strictly scientific, and hence brought in little money. You don't write books of that kind in order to become rich; at the time real money from writing psychological books could only be earned by writing a textbook which became standard reading in American universities. This I could not do, for you must be able to accommodate your presentation to the foibles and prejudices of the teachers of your subject. No book which criticized Freud or Rorschach, or refused to honour any of the other shibboleths which were characteristic of American psychology at the time had any chance of being accepted, however justified the criticisms might be. Then, an entirely new venue opened up for me.

This, like so much else, I owed to Aubrey Lewis. He was visited by Allen Lane (later Sir Allen), who had started the paperback revolution in England by founding the Penguin Press. He was just beginning to develop another venture, the Pelican Press, also devoted to paperbacks, but on more serious subjects. He asked Aubrey Lewis whether he thought it worthwhile trying out books on psychology and psychiatry as part of his new series. He wanted Aubrey Lewis to recommend someone who could write a popular book on these topics for him. Lewis recommended me, and Allen Lane asked me to produce a book on psychological topics which would be scientifically sound but intelligible to the layman, and above all, interesting.

England had produced quite a few popular writers of outstanding ability – there had been Jeans and Eddington in physics, and Haldane,

Hogben and Huxley in biology. I had read their books with considerable interest and enthusiasm, and I shared their view that science was not an esoteric enterprise to be kept in mystical seclusion from the rest of the population, but ought to be read and discussed by intelligent people everywhere. It should be possible to explain anything in psychology clearly and succinctly to a bright ten-year-old without any prior knowledge. I accepted Sir Allen Lane's offer, and wrote *The Uses and Abuses of Psychology*.

It took me a fortnight to write *Uses and Abuses*. It is important to realize what the term 'writing' implies. The 'writing' begins in the remote past, when one is reading and learning the elements of one's craft. The next step would be to gather material to write articles, or to use in one's lectures. By the time one starts the actual writing, or in my case dictation, it should already all be there in one's head – facts, theories, the organization of the whole thing. The topics I dealt with in *Uses and Abuses* – like intelligence testing, occupational and industrial psychology, abnormal behaviour, the effects of psychotherapy, the use of psychological tests, social attitudes and their measurement, Gallup Polls, and many others – were the material I had been lecturing on to the registrars for the DPM course for several years, and to dictate these chapters was not different to giving my lectures. I simply dictated each chapter as it came along, my secretary Shirley typed it out, and I made an absolute minimum of revisions, correcting the punctuation, and altering a noun or a verb where that had been repeated twice in the same sentence.

The book was almost excessively successful. It was widely reviewed, it sold at an astonishing rate, and was reprinted over twenty times in the next few years; finally, it was translated into many foreign languages. Many well-known psychologists and psychiatrists have told me that it was reading *Uses and Abuses* when they were at school that persuaded them that they ought to go into psychology or psychiatry, and certainly for many people this was their first introduction to psychology, there being nothing similar available which was both academically sound and not written in the peculiar jargon beloved by psychologists and psychiatrists.

The book was published in 1953; in 1956 I published a sequel, *Sense and Nonsense in Psychology*, which was similarly successful, being reprinted many times, and translated into many languages. It dealt with topics like Hypnosis and Suggestibility, Lie Detectors and Truth Drugs, Telepathy and Clairvoyance, and The Interpretation of Dreams; there were also chapters on the Measurement of Personality, Personality and Conditioning, Politics and Personality, and The Psychology of Aesthetics.

Rather late, in 1965, I published *Fact and Fiction in Psychology*, again written in much the same style, with chapters describing a Visit to a

[164]

Psychological Laboratory, Personality and Eysenck's Demon, Little Hans or Little Albert ('Little Hans', of course, being the little boy whose phobia Freud used as an introduction to psychoanalysis of children, while 'Little Albert' was the boy Watson used to demonstrate the conditioning of neurotic disorders). There were also chapters on New Ways of Curing Neurosis, Therapy or Brain-washing?, Accidents and Personality, and finally, Crime, Conscience, and Conditioning, a popularization of my theory that one of the major reasons why most people don't commit crimes is their possession of a conscience, and that this conscience is created through a process of conditioning in their youth, the unconditioned stimuli being punishment provided by parents, teachers and peers for evildoing.

This trilogy sold millions (literally!) of copies, and raised my income to a respectable level – more than trebling the rather poor salary paid to a university professor in England. Unfortunately, the Labour Government slapped income tax of about 80 per cent on my earnings at the top level; had I emigrated to a tax haven and continued to write bestsellers, very soon I would have become a multi-millionaire!

Why were these books so successful? They certainly had to fight against difficulties which Hogben, Haldane and Huxley did not have to fight against. They were writing about mathematics, evolution, and biology; every educated person knows something about these topics, and regards them as scientifically important and socially valuable. The only thing most people knew about psychology was some (usually misunderstood) snippets of Freudian psychoanalysis; they would also normally have a healthy doubt about the scientific nature of psychology, or even the possibility of studying human beings scientifically.

I had to start erasing misconceptions before even beginning to deal with the positive side. Thus there had to be a good deal of debunking, which Haldane and the others did not have to do. One reviewer in fact quoted a short colloquy from Boswell: 'Dr Johnson: Well, we had a good talk. Boswell: Yes, Sir, you tossed and gored several persons.' Unfortunately the tossing and goring was very necessary, but it does not make one many friends!

A few reviewers complained about my not doing adequate obeisance to Sigmund Freud, but the majority took my criticism of psychoanalysis quite reasonably. Altogether, after the publication of these volumes, I became, for the newspaper readers at least, the voice of psychology, and few days passed when some newspaper, radio or television person did not ring up to ask me questions on the most impossible topics, like: 'Can you tell a person's sexual behaviour and interest from the kind of tie he wears?' or 'Can you tell a person's personality from his eating preferences?' On the whole I declined to answer these questions, but this does not normally prevent newspapers from writing articles on such nonsensical topics, usually quoting some psychologist or psychiatrist who likes to see himself in print.

Allen Lane was enthusiastic, and decided to go wholesale into the general field of psychology. This turned out to be a great mistake; Pelicans got landed with a whole series of left-wing educationalists who knew very little if any psychology, had no interest other than to grind their Marxist axes in public, and wrote a jargon too terrible to contemplate. I still remember one wonderful quotation, which argued that: 'The lower organs of the Party in Britain must make still greater efforts to penetrate the backward parts of the proletariat.' There speaks a true Marxist. The public was quite able to discriminate between political nonsense written with an ulterior motive, and genuine science, and stayed away from this avalanche of absurdity.

Sir Allen and Pelican published two more popular books of mine, although rather later. The first of these was *Psychology Is About People*, which came out in 1972; the other was *Decline and Fall of the Freudian Empire* which appeared in 1985, published by the Viking Press, the hardback name for Pelican. Of all my popular books I think this is the best, although it was frequently attacked for daring to criticize psychoanalysis in general, and Freud in particular.

Another kind of popular writing opened up in the late 1950s when I had a further windfall. A television company wanted to put out a programme which would contain in the first section typical IQ test items, and in the second section typical general knowledge items. They asked me to provide the IQ items, paying £3 for each. As such items only take about a minute to write, I accepted this as a welcome addition to the family income, and the programme, which ran for quite a long time, was very successful and a popular choice. I tried to make it as interesting and amusing as possible, while retaining the genuine nature of IQ tests. When the series ended I was left with the thousands of problems which had been used. I didn't quite know what to do with them, and stored them away in the attic, when I suddenly had a brainwave – why not publish them with Pelican in paperback form?

Thus was born *Know Your Own IQ* in 1962, and *Check Your Own IQ* in 1966. The first of these included eight tests, each consisting of forty items, to be done in half-an-hour and giving the reader an estimate of his IQ. I standardized these tests before making up the book. For *Check Your Own IQ* I used five tests of general intelligence, one for verbal ability, one for numerical ability, and one for visual-spatial ability; I also had two extra difficult ones which I called 'Limbering Up For Intellectual Giants'. Each text was preceded by a lengthy explanation of what the IQ can and cannot do, as well as other information on intelligence which I thought might be useful for potential readers. Like the others, these books frequently appeared in the bestseller list.

I called all these books 'entertainments' because, while they had a definite educational purpose, I wrote them to be entertaining as well as educational. I have already mentioned one of the difficulties in writing about psychology. Another one would be obvious to anyone who compares psychology with psychoanalysis. The great advantage of psychoanalysis is that it is written in terms which are readily intelligible to the layman. To say: 'The young male child wants to sleep with his mother and kill his father' may be nonsensical, but it is fairly clear what is meant. Mostly readers will feel that having read Freud's *The Interpretation of Dreams* or his *Totem and Taboo* they know what he is talking about, and that they can talk intelligently about it.

Now take a very straightforward and factual statement in psychology, like: 'Schizophrenics, unlike normal people, show little if any latent inhibition.' The lay reader may know what schizophrenia is, at least in outline, but he is unlikely to know what 'latent inhibition' may be – I doubt if most psychologists will know what the term means. Inevitably, the term will have to be explained, but the explanation itself will be in terms of conditioning paradigms which will be unfamilar to the reader. This is only one difficulty; in many cases the argument becomes mathematical or statistical, and most readers will switch off the moment figures or tables are drawn into the argument. To avoid doing so, and yet to explain meaningfully what psychologists have found, and what their theories are, is not easy. I have tried my best, but I don't think that complete success is attainable.

The reception of my 'entertainments' among my colleagues was more critical than I had expected. They did not criticize the actual points I had made; what they objected to was the effort to make psychology popularly understandable. I suspect they wanted to preserve a certain mystique to surround their cabalistic practices.

Most of the work I have mentioned so far was done in the 1950s, and it coincided with an important event which was to produce another great battle for me, although I did not realize it at the time. At some scientific convention I met a Ms M. Tarrant, who introduced herself as a Director of Mass Observation. The term did not arouse any favourable reaction in me; it had been used during the war by some sociologists who pretended to apply scientific methods to measure social attitudes by means of getting large groups of ordinary people to keep diaries and write down a variety of things they had done, or heard, or seen. This was a journalistic enterprise, not a scientific one, and I had severely criticized the books which had been published summarizing this work. Since then Mass Observation had become an ordinary commercial research organization, using orthodox methods, but I didn't know that at the time. Ms Tarrant told me that she had been asked to get three or four scientists together for a radio discussion on smoking, and would I take part? I agreed, and decided that first I would read a bit about cigarette smoking, the debate that was just starting about its effects on health, and other aspects of smoking. In my mind, I tried to link up smoking with some of my work on personality.

I had been looking at the experimental side of personality study – i.e., how best to describe personality and how to explain the individual differences that we found in terms of concepts like 'Pavlovian Excitation and Inhibition'. On the social side, on the other hand, there were variables like criminality and anti-social conduct, smoking and drinking, neurotic and general emotional behaviour, sexual behaviour, and many others of a similar kind. In all of these there were marked individual differences, and it seemed to me that they were very likely linked with personality differences, and could be explained along the same lines. Smoking might very well be one of the social consequences of individual differences in personality, leading some people to smoke, others to be rather hostile to smoking, and I sat down to try and work out the rules.

I came up with two hypotheses. It was known that nicotine, at least in small quantities, produced cortical arousal (a state of the brain in which the individual is highly alert). In my general theory cortical arousal was characteristic of introverts, while lack of such arousal was characteristic of extraverts, and the possibility seemed to arise that extraverts would smoke cigarettes in order to increase their level of arousal to tolerable amounts, thus overcoming the boredom so characteristic of low levels of arousal. Equally it was assumed that smoking (in larger doses) reduces tension, and so, perhaps if people were high on neuroticism and anxiety, they would smoke in order to reduce their anxieties. These two effects might seem contradictory, but it was suspected, and later proved, that nicotine is in fact biphasic; in other words, in small quantities it is arousing, in larger quantities it is a depressant. However that may be, during the discussion I suggested this as a possible reason why people smoked. I was unwilling to accept the so often heard argument that smoking was addictive, because neither then nor now does the term have any scientific content. I like playing tennis and writing books on psychology; does that mean that I am addicted to tennis and book writing? The term 'addictive' has so many different connotations, and is defined in so many different ways, that it has become meaningless. It seems much more reasonable to look for positive effects of smoking (or drinking, or eating sweets, or whatever) which might explain why people were indulging in those particular pastimes, even though they might also have many undesirable consequences.

After this discussion, Ms Tarrant told me that the Tobacco Research Council were interested in financing research, to be done by Mass

Observation, into personality correlates of smoking; was I willing to direct this research? Needless to say I was keen on trying out my theory, and two large-scale studies were in fact done on random samples of the population, interviewed by paid employees of Mass Observation. The subjects of the study were asked about their smoking habits in some detail, and we also administered one of my personality inventories. The outcome showed very clearly that there was indeed a regular increase in cigarette smoking as the extraversion scores of the subjects increased. Pipe smokers tended to be introverted, on the other hand; with people who had given up cigarettes somewhere in between. For neuroticism the data were rather less favourable to my theory, but later studies have shown that there also, particularly for women, was a significant relationship – the more anxious and tense the woman, the more cigarettes would she smoke. The results were written up for the *British Medical Journal* and appeared in 1960. This study had two rather interesting consequences.

The first of these was that I became a consultant for Mass Observation, and directed a number of studies for them – e.g., into popular women's journals and beer drinking, in which attempts were made to use factor analysis and other modern methods of statistical treatment to tease out factors underlining the preferences of people for one or other journal, or beer, or whatever, and where possible to relate these to personality factors. This unusual approach was regarded as pioneering research in the industrial and commercial fields; unfortunately the results could not be published as obviously the firm that was paying for the work did not want its competitors to know about the results. However, the work gave me a good deal of insight into commercial practices and popular reactions to products and advertising, as well as easing our financial difficulties.

Another, rather more amusing, light was thrown on the thinking of business people when a manufacturer of sweets engaged one of my students, later Professor Cyril Franks, to investigate the reasons why the mints he was producing were nothing like as successful as the famous Polo Mints ('Lifesavers' in the United States).

Having interviewed large numbers of consumers and sales staff, Cyril reported that the reason was very simple: people got more mint for a penny if they bought the Polo Mints than if they bought this man's confectionery. This factual explanation produced a furious outburst. Apparently the manufacturer was firmly convinced that Polo Mints were selling better because they had the hole in the middle; this, he believed, had symbolic Freudian meanings, which accounted for the preference of the customers! Cyril tried to tell him that if this were so, then surely the preference should be larger for males than for females, but he wouldn't listen, and peremptorily dismissed Cyril. A year later he went broke.

I have heard similar stories from psychologists who had to research into cigarette smoking, and who found that manufacturers also seemed to believe in the symbolic influence of the shape of the cigarette.

Another outcome of my meeting with Ms Tarrant was a continuing interest in my research shown by the Tobacco Research Council, which funded a whole series of investigations into the relationship between personality and smoking, and the effects of smoking. One of these effects was supposed to be lung cancer and many other types of cancer, as well as coronary heart disease and a variety of other fatal or non-fatal medical diseases. R. Doll, in England, and E. C. Hammond, in the United States, had turned this belief from a hypothesis into virtual certainty in the minds of many people, aided by a virulent press campaign and the setting-up of a medical propaganda machine. Looking at the evidence, I detected many weaknesses, both methodological and statistical, and I found that leading statisticians and other experts who had looked into the question were quite scathing about the quality of the research. Men like R. Fisher, probably the most famous statistician of the century, J. Berkson and J. Yerushalmy, also expert statisticians, and P. R. J. Burch, a medical physicist, whose book on *The Biology of Cancer* has become rightly famous, K. A. Brownlee and many others might be mentioned here; and when I wrote my book on *Smoking, Health and Personality* in 1965, I was largely following in their footsteps in coming to the conclusion that the evidence was not sufficient to prove that smoking caused cancer or coronary heart disease, or even lung cancer. This conclusion was attacked furiously in the medical as well as the popular press, and it was suggested that I was encouraging smoking, denying that it had evil consequences, and was acting irresponsibly.

Let us consider these points. It is well known that even if smoking is causally related to lung cancer, it is neither a necessary nor a sufficient cause for it. It is not a necessary cause because one person in ten who dies of lung cancer is a non-smoker; hence other causes must be responsible for his lung cancer. This becomes even more obvious when we consider non-Caucasian populations, where the ratio of smokers to non-smokers in those afflicted with lung cancer is not 10 to 1, but in the case of Japanese, Chinese, Thai and similar groups it may be more like 2 to 1, and may even become insignificant. Racial differences are crucial, but are mostly disregarded by commentators ignorant of the facts.

Smoking certainly is not a sufficient cause of lung cancer; of ten heavy smokers, only one dies of lung cancer! This means that for this one person out of ten, there must have been other causes which led to his being singled out to die of lung cancer, as opposed to the other nine heavy smokers who did not. These facts alone should make us cautious in using the slippery concept of 'causation' in relation to smoking. Smoking may play a part in a complex and lengthy causal chain; it certainly is not *the* cause of cancer (or coronary heart disease).

One obvious problem with all epidemiological studies of the effects of *one* risk factor is the simple fact that this factor is strongly correlated with many others, so that a demonstration of a statistical relation between Factor X and death from cancer, say, may really be due to Factor Y, or Z, both of which are highly correlated with Factor X. As an example, take cancer of the cervix, which has been linked with smoking. But smoking is strongly linked with early sexual activity and promiscuity. American high school students who smoke have a much higher probability at all ages of having had sexual intercourse than non-smokers. Thus cancer of the cervix is perhaps causally linked with frequency of sexual intercourse, and promiscuity, and only statistically with smoking? Or perhaps the drinking of alcohol, also correlated with smoking and sexual indulgence, is the true cause? Or perhaps extraversion, which is correlated with all three? I am merely pointing out the complexity of the problem, and the lack of care that has usually gone into unravelling the many strands. There is unlikely to be a simple answer.

But is it not true that giving up smoking leads to a lesser probability of dying of lung cancer, or cancer in general? The answer is uncertain, but the effect, if any, is certainly not very marked. Some studies have indeed shown such an effect, but these studies suffer from a curious methodological fault. They *assume* that smokers who continue to smoke, and smokers who give up smoking, are similar health-wise and personality-wise at the time when the quitters give up smoking, but it has been shown quite definitely that this is not true. In actual fact the quitters are more like non-smokers with respect to health and personality at the point when they give up smoking, as compared with those who continue. Hence the better health of those who give up smoking may not be due to their giving up smoking, but to their having better health already at the time of quitting. Like most of the evidence, that on quitting is largely inconclusive, and characterized by poor methodology. The best studies show little or no effect.

But is it not true that there has been a tremendous increase in lung cancer following the increase in smoking, with a time lag of twenty to thirty years? Well, again, the evidence is pretty inconclusive. Epidemiological studies are usually based on death certificates, and these are extremely unreliable, as many studies have shown. Particularly relevant are the facts that death from lung cancer was severely under-diagnosed at the beginning of the century, and is now severely over-diagnosed, when comparing death certificates with autopsies, which are much more reliable. Thus at the beginning of the century, out of 100 people who died of lung cancer and were diagnosed so on autopsy, only four were so diagnosed on the death certificate.

What makes the matter worse is the fact that diagnosis, and cause of death as shown on the death certificate, are seriously influenced by whether the patient was a smoker or not, and this also determines the kinds of tests which are being carried out. Thus we may here be dealing with a self-fulfilling prophesy, rather than with a true causal relation.

Inhaling is another problem for those who believe that smoking causes lung cancer. If this were true, then obviously people who inhale should be much more likely to die of lung cancer than people who smoke but do not inhale. Yet, as Fisher has already pointed out, this is not true; if anything, smokers who do not inhale are *more* likely to die of lung cancer than those who do. This anomaly has never been explained satisfactorily.

There are many other difficulties with the belief that 'smoking causes lung cancer and coronary heart disease', and I have outlined these in detail in a chapter on 'Smoking and Health' in a book on *Smoking and Society* published in 1985. Note that I have never stated that cigarette smoking does *not* appear to be causally related to cancer and coronary heart disease; to deny such a relationship would indeed be irresponsible and counter to the evidence. I have merely stated that the available evidence is insufficient to prove a causal relationship, and this I believe to be true. This is not the place to argue the case; readers who feel unconvinced are invited to look at my chapter, and consider the evidence.

All this would not matter so much if it were not for the fact that we have found recently that heavy smokers who believe that 'smoking causes cancer' are much more likely to die of cancer than are equally heavy smokers who do not so believe. As Claud Bernard, the famous French psychologist, once said: 'In ignorance, abstain!' Until we know far more about the causes of cancer and heart disease, we should not go around frightening people unnecessarily, or lead them to believe that we know more about these matters than we do.

If personality was related to smoking, might it not also be related to susceptibility to cancer and coronary heart disease? And if so, might there not be a genetic influence on smoking and disease, as well as on personality? My research on these matters was published in a book called *The Causes and Effects of Smoking*, in 1980, containing a large-scale study of the genetics of smoking which I undertook jointly with Dr Lindon Eaves, the well-known geneticist. It demonstrated that while the taking up of cigarette smoking was not determined by genetic factors, its continuation was. Much of the material in the book supported the view that personality was indeed crucially linked with smoking, and it might also be linked with disease. Some of the studies surveyed were of particular interest in showing cross-culturally that personality showed much higher relationships with lung cancer than did smoking. The importance of the fact that neuroticism showed a negative relation with lung cancer will become apparent presently.

It seemed to me at that time – i.e., towards the end of the 1950s – while smoking might or might not have a causal influence on cancer and coronary heart disease, clearly other factors were at least equally important, and might be much more important. What might these factors be? There has been a belief throughout recorded history that people suffering from cancer were characterized by a certain type of personality; on the one hand, they were nice, unassertive, compliant people, unexpressive of negative emotions like anger, fear and anxiety. Secondly, they were people who tended to react to stress by giving in, by failing to overcome the difficulties they encountered, and by developing feelings of hopelessness and helplessness. There was some observational, descriptive and anecdotal evidence, but no hard data. Aided by the Tobacco Research Council, I got together with Dr David Kissen, a well-known Scottish oncologist, and we designed a study which would throw light on this topic. We selected as our experimental subjects patients who came to Kissen's chest clinic, complaining about pains. These were then given one of my questionnaires, paying particular attention to the neuroticism or anxiety scale, the expectation being that if these old theories were true, then those with low scores – i.e., non-expressive of anxiety (repression), would be more likely to be diagnosed as having lung cancer than those who had high scores.

Of the patients tested, 116 turned out to have lung cancer, 123 not to suffer from lung cancer but from some benign disorder. The cancer group had much lower neuroticism scores than the non-cancer group, a statistically significant difference. This study turned out to be the beginning of a very important series of investigations, undertaken twenty years later together with Dr Ronald Grossarth-Maticek.

I tried to follow up my work, naively assuming that oncologists would be interested in what after all is a remarkable finding, namely, the involvement of personality and stress in the causation and the growth of carcinomas. I had not reckoned with the hostility of the medical establishment to the intrusion of new and disturbing ideas. I approached several experts, all of whom refused to collaborate in any kind of research, and even refused to allow me to give questionnaires to their patients! They did not give any reasons for this refusal, but it effectively made it impossible for me to continue work along these lines, although I thought that this might be of some importance.

I encountered opposition from the medical profession with a problem in relation to another interesting theory I had run into. There are marked differences in the incidence of lung cancer in various races and nationalities, and while some of these are undoubtedly linked to genetic factors, there was also the possibility that the type of tobacco smoked might be responsible. It was well known that smoking cigars showed much lower correlations with lung cancer and other diseases than did smoking cigarettes, and it is also known, of course, that the tobacco which goes into cigars is cured in a different way to that which goes into cigarettes. Cigarette tobacco is flue-cured, whereas cigar tobacco is sun-cured. Interestingly enough, the tobacco in those countries where there seemed to be little cigarette-linked lung cancer was also sun-cured rather than flue-cured. Sun-cured tobacco might therefore be safer than flue-cured tobacco, but there is no direct empirical evidence for this. I thought I might be able to provide that evidence, and I got in touch with a small German firm which produced both flue-cured and sun-cured tobacco to put into their cigarettes.

My idea was to do a study of people who smoked the products of this firm, and look at the proportion of lung cancer sufferers who had smoked the sun-cured and the flue-cured variety, respectively. The proposal was of course rather more complex, but that was the underlying idea, and the firm agreed enthusiastically to support the study financially. There was only one last purely formal step to be taken; they had to refer the matter to a giant concern which owned them, for ratification.

This was the last I ever heard of the proposal. I was told informally much later on that the giant concern itself had simply put a veto on the matter because they were producing entirely flue-cured tobacco for their cigarettes, and didn't want the results to demonstrate that these cigarettes might be less healthy than others! (The reason for preferring flue-cured tobacco, of course, is that it is much cheaper and quicker to produce than sun-cured tobacco; this is presumably why cigarette firms stick with it.)

All of these events seemed to me to leave a bad smell behind. Cancer and coronary heart disease kill more people in our society than any other disorders, and if they were indeed causally linked with smoking, then clearly something ought to be done. Personality might be an important intervening variable, but the medical establishment put their veto on this type of research. The type of tobacco smoked might have an important influence, but the cigarette industry put their veto on research into that. Nobody seemed to care about the truth, or about the lives of those who seemed destined to die of cancer and coronary heart disease; that seemed to be the least important consideration for either the medical establishment or for the cigarette industry.

Now there came a twenty-year interlude in my work on personality, smoking and disease, and I will take the story up again in due course. When my book *Smoking, Health and Personality* appeared, the Tobacco Research Council decided not to continue the research grants they had been giving me. This may have been because the British tobacco industry, which finances the Research Council, had decided to react to the onslaught of the medical profession by lying low. To them my research and my writing were a nuisance, and they decided to stop it.

Much occurred during the twenty years intervening between my work on smoking, cancer and personality with David Kissen, and the work I was to begin with Ronald Grossarth-Maticek. In 1964 we moved into the new Institute of Psychiatry building, which had been put up next door to the Maudsley Hospital. We had many research students who acquired their Ph.Ds.; we educated whole generations of clinical students in abnormal psychology and behaviour therapy. Much research was done, mainly on personality, and later on intelligence, and other topics; about these I will report in another chapter. Here let me go on to complete my account of the battle of the cigarettes by describing my first meeting with Grossarth-Maticek in 1980.

Following my study with Kissen a large number of people reported similar results, and finally a kind of agreement was reached on the personality of the cancer patient – he appeared over-cooperative, appeasing, unassertive, over-patient, avoiding conflict, seeking harmony, compliant, with a defensive response to stress, and a failure to express negative emotions, like anger and anxiety, openly in a socially approved manner.

In a similar manner, there had appeared a typology of the coronary heart disease patient, who was often labelled 'Type A' – 'Type B' being the healthy type, by comparison. Type A behaviour was supposed to include a large number of components, particularly competitiveness, time urgency, aggressiveness, drive, achievement-striving, pre-occupation with deadlines, ambition and desire for advancement, impatience, hostility, hard-driving, restlessness, and a high activity level. In actual fact these components do not correlate all that well together, and in combination they have been found to be a mixture of neuroticism and extraversion. The concept of Type A – Type B behaviour was originally formulated by medical researchers who had little idea of the psychometric properties which measuring scales should possess, and while their notions had a good deal of appeal to begin with, recent work has rather doused that enthusiasm.

Most of the early work on cancer and coronary heart disease, and their relation to personality, was based on people already ill; possibly it was the illness that caused the personality and behaviour patterns, rather than the other way about. This is perhaps unlikely, but it is not impossible, and obviously it was necessary to get information from prospective studies – i.e., studies in which healthy people were allocated to a given type and then followed up over a period of years, to see who died of what disease. Only in that way could one decisively support theories such as these. With the Type A – Type B behaviour patterns, the outcome must be said to have been disappointing. Some follow-up studies did show predictive value, some did not, but in any case the predictive accuracy was rather poor, and it was obvious that if there was anything in the notion of Type A, it was confined to some of the constituents, with most of the traits supposed to characterize it being irrelevant. Research has suggested that the most relevant aspects were anger, hostility and aggressiveness, and these of course are very much opposed to the characteristics of the cancer personality. Some investigators have called the cancer personality 'Type C', to contrast it with the coronary heart disease Type A, and the healthy Type B, but it should be understood that when we nowadays talk about Type A behaviour, we are really discussing a subsection of that behaviour expressing itself in anger, aggression and hostility, rather than the older conception which included many more traits.

I was of course familiar with all these studies when I came across a report by a Dr Ronald Grossarth-Maticek, in which he discussed results from a prospective study he had carried out in Crevenka, Yugoslavia. Subjects had been given a personality inventory at the beginning of the study, and had answered questions about smoking and drinking habits, diseases experienced, treatment received, medicines taken, etc. They were then followed up over a period of ten years, and at the end of that period information was gathered about death and cause of death.

Among the scales used in this study was one which Grossarth-Maticek called the Rationality-Anti-emotionality Scale (the R-A Scale). This seemed to measure pretty much the opposite of my own Neuroticism Scale; where those scoring high on neuroticism were very expressive emotionally, showing strong anxieties and fears, people high on the R-A Scale were exactly the opposite – they refused to admit to feelings of fear and anxiety, they pretended that their life was governed entirely by rational motives, and that intellect was more important than emotion. According to the theories Kissen and I had developed, low scorers on the R-A Scale, like high scorers on the Neuroticism Scale, should be protected from cancer, whereas high scorers on the R-A Scale, like low scorers on the Neuroticism Scale, should show a higher incidence of cancer. When we record the observed number of deaths, and the number of deaths expected if there were no relationship between cancer and scores on the R-A Scale, there is in fact a very close relationship, and it is in the predicted direction. Thus Grossarth-Maticek's results agreed perfectly with those reported by Kissen and myself.

What also interested me was the synergistic relation between personality and smoking in predicting cancer. Let us look at the number of deaths from cancer, as compared in each case with the number of cases and risks. Thus of 157 probands with an R-A score of 0, none died of cancer, even though 38 smoked more than 20 cigarettes a day. Of 117 who never smoked, but had an R-A score of 10 or 11, only 1 died of cancer. Thus a healthy personality *or* abstinence from smoking seemed to protect probands from dying of cancer. But of 139 who smoked heavily *and* had R-A scores of 10 or 11, 31 died of cancer; it was the combination of personality and smoking that predicted death from cancer. This too agreed with the formulation of the problem I had arrived at.

Naturally I was excited – it is rarely that one finds such a wonderful replication of one's own findings, with, in this case, the additional benefit that the study had been a prospective one, not showing the same faults as ours, namely the possible contamination of personality scores by disease. The author was at the time resident in Heidelberg, having emigrated from Yugoslavia, so while attending a conference in Mannheim I paid a visit to Grossarth-Maticek. He received me most hospitably, was familiar with my work and poured out his heart to me. Apparently he had received the same cold shoulder as I had from the medical establishment; they didn't want to know anything about personality, or stress, or any other psychosocial variables. To them, smoking caused cancer and coronary heart disease, and to eliminate those they had to eliminate smoking; anything else was the Devil's work, and must be discouraged at all cost.

He had financed his work largely from monies given to him by one or two moderately rich relatives, and had otherwise received nothing but rebuffs when he had tried to obtain funds for his research from official sources, like the Cancer Society. He was on the verge of giving up. He was only too keen to show me all the data he had accumulated for tens of thousands of cases, and I spent hours poring over these records, trying to elicit an accurate impression of all the work done, and the scientific value it might possess. I was impressed with his immense industry. If he had indeed done all that he said, I would be honour-bound to try and help him as best I could. I promised to come and visit him again, and started talking to German experts about his work.

They were universally discouraging, making all sorts of accusations and criticisms. I was told, for instance, that no-one in Yugoslavia had heard of his work there; that one of the collaborators he listed as co-author did not exist; that not being associated with the University he could not have obtained the death certificates on which his records were based, and so forth.

I spent some time trying to get evidence with respect to these rumours, which had never seen the light of day in any scientific publication. I found that his work was indeed very well-known and highly regarded in Yugoslavia. At a later date he and I were both invited by the President of the Yugoslav Academy of Arts and Sciences to give lectures there, and not only the President himself, an internationally-known scientist, but many oncologists, epidemiologists and others told me of the high regard in which his work was held, and their willingness to cooperate in any future studies. (He was later offered a Professorship in Yugoslavia.) His collaborator, who was said not to exist at all, was easy to find; I met him in Mannheim, where he was working in a hospital. The question of the death certificates was equally easily settled; the Oberbürgermeister of Heidelberg himself told me that he had given permission for the data to be handed to Grossarth-Maticek, and added that he and his advisers were very much impressed with the value of his work.

I spent a good deal of time making sure – as far as that was possible – that none of the objections with which I had been regaled had any truth in them. Certainly Ronald himself was eager for me to look at all his data, carry out any kind of investigation I wanted, interview anyone who had worked with him – indeed, it would be impossible to be more open about one's work than he was. I concluded that a terrible injustice was being done to a man of considerable integrity and honesty. It was also clear that there were methodological and other weaknesses in his work (as indeed there are in any epidemiological study which I have ever seen!), but that the strengths vastly outnumbered the weaknesses, and that his whole work was indeed unique in the annals of epidemiology.

The obvious need was for financial support to make possible the follow-up of all the people whose personality, degree of stress, smoking habits, drinking habits, cholesterol level, blood pressure, etc. had been tested in 1972. German medical orthodoxy refused to finance this work, and I had quite a job to convince J. R. Reynolds and Phillip Morris – two large industrial combines with special interest in cigarette production – to fund us. They agreed finally, and the work could continue.

I have now spent some eight years working on this material with Ronald, and I am convinced that even though some details may be mistaken, the general outline is sound and replicable. But of course the best support for a scientific finding is independent replication, and about this I will have to say a few words at the end of this chapter. At this point let me rather give an outline of the major findings as they appear at the moment.

Three major studies have been analysed to date. The first of these studies, carried out in Crevenka in Yugoslavia, has already been described. The second study, done in Heidelberg, used a fairly random group of people with a pre-set sex ratio and between certain age levels. (A truly random sample would contain far too many young people who would not be expected to develop cancer or coronary heart disease over the next forty or fifty years; these are diseases of old age, and mostly take their toll of the over-60s. Hence an investigator who starts with a group that is relatively young is liable to die before his subjects do!)

The third group was nominated by the members of the normal Heidelberg sample; as being highly stressed due to loss of loved ones through death, or through separation, suffering unemployment or stress at work, being depressed or having suicidal thoughts, etc. This group was similar to the normal group in age and sex composition, smoking habits, etc., the only major difference being that of stress; it seemed an ideal opportunity to study the alleged powers of stress to cause disease and death.

To classify the individuals in these three groups, a typology inventory was drawn up which gave detailed description of behaviour and personality characteristics of normality, cancer-prone personality, coronary heart disease-prone personality, and a fourth rather psychopathic type which, from the point of view of physical disease, was also thought to be relatively healthy. This was 'Type 3'; 'Type 4' was the healthy, autonomous type, with 'Type 1' the cancer-prone and 'Type 2' the CHD (coronary heart disease)-prone type.

Each person was assigned to one of four types. Type 1, the cancer-prone type, is characterized by a lack of autonomy, lack of emotional expressiveness, the repression of anxiety and anger, and reactions of hopelessness and helplessness in the face of interpersonal stress. Type 2, the coronary heart disease-prone type, is characterized by strong feelings of anger, aggression and hostility when faced with interpersonal difficulties and problems. Type 3 is not very well understood; persons of that type seem to alternate between reactions typical of Type 1 and Type 2, and being thus in the middle rather than at either extreme may be protected from disease. Type 4, last but not least, is the normal, autonomous type, capable of expressing emotions and coping with stress more or less successfully.

Subjects in each group were allocated to one type or another at the beginning of the study, and were then located after ten years and the cause of death ascertained for those who had died. The results of the Yugoslav study are shown in Figure 5.1; they show the percentages of the four types who died of cancer and of coronary heart disease respectively. The figures also show that Type 1 tend to die of cancer rather than coronary heart disease, while Type 2 die of coronary heart disease rather than of cancer, with the healthy types showing far fewer deaths. The results demonstrate pretty clearly that personality and stress are closely related to disease and death, and even to specific types of disease.

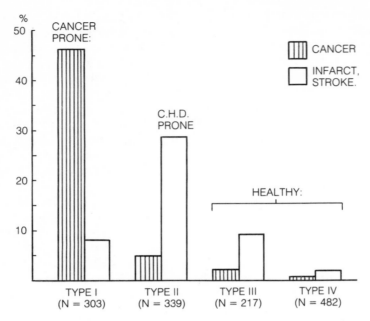

FIG. 5.1   *Deaths from cancer and CHD according to personality*
type; Yugoslav study.

Results from the Heidelberg groups are very similar. What is noteworthy is that although the stressed sample does not differ in essentials (age, sex) from the normal sample, the death rate is 40 per cent higher, showing clearly that stress can kill. What of smoking? Two major results emerged from the detailed analysis of the figures. The first was that smoking appeared much less effective in predicting cancer or coronary heart disease than did personality and stress. On a purely statistical basis the causal efficacy of smoking – if this can be deduced at all from a simple correlation – is very much less than that of psychosocial factors; about one-sixth in fact.

Equally important is our second finding, namely, that the only correlation between smoking and death from cancer or coronary heart disease occurs in people who were already predisposed to die of these diseases – i.e., Types 1 and 2. Low correlations between smoking and disease were found in people of the healthy type. Thus, although smoking may make disease more likely in those already predisposed, it doesn't cause it by itself.

Does all this *prove* that personality and stress actually cause cancer and coronary heart disease? The concept of 'proof' is a complex one, and also extremely subtle; but to simplify matters somewhat, one might say that scientists are more inclined to accept a relationship as causal, rather than merely statistical, if they can modify it experimentally. If it could be shown that people are less likely to die of cancer and coronary heart disease if they stopped smoking, a causal relation would seem more probable than if this relation was merely based on simple statistical correlations. Of course even such intervention might not be conclusive. Thus a person giving up smoking might take up jogging and other sports, and might adopt healthier eating habits, and it might be those which were responsible for reducing his liability to disease. It is difficult to arrive at *certain* conclusions, but intervention studies offer a way of making a causal interpretation of statistical results more likely.

Would it be possible to use a specially adapted form of behaviour therapy to alter the behaviour of cancer-prone and coronary heart disease-prone people in such a way that they could learn to express their emotions in a socially acceptable manner, and to acquire social skills and acquired appropriate strategies in the face of stressful interpersonal situations? The aim here would be rather different from that of behaviour therapy as applied to the usual psychiatric problems, where the attempt is made to eliminate phobias, anxieties, and other fears, to alter obsessive-compulsive behaviour patterns, or to eliminate other types of neurotic behaviour. The task here would be to make people more autonomous, more capable of coping with interpersonal problems and difficulties. Two experiments were designed to try out this new type of treatment, labelled 'Creative Novation Behaviour Therapy' by R. Grossarth-Maticek. Of the people who had been studied in the Heidelberg investigations, 100 were chosen as a cancer-prone group, and ninety-two as a coronary heart disease-prone group. Each of these two groups was divided in two, a control group which received no treatment, and a therapy group which received between twenty and thirty hours of individual therapy. Thirteen years after the cessation of therapy, we succeeded in determining the status of all 192 subjects, with respect to death and cause of death. The results are shown in Table 5.

It will be seen that of fifty controls in the cancer-prone group, sixteen died of cancer and fifteen of other causes; in the therapy group none died of cancer, and five died of other causes. Thus nineteen survived in the control group, forty-five in the therapy group. This tremendous difference demonstrates the efficacy of behaviour therapy. Similarly in the coronary heart disease-prone group, of the controls sixteen died of coronary heart disease, and thirteen of other causes; in the therapy group, three died of coronary heart disease, and six died of other causes. Seventeen were still alive in the control group, thirty-seven in the therapy group. Again, this is a large and important difference, demonstrating the efficacy of the therapy involved.

Cancer-prone Group			
	Still alive	Died of cancer	Died of other causes	Total
Control	19	16	15	50
Therapy	45	0	5	50
	64	16	20	100

Coronary Heart Disease-prone Group			
	Still alive	Died of C.H.D.	Died of other causes	Total
Control	17	16	13	46
Therapy	37	3	6	46
	54	19	19	92

TABLE 5 *Deaths from various causes in a control group, and a treatment group receiving special behaviour therapy as a prophylactic treatment.*

Although death certificates are somewhat unreliable as regards the cause of death, they are, however, completely reliable as far as the fact of death is concerned. If we only look at this we find that in the combined therapy groups – i.e., of the 192 people who entered the experiment, thirty-six are still alive in the control groups, eighty-two in the therapy groups. Fourteen died in the therapy groups, sixty in the control groups. These figures speak for themselves.

Two other experiments were done to test the efficacy of therapy. In one of these 245 pairs of cancer or coronary heart disease-prone subjects were formed and equated as far as possible for age, personality type, socio-economic status and sex; in each pair, one was randomly allocated to therapy, another to a control group. Treatment in this case consisted of group behaviour therapy, along the same lines as the individual therapy already described, but given to groups of some twenty-five people at a time who met for a variable number of sessions. Eight years after the therapy had taken place, six were untraceable in the therapy group, eleven in the control group. In the therapy group, forty-eight had died, eighteen of cancer, ten of coronary heart disease, and twenty of other causes; in the control group, 108 had died, 111 of cancer, thirty-six of coronary heart disease, and thirty-three of other causes. Thus group treatment may be as effective as individual treatment against cancer and coronary heart disease.

In a final experiment, short-term behaviour therapy was given to 600 cancer or coronary heart disease-prone people in a therapy group, 500 constituted a control group (no treatment) and 100 were in a placebo group – i.e., receiving a meaningless type of treatment based on dynamic principles. In addition to the four-to-five-hour treatment, each person in the therapy group received a printed pamphlet detailing the aims of autonomy training, and describing the best ways of attaining these aims. Subjects in the placebo group received a similar printed page containing 'dynamic' advice. The total number of deaths in the control group was 83 per cent, in the placebo group 81 per cent, and in the therapy group 32 per cent, again demonstrating the efficacy of the method in preventing death from cancer and coronary heart disease.

It is clearly possible to use behaviour therapy in order to avoid cancer and coronary heart disease; is it also possible to prolong life in patients already suffering from cancer? Two experiments show that the answer is yes. In one of these twenty-four pairs of cancer patients were formed, equated in terms of age, type of cancer, treatment and other relevant variables; one patient in each pair was randomly allocated to a control group, one to a treatment group. The average length of survival was 5.07 years for the therapy group, 3.09 years for the control group. This agrees with some recent American work, which demonstrated that a type of group therapy succeeded in just about doubling the life span of terminally ill cancer patients, and leaves little doubt that behaviour therapy ought to form part of the treatment planned for cancer patients.

In yet another study, 100 women were included (out of a rather larger number); fifty of these had chosen to accept chemotherapy, fifty had rejected it. Half the members of each of these two groups was also offered, and accepted, behaviour therapy; half were not offered behaviour therapy. We thus have four groups of twenty-five, receiving either no therapy, only behaviour therapy, only chemotherapy, or both types of therapy. Ideally the receipt of chemotherapy would also have been randomized, as was the receipt of behaviour therapy, but of course that would have been impossible on ethical grounds – one could not withhold a treatment known to have some effect on survival, simply in the interests of having a better experimental design!

The result, expressed in terms of survival in months, was very clear-cut. The group receiving no treatment of any kind survived for eleven months, those receiving chemotherapy only for fourteen months, those receiving only behaviour therapy survived for fifteen months. Thus these two treatments were equally effective and significantly more so than no treatment. Both treatments together produced a synergistic effect, the survival time now being twenty-two months; this is significantly more than simply adding together the effects of chemotherapy and behaviour therapy. Thus there is some evidence that behaviour therapy may be useful in prolonging life, as well as in preventing disease.

How can we evaluate all this work? To people brought up on the

Cartesian notion of two separate entities, body and mind, the results may seem improbable. But this notion of two separate entities is almost certainly wrong. Just as the physicists had to learn that space and time are not entirely different entities, and now deal with a space-time continuum, so we will have to learn to deal with a mind-body continuum. The evidence is now overwhelming that behaviour (including cognitive behaviour!) can influence disease processes, and we should not allow philosophical prejudices to stand in the way of recognizing this fact.

We have developed, and provided some evidence for theories which can explain just how psychological factors can influence the immune system and the development of sclerosis and thus indirectly determine changing probabilities for the development of cancer and CHD; this is not the place to discuss these very recent developments.

Obviously the whole interplay of causal factors leading to cancer or CHD is immensely complex, and we are only at the beginning of achieving any sort of understanding. But I believe these results are of considerable scientific, medical and social importance. It is said that among the ancient Chinese, doctors were paid while they kept their patients healthy; they were not paid when the patients fell ill, and required treatment. Modern medicine lays very little stress on prophylaxis, and really only comes into its own when a person falls ill. It seems to me that a return to the Chinese practice might be indicated, for two main reasons. In the first, if we can indeed prevent death from cancer and coronary heart disease by treatment through behaviour therapy, we could prevent a large proportion of deaths from cancer and coronary heart disease. It would also be cost effective; compare the very low cost of treating cancer-prone and coronary heart disease-prone persons by means of group behaviour therapy with the tremendous cost of medical treatment, medicines, operations, hospital stay and all the other costs involved in treatment of the disease once it has established itself. We could in this way reduce the cost of the National Health Service, or the cost of medical insurance, drastically, while keeping many people well and healthy who might otherwise have fallen ill and died. Thus the social import of these results is incalculable, and deserves to be looked at very seriously by those responsible for the National Health Service.

The new discipline of 'Medical Psychology' – i.e., the application of psychological principles and treatments in medical fields outside psychiatry, has now found firm roots and the discipline is growing at a fast pace. These developments suggest the possibility that perhaps the principles involved might also find application outside the medical field altogether, and as one example of how this can be done I will here consider a study by Grossarth-Maticek, myself and H. Vetter which dealt with the causes of prejudice, and the possibilities of using behaviour therapy to reduce and possibly eliminate such prejudice. The theoretical basis of this research may be briefly outlined as follows. Prejudice against other races, other religions, other social organizations, etc. is nearly always linked with aggression; the prejudiced individual wishes to diminish the influence, power and importance of the group against which he is prejudiced. There is a well-known theory in psychology which links aggression with frustration; the original frustration-aggression hypothesis suggested that frustration always leads to aggression, and aggression is always the result of frustration. The original form of the hypothesis is almost certainly wrong. Research has demonstrated that frustration does not always lead to aggression, but may cause alternative reactions, such as depression. Similarly, aggression is not always the result of frustration, but may have other causes. The newer form of the theory, now more widely accepted, is that frustration often leads to anger, and that anger may, and frequently does, lead to aggression.

Types 1 and 2 – i.e., the cancer-prone and the coronary heart disease-prone types, would seem particularly prone to frustration, in view of their inability to cope with stress, and hence would seem more likely than the 'healthy' Type 4 to show prejudice. Type 3, although less given to health problems, would also seem liable to the development of prejudice, because he has not developed a truly autonomous way of dealing with stress. Hence, we tested the hypothesis that Types 1, 2 and 3, as opposed to Type 4, would be most likely to show prejudice.

In this study, 6,796 males, aged between forty-five and fifty-five years, were interviewed and asked questions concerning eight possible objects of prejudice; they were also divided into personality types according to the system already described. Objects of prejudice ranged from Communist ideology, through the role of the United States, the Christian religion, the Slavic people, the Arabs, the Jews, parliamentary democracy, to other races in general. It was found that of Type 1, 36 per cent answered at least one question in a prejudiced direction; of Type 2, 65 per cent did so, of Type 3, 45 per cent. Of Type 4, less than 1 per cent demonstrated prejudice on any of the questions. Thus Type 2 is the most prejudiced, followed by Type 3, then Type 1, with Type 4 being almost free of prejudice.

We hypothesized that if frustration was a characteristic of Types 1, 2 and 3, and if frustration was causally implicated in producing prejudice, any treatment by behaviour therapy designed to lower frustration would also incidentally lower prejudice. Following this idea, people showing at least one strong political prejudice in the questionnaire were divided on a random basis into a control group and a therapy group, each consisting of 265 persons. Pairs were formed on an age basis, and one member was randomly assigned to the treatment group, the other to the control group. We also equated for type of prejudice; in other words, both members of a pair were anti-Semitic, or whatever. Training was given to groups of twenty to thirty persons at a time, and lasted altogether between twenty and twenty-five hours. Roughly speaking, the training consisted of five hours' theory, regarding the differences between autonomous and independent behaviour, self-regulation, etc. Ten hours were spent on the identification of dependence on other people, and the discovery of alternative behaviour patterns which should be aimed at in order to avoid such dependence. The last ten hours were spent on formulating precise aims for each person, suggesting coping mechanisms, and dealing with general and specific methods of attaining the person's aims. After this training was completed, the prejudice questionnaire was repeatedly applied to these groups after six months, one year and two years from the completion of the training. It is important to note that the therapy training was offered in the course of an investigation into the possibility of using such training as a prophylactic measure against cancer and coronary heart disease; it was not given as a 'cure' for racist prejudice, and indeed, during the training, political and social attitudes were never mentioned. The therapy was offered, and accepted, as an aid to physical health, and it was accepted or rejected *exclusively* on this basis. Of the 440 pairs originally approached, 175 refused to take part in the training; a pair was excluded from the experiment if one of the two refused participation.

Figure 5.2 shows the changes which took place in the treatment group over time after the completion of the treatment. It will be seen that there was a marked increase in the number of people 'without prejudice' – i.e., those not endorsing a single item in the scale. The major improvement is during the first six months; thereafter improvement is less marked. The control group shows no change whatsoever.

Figure 5.3 shows the results for anti-Semitic prejudice, and again it will be seen that while the control group shows no change, the treatment group shows a very marked decline in anti-Semitic prejudice. The results make it clear that it is possible to alter a person's prejudice by means of suitable psychological treatment; this is an important conclusion from the social as well as the scientific point of view.

In a sense this study brings us back to the investigation of social attitudes and *The Psychology of Politics* which I described earlier in this book. At first sight there seems little in common between the study of social attitudes and prejudices, medical diseases like cancer and coronary heart disease, and behaviour therapy; yet they are connected through the intermediate link of personality. I have often been astonished to see that while apparently my research interests were going in all

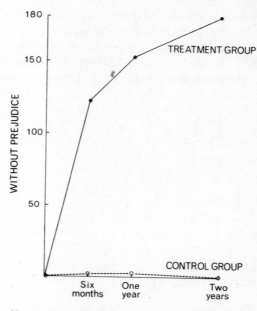

FIG. 5.2   *Changes in prejudice as a function of behaviour therapy.*

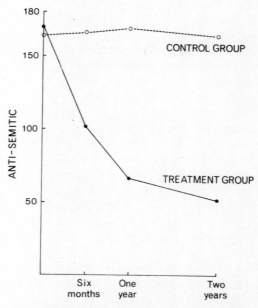

FIG. 5.3   *Changes in anti-Semitism as a function of behaviour therapy.*

sorts of different directions, there was also a unity underlying them which finally brought them together again. I certainly had not anticipated it when I started out on research into social attitudes, analysing Flugel's data, or when I worked with David Kissen on the personality of cancer patients. Much, of course, remains to be done.

CHAPTER 6

Intelligence and Personality: the fight for a new paradigm

Without theory, practice is but routine
born of habit. Theory alone can bring
forth and develop the spirit of invention.

L. Pasteur

As I became more widely known I began to have some odd encounters
and adventures. Consider the following. During the sixties, I received a
telephone call inviting me to have a public debate with Dr D. G. Cooper,
a well-known anti-psychology psychiatrist who shared many of his
opinions with R. D. Laing, who is probably even better known. The
debate was to be held at University College, my old Alma Mater, and was
to be about psychiatry and behaviour therapy. I should have twigged
that there was something curious about the occasion when in confirming
the date the organizer said: 'By the way, Dr Cooper won't actually debate
with you; he will shout slogans to the sound of a violin!' I weakly
inquired whether I could bring along my own trumpeter, but permission
was refused!

When Sybil and I got there we could hardly get in. Cooper was already
there, a huge man with what seemed a bear rug slung over his shoulder.
As I stepped down the stairs of the amphitheatre he got up, grasped my
hand and kissed it, a rather novel kind of greeting for me – even on the
Continent you usually limit your hand-kissing to members of the fair sex!

From there on the situation deteriorated. Cooper behaved in a bizarre
manner, and left the talking to an acolyte who seemed only interested in
the evils of the Vietnamese war, his cleverness in avoiding service, and
burning his calling-up papers. This seemed to go down well with the
audience, many of whom were clearly well away in drug-induced

happiness. There seemed a good deal of agreement that I was at least partly responsible for the Vietnamese war, and one member of the audience asked me with tears in his eyes to intercede with Mr Wilson, the then Prime Minister, to stop the war. I said that I was as opposed to the war as they were, but that there was very little I could do about it. I then tried to get to what was supposed to be the theme of the debate, but with Cooper somewhat somnolent I had little response to my arguments in favour of behaviour therapy. But I still recall one member of the audience who at the end of my talk beat his fist on the desk in front of him and shouted: 'That I should agree with Eysenck!' – like you might say: 'That I should agree with Hitler!' An odd evening, but not untypical of the times.

I took part in many TV programmes, beginning in the fifties, when my Pelican books had made me fairly widely known. There were hour-long interviews on the BBC *Horizon* programme, an ITV programme, and a German programme, dealing explicitly with me and my works, but for the most part I was one of several people being interviewed, or taking part in a discussion. In this way I met many famous TV personalities, such as Jonathan Miller, Malcolm Muggeridge, Percy Cudlipp, Baroness Wootton, and many more.

I was quite popular among the arrangers and producers of such programmes, for several reasons. I never had a shred of nervousness; the whole thing was a game to me – which of course it is! I could talk precisely to time; if asked to talk for two minutes on a given subject, I would talk for exactly two minutes, within a margin of less than five seconds. I never lost my cool, but exuded sweet reasonableness. And above all I always knew what I was talking about, refusing invitations to take part in discussions on themes I was not thoroughly at home with, or where there were simply no facts to discuss!

In addition to all the battles I have described in previous chapters, I have also done a good deal of work in the experimental area. My book on *Experiments in Motivation*, for instance, combined experimental studies of important problems with the use of strong, real-life motivation; these studies are seldom mentioned in the literature. Most important, however, has been my work on reminiscence, published in book form, together with Chris Frith, under the title *Reminiscence, Motivation and Personality*. Reminiscence is an interesting phenomenon; there is little or no improvement in performance while a subject is practising a motor task (usually the pursuit rotor, in which the subject tries to keep a metal rod in touch with a small metal disc on a rotating gramophone turntable). Introduce a rest-pause, and performance will show a considerable improvement immediately practice is resumed. The performance curve shows an immediate upswing, continued for about a minute, and then a downswing even though the subject is continuing to practise! The relevant phenomena are well-established, but I found that the traditional theory of inhibition produced by practice, and abolished by rest, was inadequate to account for the facts; Chris Frith and I put forward an alternative theory according to which practice has to be consolidated before it shows up in performance, and consolidation occurs during rest. We managed to show that this theory accounted for the facts much better than the inhibition theory, but there has not been much interest in the theory, or even the phenomena, in recent years.

My work on intelligence and personality naturally took me into the field of education, and there, in the seventies, I took a (very minor) part in the battle of the 'Black Papers in Education'. The story is important because it concerns the future of our children, and hence our whole culture and civilization. I got involved in part because of my professional knowledge and expertise, but in part because our own children sampled British education and found it wanting! The sampling was pretty random, involving public schools, grammar schools, and comprehensives; our opposition to the latter was not on the basis of preconceived opinion, but resulted from our own experiences of the extremely low quality of education our children received there. They managed to pull through and receive good university degrees, but only because of hereditary high IQ and good home support; I shudder to think what would have happened to kids of average IQ and little home support! Our traumatic experience with comprehensives opened our eyes, and our younger children were sent to the grammar and public school system.

Historically, England, like Germany, had a tripartite system of education, providing different kinds of schools for different kinds of children. At the age of eleven, children would be allocated to secondary schools deemed most appropriate for their interests and abilities, grammar schools catering to the more academically-oriented children, while secondary modern, or technical schools served other types of children. The system worked well educationally, but was subjected to considerable criticism by politicians who were committed to educational equality – not only equality of opportunity, but also equality of outcome, which of course is a psychological nonsense. The system was anathema to the Labour Party, and while Anthony Crosland was Labour Secretary of State for Education and Science in Harold Wilson's first Labour Government, he said to his wife: 'If it's the last thing I do, I'm going to destroy every fucking grammar school in England. And Wales. And Northern Ireland.' When she asked: 'Why not Scotland?', Crosland replied: 'Because their schools come under the Secretary of State for Scotland.'

[191]

In public of course Crosland was more economical of the truth, describing the aim of his policy as 'to preserve all that is valuable in grammar school education for those children who now receive it and make it available to more children'. Harold Wilson himself had stated, only two years earlier, that 'the grammar school will be abolished over my dead body'.

The egregious Crosland was followed by the even more appalling Shirley Williams, who declared: 'I passionately believe that the comprehensive school is a proper complement for what I think will ultimately be a classless society.' Thus secondary education was slowly murdered in England in the name of an experiment to produce a classless society.

Now an inescapable part of an experiment is the monitoring of its effects; in other words, having declared that comprehensive schooling would improve the quality of education, it was obviously necessary to discover exactly what happened to the quality of education in the years following the revolution. The Department of Education and Science (DES) was fully committed to the new venture, and at first put in motion some tentative efforts in that direction. When it became clear in the seventies how awful the consequences of comprehensive schooling in fact were, they quickly withdrew, and pursued a policy of silence and censorship, not publishing any figures and making it as difficult as possible for anyone to discover what the real consequences of their policy were. I recall asking Mrs Thatcher, who had been Minister for Education in the Heath Government, why she had not put in operation a large-scale research effort to discover what was happening in secondary education. She answered very simply that she had asked her civil servants in the DES to prepare and carry out such a policy, but when after a year or so she asked them for the results, they had in fact done nothing!

It was obvious that something radical and frightening was happening to secondary education in Great Britain, and a number of educationalists, sociologists and psychologists (including myself) worried about these developments got together under the leadership of Brian Cox, a professor of education, who published a series of 'Black Papers' in education, drawing attention to these evils as we saw them, trying to give objective accounts of what was happening, and generally warning the public of the dangers of existing policies. These Black Papers were furiously attacked by the National Union of Teachers, a left-wing organization, and by papers such as *The Guardian* and the *Times Educational Supplement*. These criticisms and attacks were entirely non-factual and did not provide any data to demonstrate that we were wrong.

Caroline Cox and John Marks later published the results of their wide-ranging empirical studies of educational achievements of pupils in comprehensive (as compared with other types of) schools. Their report, entitled 'Standards in English Schools', came to devastating conclusions about the quality of education provided by the comprehensives, and the failure of their pupils to reach acceptable standards. The shabby treatment their report received by civil servants, the NUT and the Press is recounted in their book *The Insolence of Office*; this should be read by anyone who imagines scientific data are treated objectively by left-wing partisans!

The battles I have recounted did not occupy the centre of my attention, as most of the work done by myself, my colleagues and my research students was concerned rather with personality and intelligence. The use of the term 'personality' is often ambiguous; for some, such as R. B. Cattell, it includes intelligence, while for others it only refers to the non-cognitive aspects of behaviour. I will here continue the more usual habit of referring to non-cognitive aspects of behaviour under the term 'personality', and to the cognitive ones as 'intelligence'. I have already mentioned some of the major principles according to which I organized my work and thinking; in this chapter I wish to outline more in detail what it was I attempted to achieve, and did achieve.

In my work on personality I was particularly lucky to have Sybil working with me. Wives working in science with their husbands seldom get the credit they deserve, but Sybil's contribution is well enough known and appreciated by experts working in this field for her to have been offered nomination as President of the International Society for the Study of Individual Differences – which she modestly declined!

My son, Michael, has also gone into psychology, carving out a rather independent career in the fields of memory and cognitive psychology. He worked as a lecturer at Birkbeck College, later on to become Professor and Head of Department at the Royal Holloway and New Bedford College, one of the five large Departments of Psychology in the University of London. Gradually he appreciated the importance of individual differences in the study of memory and cognition generally, and we worked together on several books, the most notable of which is *Personality and Individual Differences: A Natural Science Approach*. I found his expertise in experimental methods and in particular theoretical analysis invaluable, and there is no question that he has already achieved a high standing among his peers.

Phil Rushton has recently published a table of British psychologists with 60 or more citations in the 1985 Social Sciences Citation Index, which may be taken as a measure of scientific standing. The table from his study is reproduced on page 284, but with the inclusion of Don Broadbent who, working for the Medical Research Council rather than being a member of the Psychology Department, was omitted. Both Sybil and Michael are well up in this table – as indeed are many of my former students, such as J. A. Gray, J. Sandler, G. D. Wilson, D. H. Venables, and W. Yule. We will come back to the SSCI in Chapter 8, because it gives much useful information; here I am only quoting the table to show that my estimate of Sybil's and Michael's contribution is not entirely subjective, but has a more objective basis!

Personally I developed more and more in a direction once predicted by Einstein, who said: 'A man who devotes his best efforts to objective research becomes, from the social point of view, an extreme individualist, who relies, at least in principle, on nothing but his own judgement.' I became more and more disillusioned with politicians and all their works. The Labour Party was busily destroying the excellent primary and secondary school system that had been built up over the centuries, and the Tory Government which succeeded it set about the destruction of the universities with equal enthusiasm. I understood less and less the way so many people rely on party slogans, and give up their right to independent judgement. Perhaps it is what Erich Fromm once called 'fear of freedom'; life may be more comfortable that way, but I could not live without freedom to make up my own mind.

Why did I choose to devote most of my scientific work to the study of individual differences? Look at Figure 6.1, which is a rough model of human (or animal) behaviour. Central to this is the organism (O) which is a product of genetic (G) and environmental (E) influences. This organism encounters a number of stimuli, some of which are physical (S_p), some of which are social (S_s), and some of which are internal (S_i), i.e., stimuli which emanate from the person's viscera. In response to these stimuli, the organism then emits responses, which may be mediated by the autonomic nervous system – i.e., are emotional in nature (R_a), which may be cognitive – i.e., thoughts or ideas (R_c), or which may be motor movements (R_m). These responses finally lead to an affect or state ($E^\pm$)

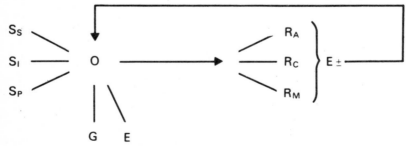

FIG. 6.1   *A model of the human person interacting with the environment.*

which may be either pleasant (indicated by the plus sign) or unpleasant (indicated by the minus sign). The pleasantness or otherwise of this state constitutes a positive or negative reinforcement produced by the whole chain of events; this in turn modifies the organism (through learning and conditioning) in such a way that in future it will seek or avoid the stimuli which herald the final affect or state.

Note that in this very rough and ready model the organism occupies a central place. Now, unfortunately, experimental psychologists have tended to disregard the obvious differences between one organism and another in studying the effects of stimuli upon responses, neglecting to note that these reactions are modified by the nature of the organism. The study of individual differences in the organism, and their interaction with stimuli and responses, is an integral part of scientific psychology, and central to it. Identical stimuli are perceived and reacted to differentially by a bright person or a dull, an extravert or an introvert, an emotionally unstable or stable person. To find out the laws according to which this may happen, and to isolate the major dimensions along which we can classify people, seems to me a fundamental and critically important part of psychology.

To look simply for direct relationships between stimuli and responses, as many experimental psychologists still do, is not the most advantageous method of discovering new and important truths. Consider education. Many new methods of teaching are proposed every year, but when these are compared with traditional methods, it is usually found that there is little difference in school achievements of children exposed to these different methods.

It is of course possible that there really are no differences, but it is also possible that some methods are more suitable for some types of children, others for other types of children. Let us consider 'discovery learning', which is now widely used and contrasted with 'reception learning'. In reception learning you simply tell the children what the facts are, and they commit them to memory. In discovery learning they are required to discover the facts for themselves, being given some help by the teacher. Many great claims have been made for this discovery method, but the evidence does not suggest that it is superior or inferior to reception learning.

A hypothesis was proposed by Professor Leith that extraverts would be much more interested in discovery learning, because of their greater readiness to become bored by routines and their greater likelihood to respond to stimulus variation. Introverts, being disturbed by changes of set but able to maintain attentiveness to a highly-prompted task would be more likely to prefer reception learning. Tests showed that this was indeed so. Using methods of discovery learning, extraverts were greatly superior to introverts in their achievement; using methods of reception learning, introverts were superior to extraverts. Averaging the two groups together showed no difference between the two methods! I have given many other examples of personality and teaching method interaction in an article on 'The Development of Personality and its Relation to Learning' of 1978 (Melbourne Studies in Education).

Similar principles obtain in industrial psychology, social psychology, clinical psychology and indeed any applied area; extraverts react very differently to introverts, stable to unstable people, etc. However, this is still not generally recognized in the field of experimental psychology proper, where it has been found to apply with equal strength.

Why did experimentalists, educational psychologists, social psychologists, clinical psychologists, and indeed most psychologists, fail to take individual differences and personality seriously? There are several reasons. The first, and probably the main one, was that there were so many different theories about the nature and measurement of personality that one could simply not get even a minimum amount of scientific consensus, and without such consensus of course it is difficult to make use of concepts within the field. The notion of 'introversion', for instance, was quite popular, but people found it difficult to distinguish it from 'anxiety' or 'neuroticism' – Jung had thought them quite different, but Freud had considered introversion just a preliminary stage in the development of neuroticism. Questionnaires of introversion correlated as highly with questionnaires apparently measuring neuroticism as they did with other questionnaires presumed to measure introversion. In other words, there was complete chaos in the field. This did not encourage anyone to take it seriously.

Again, much of the work on personality was related to psychoanalysis, and the surrealistic nature of the psychoanalytic theories did not make experimental psychologists eager to take them on board. Also of course there was not a lot you could do with notions of the unconscious – they could not be measured or even verified sufficiently to make them intelligible to the experimental psychologist.

Last but not least, there was a strong objection embodied in the Zeitgeist to the very notion of individual differences. A belief in general equality was prevalent, and the notion that some people were more intelligent than others, or more introverted, or more extraverted, or more stable was not favoured.

It seemed clear to me that there were two major problems in research on individual differences in personality. The first of these was a taxonomic one – what are the best concepts to describe personality? The second a causal one – how did it come about that some people had one type of personality, others another? Obviously the taxonomic problem came first; without being able to describe and measure the major dimensions of personality, one could hardly investigate the causal influences which served to mould them. Involved with the problem of taxonomy was the problem of measurement; I had well in mind Clark Maxwell's famous saying: 'We owe all the greatest advances in knowledge to those who endeavour to find out how much there is of anything.' Once we could isolate and measure the major dimensions of personality, we would be well launched on the study of causality.

First of all I looked for a model that might accommodate whatever findings I might have to report. After much reading and thinking I decided on the *hierarchical* model, as shown in Figures 3.1, 3.2 and 3.3 in Chapter 3. In other words, personality can best be described in terms of a large number of traits, such as assertiveness, sociability, impulsiveness, depressiveness, punctuality, etc.; these traits are not independent, but are correlated and form clusters, factors or dimensions such as extraversion-introversion, or emotional stability-neuroticism. Each trait in turn is produced by the observed intercorrelation of a number of behaviours. Thus a concept of 'sociability' is made up of a variety of different behaviours, such as finding it easy to talk to people, liking to go to parties, enjoying meeting new people, etc. Each of these activities in turn is based on the fact that on a number of different occasions similar behaviours are observed – i.e., a person who likes to talk to others on one occasion is likely to enjoy doing so on other occasions as well.

Thus we have four levels of description. At its lowest level: 'single occurrences', such as: 'As I was sitting in the train going to work, I got talking to someone sitting opposite me, and quite enjoyed our talk.' At the second level: some estimate of the frequency with which our subject met and enjoyed talking to other people. At the third level: the intercorrelations between this type of behaviour, and other types of social behaviour, thus defining the trait 'sociability'. And at the top level: the intercorrelation between such traits as sociability, activity, assertiveness, liveliness, etc., defining the type-concept of extraversion.

Implicit in this model, which I published in 1947, together with a lot of supporting evidence, were notions which became popular some twenty or thirty years later. The first of these was that of *'aggregation'*. This simply states that the larger the number of incidents which you are using to measure a given trait, the greater is likely to be the reliability of that measurement, and hence its predictive accuracy. Also implicit in the model was a distinction between traits and states, already made 2,000 years ago by Cicero, but later largely disregarded by psychologists. A *trait* is a dispositional factor that regularly and persistently determines our conduct in many different types of situations. In contrast, states may be defined as singular occurrences: I may be a sociable person in general, hence high on the trait of 'sociability', but on this particular occasion I may for some reason or other feel disinclined to act in a sociable manner, and hence be in a state of 'unsociability'. This distinction corresponds to one of levels in the hierarchical model – higher levels are defined in terms of traits and types, lower levels in terms of states.

Having decided on a model, I also decided on a method, namely that of correlational analysis and factor analysis (i.e., a statistical technique to reduce a large number of correlations to a few factors indicative of the number of dimensions and of their nature). Clearly the various levels were defined in terms of intercorrelations between actual behaviours, either observed, rated, or self-reported by the person concerned. The interactions or correlations between such behaviours could obviously be established, and formed the basis for the hierarchical model. Thus to my mind the whole model was *behaviouristic* in the broadest sense – i.e., based on behaviour; in that it differed very much from psychoanalytic models which were based entirely on interpretations made by the analyst, usually of such things as dreams, verbal slips, etc. I was surprised when I found that behaviourists in general were hostile to the very notion of personality and individual differences, and tried to disregard it, or at best downgrade it as relatively unimportant.

I next had to decide on the criteria to be adopted for regarding the results of my research as making a genuine contribution to psychology, and establishing a paradigm, as we would now call it. There were available any number of models of personality, as well as any number of theoretical concepts; what made the choice difficult was simply that there were no criteria for deciding which model was better than any other. When Hall and Lindzey brought out their widely-read book on *Theories of Personality*, the chapters were simply eponymous model descriptions as envisaged by various authors, such as Lewin, Sheldon, Cattell, Skinner, Freud, Bandura, Jung, and many others. There was no attempt to evaluate the evidence for and against each particular theory, or to lay down criteria against which to evaluate them; and solid, scientific theories were rubbing shoulders with the most airy-fairy subjectivism. Clearly there was no way in which we would ever arrive at a paradigm along these lines of abject eclecticism!

The Hall and Lindzey book and its successors were of course not available when I was mulling over these matters at the Mill Hill Emergency Hospital, but the situation was exactly as they were to describe it later on – a multitude of contradictory and incompatible models searching for adherents in a kind of Dutch auction unworthy of a scientific discipline. I put down the criteria for a scientific theory of personality, as I saw it, along the following lines.

A scientifically acceptable theory must be based on a model which is

[198]

testable – i.e., which makes specific predictions which can be confirmed or refuted. This of course is nothing but Popper's claim that theories which are not testable, and cannot be rejected on empirical grounds, have no place in science. Popper named Marxism and astrology, as well as psychoanalysis, as being pseudo-sciences because they made no testable predictions, but in this he was mistaken. Astrology makes many quite specific predictions, practically all of which have been shown to be contradicted by the facts. Similarly, Marxism has made many predictions, such as that the proletarian revolution would break out first in the most highly developed countries, such as England; most of these Marxist predictions have also been contradicted by the facts. Similarly, Freud predicted that only psychoanalysis could lead to lasting improvement in neurotic conditions; this claim too has been shown to be incorrect. In other words, these examples of what Popper considers pseudo-sciences should have been admitted by him to the ranks of proper sciences because they did make specific and testable predictions. It is for this reason that I added to the requirement of theories being testable that of actually producing a sufficiency of positive results to make further research worthwhile.

Given a model that was testable, and made predictions which could be verified or refuted, we would then require positive results from such testing, not only from the author's own work, but as a result of the work of other researchers, using different methods, different instruments, and different populations. If the P-E-N system (psychoticism, extraversion, neuroticism) I described in Chapter 3 was indeed a fundamental paradigm of human personality, then the proper analysis of data collected using the MMPI, or the CPI, or the 16-PF, or other widely-used instruments, should also show up identical or at least similar factors. There is now ample evidence that this is indeed so, and that these three major dimensions emerge from practically any large-scale analysis of traits published in the literature.

The requirements enumerated above are fairly obvious; the next one is dependent upon belief that the major dimensions of personality would be characteristic of man as a *biosocial* animal (i.e., both biological factors – hunger, thirst, sex – and social factors – laws, customs – influence human behaviour), and hence have biological validity, as well as being in part determined by environmental, social and cultural factors. The biological foundation for the major dimensions of personality suggested that they would be firmly based on heredity, and some of my early work was devoted to establishing this point, against the firm belief, then practically universal, that genetic factors played little part in individual differences. In the studies I carried out using the British Twin Register at the Maudsley, I was lucky to have the collaboration of two eminent behavioural geneticists, Lindon Eaves and David Fulker from the Genetics Department at the University of Birmingham, then in the forefront of work on behavioural genetics. I was very impressed with them – indeed, I concluded that they both knew far more about the subject than I did! Fulker later on came down to run my animal laboratory for me, taking over from Peter Broadhurst who had done a lot of work on the genetics of emotionality in rats, and went in turn to start the Psychological Department in Birmingham and become its first Professor. Lindon Eaves collaborated with me for a while from his base in Birmingham before joining the Psychological Department at Oxford, and finally emigrating to a research Chair in Richmond, Virginia, in one of the biggest and best genetics departments in the world.

Our work has been described in great detail in *Genes, Culture and Personality: An Empirical Approach*, written by Lindon Eaves, myself and Nick Martin, with the help of a whole set of young, mostly British, behavioural geneticists who had emigrated to join Lindon Eaves.

What were our main findings? In the first place, additive genetic factors played the most important part in deciding on a person's position along the three major dimensions of personality, contributing something like 50 per cent to the total of phenotypic (i.e., the observed behaviour) variance. There was little evidence for assortative mating; like does not seem to marry like (or unlike!) with any marked frequency, although there is a slight tendency for psychiatrically abnormal people to marry others also psychiatrically abnormal. There was a little evidence for dominance as far as extraversion is concerned, but none for the other variables.

The major point of interest in our studies, however, related to the locus of environmental determinants. Geneticists distinguish between two types of environmental influences. The first ('between family environmental variance', or 'shared environments') refers to the differences in upbringing experienced by children in one family as compared with another. Thus children in the same family share the same parents, the same home environment, probably go to the same schools, have the same friends, etc. It is this that has had to bear the major portion of psychological theorizing about individual differences; we were the first to find that it contributed practically nothing to phenotypic differences between individuals! In other words, our work disproved most, if not all, the existing theories of personality, including the psychoanalytic. Family influences do not affect personality of children! All the environmental variance seemed to be concentrated on what is called the 'within family environmental sector' – i.e., environmental factors which differentially affect children within the same family.

Such factors might be ante-natal – i.e., refer to events in the womb, or they might relate to accidents occurring at birth, or might be linked with events in the life of children of the same family which were unique to one or other child, such as having a good or bad teacher, suffering an illness, having a good or bad marriage partner, etc. Factors of this kind are unusually difficult to study, so that we know very little about those environmental factors which determine individual differences in personality.

These findings establish what is sometimes called the 'genetic architecture of personality'. In other words, we are not only or even mainly interested in heritability, but in the finer details of genetic and cultural transmission. The tremendous advances in the statistical analysis of twin data have made it possible to construct and test varied models incorporating all these factors. To do this adequately requires large numbers of twin pairs. Recent studies in Finland, using 15,000 pairs, in Sweden, using 12,000 pairs, in Australia using 8,000 pairs, and in the United States embodying somewhat smaller numbers, all corroborated our findings. The main outlines of the contribution of heredity and environment to individual differences in personality are now becoming clear, and leave little doubt about the biosocial nature of the major dimensions of personality – or indeed of specific traits, such as impulsivity, sensation-seeking, altruism, aggressivity, etc.

The next point on my list of criteria was that given a firm biological foundation for the major dimensions of personality, we would expect a person's position on these dimensions to remain relatively invariant; once an extravert, always an extravert! Such a prediction might have to be modified where extreme environmental pressure was applied to an individual, such as being sent to a Concentration, or Soviet Gulag, Camp, but under normal conditions one would expect consistency.

Another criterion that seemed to me indispensable in judging the paradigmatic value of the given model was that it should apply across different cultures. All the studies mentioned in relation to our first criterion – i.e., that the same dimensions should appear in large-scale investigations – were tested in relation to young European–American populations, that is, populations sharing a common culture and background, as well as similar Caucasian ancestry. If there was a firm foundation in biology for these dimensions, they should appear equally strongly all over the world, regardless of culture or race. Work on this complex hypothesis was carried out over many years by Sybil, who made this topic of cross-cultural personality study her very own. She administered our major questionnaire, the EPQ, to at least 500 males and 500 females in thirty-five different countries, embracing all different forms of cultural, political and racial differentiation. Thus, in their own language, she tested African subjects living in Uganda and Nigeria;

Japanese and Chinese, both Mainland China and Hong Kong; subjects in Socialist countries like the USSR, Czechoslovakia, Hungary, and Yugoslavia; the major European countries like Germany, France, Italy, Spain, etc.; in Scandinavia; South America; the English-speaking countries like the USA, Canada, Australia, and of course Great Britain.

In each country a factor analysis was carried out of the intercorrelations between the items, and the resulting factors compared with each other, each country with each, using indices of factor comparison. On the average these indices gave a value of 0.98 – i.e., only marginally different from perfect agreement which of course equals 1.00! This was surprisingly strong support for the hypothesis and led us to conclude that the major dimensions of personality are equally apparent in different cultures. Of course, countries differ in their *position* – thus the Japanese are very high scorers on introversion and neuroticism, compared, say, with citizens of the USA.

In my musings I went one step further and suggested another criterion for the acceptability of major dimensions of personality, namely that they should be apparent not only in humans, but also in animals. I have published a study, together with A. S. Chamove and Professor H. F. Harlow, on personality in monkeys. Rhesus monkeys were observed on a regular basis for about two years, and their behaviours noted. The resulting ratings were then factor analysed, and three major factors extracted which could reasonably be regarded as similar to psychoticism, extraversion and neuroticism. Characterized by their behaviour, animals tended to be either aggressive (P), sociable (E) or afraid (N). Indeed, these three seemed to be the only fundamental ways in which people or animals can interrelate socially, and from a purely logical point of view, one might have anticipated the emergence of these three factors.

Most of our animal work, however, was concentrated on rats, trying to measure individual differences in behaviour and determining the ways genetic factors influenced these. Our first interest was in the distinction between emotionally reactive and non-reactive rats – i.e., an analogue of neuroticism, using the open-field test, in which the rat is put in a round enclosure, brightly lit and flooded with loud noise. There are two scores: the amount of defecation produced by his fear response, and the amount of ambulation, usually reduced by the animal's fear – fearful animals don't walk about! Starting with a uniform stock, we would select the most fearful animals and interbreed them, as well as the least fearful who would also be interbred. Following this procedure for generation after generation, we obtained strains of reactive and non-reactive animals, very different in appearance and behaviour.

The work on the Maudsley reactive and non-reactive strains has been continued since my retirement by my successor, Professor Jeffrey Gray.

He has explored molecular genetic techniques, which have proceeded to the point where they could now, in principle, be applied to characteristics that are polygenetically inherited (i.e., are determined by several genes) and which had up till now been regarded as amenable only to the approach of statistical genetics. Successful demonstration of this approach showed that characteristics such as emotional behaviour would have major implications for a whole range of problems in behaviour genetics.

Clinically, the potential implications of such a demonstration are great. Suppose it could be shown that highly emotional animals carry a gene or genes that are the same as those present in human beings characterized by a high susceptibility to anxiety. The role of such genes in brain function and the control of behaviour could then be studied further in the rat, paving the way to an understanding of how the equivalent genes cause anxiety (with their influence on brain function) in man, and making it possible to diagnose basic psychiatric disorders. Gray has made important advances in this type of study, but these are too technical to be described here.

I think it is a great pity that so little work has been done on the measurement of personality in animals, or its genetics. This is probably because for many people it sounds almost absurd or indeed insulting to talk about 'personality' in animals, though no one familiar with dogs, cats, horses, or indeed rats, and ever lowlier animals would doubt that there are great differences in behaviour between them. The great advantage of animals, of course, is that controlled genetic studies are possible, as they are not with humans, so that we can get a much better insight into the genetic architecture present. One has to be very cautious about extrapolating from animals to humans (or vice-versa!), but the existing literature leaves no doubt about the considerable degree of overlap.

These were the main criteria I wanted to apply to research in the personality field. I believe that on the whole the effort has been successful. Extraversion and neuroticism are perhaps better established than psychoticism, more reliably measured, and their nature better understood, but granted that the model is as yet nothing like perfect, I believe it is along the right lines, and that while future work will undoubtedly improve it, it is unlikely to substitute for it something entirely different.

So much for the descriptive side. Can we say anything about the causal aspects? Here again it seemed to me that an acceptable paradigm, having regard to the biosocial nature of man, should have something to say about the biological determinants (physiological, neurological, hormonal) which might lead to extraverted or introverted, fearful or courageous behaviour. My own contribution has largely lain in the elaboration of a theory concerning extraversion-introversion. I first attempted to do so by reference to theories of excitation-inhibition, following a Pavlovian model, in my book *The Dynamics of Anxiety and Hysteria* (1957), but this was not entirely successful, and I finally went the whole reductionist hog and tried to account for extraverted and introverted behaviour in terms of the concept of cortical arousal. This fairly modern concept is illustrated diagrammatically in Figure 6.2.

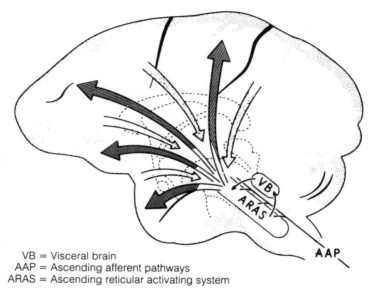

VB = Visceral brain
AAP = Ascending afferent pathways
ARAS = Ascending reticular activating system

FIG. 6.2   *Model of the brain showing the areas responsible for differing degrees of extroversion-introversion (ARAS) and neuroticism-stability (VB).*

We have the ascending afferent pathways going into the brain, carrying messages from all over the body. These pathways go to various parts of the brain, but they also send collaterals into the so-called ascending reticular activating system, which in turn sends messages to various parts of the brain warning them of the incoming stimulation, and instructing them to keep awake (in a state of arousal). Without this activity on the part of the ARAS, the brain would go to sleep, and not react to incoming messages.

My theory was very simply that under-activity of the ARAS produced low cortical arousal as a consequence of sensory and other stimuli, and led to extraverted behaviour, while heightened activity of the ARAS produced a good deal of cortical arousal in response to incoming stimuli, and led to introverted types of behaviour. On this hypothesis, extraverts who interact with other people, indulge in sensation-seeking, etc., because they are under-aroused and bored by the stimuli which impinge on the cortex in the ordinary course of their lives. At the other extreme introverts avoid social contacts and strongly arousing stimuli, and are not sensation-seeking precisely because they also react with strong arousal to ordinary stimulation, and would be over-aroused if they did not take avoiding action. There is now a very large literature on this theory, testing it both along physiological and psychological experimental lines, and results have on the whole been confirmatory, although there are still anomalies.

My studies of personality and individual differences inevitably led me to look at behaviours of social importance which are intimately linked with P, E and N. Thus, for instance, anti-social behaviour and criminality have been found to be fairly closely associated with all three personality dimensions, high scores on P, E and N correlating with criminality; and anti-social behaviour in youngsters. Accident proneness is another area where P, E and N show prominent effects – high scores on these factors undoubtedly predispose a person to behaviours likely to lead to accidents.

Smoking, drinking and wenching are also closely linked with personality. Work on *Sex and Personality* led me to research what makes a good marriage, which emphasized personality features (written up in my book '*I Do*'). There is no doubt that much social behaviour is governed by factors related to the major dimensions of personality, and no proper understanding of social behaviour is possible which leaves out these determinants. Much of my later work has been devoted to trying to gain an understanding of these complex relationships.

When I first explained my theory of arousal, most people found it somewhat contradictory. How is it, they said, that high cortical arousal is associated with low activity, the retreat from social life, and a generally low-arousal life style? The answer of course is that the cortex controls and inhibits the lower centres of the brain, so that high arousal in the cortex means a greater inhibition of behaviour. This is obvious when we consider alcohol; this is a depressant drug, lowering cortical arousal, but making people behave in a more extraverted fashion. (This example is in actual fact much more complex than appears at first; the effects of alcohol are not only pharmacological, but may be mainly psychological – people become much more extraverted in their behaviour after they have drunk a non-alcoholic drink which they believe to contain alcohol!)

This analogy can be broadened to study the effects of stimulant and depressant drugs generally as leading to extraverted or introverted behaviour. Similarly, there are groups of drugs which reduce or increase anxiety, and are therefore relevant to N, and drugs like LSD which increase psychotic-like behaviour, and others like phenothiazine which reduce it.

At the beginning of my career I had to fight the wholesale environmentalists, behaviourists who had no place for individual differences in their system, and factor analysts who preferred large numbers of small factors to a few major dimensions. During the middle years we had the astonishing advent of Mischel, who advocated the doctrine of situationism – i.e., that behaviour was determined by situations, *not* by personality traits or types. This is a nonsensical statement, because the measurement of personality traits occurs precisely in situations similar or identical for everybody, so that the situation cannot be blamed for differential reactions! Obviously there is always an interaction; behaviour can only occur in situations of a defined type – we cannot measure sociability in a situation that does not contain other people, or persistence in a situation where it is irrelevant. As in the case of nature-nurture, neither can exist without the other, and the essential task of the scientist is to try and assign some numerical value to the relative contributions of both.

Turning now from personality to intelligence, I must emphasize that certain discoveries often attributed to me by newspapers have really nothing whatsoever to do with me. I have *not* invented the IQ – William Stern did that four years before I was born. I did *not* discover that genetic factors played a large part in the genesis of individual differences in intelligence; Woodworth was already able in 1941 – i.e., just after I had received my Ph.D. – to summarize a large amount of research done on adopted children, identical and fraternal twins, and identical twins brought up in isolation, and conclude that about 70 per cent of the total variance in intelligence was contributed by genetic factors, and about 20 per cent by familial ones. (Ten per cent are due to non-familial environmental factors.) Indeed, I have never done any research myself on the genetics of intelligence; I have merely written about research done by others. Nor have I done any research on racial differences in intelligence, whatever the ill-informed may say. I believe I have made some contributions to the scientific study of intelligence, but not in the areas of genetics or race.

The position of intelligence in psychology is altogether odd and paradoxical. For many people the measurement of intelligence through IQ tests was regarded as the greatest achievement of modern psychology, proving once and for all that mental qualities could be measured with a fair degree of precision, reliability and validity. On the other hand, others have severely criticized the concept, asserting that intelligence didn't exist, and had no scientific meaning, because there was no agreed theory or definition concerning it. Does intelligence exist? Of course it does not *exist* in the sense that stones and pigs and psychoanalysts exist. Intelligence is a scientific concept, analogous to such concepts as gravitation, humidity or mass. These are all scientific concepts, and as such, carry no more implications of existence than does intelligence. Concepts may be useful or useless; they do not imply physical existence.

How about the lack of an agreed theory? True, there are several theories, some contradicting others, and there is certainly no general agreement. Is that a fatal objection? Such a view would certainly run counter to anything that the history of science could teach us. Concepts develop for centuries before a great theory arrives, and often the views on which they are based are known from the beginning to have faults. Gravitation is a good example. Newton's 'action at a distance' theory was already known to him to be absurd, but it served a useful purpose. Even now, 300 years later, there is no agreed theory of gravitation. What we have are two dissimilar theories between which it is impossible to make a rational choice. On the one hand, we have Einstein's view according to which gravitation is a distortion of the space-time continuum, and on the other we have the quantum mechanics interpretation in terms of particle interaction (gravitons). Physics has done all right in its use of the concept of gravitation, even in the absence of an agreed theory; why should we expect psychology to be different? We have had much less time to develop a theory for what is probably a much more complex concept, and we have not had the service of the outstanding geniuses, from Newton to Einstein and Planck, who have worked on the concept of gravitation. To ask us for an agreed, universal theory at this stage is absurd.

But would it not be necessary to have an agreed definition of intelligence? The usual definitions offered by psychologists turn out for the most part to be examples of what intelligence might be expected to do, rather than definitions of any underlying concept. Consequently, definitions in terms of learning, remembering, problem-solving, following instructions, educational success, worldly achievement, reasoning, thinking, or originality, are not even attempts at *definitions* of intelligence. What would we think of a physicist who tried to define gravitation in terms of the apple falling on Newton's head, the shapes of the planets, the occurrence of tides or black holes, the equatorial bulge of the earth, planetary movements, the laws of gunnery or the formation of galaxies? These are all examples of the *operation* of gravitational forces; they are not definitions, and any physicist who tried to define gravitation in those terms would be laughed out of court. So would any critic of the concept of gravitation who argued that because different physicists used different examples of the effect of gravitational forces, the concept was therefore useless.

I have argued that psychologists have used the term 'intelligence' with three related but essentially different meanings, and that it is vital to separate these, and be clear about which one we are arguing. These three meanings are illustrated in Fig. 6.3. The most fundamental is that of *biological intelligence*, determined by genetics and mediated by physiological and biochemical factors. Biological intelligence may be measured, as I shall point out later on, by means of the electro-encephalogram, by means of averaged evoked potentials, by means of the contingent negative variation, the galvanic skin response, reaction times, etc.

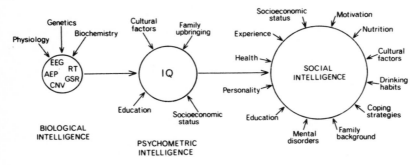

FIG. 6.3   *Three meanings of the term: intelligence.*

Psychometric intelligence or IQ is a somewhat different conception, fundamentally determined by biological intelligence, but also by cultural factors, family upbringing, socio-economic status, education, etc. Its dependence on biological intelligence is indicated by its heritability, which we will talk about later on; its dependence on environmental factors is shown by the fact that heredity only accounts for some 70 per cent of the total variance, leaving 30 per cent over for the environmental factors already mentioned.

Finally, we have the concept of *social intelligence*, or as it is sometimes called, 'practical intelligence' – i.e., the application of intelligence in life and employment situations. This again is determined to a large extent by IQ, but also by a large number of additional factors, such as those indicated in the diagram. A person's intelligence may be high, but if he has alcohol problems, suffers from mental disorders, has a poor education, is highly neurotic, has poor health, or has low motivation, he is unlikely to do himself justice. L. M. Terman, in his *Studies of Genius*, studied some 1,500 American children with IQs above 140; in a follow-up it was found that the great majority did very well in their careers, but a small proportion was quite unsuccessful. Practically all of these had been noted by their teachers as suffering from nervous instability or neuroticism. Thus personality too is an important variable in deciding whether high IQ is prevented from achieving high success in the world.

It will be obvious that when people are arguing about 'intelligence', and one person talks about biological intelligence, the second about psychometric intelligence, and the third about practical intelligence, then obviously they will not achieve any agreement. Any discussion must begin with a realization of which particular concept of intelligence we are talking about. When Burt defined intelligence as 'general, inherited, cognitive ability', he obviously had biological intelligence in mind; it is no criticism to argue that social intelligence is determined by many other factors, most of which are not inherited, and many of which are not cognitive.

I have mentioned that roughly 70 per cent of the total variance in IQ is contributed by genetic factors, 20 per cent by common environments, and 10 per cent by accidental features of the environment. These figures should not be taken as absolutes; heritability is a population estimate – i.e., it applies to given populations, at a given time. Changing environments may change heritabilities. A good example is a recent study of the heritability of educational achievement in Norway, comparing two groups of twins, one studied around the time of the Second World War, the other studied recently. It was hypothesized that because of the much greater egalitarianism in education now, as compared with earlier times, this would have increased the heritability of scholastic achievement, and indeed it was found that for the boys studied heritability increased from about 40 per cent to about 70 per cent. (For girls the change was much less.) In other words, heritabilities are not absolutes, and they may well differ from one country to another and from one age to another. Make nurture more equal, and you will increase the importance of nature, and vice-versa. We measure relative importance of nature and nurture, and that changes from time to time, and from one country to another.

Whenever there is a discussion about the inheritance of intelligence, the name of Cyril Burt, and his alleged fraud in inventing and faking data on identical twins brought up in separation, inevitably comes into the conversation. Many people believe this alleged fraud disproves any theories concerning the inheritance of intelligence and demonstrates the importance of educational, cultural and other environmental factors. The actual facts are extremely interesting.

After Burt had retired from his Chair at University College, he

[209]

published an article in 1966 on monozygotic twins brought up in separation; he claimed that since his earlier work on such twins, the number had more than doubled! After Burt's death, doubts were raised about this work, and also some other studies of Burt's, by Allan and Ann Clarke, two of my former students, whose criticisms alerted the Medical Correspondent of the *Sunday Times*, Oliver Gillie, to write an article which appeared prominently on the front page, with a sensational headline: 'Crucial data was (sic!) faked by eminent psychologist', with a photograph of Burt alongside.

For details of these accusations, readers should consult L. S. Hearnshaw's book *Cyril Burt: Psychologist*. Hearnshaw was a colleague and friend of Burt's, who had been asked to write Burt's biography by Burt's sister. The book examines the accusations on a factual and impartial basis, and concludes that while the evidence is circumstantial, it does seem to have a basis in fact. Hearnshaw had access to Burt's diaries, letters, and many other data which make his judgement exceptionally valuable and telling; it should be mentioned, however, that several eminent educationalists and psychologists have argued that Burt was in fact innocent, although he became careless in his old age and allowed many printing errors to slip through

When the original accusations were made I felt that the evidence was insufficient to condemn Burt, and I said so. However, when Hearnshaw's book appeared I felt that the evidence he adduced was incontrovertible, and that Burt had almost certainly invented some of his data and been exceedingly careless in his collection and treatment of others. I still believe that this is true, although some of the accusations against Burt, many of these comical rather than serious, seem to me misplaced.

Quite recently R. B. Joynson has published his book, *The Burt Affair*, which meticulously goes over the evidence, coming to the conclusion that Burt was innocent of the crimes he was accused of. He makes a strong case, but of course where the evidence is inevitably circumstantial, certainty can never be achieved one way or the other. Perhaps we should agree on the old Scottish verdict of 'Not proven', delete doubtful data from our textbooks, and cease to worry about the case. This leaves untarnished Burt's theoretical contributions, always the most important scientifically, and his early work on the taxonomy of intelligence.

Let us assume that everything that has been alleged against Burt is true; how then does this reflect on the truth or falsity of the claims made for the genetic basis of intelligence? The answer surely must be that it is completely irrelevant. An estimate of heritability for IQ of something like 70 per cent was made by Woodworth already in 1941, basing himself on a large body of evidence from monozygotic twins separated at birth, comparisons between monozygotic and dizygotic twins, and adopted children; no studies of Burt are quoted in this monograph, so that the facts were already established before Burt took a hand. Similarly, in 1979, David Fulker and I reviewed the evidence in *The Structure and Measurement of Intelligence*, explicitly excluding any works of Burt's from our analysis, and came to conclusions very similar to those of Woodworth, although now based on vastly larger numbers of cases, analysed along much more sophisticated lines, and including types of evidence not considered by Woodworth, such as degrees of consanguinity, inbreeding effects, etc. The estimates made by Burt on the basis of his real or imaginary data agree very well with those made by Woodworth, and Dave Fulker and myself; their omission makes no difference to the conclusions reached.

But how about the other side – those who believe that intelligence can't be inherited? Many environmentalists have claimed to have increased the IQ of the children they studied by various educational means, thus apparently disproving the claims of the geneticists. Herman Spitz, in his book *The Raising of Intelligence*, has looked into these claims, and has found them based either on very poor and inadequate methodology, or arising from fraudulent manipulations of one kind or another. A brief look at some of these may prove interesting.

In 1946, Bernardine Schmidt published a monograph concerning 322 retarded boys and girls, twelve to fourteen years of age, with IQs ranging from twenty-seven to sixty-nine. Two hundred and fifty-four children who were in three special centres in the Chicago school system comprised her experimental group, during an eight-year study. Schmidt claimed that a special programme of education resulted in gains of some forty points of IQ for those children included in the study, as compared with the controls not so included. The *Reader's Digest* and *Woman's Home Companion*, as well as many other newspapers and popular journals, enthusiastically took up these results. Alas, when serious researchers tried to contact the centres and persons concerned, they were unsuccessful, and the experts who looked into the work concluded that the best estimate of the Bernadine Schmidt study was that it was largely, if not entirely, fraudulent and that there was no 'miracle' in Chicago – the name newspaper correspondents had given to these fantastic results! Thirty-five years later, Marva Collins, a schoolteacher, made claims as remarkable, if not more so. The newspapers published her claims; on television there was a 'docudrama' on her; *Sixty Minutes* did a feature on her, and she was invited to lecture throughout the country – at $10,000 a lecture! Alas, her claims were equally based on completely fraudulent data, and Spitz comments that 'this sadly familiar affair . . . demonstrates how one's wish to believe can cloud our critical faculties'.

Clearly there have been frauds on both sides, more on the

environmentalist than on the genetic side, but the treatment of these fraudsters has been very different. Everyone knows about the alleged fraud committed by Burt; who now knows about Bernardine Schmidt or Marva Collins? Newspapers, journals and even psychological textbooks were only too keen to publicize data, however implausible and however inadequate the publication, as long as they served to support the prejudices of the writers. They played down anything that favoured hereditarian doctrines, and played up anything that was favourable to environmentalistic theory.

All fraud in science causes damage, mainly to the implicit trust that scientists must have in each other's honesty. However, the substantive damage done by fraudulent scientists depends very much on the degree to which their fraudulent conclusions differ from widely accepted paradigms. It may be said that Burt's conclusions were identical with what is and always has been regarded as factually correct by experts in the field, both quantitatively and qualitatively; hence his data did not cause any change in the general paradigm. The fraudulent findings of Bernardine Schmidt, Marva Collins and others, however, throw doubt on the scientific concensus, and claim to be able to do things which in actual fact are unlikely to be feasible or possible with existing methods. They thus raise false hopes, upset the scientific consensus, and attempt to introduce a new and factually inadmissible paradigm. The damage they do is far greater than that done by Burt, who mainly injured his own reputation, and destroyed his own credibility.

My own contribution to intelligence testing is closely related to the measuring of intelligence. Many American researchers had more or less decided that intelligence was essentially what a person has learned in school and possibly in life outside school. This links up with one of the two meanings that the term 'intelligence' has in common language. It may refer to simple knowledge; or it may mean the capacity for understanding. Thus in Victorian times the term 'intelligence' was used as synonymous with news and information; we still talk about 'gathering intelligence', or 'an intelligence network'. This double meaning has been incorporated in the literature on intelligence by referring to 'crystallized ability' – i.e., largely information and knowledge received over the years, and 'fluid ability' – i.e., intelligence as a dispositional trait, enabling its possessor to acquire information. The two are related, because what is acquired is likely to be greater in those more capable of acquiring knowledge; but when we look at the tests which most clearly identify the general factor in analyses, these always turn out to be tests of fluid ability, which are thus most closely identified with the scientific meaning of intelligence.

In a paper I published in 1967, I argued that mental speed was possibly the central factor in any discussion of the nature of intelligence, and that there was some evidence suggesting that a revival of Galton's conception of reaction time measurement as being fundamental to intelligence was overdue. This suggestion was taken up by Arthur Jensen, in the United States, and also by various other groups, so now it seems that measures of reaction time do in fact correlate quite closely (unexpectedly so!) with IQ tests.

Of particular interest is another fact, which at first sight may seem rather odd. We measure reaction times not just once, but run a series of fifty or more tests in order to get a meaningful average. Individual measures of reaction time are variable, and we need a fair number to get a score that is reasonably constant. But of course we can also measure a particular individual's *variability* – i.e., we can see whether the fifty reaction times we measure are fairly close together, or range from very fast to very slow. What has been found is that the measure of variability correlates even more highly with IQ (negatively) than does reaction time itself. In other words, a person who is dull as measured by an IQ test is not only slow, but also very variable in his reactions. Let us at the moment merely keep this fact in mind; an explanation will be suggested presently.

Another measure has been quite widely used recently, analogous to reaction time. This is called *inspection time*, and it involves speed of perception rather than speed of reaction. Two lines are shown to the subject for a very short period of time, one very much longer than the other, and he is required to press a button on his right when that line is longer, on his left when that line is shorter. The experiment starts with a presentation of the lines so lengthy that the individual makes no errors, and stops when presentation is so short that he can no longer distinguish between the two. His inspection time score is at the point where he gets 97.5 per cent of all the presentations right. He does not have to react very quickly, and can take his time. Inspection time correlates as highly as does reaction time with IQ, and again to most people this was rather unexpected.

Of course, reaction times and inspection times, although relatively primitive indices of cognitive involvement, are not strictly speaking biological measures. When the encephalograph came to be recognized as an important measure of brain activity, many attempts were made to use it for the exploration of cognitive ability, but until fairly recently little of substance was discovered. Now we know that reasonable correlations do exist between IQ and certain wave configurations on the resting EEG, in size roughly equal to those obtained for reaction time and inspection time measures. But of most interest in recent years has been a rather different measure, namely the so-called 'averaged evoked potential'.

[213]

This is a measure of the flurry of waves which is produced on the EEG when a sudden visual or auditory stimulus is produced. Normally we look at the first 250 milliseconds which elapse after the stimulus has been presented; little of further interest is added by extending the analysis to 500 milliseconds or more.

Figure 6.4 shows from some of our own work the evoked potentials of six very bright and six very dull children; their IQs are given in the figure. It has been customary to analyse amplitudes and latencies of these waves in order to obtain an IQ correlate, and correlations of .3 or .4 had been obtained. After working with these methods for several years, Alan and Elaine Hendrickson, two Ph.D. students of mine, suggested a rather novel way of looking at the data. If we consider Figure 6.4 for a minute, we can see there is a very marked difference between the waveforms on the left, and those on the right, relating to their *complexity*. Those of the high IQ children are very complex, whereas of the low IQ children the curves are very simple, bland. This complexity or simplicity is due to the amount of *variability* of the measures taken. As with reaction time, there is a poor signal-to-noise ratio, and we have to average a large number of determinations in order to obtain the averaged waveform shown in the figure. In order to get a complex waveform, there has to be a certain degree of uniformity of successive occasions of measurement; if we don't get peak falling on peak, and trough falling on trough, then we will get the very bland sort of curves we find among low IQ children. The

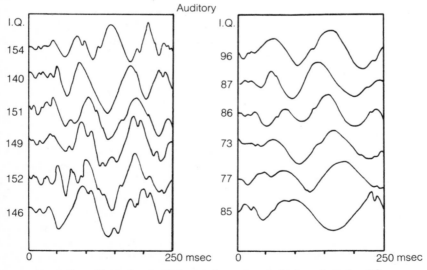

FIG. 6.4 *Evoked potential waveforms for six high and six low IQ subjects.*

Hendricksons did find that variability was much greater among lower IQ than among high IQ children, leading to the greater complexity of the latter. Thus we have here a highly interesting agreement between apparently quite different types of measurement, namely reaction time and averaged evoked potential, with variability always accompanying low intelligence. Variability in turn may be due to errors in cortical transmission.

My original suggestion had been that *speed* of information processing was the factor that causes differences in IQ; now I am saying that perhaps a person's disposition to produce errors in the transmission of information through the cortex was the responsible agent. It is possible to reconcile these two hypotheses.

Information-processing does not occur through a single nerve, but through a whole array of different nerves. This, of course, is to safeguard the accuracy of the message by multiplying the channels through which it passes. Finally, as argued by the Russian psychologist, Sokolov, these messages converge on a comparator, which compares them, and if they all agree, gives the signal for a motor reaction to occur. Now clearly if errors occur in some of the transmissions, the messages will not agree, and the comparator will have to wait until further evidence is produced to decide the issue, thus slowing down the reaction. So errors in the transmission of information through the cortex cause variability in the rate of response, and slowness. This is only the beginning of a genuine theory of intelligence; it will require much modification and extension before we can account for all the known facts.

The large genetic component in producing differences in intelligence stuck in the gullets of egalitarian leftists; what really infuriated them was the extension of this argument by Arthur Jensen to racial differences. I was drawn into this because in 1971 I published a book on *Race, Intelligence and Education*. This book was written because of the considerable uproar caused by the publication, in 1969, of an invited article by Arthur Jensen in the *Harvard Educational Review*, in which he emphasized the role of genetic factors in intelligence, and mentioned briefly the possibility that black-white differences in IQ (usually around 15 points) might in part be due to genetic causes. In the preface to his book *Genetics and Education* Jensen has described in detail the persecution he suffered as a result of his scholarly and fully documented article. He and his family were threatened with death by bombs being planted in their house; he was personally attacked, his invited contributions to scientific conferences shouted down; reviewers misrepresented what he had said and made him out a racist and a Fascist. He was unable to continue his research, as educational establishments refused him access to schools and universities. His life was made a total misery, for many, many years.

I wrote my book in order to introduce some sanity into what had become a political, ideological debate. All I did was to collect the relevant facts, and put them together, leaving it to the reader to judge. There clearly was no doubt about the poor performance of blacks on IQ tests; this is universally agreed. What is in dispute is the *cause* of the difference. As I pointed out, there is no direct biological test of possible genetic differentiation; all the evidence must be circumstantial. There were strong reasons to interpret this evidence in genetic terms, but equally it was clear that the evidence was not conclusive.

African-speaking whites in South Africa, for instance, used to score very much below English-speaking whites a generation or two ago; now the two groups have pretty equal IQ scores. Whatever the reason for this change, it suggests that differences between groups may not necessarily be genetically caused, and may be susceptible to change.

However that may be, I suffered a fate very similar to Jensen; I have told the story of misrepresentation, physical attacks, broken-up meetings, threats of bombing and worse in an article in *Encounter*, under the title 'The Danger of the New Zealots' (1972, 39, 12, pp.77–91) and will not repeat myself here. My wife and children suffered equally under this persecution, and Sybil specifically requested that I should not bring up all the old bitterness again. I do advocate open discussion, along scientific lines, of the problems caused by differences between racial, national and religious groups; I am certain only of one thing – the problem will not be solved by slogans, and in ignorance of the true facts. As Adam Smith has said: 'Science is the great antidote to the passion of enthusiasm and superstition', and only scientific research into these matters will enable us to find solutions. The passion which boiled over when I was attacked bodily at a lecture at the London School of Economics is illustrated in the picture section, and ridiculed in the Osbert Lancaster cartoon.

I am not optimistic about the likelihood of this becoming a possibility in the near future. At one stage I thought of giving this autobiography the title 'Geese are Swans, and Swans are Geese', after the famous poem by Matthew Arnold. It goes as follows:

Creep into thy narrow bed,
Creep, and let no more be said!
Vain thy onset! all stands fast;
Thou thyself must break at last.

Let the long contention cease!
Geese are swans, and swans are geese.
Let them have it how they will!
Thou are tired; best be still!

[216]

*Now, gentlemen, let us continue our appraisal of the law of
diminishing returns in a post-Freudian context.*

They out-talk'd thee, hiss'd, tore thee;
Better men fared thus before thee;
Fired their ringing shot and pass'd.
Hotly charged – and broke at last.

Charge once more, then, and be dumb!
Let the victors, when they come,
When the forts of folly fall,
Find thy body by the wall.

I finally decided that this sounded too defeatist. Although it still encounters determined resistance, research *is* continuing into this difficult field and the National Academy of Sciences in the USA has officially declared such research to be worthwhile and scientifically important. Perhaps one day the *argumenta ad hominem* will give way to *argumenta ad rem,* and we will deal with facts rather than shibboleths, propaganda, and abuse.

Not all that happened to me was as unacceptable as this persecution; a number of amusing incidents brightened up the inspissated gloom.

I was asked to give a lecture at the University of Birmingham, the theme of which was the contribution which psychology could make to our political life. Before it started, a group of students distributed a leaflet entitled 'SEEK TRUTH TO SERVE PEOPLE'. The theme was set in the heading: 'DENOUNCE FASCIST EYSENCK, INTELLECTUAL PROSTITUTE PROMOTING UNSCIENTIFIC AND ANTI-PEOPLE IDEAS IN THE SERVICE OF IMPERIALISM!' The first paragraph will give a taste of the flavour of this broadsheet:

In an act of open provocation against the working people and all progressive honest scientists, a Fascist and intellectual prostitute, parading as a 'professor of psychology', is coming to Birmingham University on the 16 November. The progressive Intellectuals Study Group (Birmingham) condemns the visit of H. J. Eysenck to Birmingham to promote himself and anti-people and unscientific ideas in the service of imperialism.

The broadsheet went on in this vein:

Wildly dreaming that the bourgeoisie will continue sucking the blood of the people forever, Eysenck does propaganda for the practical measures whereby the bourgeoisie can further manipulate the people.

[218]

Having thus introduced me to the audience, the writers continue:

> Eysenck is one of a band of sold-out careerists who are parading as writers, scientists, scholars, etc. They have come forward to prostitute themselves in the services of imperialism. Through the promotion of unscientific and anti-people ideas they are creating the ideological basis for the development of Fascism.

Fortunately, help is at hand. Admittedly, 'the Fascist ideas will not collapse of themselves.' But never fear: 'they will be smashed if we (1) put Mao Tse-tung thought in command of everything, (2) rely on the people and release their revolutionary initiative.'

So now we know.

The Birmingham meeting was also the occasion for the militants to produce the oxymoron to end all oxymorons. On the walls of the library building they had written in very large letters: 'Uphold genuine academic freedom: Fascist Eysenck has no right to speak.' The photograph records this historic occasion: never before or since has my name desecrated the hallowed halls of any university building!

At Leicester I was invited to speak about 'The Inequality of Man'. The hall was crowded even though I was told that the 'New Left' groups in Leicester had protested wildly against my being allowed to come and 'make propaganda for my racist ideas'; as it happened I did not deal with race at all in my talk. This rather discomfited the large Communist contingent, but at the end their spokesman (or rather woman) managed to get out of this impasse. 'I protest,' she cried, 'against this Fascist imperialist Eysenck coming here, and not even having the courage to put before us his racist ideas about the inferiority of coloured people!' To do them justice, even the more left-wing laughed at this turnabout, and the evening proceeded to its normal conclusion.

On another occasion I gave a lecture on intelligence and genetics in a BBC television programme, at the end of which members of the audience were asked to comment. One member stated that he had a perfectly logical argument to show that the notion of the IQ was absurd. Take God, he said, God has always existed; therefore his chronological age is infinity. But God is also all-wise; consequently his mental age is infinity. Now the IQ is the ratio of mental age over chronological age; infinity over infinity is zero, therefore God's IQ is zero, which is nonsense. *Ergo*, the notion of the IQ is nonsense.

Readers are perhaps entitled to ask whether views I have put forward on intelligence are just maverick notions representing no one but myself, and perhaps a small minority of psychologists like Jensen and Herrnstein. Where are these views in the mainstream of psychological research? Snyderman and Rothman, in their recent book on *The IQ*

Controversy, report on the results of a large-scale survey of experts in their field, coming from the areas of developmental psychology, educational psychology, evaluation and measurement, school psychology, educational sociologists, behaviour geneticists, cognitive science experts, counselling psychologists, and industrial and organizational psychologists. In this consensus, there is majority support for every single one of the main contentions I have put forward in my writings, both scientific and popular. This does not mean that these beliefs are necessarily correct; experts are not infallible, and may be wrong. Nevertheless, the point is an important one.

In this very brief account of my work on personality and intelligence, I have only given the main outlines, without being able to dwell on any details, criticisms, or extensions to neighbouring fields. I would like, however, to discuss a few points that relate indirectly to the difficulties many people have had in accepting the major findings of psychological research in these fields, namely the overwhelming importance of genetics. It is clear that many people feel strongly about the principle of equality, and the debate relating thereto goes back a very long time – over 2,000 years, at the very least. Thus a fragment of a book *On Truth* seems to have given the earliest explicit explanation of human equality in Greek philosophy when it said: 'We are all by nature born the same in every way, both barbarians and Hellenes.' And on the other side Aristotle, in his *Politics*, attributed to Antisthenes a sardonic fable: 'When the hares made speeches in the Assembly and demanded that all should have equality, the lions replied: "Where are your claws and teeth?"'

The major argument in modern times is between those who define equality in terms of social *status*, and those who define it in terms of equality of biological inheritance. Equality of social status has always been a socialist idea, and it is certainly possible to argue about its desirability, or the possibility of achieving it. Equality of biological abilities and traits is a chimera which no thinking person should entertain for one moment. This statement has nothing to do with any political or social preconceptions. As Lenin pointed out: 'When one's experience and reason testify that men are *not* equal, then one understands under equality the equality of *abilities* or the equivalence of bodily strength and mental capacities of men. It is quite obvious in this sense that men are not equal. No single reasonable man and no single Socialist ever forgets this.' Lenin goes on to characterize as an 'absurdity' the idea of extending equality into these spheres, and concludes by saying: 'When Socialists speak of equality, they understand by that *social* equality, the equality of social position, but not at all the equality of physical and mental abilities of individual persons.'

[220]

Similarly, when the American Declaration of Independence declares: 'We hold these truths to be self-evident, that all men are created equal, that they are endowed by their Creator with certain unalienable rights, that among these are life, liberty, and the pursuit of happiness', they clearly had in mind equality of status, equality before the Law, and equality as citizens; they are endowed with unalienable rights, not with equal intelligence!

On this issue, I may perhaps claim that the forts of folly are beginning to fall, and that science has won a modest victory. But the fight is still far from won, and the *Zeitgeist* is still hostile to what we all know to be true in our hearts, namely that genetic factors are at least as important as environmental ones in determining intelligence and personality and probably more so.

What a comprehensive environmentalist would have to believe is that, given the right environment, I could have painted like Titian, composed like Beethoven, become a scientist like Newton or Einstein, equalled Gauss as a mathematician, boxed like Tyson, played tennis like McEnroe, sung opera like Caruso – but enough is enough. Indeed, what first convinced me of the importance of genetic factors was the extent of the things *I couldn't* do. I never learned to draw at all; I tried hard, but even now any average five-year-old who is gifted in this direction can do it much better than I can. I can't carry a tune, or play an instrument, although I was quite motivated – it would be difficult to find anybody less gifted in this direction!

How about the actual background of geniuses? Occasionally we find that they come from a congenial background – Bach and Mozart came from musical families, Bernouilli from a mathematical family, etc. These cases prove nothing; they could be explained equally well on environmental as well as genetic grounds. But there are cases where there is obviously no environmental support for the budding genius whatever. Hector Berlioz, for instance, was born the son of a provincial doctor in a small town near Grenoble, where the great events were the annual vintage and the bi-annual sheepwashing. The young Berlioz heard no music at all except at Mass, and in the fields where the shepherds sang; occasionally the town band played excruciatingly out of tune. When the youngster decided to devote his life to music, he had to struggle against family opposition. His mother felt music was the work of the Devil, his father was an incorrigible Philistine and was in no way persuaded of the destiny of the artist. Hector was forced to become a medical student, only slowly and painfully forging an artistic career.

This complete absence of environmental clues to the developing genius is the rule rather than the exception. Faraday was the son of an itinerant tinker; there was no suggestion even in his early life of anything even remotely connected with science. Newton came from a family of small farmers, his father dying before the birth of his son; the widow then married the Reverend Barnabas Smith. There was not the remotest interest in science in his family or background. Gauss, 'the Prince of Mathematicians', was the son of poor parents, being born in a miserable cottage; his grandfather was a poor peasant, his father a gardener, canal-tender and bricklayer without distinction of any kind. His maternal grandfather was a stone-cutter. Is that the background we would prescribe for a budding mathematical genius?

Look at the conditions under which Napoleon, Hitler and Stalin grew up – can anyone discover there the seeds of their evil doings? What is it in the background of Nelson, Lincoln or Churchill which caused them to be so outstanding in their fields? These are the questions that environmentalists have to answer in order to be taken seriously. Can we do nothing to improve IQ? There is a lot of recent evidence that a bad diet, producing enough calories but deficient in certain vitamins, can lead to poor IQ performance which can be raised by ten to twenty points by suitable additions to the diet. Altogether, improvements in diet seem to have been followed by increases in IQ all over the world.

With such examples before them, in addition to the immense amount of scientific evidence, why do so many people still reject the notion that heredity plays an important part in their lives? One reason, based on an erroneous conception, is that if heredity largely determines intelligence, then surely we must be locked into an eternal caste system, in which the children of the less well endowed have no chance of escaping from their fate as hewers of wood and carriers of water. According to this conception, very dull parents have very dull children, very bright parents have very bright children and so on. If this were indeed the case, then one might have the right to feel upset and pessimistic. However, genetics teaches us that where heredity is less than 100 per cent, there is regression to the mean – in other words the dull and very dull have children who are brighter on the whole than the parents, while the bright and very bright have children who are duller on average than the parents.

This is shown in Figure 6.5 where it will be seen that for four very dull parents, only one of the children is very dull; two are dull, and one is average. Of the children of four very bright parents, one is very bright, two are bright and one is average. Thus there is a great deal of shifting about from one generation to another, as far as intelligence is concerned.

How does it come about, in the face of regression to the mean, that the range of intelligence does not shrink from one generation to another? The answer is that the very large number of average IQ parents have children some of whom are very bright, some of whom are very dull,

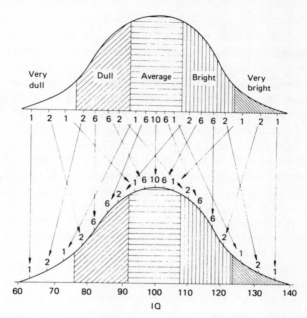

FIG. 6.5   *Inheritance and intelligence as it actually works.*

even though the majority are average. So for 24 average IQ parents there will be one very bright child and one very dull child, with six children who are bright or dull, and ten who are average. Corresponding to this regression in intelligence, and no doubt largely determined by it, is the degree of social mobility that characterizes other civilizations. In a study of American white males surveyed in the 1960s, for instance, 21 per cent of children born into the lower manual worker category moved right up the socio-economic status scale to reach the highest status (higher 'white-collar' workers); of those born into the highest status category however, only 54 per cent remained in it. Regression to the mean, and social mobility based on it, are only explicable in terms of genetic factors. Segregation of genes ensures generational change, and that social mobility will prevent the emergence of any caste system.

It has been shown that IQ is highly correlated with glucose uptake in the brain. Perhaps research should be directed to improving this uptake, in the hope of raising IQ. The very fact that heredity plays such an important part in the genesis of individual differences in intelligence suggests that biological methods may be more appropriate in improving mental efficiency than our educational or cultural methods. Perhaps a combination of the two might give us optimal results. The sullen refusal to follow this lead has resulted in a poverty of empirical studies exploiting what we already know about the biological conditions favouring high IQ; it is high time that we took seriously the messages scientific research has been giving us over the past fifty years.

Readers may feel that while I advocate the conception of man as a biosocial animal, I have concentrated most of my energies on the biological side. This is not true. In our animal work we did a good deal to clarify the genetics of emotionality, as already explained, but we also looked very carefully at environmental factors. Justin Joffe, for instance, did his Ph.D. research on the topic of *Prenatal Determinants of Behaviour*, to use the title of the book he published as a result of his studies. If, as now seems firmly established, environmental effects on personality are within family, rather than, as used to be assumed, between family, then it seems possible or even likely that intra-uterine events may play a large part. Such 'constitutional' factors are not genetic, but they are rather different from our usual notions of environmental influences – cultural, educational, and so forth.

In a series of brilliant studies Justin showed how important such constitutional factors were; in experiments with rats, giving the mother-to-be electric shocks had an important influence on the behaviour of the pups when born. In humans, too, such antenatal influences have been shown to act as 'primary biases' in assessing heritability; they have been shown, for instance, to lower the correlations between identical twins, but without partaking of the nature of 'environmental' factors properly so called. It may sound like a joke to say that someone is anxious because his mother was frightened when she was carrying him, but Justin's results demonstrate that such an outcome is perfectly feasible!

Other examples of environmental studies? We are at present engaged in an experiment trying to replicate and extend studies purporting to show that calcium and vitamin additions to the diet of children can increase their IQ – there are calcium deficiencies even in the diets of normal middle-class children. Equally, I am consultant in an experiment, encompassing four countries, seeking to confirm theories that nutritional supplementation has a powerful influence on intelligence and anti-social behaviour.

Most important has been my work on behaviour therapy; this is entirely devoted to the undoing of that mixture of hereditary and environmental factors we call 'neurosis'. That it has proved more effective in doing so than psychoanalysis may be due to our starting from a biosocial perspective in our work, rather than attributing all such evils to early familial inter-relations.

In the field of social attitudes, too, our demonstration that genetic factors are importantly involved in producing individual differences is balanced by our work on prejudice, with the demonstration that prejudice can be reduced very powerfully by methods of behaviour therapy. It would simply be untrue to say that my work has concentrated entirely on the genetic-biological side; I have always tried to look at the social-environmental side as well. Indeed, to a behavioural geneticist it would seem impossible to study the one side meaningfully while excluding the other. Everything we think and do and feel is influenced to varying degrees by nature and nurture, and it must be the task of science to unravel in each case the enormously complex web of influences and factors which together produce the phenotypical patterns of conduct-behaviour we observe, and which is our starting point as psychologists. It has been the endemic sin of psychologists over the past fifty years to have disregarded this rule, and to have given environmentalistic theories and explanations a monopoly position; we have paid for this disregard of genetics by consistent failures in our attempts to *explain* and *alter* human behaviour.

What I have said so far about intelligence and personality applies in equal measure to sex. I have always been a pro-feminist, in the sense given to the concept by John Stuart Mill; I strongly believe that women have been discriminated against very badly, and have a very hard time in a man's world. I approve of laws attempting to redress the balance, and applaud all efforts to enforce equal pay for equal work. But my belief in equality of status does not include belief in biological equality; the evidence strongly suggests that men and women are profoundly different biologically, and that while role-playing and other social factors enhance this difference, they do not cause it in the first place. I wrote a book on this theme with Glenn Wilson, entitled *The Psychology of Sex*, which sets out in detail the evidence for this belief. The evidence is partly biological, partly social.

On the biological side, studies have shown that when females (humans or other primates) receive, accidentally or by design, too strong a dose of androgens (male sex hormones) during the last two months of foetal life, they grow up showing behaviour typically *male* in nature, and quite different from the control females not receiving the androgens. Such masculinized girls are very tomboyish, prefer to play with boys already at an early age, like rough-and-tumble games, dislike chic, pretty or fashionable feminine clothing, and prefer theirs to be utilitarian or functional. They show little interest in accessories like jewellery, perfume and hairstyling. There is an indifference to dolls, and a preference for cars, trucks and guns. Later on there is a lack of interest in infants; they do not enjoy doing things for the care of babies and do not anticipate doing such things, even as paid babysitters, in the future.

Many of the androgenized girls stated they would rather not have children; they preferred careers to marriage, while the controls regarded marriage as the most important thing in their future. *Mutatis mutandis,* similar differences have been found in female monkeys as the result of androgen injection. Male behaviour, socially and sexually, does seem causally linked with early hormone levels prior to birth.

On the social side, the best evidence comes from Israeli Kibbutzim – i.e., children who were brought up in an environment stressing sexual equality, playing down the influence of the family, and providing role models emphasizing equality of work. In spite of this high degree of brain-washing, the children reverted to type, almost exaggeratedly so; girls played with dolls, boys with trucks and guns; girls went for adornment, quite against all the social pressures to which they had been exposed; finally, boys and girls opted for a traditional family life, as against the communal living preached and practised by their parents. Altogether, when social precept opposed biological promptings, social precept lost out all along the way. This is an important social experiment, replicated many times, that we disregard to our cost.

The tragedy of course is that many of the women who started out as outspoken proponents of the Kibbutz ideology regretted later on all the things they had given up. Mothers would regret bitterly not having lived a complete family life, and enjoyed adornment, romantic love and role fulfilment.

Again, as in the case of race, we are talking about averages; there is much overlap, and many exceptions. What I want to emphasize, however, is that much harm can be done by trying to persuade women that they are *identical* (except for the *petite difference*) with males, and should adopt male values, behaviours and characteristics. When girls accept such teaching, they may wake up too late to find their best chances of happiness gone. Each one of us should have the chance to choose his or her destiny without pressure to adhere to some ideal chosen for him or her on the basis of some quite unscientific and arbitrary ideology. Thus I would reject extreme feminism, based on ignorance of biological reality; equal but different is the verdict of nature, and we depart from it at our peril.

Just as my book on race earned me the epithet of 'racist', so our book on sex earned Wilson and me the epithet 'sexist'. When Wilson showed the manuscript of our book to an American publisher, he was excited and keen to publish it. However, his reader warned him that the book would be regarded as 'sexist' by females on campus, and boycotted by them; she advised rejection. Americans have been effectively protected against the truth ever since; the book never found an American publisher! So much for the First Amendment! There are shibboleths in our society which it is dangerous to disregard; ideology is stronger, if only in the short run, than science, and facts which do not fit in with ideology are censored and cast out into the void. Fortunately a less stringent tone is becoming noticeable in regard to both race and sex; perhaps, in a few years' time, it may be possible to discuss and research these topics seriously without being attacked physically, having one's writings censored, and being labelled 'racist' or 'sexist' for pointing out indisputable facts. Perhaps.

There was one further occasion (around 1970) when I incurred the wrath of a militant group, this time the ALF (Animal Liberation Front), a group of extreme opponents of vivisection who actively attacked animal research workers by planting bombs under their cars, broke into their laboratories and wreaked havoc there, liberated animals in medical laboratories (thus exposing them to starvation outside), destroyed computers (even those that had nothing to do with animal research), and generally made pests of themselves. I had started an animal laboratory at Bethlem Royal Hospital, our sister hospital in Beckenham, and thus became the victim of the hostility of these weirdos.

One evening my daughter came home rather late, after we had all gone to bed, to find that the yellow walls of our house had been daubed with red paint by the ALF. The photograph shows some of their words; the suggestion 'Murderer' was one of the more complimentary words used by the artist responsible. It took a long time and a good deal of money to have the house repainted; what our neighbours thought I shudder to think!

Had I in fact been guilty of vivisection, some degree of hostility might have been understandable. Actually of course I have never cut up any animals in my life; not only did I not have the training or competence to do so, or the necessary permit from the Home Office; I could not see that a psychologist, whose job it was to study the behaviour of the whole intact animal, had any business to go about destroying his object of study.

Indeed, I have always had some sympathy with the more sensible kind of anti-vivisectionist. I know that vivisection is occasionally necessary for medical research, or for genuine scientific advances, but I abhor the cruelties which are sometimes inflicted, often unnecessarily (more so in the USA than in the UK, where the Home Office have to approve all animal research). I could certainly never bring myself to carry out such work myself, nor would I encourage any of my co-workers or students to do so.

It would probably be true to say that I am more tender-hearted than most, as far as animals are concerned. I never kill a spider that happens to find its way into my house, but carefully catch it in a tumbler and evict it into the garden. When I find a caterpillar in the road, or on the pavement, I carefully allow it to creep into my hand, and then carry it to safety in some leafy garden. Cruelty to animals is one of the few things which really upset me, and by inclination I sympathize with vegetarians – although I am afraid that the flesh is weak! To be browbeaten in this horrific manner by the ALF, with whose aims I am in general sympathy, was an odd and uncomfortable experience; it upset the rest of the family more than it did me, but it certainly did not make me feel more friendly to this group of people whose alleged love of animals did not seem to include fellow humans – who after all are also a kind of animal!

It is odd, and indeed paradoxical, that my most determined opponents should have been people with whose aims I completely agreed. Why the rejection of science and empirical evidence by so many? Perhaps Sir Francis Bacon was right when he suggested in his *Advancement of Learning*:

> To have the true testimonies of learning to be better heard, without the interruption of tacit objection, I think good to deliver it from the discredits and disgraces it hath received, all from ignorance; but ignorance severely disguised; appearing sometimes in the zeal and jealousy of divines; sometimes in the severity and arrogance of politiques; and sometimes in the errors and imperfections of learned men themselves . . .

CHAPTER 7

The Battle for the Stars

Nothing is so firmly believed, as that what we least know.

Montaigne

The battles about behaviour therapy, cigarette smoking and race were not the only ones in my career; in this chapter I will report on my association with parapsychology (extrasensory perception or PSI) and astrology. Here too battle lines were drawn, and here too I could not escape controversy. Fortunately all these battles took place against the background of a happy family life; it is difficult to over-emphasize the importance of a secure and loving home to which one can return after facing ridicule, dislike and often outright hatred in one's working life!

Our four children were growing up, and we spent most summers, and other holidays as well, in a little bungalow we bought on the Isle of Wight, in a small village called Lake, between Sandown and Shanklin, two large holiday resorts. The bungalow had a large garden and we grew our own vegetables; collecting peas and beans in the morning for the midday meal, or digging up potatoes, were some of the delights of ownership. We did a lot of walking, of course; all the children were taught to swim; we played badminton in the garden, a game we later on continued in the Maudsley gymnasium during the winters. I taught Darrin to play tennis, and we used to play a lot on the Island. We also played beach cricket, went around the Island by car, made friends and generally enjoyed our life there. It was ideal for the children to spend their holidays by the sea, not in hotels, but in their own living quarters, and we didn't sell the bungalow (with a 1,500 per cent profit!) until the kids were too old to enjoy such simple holidays.

As in so many other things, we were very lucky to have produced really nice children; genetics worked its usual miracles, segregating parental chromosomes in many different ways to produce four entirely different human beings. Children can be a great trial – growing up to be criminals, taking drugs, dropping out, being ill, and in many other ways. Apart from some slight hiccups, our children avoided all these pitfalls, worked hard, got married, had children, became responsible adults and parents, and remained within the bonds of the family. Most, if not all, of the credit must of course go to Sybil for this.

It is unfortunate for the purposes of an autobiography that a happy marriage tends to appear boring to outsiders. So is a happy family life; there are no startling events, no great tragedies, no upheavals. Quiet happiness is difficult to describe, and not very interesting to read about. As Tolstoy pointed out: 'All happy families resemble each other, each unhappy family is unhappy in its own way.' Exactly.

I concentrated more and more on my work, and abandoned the tendency of my younger years of trying to reorganize the world. I had started a number of hares during the early years. At University College, as a student, I started the Psychological Society there and became its first President. I was active, with Monte Shapiro, in starting the Social Sciences Section of the A.Sc.W. (The Association of Scientific Workers), a Trades Union of scientists; and in starting a Social Psychology Section at The British Psychological Society. Of these activities I remember the A.Sc.W. best. We held our first meeting, to decide on the nature of the Section, at the Bonnington Hotel; thereafter, meetings were held in Half Moon Street in Mayfair, notable for the prostitutes parading along it. At first I was quite enthusiastic about this endeavour, but slowly it dawned on me that the Section was Communist dominated, and had political – rather than trades union – ambitions. I soon lost interest and dropped out.

I was asked to become the first President of the newly-founded International Society for the Study of Individual Differences (ISSID) in 1983; little work was involved, and I thought the Society was very much needed in counteracting a *Zeitgeist* which was antagonistic to the very idea that all individuals might not be exactly equal and identical.

During these years I also enjoyed my second Visiting Professorship in the United States, at the University of California at Berkeley. I met many interesting people there, including Mary Cover Jones, who had been Watson's student when he first introduced the notion that neurosis was essentially a conditioned response, which could be cured by extinguishing these conditioned responses. She obtained her Ph.D. by putting this theory into practice, and was the first person to practise what we now call 'behaviour therapy', with considerable success. I also met Donald Hebb, and we had many interesting talks. But the whole department was full of eminent people who made important contributions to psychology such as Tolman, Krech, Postman, Rosenzweig, Gough, Egon, and Elsie Brunswick and many others. This, aided by the wonderful climate and the scenic beauty, made my stay a memorable one. (Berkeley is situated on the other side of the bay opposite San Francisco, and the bay, with the tall buildings of the city beyond, is a wonderful sight as it changes its character with the time of day – fog making it a fairyland spectacle in the morning, sunshine a beautiful apparition at noon, and starlight a magic sight in the evening.) I left San Francisco and rented a small bungalow overlooking the bay, and spent a good deal of time lying in the sun, or watering the garden. The neighbours used to watch me doing this in astonishment; I only realized as I was leaving that water is very expensive in Berkeley, as it has to be brought in through pipes from faraway rivers, and that I had spent a fortune on behalf of the unfortunate owner of the bungalow!

The students I had to teach provided a revelation. American State Universities, unlike British ones, did little by way of selection; anyone with a High School Certificate (which doesn't mean very much) seemed eligible, and in fact the standard was so low that the first year seemed to be devoted to bringing people up to British Matriculation standard; it also acted as a selection device, with very large numbers being rejected. It still seems to me that the British system of using A-levels as a selection device for university admission is a much better way of organizing the selection process; it avoids raising hopes, and then frustrating students by throwing them out after the first year! Even so I was surprised at the low level of the students, compared with those I had been teaching in London. There were of course no undergraduates at the Institute of Psychiatry; we were entirely a postgraduate institution and hence only accepted students who already had a First-Class Degree in Psychology. However, I did teach undergraduate students at University College, after Burt retired.

When Sir Cyril Burt was due to retire in 1950 he was obviously considering ways of having the department continue along the lines Spearman and he had laid down. He must have come to the reluctant conclusion that I was the only man who could do this because he overcame his quite obsessive hatred of me and tried to interest me in becoming his successor. University College, too, made some advances, and because this had been the home of the 'London School', and my own Alma Mater, I certainly felt tempted. I suggested that I would be willing to accept the Chair, provided I could continue as Head of the Department at the Institute; I even offered to do one or other of these two jobs without payment. This did not seem unreasonable to me; many universities in the United States had such arrangements, and my old friend Joe Zubin was a Professor at Columbia University and successfully worked at the New York Psychiatric Hospital as well. However, both University College and the Institute in the person of Sir Aubrey Lewis, were outraged. Both thought that they were leading institutions in their respective fields, and that it was an honour to be running one of their departments. Both indignantly turned down my proposal. I think this was a mistake. It could have provided an excellent link between undergraduate and postgraduate teaching for the students; and the vast growth of clinical psychology, which for many years was to provide the major offer of jobs for graduates in psychology, would have made this link very attractive to the best students at University College. However, it was not to be, and I stayed at the Institute.

University College finally elected as Burt's successor a friend and colleague of mine, Roger Russell. He had done excellent work in animal psychology in the United States, before I brought him over to the Institute to start and run our animal laboratory, located at Bethlem Hospital. This was the only animal laboratory in England at the time, and Roger made a wonderful job of it, being an excellent experimentalist. He managed to teach several of the students the way animal work should be done, and thus enabled me eventually to find a successor who would carry on the work.

The offer of a Chair at such a prestigious department could not be resisted, and Roger became Burt's successor. Despite Roger's qualities it seemed to me a silly appointment. A department with such a monumental history as the birthplace of psychometrics should continue in that tradition. Roger was an experimentalist, particularly in the animal field; his interests and his teaching would be quite at variance with the tradition of the department. Also, I didn't think that he would stay there long; British university salaries are so poor compared with American ones that it did not seem likely that Roger could make ends meet. As was to be expected he resigned after just a few years, and the department, from having been with Cambridge the foremost in the country, dropped disastrously in its rating. The following comparison is taken from the 1975 Social Sciences Citation Index, and illustrates the depth to which University College has fallen. During that year the Institute of Psychiatry Psychology Department (my department) had sixty-two publications, while University College had ten. The Institute had 886 citations, University College 92. These figures speak for themselves. The position has not improved since 1975. This is a great pity; a tradition like that of the London School, dating back to Sir Francis Galton, Karl Pearson, Spearman and then Burt is worth preserving.

My own work on intelligence and personality, which I have recounted in the preceding chapter, followed along the lines laid down by the earlier members of the London School. In addition, as I have mentioned,

I indulged in some work related to parapsychology and astrology. My studies and my theorizing in these fields have been received with astonishment by colleagues and friends. Wasn't parapsychology, and astrology even more so, just a nonsense that ought to be excoriated rather than taken seriously? How could a scientist be found mixing with these unscientific oddballs, caught in the musty, fusty miasmas of Victorian seances and medieval star-gazing?

Motivational factors are difficult to discuss, because we do not really know how to provide good evidence that might take the place of speculation. As psychologists know better than most, the dangers of relying on introspection are that you are liable to find what you seek, which in most cases is a socially acceptable reason for doing what you are doing. Let me defer this question and rather concentrate on what I have actually done in these fields.

Before doing this, however, I would like to draw attention to a similarity between the work I originally did on hypnosis, and the work I did later on in parapsychology and astrology. In scientific research, one of the most important factors in deciding what to investigate is a person's attitude to the subject on a scale from adventurous curiosity to improving existing practices. Most scientists are in the latter tradition; they work in a widely recognized field, use established methods, attack problems that arise from existing theories, and do what Thomas Kuhn has called 'the ordinary business of science'. Such work is an essential part of science.

However, I have always been more interested in areas outside these narrow confines, areas where important problems arise, but where there is very little in the way of acknowledged results, agreed methods, or problems arising from established theories. Hypnosis, when I started working on it as a student, was such a field. The very existence of hypnotic phenomena was denied by many, and they are still considered artefacts by some. There was no agreed body of knowledge, established method of investigation, or widely recognized theories. 'Each for himself!' was the motto of investigators, and as my own experience was to show, even a young student knowing very little about the subject could make an important contribution. But the main attraction of a field such as hypnosis (or parapsychology, or astrology), is the promise it contains of entirely new and extremely important knowledge that might be gained by a study of the (alleged) phenomena in question.

Consider hypnosis. There are many phenomena here which are thoroughly attested, and no longer in doubt. There is a famous case of the patient who was suffering from ichthyosis, a disease in which the body is covered with scales. There being little medical help in this condition, the psychologist tried to get rid of the scales by means of hypnosis. If he were successful, he knew others might argue that these scales would have disappeared of their own accord; so he first suggested that the scales would vanish on the right side of the body only. When this was accomplished, he also got rid of the scales on the left side by making suitable suggestions. This study indicates, with unusual clarity, the potential powers of hypnotic suggestion. It has equally well been established that major surgery can be carried out under hypnosis without the patient feeling any pain – an incredible achievement. Among minor demonstrations it has been shown that warts can be got rid of through hypnotic suggestion, and it has even been found that with suitable suggestions the size of the female breast can be enlarged under hypnosis! It seemed to me that here was a field that really cried out for experimental analysis, the development of good theories, and the application of proper experimental methods. Yet most of my colleagues and teachers warned me against working in this field because it was considered to be full of 'quackery' – no genuine scientist would be willing to work in it and expose himself to such accusations. As I was to discover, my efforts to continue with this work at the Maudsley Hospital were frustrated by the medical staff who refused to let the hospital be associated with such 'quackery', and I didn't then have the status to stand up against such pressure. Since then things have changed a little, but even now I know of no department of psychology, and no teaching hospital in England, where research is being carried out on this vitally important topic.

Similarly, if there is any truth whatsoever in the suggestions made by parapsychologists and astrologers about their 'sciences', then clearly we have here an enormously important contribution to knowledge.

It would be wrong to assume that because science rejects certain formulations and ideas, these must therefore be right, and eventually flourish. The vast majority of ideas, theories, and assumptions rejected by orthodox science fully deserve to be rejected, and it is only very occasionally that science has to reconsider its position.

Perhaps Pascal's famous argument for believing in God is apposite here. He argued that the benefits of being in Paradise, as compared with the sufferings of being in Hell, are infinite; consequently even the smallest probability that God exists should be sufficient to make one believe in Him, in order to avoid going to Hell, and to ensure the passage to Heaven! The argument may appeal more to mathematicians, like Pascal, than to genuinely religious people, and I cannot pretend that I have ever found it persuasive. Nevertheless, in revised form it does apply to the possible discovery of important new truths in parapsychology and astrology.

As a student I had already become familiar with the work of J. B. Rhine in parapsychology and his attempts to prove the existence of extrasensory perception through card guessing games. When Sybil and I were in the United States during 1949–50, we went to visit Rhine and his wife, looked at his laboratory, and talked with his co-workers. We formed the opinion that while these people might be wildly wrong in their researches, they were certainly hardworking, honest scientists who were concerned with finding the truth. There was no doubt that they had made mistakes, and would make many more – but then we all do. There seemed to me enough material to make one wonder about the possibilities of clairvoyance, telepathy, precognition and psychokinesis (the actual manipulation of physical entities by means of psychological powers). I certainly did not believe that this research had established the existence of any of these varieties of ESP, or 'PSI' as it came to be named, but it did seem to me entirely wrong to dismiss it all, as was done by many people who hadn't even bothered to read the research records, or the books published on the topic.

But what of the possibility of cheating and faking? There certainly have been many cases where mediums particularly have been exposed, and there have also been well documented cases where scientists concerned with parapsychological experiments have been shown to have faked their data. But this should be seen in the light of the fact that many scientists in physics, biology, psychology and other recognized scientific disciplines have been shown to have cheated, to have forged data, or to have altered their results in other ways. But it cannot be assumed that because a few people in a given discipline have cheated, everyone has cheated. Critics also tend to forget that some of the most virulent critics of parapsychology themselves have been shown to have cheated. Brian Inglis, in his book on *Science and Parascience*, gives a number of examples. Consider for instance Houdini, the famous magician who was a sworn enemy of psychic research and spiritualism. He spent much of his time 'exposing' spiritualists, among them 'Marjorie', a medium who produced some very astonishing phenomena which are well attested. Houdini tried to show her up as a fake, using methods that are clearly well beyond what we would recognize as scientifically permissible. Marjorie, encased in a wooden hut of Houdini's own construction, was supposed to ring a bell while both her hands were being held by Houdini and a friend of his. Houdini wedged a small rubber eraser into the bell to make this more difficult to happen; he disclaimed responsibility, but as he had been responsible for checking the bell, it was difficult to accept this as an explanation.

On another occasion, a wooden ruler was found in the cabinet which might have been used by Marjorie to convey to her mouth in order to ring the bell, and perhaps play other tricks. Houdini denied that either he or his friend was responsible, but the friend, who was Houdini's assistant, later admitted 'I chucked it in the box myself. The Boss told me to do it. 'E wanted to fix her good.'

My contribution to the field of parapsychology has been a modest one. I carried out one fairly large-scale experiment; I contributed a theory which has been pretty well substantiated; and I wrote a book (with Carl Sargent), *Explaining the Unexplained*, which reviews the available experimental evidence.

The experiment was in relation to the alleged phenomena of precognition – i.e., the ability of people (and animals) to look into the future and arrange their activities accordingly. This is perhaps one of the most unbelievable but also exciting claims of parapsychology, and there had been two studies of precognition in the literature reporting positive results. Both dealt with rats, and their ability to foresee just where they might receive an electric shock in the future, and avoid that place. I discussed the possibility of replication with Rhine, and designed an experiment using a shuttlebox, consisting of two halves, which would be separately electrified in a random manner. The rat was let loose in the box; if it had precognition as to which of the two halves was to be electrified, it could avoid the electric shock by going to the other half. I used several strains of rats, and several different intensities of shocks, in order to see if the phenomenon – assuming that it existed at all – was in any way dependent on the severity of shock, or related to the strain of animal. The outcome was clear-cut; there was no effect whatsoever, rats going to electrified and unelectrified parts of the box with equal frequency.

The experiment, which was conducted with the help of some of my colleagues in the animal laboratory, seemed so decisive that I sent it to the *Journal of Parapsychology*. To my surprise they turned it down, criticizing the statistics and suggesting other ways of analysing the data. I found this unreasonable. The statistics were quite simple and traditional; the analysis had been carried out by David Fulker, one of the most gifted statistical geneticists in the country, and I had cleared it with two eminent statisticians who found nothing to criticize. I decided that perhaps the negative result had irked the editor, and I published the paper instead in a well-established psychological journal. The rejection of our paper did make me wonder about the fate of negative results in parapsychological research, when submitted in article form to the journal; did they make it a habit only to accept positive results? This would not be unusual; much the same was true of psychological journals, but it does make the appraisal of statistical significance of reported results rather difficult.

My theoretical contribution occurred in 1967, when I had been invited to give a lecture to the Society for Psychical Research in London. I had just developed my theory linking extraversion with lack of cortical arousal and it seemed to me that if any parapsychological abilities existed, they would be primitive; if that were true, then the activity of the neocortex would tend to suppress them. Now introverts, having a greater degree of cortical arousal, would also show greater activity in the neocortex. This suggested that extraverts, having lower arousal and a lower degree of cortical activity, would be more likely to show evidence of parapsychological phenomena than would introverts. I found some evidence for this hypothesis in the literature, particularly the fact that parapsychological phenomena tended to occur with particular frequency in states of low arousal.

Since then ninety-five per cent of all significant findings have supported my hypothesis, one in three experiments giving significant results. Whether the agreement between hypothesis and fact is due to the causes I have suggested is of course another matter; there are other reasons why extraverts might be more successful in activities which, after all, always involve other people. Much more searching inquiries are needed before my hypothesis can be verified. However, it certainly seems to be in the right direction, and thus constitutes the beginning of hypothesis-formation in a field where most work has been entirely heuristic.

The invitation by the Society for Psychical Research had come about because of a chapter I wrote on telepathy and clairvoyance in my Pelican *Sense and Nonsense in Psychology*. This was one of few acknowledgements by scientific writers that there might be some truth in psychical phenomena. When I met Carl Sargent, who had gained his Ph.D. in experimental parapsychology at the University of Cambridge, and whose post-doctoral research had been concerned with ESP, he suggested we might get together to write a book on the topic, reviewing all the evidence. This we did, in *Explaining the Unexplained*, and I believe it presents the facts fairly and without prejudice. Whatever reservations one might have about specific parapsychological allegations, it seems to me indisputable that there are phenomena here which cannot be explained in terms of orthodox science, and which require further investigation. Methodology and statistical analysis of such phenomena have improved to such an extent that the older objections are certainly no longer applicable. In particular the use of computers both to run the experiment and to analyse the data – without any human interference – has made arguments about involuntary influences favouring ESP results inapplicable. It has become routine to mark all items that are being used, and to make a photographic recording of the whole procedure, so that any activities on the part of the subject that might elude the investigator can be discovered on the film. Also, the use of magicians to help in the design of the experiment, and its execution, has also become widespread; they would presumably be best able to discover evidence of faking and cheating.

Particularly interesting, too, is the collaboration of metallurgists, who carry out laboratory investigations of spoons and other metal objects bent in the course of experiments on the so-called Geller-effect.

Sargent and I also published another book, *Know Your Own PSI-Q*. Here we have set out a number of ways in which an individual can test his own abilities in parapsychology. (Sadly, this has been nothing like as successful as my *Know Your Own IQ*, or *Check Your Own IQ*; perhaps this is due to the fact that it never came out in paperback. Or of course it might be due to the fact that to most people the term 'PSI' still does not mean very much. Or perhaps people are just more interested in their intelligence than in their parapsychological ability. Who can say?)

What is true of parapsychology is probably even more true of astrology. In recent years there has been a considerable change of opinion with respect to parapsychology, and something like one in three professional scientists is willing to concede that there may be something in it. But, it would be difficult to find any scientists at all who have anything but contempt for astrology.

In September 1975, *The Humanist*, an American magazine devoted to discussions of psychic problems and irrationality, carried a lengthy statement entitled 'Objections to Astrology'. It was endorsed by 186 leading scientists including eighteen Nobel Prize-winners. This statement was considered as evidence of a sceptical frame of mind on the part of the scientists who signed it, but this is surely a misuse of the term. Authors and signatories of the statement alike had not looked carefully at the empirical evidence, discovered methodological and statistical faults, and on the basis of an exhaustive examination came to certain conclusions; they had simply made an a priori judgement. Carl Sagan, a scientist who declined to sign, made the point well in the following letter to *The Humanist*:

I find myself unable to endorse the 'Objections to Astrology' statement (September/October, 1975) – not because I feel that astrology has any validity whatever, but because I felt and still feel that the tone of the statement is authoritarian. The fundamental point is not that the origins of astrology are shrouded in superstition. This is true as well for chemistry, medicine, and astronomy, to mention only three. To discuss the psychological motivations of those who believe in astrology seems to be quite peripheral to the issue of its validity. That we can think of no mechanism for astrology is relevant but unconvincing. No

[238]

mechanism was known, for example, for continental drift when it was proposed by Wegener. Nevertheless, we see that Wegener was right, and those who objected on the grounds of unavailable mechanism were wrong . . .

What I would have signed is a statement describing and refuting the principal tenets of astrological belief. My belief is that such a statement would have been far more persuasive and would have produced vastly less controversy than the one that was actually circulated.

Here speaks a true sceptic.

What we thus have is not astrologers versus scientific sceptics, but two sets of fanatics, one believing on the basis of suspect evidence in the truth of astrology, the other on the basis of complete ignorance of what evidence there might be for disbelieving in astrology. The true sceptic is equally sceptical of both sets of fanatics, and would wish to look at the evidence before coming to a conclusion. This is what I set out to do when I wrote *Astrology: Science or Superstition?*, together with Dr D. K. Nias, a colleague at the Institute of Psychiatry. In this book we examined in detail all the empirical studies which had claimed to find positive evidence for astrology, as well as the major studies failing to find such evidence. We looked for methodological and statistical errors, which we found in plenty – not only on the part of astrologers claiming positive results, but also on the part of critics claiming negative ones!

Turning to some typical errors committed by astrologers in their research, C. Cole, a Cornell University zoologist, quotes a cautionary tale entitled: 'How to discover the secret rhythms of the digestive system of the unicorn.'

Since he was unable to obtain any actual unicorns for his experiment, he decided instead to use a series of random numbers to represent the metabolic changes in the missing animal. The aim was to see whether these numbers could be made to yield some kind of recognizable pattern.

Cole constructed first a graph covering five days in the unicorn's life, and on it he plotted his series of numbers to stand for the unicorn's metabolic rates over that period. There was, of course, no pattern, since the numbers were truly random. To simplify the graph, Cole averaged groups of figures, but still no pattern emerged. It is inconceivable that the unicorn should really be such a haphazard beast, so Cole continued his search. Arguing that the unicorn's cycle might well be governed by the moon, he adjusted the scale for the hour of the moon's rise and – look! – an unmistakable daily rhythm emerged. When the graph was 'smoothed' (a common and legitimate statistical practice) the pattern became clearer still, showing a peak of metabolic activity in the early morning and a trough twelve hours later. The rhythm of the unicorn's day was clear at last.

Cole had, of course, succeeded in showing what he set out to show – that if you keep on playing with any set of numbers you can eventually pull some sort of pattern out of them. As the saying goes: 'Seek [long enough] and ye shall find.' To safeguard against this effect one should decide in advance what mathematical treatment of the data would be justified, not simply go on trying different procedures until some pattern emerges. If one does discover a pattern in that way, then it is necessary to repeat the study on a new set of data, using exactly the same procedures. If Cole had performed the same manipulations on a new lot of random numbers it is highly improbable that the same rhythm would have shown up again.

Some methodological errors are of course much more subtle, and much more difficult to detect. I was involved in one study, carried out by the well-known astrologist J. Mayo, who collected data from 2,324 people, most of them interested in astrology, with whom he had been in correspondence. He set out to test two well-known astrological theories. According to ancient astrological belief, the signs of the Zodiac, starting with Aries, are alternatively positive and negative. The positive or odd-numbered signs denote masculine, outgoing, spontaneous qualities, and the negative or even-numbered signs are associated with the feminine, the self-repressive and the passive. This may be translated into modern terminology by saying that people born under the positive signs are extraverted, while those born under the negative signs are introverted.

The signs are also linked in turn with fire, earth, air and water, again starting from Aries. The earth signs (Taurus, Virgo and Capricorn) are said to be practical and stable, while the water signs (Cancer, Scorpio and Pisces) are emotional and intuitive. In other words, people born under the water signs should be high on the trait of neuroticism; those born under the earth signs should be stable. Mayo had sent a questionnaire of mine measuring these two qualities to his subjects, as well as asking their birth dates. The results were striking. For extraversion-introversion they were exactly in accord with astrological prediction, while for emotionality-stability, they departed from it only in giving too high a score for Aries. The analysis of the data was done independently by myself and Owen White, a statistician in my department at the time.

Our results seemed too good to be true. Is there an alternative hypothesis that might explain the results without invoking astrological factors? I suggested such an alternative hypothesis when I wrote up the results of the study. Perhaps subjects like these who are interested in astrology might know the personality descriptions traditionally associated with the signs of the Zodiac, and might accordingly frame their answers to the personality questionnaire in such a way as to bring them closer to the astrological ideal. Admittedly an attempt had been made in the study to test this hypothesis, without those who claimed astrological knowledge showing much difference from those who did not.

David Nias and I continued the work in an attempt to discover which of the two hypotheses was the correct one. In the first study we looked at a sample of 1,160 children, assuming the children would be less knowledgeable about the personality correlates of the signs of the Zodiac supposed to exist by astrologers. There was no evidence in this study of any relationship between personality and Zodiacal signs.

In our next study we looked at 122 adults, showing each of them twelve sets of personality traits and asking them to choose the set that best matched their own personality. In fact the twelve sets of traits were those associated with the twelve signs of the Zodiac, but almost all the subjects failed to recognize this until it was later brought to their attention.

We also tested the subjects for their knowledge of astrology. After they had chosen the set of traits they thought described them best, they were told that the twelve sets represented the twelve signs of the Zodiac and were asked to select the one that corresponded to their own sign. Those whose first choice was right were classified as 'knowledgeable', forty-six of the 122 subjects falling into this category. Those who failed three times to guess correctly were classified as 'ignorant' (fifty subjects). Those who guessed wrong first time but guessed right at the second or third attempt were classified as 'borderline' (twenty-six subjects).

The ignorant group showed no tendency whatever for their personality to match the predictions of astrology. For the borderline group the result is the same. The knowledgeable group, on the other hand, showed a marked tendency to assess themselves in accordance with astrological predictions! In other words, the astrological hypothesis was erroneous, and our alternative hypothesis was more in line with the facts.

Many others have since replicated these studies, and the outcome is very much as summarized above. I think the set of studies shows clearly some of the methodological objections Dr Nias and I made to astrological research apparently verifying astrological principles. Even when the results appear very positive, and the statistical analysis seems to be foolproof, there is seldom – if ever – any replication, and alternative hypotheses are not even considered. These two aspects of scientific investigation, however, are absolutely essential if worthwhile results are to be obtained. Even if results are significant the first time round, only replication can give us confidence that they are truly reproducible. And as long as alternative hypotheses can explain the results, we cannot be certain that astrology has been supported by the apparently positive study. We reluctantly concluded in our book that, despite our many intriguing findings, the vast majority of astrological experiments were faulty in design, methodology, or statistical analysis, and did not provide the evidence needed to support astrological tenets. We did our best to see if there were any nuggets hidden in the desert of astrological research, but despite our efforts we only unearthed one such nugget.

A French journal of popular psychology, *Psychologie d'Aujourdhui*, wanted to print an interview with me, and when I was in Paris on a visit to my mother I went to their office. The interview was conducted, and later on written up, by Michel Gauquelin, a psychologist and statistician. At the time he mentioned to me some research he had been doing in astrology, together with his wife Francoise, which had had some intriguing and positive outcomes.

Much as I liked Michel and Francoise, I was quite unwilling to believe what they had to say about their positive findings. At that time I had no interest whatsoever in astrology, assuming it to be a lot of nonsense, and it would have taken a good deal to make me give up that attitude. However, Michel gave me some books and articles to read which he had written on his work, and I took them back to London with me, confident that I would soon find the methodological or statistical errors in them. There I was mistaken; as far as I could see the work had been done very carefully, honestly, and the methodology and the statistics did not contain any obvious errors.

What the Gauquelins claimed was that famous sportsmen, scientists, soldiers, physicians, actors, and writers are born more frequently than chance would allow when certain planets were in key sectors during their diurnal rotation around the earth. We can divide the circle described by the planets around us into a number of sectors – the Gauquelins have used 12, 18, or 36, depending on the degree of discrimination required. If we use 12 sectors, the first one would be located just after the planet has risen and become visible; the fourth just after it has reached its highest point (culmination); the seventh just after the planet has sunk below the horizon, and the tenth just after it has reached its lowest point. Sectors 1 and 4 are the crucial ones, according to the Gauquelins, with 7 and 10 also showing somewhat increased frequency of births as far as these people are concerned. Different professions are associated with different planets. The superfluity of births of sportsmen, physicians, and military people are linked with Mars; soldiers, politicians, and actors with Jupiter; physicians, and scientists with Saturn, and writers with Venus, and the Moon (which for this purpose might be regarded as a planet in the same way as Mars, Jupiter, Saturn and Venus).

I could have left things there and settled back in my comfortable belief that astrology was all nonsense, but I felt that, if the Gauquelins were wrong, I should be able to find the error, or if they were right, then many important consequences for orthodox science would follow. I read all I could of the Gauquelins' work, visited them and looked at their data; and had many discussions with them, and also with astronomers, physicists and statisticians who had criticized their data.

Let us begin with what has become widely known as the 'Mars effect' – i.e., the alleged finding that famous sportsmen are more frequently born just after rise and upper culmination, and somewhat less so after the setting and the lower culmination of the planet Mars. This finding has been challenged, and several independent groups have attempted to replicate it.

Figure 7.1 shows the results of 570 famous sportsmen studied by the Gauquelins; the broken circles indicate the proportion of people born in each sector by chance (note that here we are dealing with 18 sectors); the

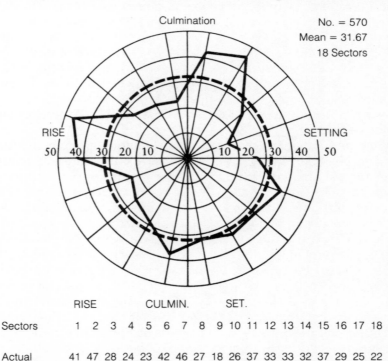

Sectors	1	2	3	4	5	6	7	8	9	10	11	12	13	14	15	16	17	18
Actual	41	47	28	24	23	42	46	27	18	26	37	33	33	32	37	29	25	22
Expected	33	34	33	33	32	31	31	31	30	30	30	30	31	31	32	32	33	33

FIG. 7.1 *The Mars Effect, shown by 570 well-known sportsmen.*

connected black line indicates the actual number of famous sportsmen born in each sector. It will be quite clear, even without statistical proof, that in the predicted sectors there is a superfluity of sportsmen, but many fewer in the intervening sectors. Thus in sector 1 and 2 we would expect 33 and 34 sportsmen, respectively, but in actual fact there are 41 and 47. In sector 6 and 7 we would expect 31 and 31, respectively, but there are 42 and 46.

Another group associated with Mars are doctors. Figure 7.2 shows 508 notable doctors, and it will be seen that here again we have exactly the same prominence just after rise, and just after culmination, as in the case of famous sportsmen. This is a replication of an earlier study of 576 famous doctors. The similarities are striking, and indicate that the effects are replicated in two independent studies.

Corresponding to a surplus in the critical positions, we also of course have a deficit for certain groups. Thus while doctors, sportsmen, military men and company heads have a surplus of births when Mars is in the critical positions, writers, painters and musicians have a deficit.

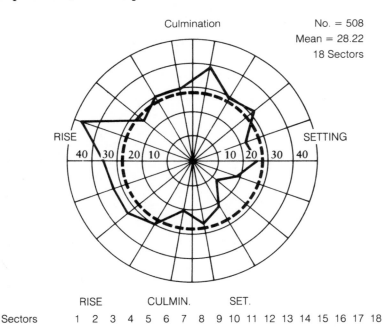

Sectors	RISE				CULMIN.				SET.									
	1	2	3	4	5	6	7	8	9	10	11	12	13	14	15	16	17	18
Actual	35	48	27	29	29	39	29	31	22	25	19	11	22	27	19	29	34	33
Expected	30	30	29	29	29	28	28	27	27	27	27	27	27	28	28	29	29	29

FIG. 7.2 *The Mars Effect, shown by 508 well-known doctors.*

Table 7 shows a survey of the principal results achieved by the Gauquelins, in each case using very large groups, and an objective assessment of eminence, namely biographical material. The numbers involved in all this research are quite incredible; adding up to almost 70,000, of whom 40,000 were ordinary people, the remaining 30,000 famous professionals in the various different professions already mentioned. All the data concerning them have been meticulously published by the Gauquelins, so that a complete reconstruction of all their work, and the checking of its accuracy, is possible. Some such checks have indeed been carried out, and will be reported in due course.

Synthesis of principal results		
	Surplus	Deficit
MARS	Doctors Sportsmen Military men Company heads	Writers Painters Musicians
JUPITER	Military men Politicians Actors Journalists Playwrights	Scientists Doctors
SATURN	Scientists Doctors	Actors Painters Musicians (?) Journalists Writers
MOON	Politicians Writers	Sportsmen Military men (?)

Surplus: high frequency of positions for the planet in the rise and culmination zones.
Deficit: small number of positions for the planet in the rise and culmination zones.

TABLE 7 *Major findings of the Gauquelin researches.*

Fig. 7.3 shows graphically one instance of a planetary surplus and deficit account, namely Saturn. This has a *positive* relation to scientists, a negative one to artists. The opposition of these two groups is very clear.

When the Gauquelins reported the Mars effect originally it invited a good deal of incredulity and criticism. A Belgian Committee, hostile to all parapsychological research, and presided over by the Astronomer Royal of Belgium, took the trouble to collect new birth data of another sample

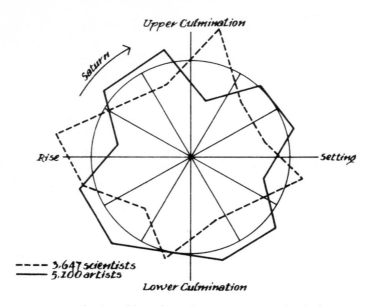

FIG. 7.3 *The dotted line shows how scientists tend to be born just after the rise of upper culmination of Saturn, while the births of artists (solid line) are least frequent at those times. It is interesting to see how closely the two curves run counter to each other. The circle shows the number of births to be expected at each time by chance alone. (Based on Gauquelin, 1978).*

of 535 athletes. They were surprised to find that their data agreed very closely with those originally published by the Gauquelins; the post-rise and culmination peaks for Mars positions appeared in their own frequency distribution just as strongly as they had in the Gauquelins' original data! (See Fig. 7.4.) One might have expected that these rather astonishing data and any criticisms they might have had would have been published by the Committee, but they refused to do so, although they did allow interested scientists to have access to the data. Round 1 clearly goes to the Gauquelins.

The second replication was carried out by CSICOP (The Committee for the Scientific Investigation of Claims of the Paranormal), an American organization equally hostile to parapsychological phenomena. They also suggested an improvement in the Gauquelins' study, recommending that for each athlete collected from the Gauquelins' sample, a number of ordinary people should be matched as controls, the controls having birthdays on the same day, and in the same place or its vicinity as the groups of experimental infants who in their later lives became famous sportsmen. This would be an experimental control about alleged

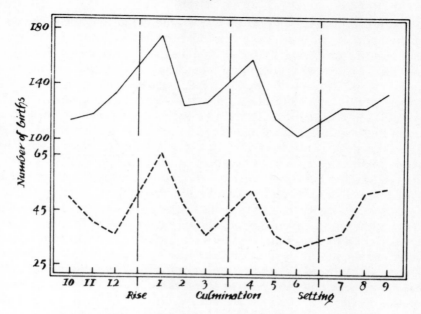

FIG. 7.4   *The two curves show the frequency of births of sports champions at different positions of Mars. The upper curve is Gauquelin's sample of 1,553; the lower curve is the independent sample of 535 studied by the Committee Para. (Based on Gauquelin, 1978.)*

demographic factors on birth distribution which had been suggested as possible extraneous reasons for the Gauquelin finding. The suggestions made by Marvin Zelen, a statistician at Harvard, were carried out by the Gauquelins at tremendous sacrifice of time and money; the results disproved Zelen's objection completely.

Michel Gauquelin undertook the collection of another European sample of athletes in 1979, and again the above chance deviations of frequency in the sensitive zones of Mars reappeared, and a final sample was added to the whole group by the Gauquelins who collected another group of sportsmen in the United States, with the overall Mars effect reappearing again. But nothing Gauquelin did seemed to be capable of persuading the critics. Could the matter be left at that stage? Fortunately a German psychologist, Suitbert Ertel, of the University of Göttingen, decided to analyse all the available data for himself, both those that had been published by all the participants, as well as some unpublished data still lying around in Gauquelin's laboratory. He found unpublished data for 1,503 sportsmen, and decided to devote his energies to testing

Gauquelin's 'eminence' hypothesis – i.e., the belief that the more eminent the sportsmen, the clearer would be the Mars effect.

Ertel defined eminence by consulting a sample of twenty-one appropriate reference books, including biographical dictionaries of international scope, books listing sporting records, etc., covering the historical period of all samples, and considering all sportsfields of the data pool. He then counted the times each athlete in the sample was listed in these sources, the range of citations for one athlete being 0 to 8. The results of this study were very clear-cut. Overall there was a distinct increase in the percentage of champions spawned in the appropriate sectors of Mars, increasing linearly with greater eminence. When looking at different sets of data individually, this was as true of the US athletes studied by Kurtz and his colleagues, as it was of the Gauquelin data. In other words, even the most hostile group, namely Kurtz, Zelen and Abell, had in their data evidence to significantly support the Gauquelins' claims, just as the Belgian Committee had found such evidence.

For myself, I found one other finding published by Ertel of particular interest, and especially supportive of the Gauquelins' claims. Figure 7.5 gives the results of a small female sample, as well as for the large male sample, showing the percentage of athletes born in the appropriate sectors of Mars, according to eminence ranks from 1, the lowest, to 4, the highest. At all levels both males and females exceed chance expectancy, but female athletes are much more likely to be born under Mars than are male athletes. Gauquelin himself had never published the data on

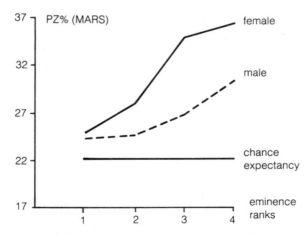

FIG. 7.5   *The Mars Effect related to degree of eminence of sportsmen and sportswomen.*

females, but Ertel dug them out from the material available in Gauquelin's laboratory, and published the data.

Not knowing that data of this were available, I had predicted the female/male difference, on the basis of the so-called 'dual threshold' theory; the theory is that most social phenomena are caused by certain dispositional traits underlying that particular behaviour. Thus criminal behaviour is to a large extent the product of certain personality traits which form a continuum from very low to very high probability of anti-social behaviour. Here there is a point, the threshold point, beyond which there is a strong probability of criminal behaviour occurring. That is the 'single threshold' hypothesis.

It is possible that different groups may have different amounts of the underlying traits; thus females are much lower on the anti-social traits than are males. In terms of the dual threshold hypothesis women require a *larger* amount of this trait in order to indulge in criminal behaviour, and the evidence shows that this is indeed so. We can now apply this hypothesis to the Gauquelin data. Clearly psychological traits which make for success in sport, like those which make for criminality, are more common in males than in females, so that really outstanding

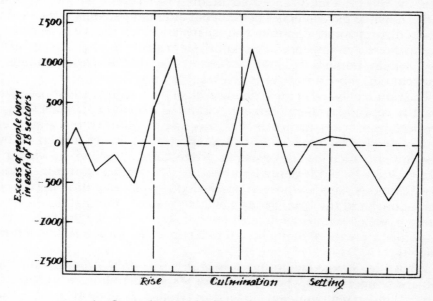

FIG. 7.6 *Gauquelin's combined sample of 46,485 people eminent in fields 'governed' by Mars, Jupiter, Saturn and the Moon. The position of each person's planet depends on the birth time, and taken all together they show highly significant peaks after rise and upper culmination.*

female athletes would be likely to show this trait much more strongly than males. This general dual threshold theory was not known to either Gauquelin or Ertel, so that they could not have 'doctored' the data to provide additional proof; Ertel simply published the data without apparently realizing their importance, and Gauquelin, as I have already said, never even bothered to publish them. These data, to me, constitute especially strong proof for the correctness of the Gauquelin hypothesis regarding the Mars effect. Taking together all the data for different groups and planets (Fig. 7.6) the evidence becomes very strong indeed.

So much for the main substance of the Gauquelins' claims and results; a great deal more could be said about them, but that would not fit into the framework of my autobiography. I would like to go on to discuss one aspect of their work which has overlapped with mine, namely the relation of personality to the effects of planetary influences on famous people. In selecting the subject for their investigations, the Gauquelins had had recourse particularly to biographies written about famous sportsmen, soldiers, actors, writers, musicians, etc., and in passing had noted all nouns and adverbs relating to personality which appeared in these works. It clearly appeared in these selections, as indeed was well-known to psychologists before, that different personalities go with different professions. Sportsmen, for instance, are 'active', 'reckless', 'competitive', 'courageous', 'energetic', 'aggressive', . . . 'full of vitality', etc., while scientists tend to be 'formal', 'reserved', 'conscientious', 'meticulous', 'observant', 'reflective' and 'retiring'.

The Gauquelins went on to divide each of their groups into those who had the appropriate temperament, and those who did not. Thus a large proportion of sportsmen had the traits just mentioned, but a smaller group, of what they call 'weak-willed' sportsmen, was characterized by descriptions such as 'inconsistent', 'dilettante', 'lacking in vigour', 'unambitious', 'gentlemanly', and so on. The former group included many famous names who had succeeded in spite of various physical limitations, and the latter group included many 'natural athletes' who had succeeded with the minimum of effort; presumably their physical attributes were more than enough to compensate for the lack of determination.

What the Gauquelins found was that it was only athletes with the athletic temperament who showed the Mars effect; those who had the wrong kind of temperament showed an actual deficiency in births in the critical sectors! Figure 7.7 shows that effect, with a solid line representing the birth of strong-willed, and the dotted line those of weak-willed champions. The difference is quite remarkable, and it is also found with other groups; planetary determination seems to go with the correct type

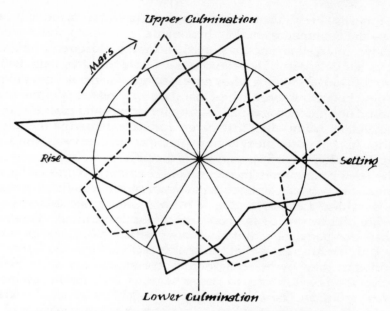

FIG. 7.7 *Mars and 'iron-willed' versus 'weak-willed' champions.*
The solid line represents the births of 'iron-willed' and the dotted
line 'weak-willed' champions. (Based on Gauquelin, 1978.)

of personality, more than with being successful as a sportsman, a
soldier, a painter, a writer or whatever!

These observations suggested that it was personality, rather than a
particular kind of profession, that was responsible for the relationship
with planetary position at birth, and Sybil and I decided to test this
hypothesis in conjunction with the Gauquelins. They sent us all the
terms descriptive of personality which they had collected, and Sybil then
looked through them 'blind' (i.e., in ignorance of the particular persons
to whom the terms referred), and marked those which could be regarded
as denoting introverted or extraverted personalities, emotionally stable
or unstable personality, and personalities characterized by a high or low
degree of psychoticism. We anticipated that Jupiter and Mars, the
planets of actors, politicians, and military men, would be linked with
extraversion, whereas the Saturn type of scientific practitioner would
show a relationship with introversion. In the same way, Jupiter and
Mars types would be related to the tough character of the high P scorer,
whereas the Saturn type would rather show the opposite characteristic.

Two studies were carried out along these lines, using first of all the
European birth data, then replicating the results with American birth
data. The results in both studies were positive, often with probabilities

[251]

indicating very high statistical significance. These data again may serve to show the genuineness of the phenomena.

Another interesting finding published by the Gauquelins relates to parent-child relations. There appears to be a distinct tendency for parents who are born under the crucial sectors of a given planet to have children who are also born when that particular planet is in the correct position. The tendency is equally strong for fathers and mothers, and of course doubly strong when both parents are born when the same planet is in the plus (+) position. When the parents were born with the Moon, Venus, Mars, Jupiter or Saturn in any of the positive areas, the chances of the child being born under the same planets are much higher. If we have a relationship between a person's planetary position and that of his/her parents, which occurs in ordinary people, and is not dependent on eminence, this must raise the possibility of discovering a direct relationship between personality and planetary position in ordinary people.

I would like to suggest that the results reported by the Gauquelins, supported as they are by replications successfully carried out by their most vociferous critics, can no longer be rejected on methodological or statistical grounds. These results suggest novel and hitherto unknown relations between terrestrial life and effects upon it by the planets. Can we find any kind of explanation? The Gauquelins have suggested that perhaps it is not the planets which determine when a child is born, or influence its destiny, but rather that the foetus itself, obeying some law of genetic make-up, chooses the time of its birth in accordance with the position of the planets (the planetary 'midwife' theory). This hypothesis runs into considerable difficulties. In conventional medicine, it is not yet known what initiates the birth process; there is believed to be a complex interaction of hormonal influences acting between mother and child, but the timing mechanism is unknown. Gauquelin's work introduces a new possibility, namely that the planets are somehow acting as celestial midwives. Some kind of signal emanating from the planets may somehow interact with the foetus in the womb, stimulating it to struggle into birth at a certain time.

However, this solution is by no means as straightforward as it might appear. If the planet sends some kind of signal that initiates the birth process, there will obviously be a lag between the signal and the resulting birth that is equal to the duration of labour. That duration varies considerably, from a single hour to many hours: first births average nine hours, second births five hours, and night labours average 25 per cent less than day labours. This compares with the average time between rise and culmination of about six hours. In other words, even if the births of all future sports champions began the moment that Mars was in one of certain specified positions, the resulting spread in the durations of labour should be enough to degrade the effect virtually beyond detection. This objection would be lessened if the planetary signal came after the onset of labour and closer to birth, but in that case the signal would be unnecessary!

On the other hand, if the planetary signal coincides with the birth moment, what initiates the birth process? And of course there remains the problem of what the signal is. Gravity or magnetism seem unlikely since the Sun has no effect. Direct electromagnetic radiation seems unlikely because it would already have been detected; in any case either terrestrial walls would block it or terrestrial sources would drown it. Furthermore, whatever the signal may be, how can the various planets have such qualitatively and quantitatively different effects? Extra-sensory or psi effects are unlikely, due to the known absence of planetary inhabitants. If it is argued that some extra-sensory power of the unborn child senses the planet's position directly, this involves the further problem of explaining why they would choose one planet rather than another, and indeed why they would want to do this anyway. After all, on evolutionary grounds it is very hard to see what advantage one birth time would have over another.

If it is difficult to believe in this particular truth of the Gauquelin hypothesis, it is even more difficult to believe that any gravitational effects from the planets can influence terrestrial events. The only even vaguely acceptable kind of hypothesis would seem to involve the magnetic field of the earth, which is influenced by solar activity, which in turn has been shown to be influenced by planetary events. However, such an explanation would run into several difficulties as well:

If the planets exert their influence through the Sun, why does the Sun itself not carry such an influence directly?

If the influence exerted by the planets, either directly or through the intervention of the Sun, is by way of some kind of radiation, why is it that main effects seem to be just after rise and just after culmination? If there was some influence through radiation, one would expect this to increase from rise to culmination in a linear fashion, then perhaps decrease in a linear fashion after culmination.

It is at present impossible to suggest any kind of physical link between planetary position and terrestrial effects, in spite of the fact that many physicists and astronomers have tried to do this, often using quantum mechanics and its laws as intermediaries.

Critics have often stated that, in the absence of a good theory, the results are unacceptable even though they might be correctly reported. This is not a rational position. We have no agreed theory of gravitation even now – Einstein's field theory involving distortion of space-time geometry, and quantum mechanics theories regarding particle interaction are still fighting it out. Newton certainly had no proper theory of gravitation when he published his fundamental work on the topic, his notion of 'action at a distance' being heavily criticized by other physicists, and even appearing contradictory to himself. If at the beginning of studying a phenomenon we needed a proper theory of it, science would never be able to get started. This is not a reasonable criticism, and we must await the emergence of a theory when we know far more about the phenomena than we do at present. Does the research of the Gauquelins actually support astrology? Astrologers divide the circle described by the planets into 12 'houses', just as the Gauquelins divide it into 12 sectors. These houses are concerned with different aspects of life; thus house No 1 deals with personality, 2 with possessions, 3 with mental interests, 4 with the home, and so forth. Unfortunately for astrology, however, the relevant 'house' does not coincide with the plus sectors of the Gauquelins; to provide proof for astrology, the crucial sector should be before rather than after the planet has risen! Thus if anything the Gauquelins have disproved this particular astrological hypothesis.

On the other hand it might be said that the particular personality traits associated with Mars, Jupiter, Saturn, Venus and the Moon are roughly what ancient astrology would have predicted, and this is certainly true. However, this is hardly enough to consider the research of the Gauquelins to have 'verified' astrology, this being the only relationship which agrees in any way with astrological prediction. I think what we might see is that the work of the Gauquelins does not herald the vindication of astrology, but rather its end, and the beginning of a new science of cosmobiology. To refer to the work of the Gauquelins as 'astrology' merely puts off scientific observers, and makes it more difficult for their work to be accepted. As a new start in cosmobiology, the climate of opinion may be somewhat fairer to their claims.

Is the work of the Gauquelins the only reason for believing that the new science of cosmobiology may be in the process of developing? There is at least one other large-scale effort to provide evidence for the relationship between terrestrial events and extra-terrestrial activities. The fundamental observations and theoretical formulations are due to the Russian historian, A. L. Chizhevsky, a near-genius in many fields, who in the early part of this century began looking for cycles in world events and trying to relate them to the sunspot cycle. He collected data from 72 countries going back to 600 BC, covering not only wars but social upheavals such as mass migrations, revolutions and epidemics.

Until recently this work, which suggested that wars and other upheavals were more frequent during periods of sunspot activity, whereas cultural events, such as the production of famous books, dramas, pictures and musical compositions were more frequent in periods of absence of solar activity, has been disregarded. Chizhevsky was poorly rewarded for his efforts, being sent to Siberia by Stalin, apparently for suggesting that it was the Sun rather than the doctrines of dialectical materialism that lay behind the great upheavals in history, and though he was finally released when Khrushchev came to power, he died soon afterwards.

Chizhevsky's work, like that of the Gauquelins, was studied very carefully by Professor Ertel, who carried out many additional analyses, extending it from the European continent to other cultures, like the Islamic, the Chinese and the Japanese. He in fact wrote a book on the topic (which unfortunately failed to find a publisher). He showed me the manuscript on the occasion of a lecture of mine given in his department, and I was so fascinated by it that I spent most of the night reading it. Ertel is a very careful, objective worker. He went to incredible lengths in objectifying his recording of wars, revolutions, migrations, and literary, musical and other cultural achievements, and found abundant evidence for the truth of Chizhevsky's theory.

I hope I have said enough in this chapter to demonstrate that my provisional and conditional belief in parapsychological phenomena and cosmobiological ones is not the product of senescent credulity, but is based on certain facts which critics have been unable to disprove. Personally I would be much happier if there were *no* parapsychological phenomena, if the planets could be demonstrated to have no influence on human affairs, and if sunspots kindly agreed not to produce wars, revolutions and mass migrations. But to me facts are facts, and you cannot dismiss them arbitrarily on the basis of how you would like things to be. The Gauquelins, Ertel, Chizhevsky and others are making a very important contribution to our picture of the world; I could only wish that their reward would be commensurate with their efforts!

To end this chapter, it may be interesting to test the accuracy of traditional astrology, and that of the Gauquelins' work, in relation to my own horoscope. Doctors Nias and Dean, in a chapter in their book *Hans Eysenck: Consensus and Controversy*, dealing with my work on astrology, have presented my astrological birth chart, which is given in Figure 7.8 and have analysed it. This is what they find:

The inner and outer rings show the Signs of the Zodiac. The middle ring shows the planets and Placidus houses, with Gauquelin's five significant planets identified by abbreviations. The chart is calculated for 5 a.m. (4 a.m. GMT) 4 March 1916 at Berlin (data from Eysenck's birth certificate). Eysenck is precisely the kind of eminent scientist for whom Gauquelin observed significant planetary effects.

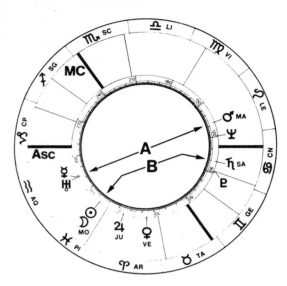

FIG. 7.8   *Astrological birth chart of Hans Eysenck.*

So to what extent does Eysenck's birth chart support the claims of Gauquelin and astrology?

To find out, we first searched Gibson's (1981) biography of Eysenck and valedictory articles (Bethlem and Maudsley Gazette, Spring 1983) for descriptions of Eysenck's personality. The result was over fifty short statements of two to twelve words each, which were then sorted into clusters according to their common meaning. The main clusters, with number of contributing statements in brackets, were as follows: quiet and reserved (7); placid, rarely gets upset (6); helpful, easy to get on with (8); self-willed (6); very self-confident (9); determined, provokes confrontation (12). In short a strong-minded, stable introvert. Gibson points out that Eysenck's quiet, soft-spoken personal manner is nothing like his public image of extreme tough-mindedness.

How does this compare with Gauquelin's findings? Gauquelin found that at the birth of eminent scientists and introverts Saturn tended to occupy the houses shown shaded, and to a lesser extent the opposite houses, while Jupiter (characteristic of extraverts and actors) tended to avoid these positions in favour of intermediate positions. Because the chart is drawn in terms of space, the houses differ in size, whereas in terms of time (which is the viewpoint involved here) they are equal. When this distortion is allowed for,

Eysenck's chart is clearly in agreement with both findings. The probability of this arising by chance is about one in ten.

In view of Eysenck's prodigious writings it is interesting that the moon (characteristic of imaginative writers) is not emphasized. However, Eysenck has told us that he is no good at *imaginative* writing and poetry, in which case there is no conflict with Gauquelin's findings.

In astrological terms the chart has a Pisces sun and moon, a Capricorn ascendent, and is dominated by the two configurations marked A and B. A is a close conjunction between Mercury and Uranus that is opposed to Mars, indicating self-will and outspokenness. B is an unusually exact (to the minute) conjunction between the sun and moon that is trine to Saturn, indicating reserve and self-control. At first sight this appears to be an uncanny match to the contrasting public and personal sides mentioned by Gibson. However, if as a control we take the exactly opposite personality, namely loud, outgoing, easily upset, submissive and lacking in confidence, inspection of astrology textbooks shows that the first three traits are exactly matched by A, and the rest by B – especially as the sun and moon are in Pisces, indicating sensitivity and passivity. Therefore, Eysenck's chart reveals little about traditional astrology other than its ability to describe almost anything in retrospect!

This provides a good ending to the chapter. Deductions from the Gauquelins are spot on; deductions from traditional astrology depend completely on interpretation, they may either be spot on or wildly off. It does not, of course, prove anything whatsoever, but in an autobiography such speculation may not be entirely out of place.

CHAPTER 8

Does Age Bring Wisdom?

There is always the one who observes, but that one has no emotions.

Diderot

At this writing, I am seventy-three years old, having retired as an unwilling victim of *agism* at sixty-seven. Would Shakespeare's words describe my situation – 'second childishness, and mere oblivion, sans teeth, sans eyes, sans taste, sans everything!'? Not really – I still have all my teeth, a full head of hair, my memory is intact, as are my taste buds – admittedly I have to wear glasses, but with them vision is all right! More hopeful has been Paul Baltes, famous for his researches into old age; according to him there is the promise of 'wisdom' as one approaches seventy. Alas! I have found little evidence of such an accretion of wisdom – my mind seems to be working much the same as always, no better and no worse! Bodily too I may have slowed down somewhat, but I still play tennis or squash every day, go for long walks, and feel reasonably robust.

If wisdom consists of asking searching philosophical questions about the meaning of life, why we are here, or a future existence in heaven or hell, I have to pass. These questions seem to me meaningless, and certainly unreasonable. Heine, the great German poet (disowned by Hitler because he was Jewish) was a well-known atheist. When he was lying on his death-bed a priest visited him and adjured him to seek forgiveness from God, who would surely grant it. *'Dieu me pardonnera. C'est son metier!'* said Heine, and expired. I trust I, too, will disregard the temptations of religion on my deathbed. Thoughts of death certainly become more insistent as one gets older. The deaths of members of a former generation, Cyril Burt and Aubrey Lewis say, do not come unexpected, but nevertheless touch a chord when they have formed an important part of one's professional life. So also with former friends like Thurstone, Luria, Kohler, Guilford, Vernon and many others. Their deaths are foreseeable, and hence seem part of the nature of things. The same applies to the deaths of my father and mother, but of course the feelings they arouse are much stronger – I still remember seeing my mother on her deathbed, still and calm, her famous beauty all wrinkled in the rictus of death. . . . Such moments are unforgettable, but at ninety-four death may be a release from an existence that has inevitably narrowed possibilities to a point where life may be more a burden than a pleasure.

It is when one's former students and colleagues die that one begins to wonder. The deaths of Gwynne Jones and Hilde Himmelweit, for instance, touched me deeply; they were too young to die.

More subtle differences come with age. Retirement is only one of them. It seems to me outrageous for the State to force people to retire at a given age, for no obvious reason. It will surely not be suggested that at the age of sixty-five a professor necessarily becomes senile, and loses his ability to teach and do research? Judges continue into their seventies, and Churchill was made Prime Minister for the first time at sixty-five! People should have a choice to retire at a given age, say sixty, or to carry on until they are not fit to continue either mentally or physically. I was lucky to have a successor who agreed to my continuing to do research in his department, and to find grant-giving bodies willing to support this research; suddenly to be condemned to doing nothing, after a long life of hard work, would be a sentence of death to me.

A more welcome transition has been that from 'Dad' to 'Grandad'. Sybil and I were both only children, and we have regretted very much the absence of any brothers or sisters, and the destruction of family life due to the divorces of our parents. We were determined to avoid the 'only child' status for our children. Michael was the first to marry, choosing for his wife Christine, also a psychologist who has published with him. They have three children, Fleur, William and Juliet, the oldest now around eleven.

Gary, the oldest of the children of my second marriage, did advanced research in Electronic Engineering, a subject in which he got a First-Class Degree; he is now working as a high-class computer specialist, and married Lilly, a Yugoslav computer specialist who proved highly compatible; they have one child, Heidi, who is precocious and bright.

Kevin, who is also working in computers, married Gill at a very young age; despite the notion that to marry young is to court disaster, they are exceptionally happy, and have two lovely boys, Damien and Raymond.

Connie married Didier in Washington, a man of dual French and Swiss nationality, who is working on the production side of television. He is also an outstanding sportsman, excelling at football, skiing and tennis. They have a son, Adrien, so that to date there are seven grandchildren with an age range of twelve years. Darrin, also working as a computer programmer, has not managed to get hitched yet, but in due course no doubt he too will contribute to this avalanche of babies.

One of the prime duties of a professor of psychology in a post-graduate department must of course be the production of large numbers of outstanding students who go into the world and accomplish something – preferably in psychology! I have had roughly 180 Ph.D. students pass through my department, and feel great pride in their achievements, the researches they have done, the positions they have reached, the honours they have received. Even the renegades and apostates who fled from science into the bosom of the psychoanalytic church, like S. Crown and J. Sandler, have made their marks – the former as editor of the *British Journal of Medical Psychology*, the latter as editor of the *International Journal of Psychoanalysis*, and Professor of Psychoanalysis at University College. A good training helps even those least willing to benefit from it!

For a long time our course was international – British students were in a minority, until the Government in its wisdom made it practically impossible for any foreigner who did not happen to be a millionaire to study at a British university. We had Germans, Poles, North Americans, South Americans, Canadians, Australians, Icelanders, Greeks, Spaniards – you name them, we had them! It was a great source of pride to me that the department was so international in its composition – science must transcend narrow nationalism if it wants to live.

I still have a warm feeling for the large number of Indian, Bangladeshi and other coloured (if that is the right word?) students who one and all succeeded in transplanting some of their teaching to foreign shores, usually as Professors and Heads of Departments.

Some of the research done by my former students is intriguing, to say the least. One of them studied the sexual habits of monkeys in India, and found that the closer to the centre of a large city the monkeys lived, the more perverse were their performances! It is difficult to formulate a theory to account for this – perhaps the more extraverted the monkey, the closer he will come to the centre of things, and also, imitating humans, the more perverse will be his sexual habits!

Some students stand out in my memory, but that does not mean that others not here named did not achieve as much, or more. One student whom none of us is likely to forget was a typical psychopath, but a very bright one – he presented an admirable thesis for his Ph.D., and I had taken great care to supervise every detail of it, to make quite sure there was no hanky-panky! He usually turned up with alcoholic fumes surrounding him like a halo, often with the marks of pub brawls on his face.

I received a letter from California, where a research group was considering hiring him to carry out some research into the psychology of prisoners. I wrote back telling them quite frankly that he was not suited to such a job, unsupervised as it would be, but typically they hired him all the same. His job was to go to the prison, interview selected prisoners, and fill in a form for each which would then be entered into a computer. The computer girl noticed that all his forms were completed according to one of three different sets of answers. To cut a long story short, he had never interviewed a single prisoner, and had simply filled in the forms while sitting drinking in a singles bar!

After he was fired, the librarian came to the Head of Department and complained that our friend had out a large number of books which he refused to return. After a lot of to-ing and fro-ing, he was offered a very substantial severance fee in return for giving back the books. All seemed to be in order when the librarian again came to see the Head, white-faced and furious. It appeared that before returning the books our friend had carefully cut out the insides, only leaving a narrow border of pages which he had glued together! By the time this was discovered he had of course disappeared. I do not count him one of my successes, but he will certainly be long remembered, longer perhaps than some more deserving students who behaved irreproachably!

But I also had other, less psychopathic students. A number have achieved international recognition, many more national acclaim; I count many of them my friends. They tend to fall into subject groups or classes, the largest being that concerned with behaviour therapy. We have here a very obvious generation gap, with three generations making their appearance. The original stalwarts who helped me found clinical psychology in the UK were M. Shapiro, Gwynne Jones, R. Payne, A. Yates, M. Israel and S. Rachman. J. Tizzard, A. Heron, N. O'Connor, and Alan and Anne Clarke did similar pioneering work in Mental Deficiency and other topics in the Social Psychiatry Unit financed at the Institute by the Medical Research Council.

The next generation would contain people like M. Berger, D. Kendrick, G. Claridge, Anne Broadhurst, R. Beech, V. Meyer, J. Inglis, D. Bannister, E. Poser, H. Brengelmann (who introduced behaviour therapy into Germany), Cyril and Violet Franks (who did much to introduce the topic in the USA), A. Arthur, Ron Ramsey (who later introduced behaviour therapy in the Netherlands), J. Humphrey (who performed a similar service in Australia), P. McLean (who did the same in Canada), M. Herbert, A. R. Dabbs, P. Feldman, and many others. Then there is a third generation, represented by people like Tony

Gibson, I. M. W. Evans, R. Hallam, J. Teasdale, A. M. Mathews, R. Hodgson, P. Slade, J. Marzillier, Fraser N. Watts, G. Powell, D. Hemsley, W. Yule, etc., etc., etc. Anyone familiar with British clinical psychology will realize how influential this group has been, and continues to be. Those who left the UK were equally influential in introducing or at least advancing behaviour therapy in the USA, Canada, Australia, Germany, and elsewhere. A brave band of brothers, even though they often disagreed with me on theoretical grounds!

The other groups are inevitably smaller, if only because there is far more financial support for clinical than for purely experimental studies. In psychophysiology we had P. Venables and I. Martin, who practically founded the study of that discipline in the United Kingdom, through their textbook, their own researches, and their students. Animal research owes much to P. Broadhurst, J. Gray, J. Keehn, J. Williams, J. Joffe and H. Holland. We also had a small group in the behaviour genetics field, with D. Fulker at the head, and M. Neale, R. Blizzard and others as his students. In statistics, we had A. Lubin, P. Slater, Owen White, A. E. Maxwell, A. Jonckhere and P. Barrett. More generally, in various areas of personality, intelligence and experimental research in its widest sense, we had H. Himmelweit and A. Petrie, my earliest research assistants; J. Easterbrook, D. Furneaux, F. Farley, C. Frith, K. O'Connor, R. Passingham, G. Wilson, D. Nias, R. Willett, E. and A. Hendrickson, J. Allsop, and many others who will be known to most psychologists interested in their particular areas of work.

An interesting question arises. Clearly our students have been very successful scientifically, and very productive. As shown in a previous chapter, almost a third of the British psychologists with 60 or more citations in the 1985 Social Sciences Citation Index are members of the Eysenck family or former students! This list does not include many former students who are working in the USA, Canada, Australia, Germany, Japan and other countries; these too have had an enviable record of scholastic success. All in all, about one in three of my students has become a full professor; another one in three has achieved academic status, or a leading position in clinical psychology. For the rest, many have gone into industrial psychology, public relations, advertising or business generally; they too have done very well, particularly financially! I can hardly think of even one failure – the psychopathic individual I mentioned in passing managed to marry an heiress, which must count as some kind of achievement!

Is this high rate of success due in some degree to the methods of teaching I introduced, or is it entirely due to the quality of the students, already apparent when joining the department? The quality of the students was no different from that shown by students in other psychology departments; if anything it was probably lower. In England, the best academically are drawn to Oxford and Cambridge; others to long-established schools, like London's University College. Existing schools tend to retain their best students for Ph.D. work, leaving only the less able to go elsewhere. Altogether, good students seldom go to newly-established, untried departments, run by controversial and distinctly non-establishment, non-conformist types like myself.

I would like to think that the way I organized the department and its teaching had something to do with the success of my students, but formal scientific proof is impossible – we can never know how they might have fared at some other university.

Retirement does lead one to wonder what one's life-work has achieved, and whether it was really worth while. After all, I have put fifty years of unremitting labour into psychological research and teaching. What has been the result – for me personally, for my department and students, and for psychology as a whole? I could give a subjective answer, but it seemed preferable to look for some more factual evidence. The best sources are the Science Citation Index and the Social Sciences Citation Index, which review the great majority of journals in their respective fields, and list the number of times any particular author has been quoted in articles appearing in leading scientific journals. The argument is that the influence of someone's work is indicated by the number of fellow-scientists who read it, and regard it as important enough to cite. It is not a perfect index of scientific eminence, but it has been shown to be valid in many ways; thus Nobel prize-winners tend to have high counts (even before the award) as have members of the Royal Society, the American Academy of Sciences, and other highly regarded scientific organizations. Citation counts can also be made for whole departments, as a help in assessing the impact of research done by these departments, or for journals, to determine their influence.

Let me begin with a study by Eugene Garfield, the man chiefly responsible for the Citation Index, who published in 1977 a list of the 250 most-cited scientific authors from 1961 to 1975. This is international, of course, and lists authors in all the major sciences, physics, chemistry, physiology, medicine, and so forth. I am included with the respectable total of 5,241 citations, easily beaten by people like L. Pauling, with 15,662 references, Gell-Mann with 9,669, or M. Born with 9,206. In this glittering list, which includes forty-two Nobel prize-winners, I came about in the middle – not too bad considering that I was only in my forties when the period in question started; since then my rate of citations has more than doubled. It must also be remembered that there are far more journals of chemistry and physics than there are of psychology, and that these figures come from the *Science* Citation Index, not the *Social Sciences*

Citation Index. There was only one other living psychologist in this group, who came out rather lower; Freud, however, came out ahead of me.

In 1978 the *American Psychologist* published a table of the hundred most cited psychologists in the 1975 Social Sciences Citation Index in which I came fifth, with Freud and Piaget leading the field. No. 3 was P. J. Winer, there because he had written a fairly elementary textbook of psychological statistics which was frequently quoted; No. 4 was A. Bandura. The list includes B.F. Skinner at No. 8, R. B. Cattell at No. 11, J. P. Guilford at No. 12, C. R. Rogers at No. 13, L. J. Cronbach at No. 17, and so on.

In another publication, Eugene Garfield again lists the hundred most cited authors in the *social sciences*, for the period 1969 to 1977. This time I managed to head the list of living psychologists, with an average citation score of 597, just ahead of Bandura (561). (In 1988 I managed to score 755 citations.) Outside psychology, or among the dead, there are a number of interesting features. Marx scored 756; Lenin 247. Chomsky scored 519, but Jung had to be content with 191. Freud with 1,369 and Piaget with 841 head the list of 'deceased' psychologists.

So much then for an objective assessment of my work over the past fifty years. High visibility, much output, a large body of citations – not unsatisfactory as a whole, but am I likely to overtake Freud in this race? If I do I'll add the figures in the second edition of this autobiography, if ever one is called for!

How about the journals I started, and have edited for a long time, or am still editing? Here we normally use an *impact factor* score, which is the mean number of citations per article published. (This tends to work against journals like mine which have a special section of 'Notes and Shorter Communications'; these are not proper lengthy contributions but present a small experiment which is of interest to specialized audiences. They reduce the ratio of mean citations per article, compared with the majority of journals not having such a section. However, we must take the statistics as we find them.) According to the 1974 Science Citation Index, the journal I edited, *Behaviour Research and Therapy* (BRAT), had an impact factor of 1.02, identical with the *Journal of Abnormal Psychology* and ahead of the *Journal of Personality and Social Psychology*, which had an impact factor of .96, the *Journal of Clinical Psychology* with an impact factor of .72, *Behaviour Therapy* with a factor of .69, the *Journal of Educational Psychology* (.66), the *Journal of Applied Behaviour Analysis* (.59), the *British Journal of Social and Clinical Psychology* (.59), the *British Journal of Medical Psychology* (.42) and the *Journal of Clinical Psychology* (.37).

It was thus ahead of all other journals in this field, although it had only been in existence for ten years and was competing against journals established over a longer period as official journals of the American Psychological Association and the British Psychological Society.

When we look at the 1987 figures from the Social Sciences Citation Index, we find that the impact factor for *Behaviour Research and Therapy* is 1.47, compared with 1.18 for the *British Journal of Clinical Psychology* and 0.74 for the *British Journal of Medical Psychology*. *Advances in Behaviour Research and Therapy*, the Monograph section of BRAT, has an impact factor 1.10. Of the journals ranked above that, three are medical, one is a popular journal, and only three are psychological – the *Journal of Abnormal Psychology* (2.34), the *Journal of Consulting and Clinical Psychology* (2.05) and *Behaviour Therapy* (1.99). Sixty-four psychiatric journals are ranked below BRAT, and 38 psychological ones. We may conclude that BRAT is among the leaders in this field.

When I was appointed by Aubrey Lewis to head the new Department of Psychology in the Institute, I promised him three things. I said I would get the profession of clinical psychology established in the United Kingdom; I promised him to make our department the best in the country, if not in Europe; and I promised to give our research students the best training in the country. Let us now consider the position of the department from the point of view of research.

I give here a table (8) listing the top twenty-five British Departments of Psychology, both for total citations and total number of publications, based on the 1975 SCC Index, summing citations each Department of Psychology member received. I have deviated in one respect from the published figures, by subtracting those for J. Bruner from those summed for Oxford University, because all the citations to Bruner's work were related to his American studies, and none to the short period he spent at Oxford; it would be absurd to regard him as an Oxford scholar.

So much for fifty years of work – success and satisfaction, combined with considerable visibility, certainly. But has psychology really developed in the direction I would like it to go? Has it come to be used by society in the way I would like it to be used? Has research progressed along the lines I would like to see it progress? These are questions which are much more difficult to answer, and I think here one would be rather less inclined to be optimistic.

There have been certain changes in the right direction, although progress has been rather slow.

When I began to emphasize the importance of genetic factors in intelligence and personality, and supported Jensen's suggestion that we should at least consider the possibility that national and racial differences might in part be due to genetic factors, the *Zeitgeist* was unalterably opposed to these views, except for experts in behaviour genetics who had the background necessary to understand the

		Total:
	Citations	Publications
(1) Institute of Psychiatry	886	62
(2) Oxford	524	31
(3) Sussex (Exp., Sociol. & Develop.)	303	27
(4) Bristol	189	19
(5) Birmingham	174	17
(6) Edinburgh	136	12
(7) Keele	134	17
(8) Strathclyde	122	11
(9) Stirling	119	8
(10) Aberdeen	115	26
(11) Cambridge	115	13
(12) University College: London	92	10
(13) Sheffield	84	13
(14) York	80	9
(15) Cardiff	79	18
(16) Exeter	79	12
(17) Reading	77	13
(18) Aston	74	7
(19) Dundee	71	14
(20) Birkbeck Coll: London	64	16
(21) Swansea	62	12
(22) Durham	58	9
(23) Inst. of Education: London	58	12
(24) London S. of Economics	53	7
(25) Nottingham	53	19
Remaining 24 Departments: Average	35	6

TABLE 8   *Citations earned and publications recorded in 49 British Departments of Psychology*

methodology and complex statistical treatment of genetic data. The media have maintained this opposition, and have succeeded in persuading the great majority of readers that people like Jensen, Herrnstein and myself, who stress the importance of genetic factors in these areas, are mavericks deviating from the majority of experts in directions which are socially divisive, dangerous and possibly racist. But what are the facts?

The primary source of evidence here is a book published in 1988 by Mark Snyderman and Stanley Rothman, entitled *The IQ Controversy: the Media and Public Policy*. The authors sent questionnaires asking detailed questions about many aspects of intelligence, its importance and relevance, its measurement, the contribution of genetics, racial differences, etc. to a large group of experts. These included members of the American Educational Research Association, the National Council of Measurement and Education, and members of different sections of the American Psychological Association concerned with developmental psychology, educational psychology, evaluation and measurement, and school psychology. They also questioned members of the American Sociological Association concerned with education, members of the Behavior Genetics Association, the Cognitive Science Society, psychologists concerned with counselling, and psychologists concerned with industrial and organizational psychology. Six hundred and sixty-one scientists completed the questionnaires which were then analysed in detail. What was the general consensus? 'On the whole, scholars with any expertise in the area of intelligence and intelligence-testing (defined very broadly) share a common view of the most important components of intelligence, and are convinced that it can be measured with some degree of accuracy. An overwhelming majority also believe that individual genetic inheritance contributes to variations in IQ within the white community, and a smaller majority expresses the same view about the black-white and SES (socio-economic status) differences in IQ. In other words, the relevant scientific community endorsed views I have expressed over the years.

Why then the discrepancy between the actual views of psychologists about these questions, and the views attributed to them by the media? Snyderman and Rothman have carried out a detailed analysis of 'what the papers say', and have arrived at some definite conclusions.

Our work demonstrates that, by any reasonable standard, media coverage of the IQ controversy has been quite inaccurate. Journalists have emphasized controversy; they have reported scientific discussions of technical issues erroneously and they have clearly misreported the views of the relevant scientific community as to the interaction between genetic and environmental factors in explaining differences in IQ among individuals and between groups. One would be forced to conclude from reading the newspapers and news magazines and watching television that only a few maverick 'experts' support the view that genetic variation plays a significant role in individual or group differences, while the vast majority of experts believe that such differences are purely the result of environmental factors. One would also conclude that intelligence and aptitude tests are hopelessly biased against minorities and the poor.

What Snyderman and Rothman say about American media can be equally well documented for British (and German, and French, etc.) newspapers and television. The distortions presented by the media are particularly noticeable when books on intelligence are being reviewed. With great regularity such reviews are handed over to people who have no status within the relevant fields of educational psychology, developmental psychology, behaviour genetics, etc., and who, inevitably, fail to understand all the issues involved.

Perhaps the fairest summary of the present position is that while scientific majorities support the views I have held and expressed, media politicians and intellectuals generally still neglect the facts, and cling to environmentalist hopes and illusions. But slowly the *Zeitgeist* is changing.

How about behaviour therapy? Here there are both pluses and minuses. Behaviour therapy is certainly now practically universally accepted as a valuable method of treatment, and is widely taught and practised. On the other hand, I was hoping that behaviour therapists would be scientist-clinicians – i.e., trying to combine the role of the scientist who keeps abreast of modern developments, who carries out research, and who tries to model his practice on what he has learned, with the role of the clinician who routinely treats patients. This has not happened; instead, we have a large group of practitioners who pay little attention to new developments, who do not read the relevant scientific journals, who disregard the need for demonstrating the efficacy of the methods they use, and who frequently combine arbitrarily different and often contradictory theories and methods.

Indeed, they have rather followed the psychiatric model which I originally criticized for failing to evaluate scientific evidence. This is certainly not what I intended clinical psychology to be. The only bright spot is that this mish-mash of methods now includes very prominently behavioural methods, and hence is likely to be more effective in the treatment of psychological disorders.

Perhaps what I was hoping for is in fact impossible. Clinical work is a full-time occupation, and it may be unrealistic to expect people engaged in it to spend a large amount of time reading the literature, assessing new methods of treatment, and new theories, and incorporating these in their practice. I have suggested the possibility of having an intermediary group with a foot in both camps, telling the theorists what the practical concerns of the practitioners are, and telling the practitioners about the most recent developments in theory and experiment, as happens in physics.

How about the smoking controversy? Here I can hardly claim any success at all. There is still, both in the medical profession and in the media, an hysterical denunciation of smoking, attributing to it all the ills of this world, and a complete failure to recognize the complexity of the issues, and the synergistic way in which risk factors like smoking, drinking, cholesterol, heredity, stress, atmospheric pollution and personality interact. It is popular to concentrate on a single enemy who is responsible for all our ills. Hitler found such an enemy in the Jew; the Ku Klux Klan found such an enemy in the negro; modern left-wingers find him in the 'racist'; and the medical profession finds him in the unlikely shape of the cigarette. Once the enemy is identified in this unequivocal fashion, reason flies out of the window, and no one is willing to listen to scientific evidence. But to say so, and to try to get the debates on a more scientific level, is certainly not popular. As George Orwell said: 'If liberty means anything at all, it means the right to tell people what they do not want to hear.'

It is difficult for reasonable, ordinary people to conceive of the hatred which can be aroused in the hypothetically quiet, rational, logical breast of the scientist by anyone who dares to doubt his *obiter dicta*. As the psychologist they 'most love to hate' (the title of an article on me in the *New Scientist*), I have been at the receiving end of such feelings too often to have any doubts myself about the violent emotions that scientific controversy can engender. For example, consider the following story:

A friend of mine was asked to review a book of mine for an APA journal. He wrote a moderately favourable review; this was returned to him by the editor (who had never questioned earlier reviews he had written), pointing out that surely he had realized that this book was by H. J. Eysenck, who had thrown doubt on the efficacy of psychotherapy; did he not think a favourable review was inappropriate? My friend declined to change his review, but it failed to appear in the journal. Another friend happened to meet the editor, and having heard about the review asked him when it was due to appear – 'I am proud to say,' said the editor, 'that I decided to kill this review of Eysenck's book!' The review never appeared.

Another example. A friend and colleague mentioned to a TV producer the then novel techniques of behaviour therapy, and interested him in presenting a one-hour documentary programme on this subject. He had it all worked out and was ready to start; all that was needed was the OK of his (American) boss. When my friend mentioned this to me I said: 'I bet the boss has been psychoanalysed, and will turn it down.' My friend clearly thought I was paranoid, but after a week he told me what happened when the producer met his boss. At first the boss was favourable, but when the producer mentioned my name, he shouted furiously: 'What – the anti-Christ himself? I'll have no such programme in my schedule!' He refused to even go on discussing it, and there was no programme on behaviour therapy on TV!

Although I have been portrayed as extremist on many issues, I feel I have always been an apostle of moderation and an opponent of extremes. In relation to genetics, for instance, I have always eschewed the extremes of 100 per cent environmentalism, but also the opposite extreme of attributing everything to heredity. In all my research I have stressed that nature and nurture always interact and that our task in any special situation is to discover what contribution to phenotypic behaviour is made by additive genetic factors, assortative mating, dominance and other genetic factors on the one hand, and by between family and within family environmental factors on the other. In other words, the problem is not one of either-or, but of quantitative assessments of the contribution of different factors.

With respect to the smoking controversy, although I have criticized extremists who blame cigarette smoking for everything, I have never gone to the other extreme of denying the possibility that cigarette smoking may be a potent risk factor for cancer, coronary heart disease and other disorders.

With respect to IQ, too, I believe that IQ measures are important predictors of educational success, and do measure many aspects of intelligence very successfully, and I cannot therefore agree with those who advocate whole-hearted rejection of all IQ measurements. I do not either fail to see the difficulties and problems which are raised by IQ measurement, or disregard the criticisms to which it is subject. Again, it is not a question of either-or, but a quantitative assessment of the accuracy of prediction made possible by IQ testing.

With respect to personality, I have already explained my rejection of the either-or position taken by many experimental psychologists, and by many advocates of individual difference approaches, each exalting the contribution of one side, and deprecating that of the other. Both, to me, are equally vital, and most important is the integration of their efforts to produce a truly scientific psychology.

What I have said so far is equally applicable to my political attitudes. I strongly believe that both an extreme socialist and an extreme capitalist position are indefensible. Full-blown socialism, as advocated in Clause 4 of the Labour Party Constitution (which advocates public ownership of industry), is bound to lead to inefficiency, poverty and dictatorship. Full-blown capitalism, relying entirely on market forces, would lead to many of the evil consequences predicted by Marx, if not countered by Trades Union organizations, and controlled by the Government. It seems obvious to me that a mixed economy is the only workable compromise, so that again we are left, not with an either-or decision, but with a quantitative decision as to the amount of free enterprise, and the amount of government control and intervention.

Does Age Bring Wisdom?

I have been equally critical of governments of the Right or the Left. I have already mentioned my criticisms of the Labour Government's destruction of the British school system; but I am just as critical of the Thatcher Government's destruction of the British university system. The Labour Government's craven surrender to the Trades Union barons is just as equally reprehensible to me as the Thatcher Government's failure to implement a proper transport policy, and support railways and other public bodies concerned with transport. I have never been a member of any political party, for the simple reason that all advocate mixed policies, some good, some bad; such a mixture I do not find attractive!

All politicians, of course, are to my mind tainted with the 'Ko-Ko heresy'! What is the Ko-Ko heresy? Let me introduce it in connection with my attempt to influence social policies.

We can start by asking: Why has psychology been so much less effective and successful than it might have been? One reason must be that research in psychology has always been starved of funds. The kind of money that has gone into physics and astronomy can only make a psychologist gasp – huge installations costing billions are not unusual, and they are serviced by hordes of technicians and scientists, all of the highest calibre. Compared to that the financial support psychologists have for their research amounts to peanuts. For our animal work on genetics of personality, and the principles of behaviour therapy, for example, we should have had a large institute using dogs and monkeys; but had to make do with a very small section using rats. We made the best use possible of our rats, but they were very much a *pis aller*, and when I think what we could have done with the proper animals for our purpose, I can only regret the short-sightedness of governments and universities which keep psychology departments on such a short rein. It is easy to accuse psychologists of not having been more successful but the inevitable answer must be that famous sentence which Churchill used to appeal to the Americans: 'Give us the tools, and we'll finish the job!'

Given this lack of support, we may ask: have I been successful or otherwise in changing views and opinions? On the scientific side, the answer is probably a moderate 'yes'. However, I always had from the beginning the hope that psychological research might be used to improve the human fate, and to find answers to the numerous social problems that beset us. We know enough about physics, chemistry, astronomy and the other hard sciences, including medicine, to make our lives longer, happier, and healthier than could have been dreamed of by our ancestors even a hundred years ago. Our troubles are very largely psychological – i.e., due to 'human nature', unreformed and uncontrolled. Wars and confrontations in international relations;

[271]

starvation and malnourishment over large areas of the earth; political strife, strikes and confrontations on the national scene; pollution, the degradation of the environment, the killing off of whales and many other species; the tremendous increase in drug taking, criminality and aggressiveness; and finally the break-up of the family, the increase in divorces, and of one-parent families – these are all due to human behaviour of some kind or another, and hence must be the concern of psychologists. So of course is the horrendous decline in scholastic achievement, the increase of violence, disobedience and truanting in schools, and the general widespread decline in educational standards. Add the tremendous burden imposed on people by stress, and by neurotic disorders, and we see why Thoreau stated that: 'The mass of men lead lives of quiet desperation.'

To some at least of our problems psychology is already in a position to suggest some answers. In my books on *The Causes and Cures of Neurosis* (with S. Rachman), and *The Causes and Cures of Criminality* (with G. Gudjonsson), I have suggested how the findings of modern psychology can be used to alleviate the evils of neurosis and criminality. Similarly the use of intelligence tests, and selection based upon them, has been shown to improve considerably the chances of bright, but socially deprived children to obtain a decent education, commensurate with their abilities. Equally, it has been shown that using concepts of personality in deciding on methods of teaching for given individuals can greatly improve their motivation and achievement. Prejudice can be tackled and significantly reduced by appropriate psychological methods. There is no limit to the contribution that psychology can make to the reduction of all the social evils I have mentioned. Yet very few people are willing to listen to what psychologists have to say, and our efforts have made little impact on social policies.

The reason for this is the 'Ko-Ko heresy'. I have named it after the High Executioner in Gilbert and Sullivan's *Mikado*. Ko-Ko, although ordered to do so, did not execute Nanki-Poo, the son of the Mikado, but told that blood-thirsty ruler that he had done so, describing the deed in considerable detail.

Suddenly Nanki-Poo appears alive at the Court of the Mikado, and Ko-Ko has to think up an explanation of what happened. For the rest, let me quote the libretto:

KO-KO: Your Majesty, it's like this: It is true that I stated
            that I had killed Nanki-Poo . . .

MIKADO: Yes, with most affecting particulars.

POOH-BAH: Merely corroborative detail intended to give
            artistic verisimilitude to a bald and . . .

KO-KO: *Will* you refrain from putting in your oar? (To
          MIKADO) It's like this: When your Majesty says,
          'Let a thing be done,' it's as good as done –
          practically, it *is* done – because your Majesty's
          will is law. Your Majesty says, 'Kill a gentleman,'
          and a gentleman is towed off to be killed.
          Consequently, that gentleman is as good as dead
          – practically, he *is* dead – and if he is dead, why
          not say so?

MIKADO: I see. Nothing could possibly be more
          satisfactory!

For the Mikado, nothing could be more satisfactory, but the point remains that what he ordered to be done, what he thinks was done, was in fact not done. This is the Ko-Ko heresy, widespread in politics, in the sense that what our rulers order to be done, they think has in fact been done, although quite often it is not done at all. For example, consider the decision made by Parliament to reduce the number of psychiatric beds, and establish the patients in the community. The community was supposed to create half-way house facilities which would take care of these former patients, and gradually introduce them to the community.

The number of hospital beds was indeed significantly reduced, but the hypothetical half-way house facilities were not in fact created, so that former patients now sleep rough, commit many crimes, and often end up in prison. When their attention is drawn to this those responsible adopt the Ko-Ko argument – it was ordered by Parliament, accordingly it must have happened, and any further responsibility is declined.

Psychological experiments have amply demonstrated that people only learn by looking at the consequences of their actions (known technically as K.R. or knowledge of results). The failure of politicians – as well as judges, educators, civil servants, parole officers and teachers – to show much interest in the results of their activities would seem to account for their inability to learn from their mistakes. The Ko-Ko heresy rules supreme, and while it does no progress is likely.

What can be done about it? We should have a group of social scientists, independent of government or civil service interference, whose task would be to use the most relevant and up-to-date scientific methodology to investigate the *consequences* of ministerial activities, and report on them. Such reports would have to be public, not reserved for the minister himself who would certainly kill it if it reflected adversely on his brainchildren. Imagine the impact of such a report on the effects of comprehensive schooling, or the Crown Prosecution Service . . . But of

[273]

course this is an ideal solution to a very real problem – the powers-that-be would never agree to expose themselves to such scrutiny.

What seems to be true of my professional image, namely that there is a marked contradiction between image and reality, is probably also true of my private image. Gibson, in his biography, has documented this quite well, and as the outsider is in a better position to judge such things than the person concerned, I will quote him directly. Thus he suggests that some students and colleagues find me a 'frightening figure'. He says: 'The paradox of his personality is that outsiders who hear him on the public platform or read his books, sometimes gain the impression that he must indeed be a holy terror to work with. In fact the man one meets at the Maudsley is nothing like his public image, but rather retiring and easy-going. Or perhaps one should say, easy-going, but of considerable cussedness on many issues.'

On another point, Gibson makes an interesting contrast, when he says that: 'Freud, with his indomitable will, never backed down when a confrontation was brewing, but he often gave signs of suffering agonies in conflicts; Eysenck gives the impression that he positively relishes a fight and goes out of his way to provoke confrontation.' This is a widespread view, but I think it is mistaken, as far as I am concerned. I quite enjoy a fair fight in the ring, under Queensberry rules, and I quite enjoy a debate on scientific issues, fairly conducted between knowledge-able people. Of course I would prefer it if others accepted my theories, but knowing that at best these would be only partially true, and needed much improvement, benevolent criticism, debate and suggestions of alternative hypotheses are all welcome. Such 'controversy' I enjoy.

What I dislike most emphatically, on the other hand, is the kind of street-fighting, no holds barred, that I encountered in the Hitler years, and the rather similar attacks I encountered from psychoanalyists, the cancer mafia, the anti-racist industry, and other groups I have mentioned in previous chapters. These groups went out of their way to disregard the adage that attacks should be directed at the issue in question, not the person! Such confrontation I can do without, and to imagine that I 'positively relish' such a fight, and go out of my way to 'provoke confrontation' in this connection is absurd. Who would want to be attacked bodily by a crowd of militants, be howled down by hundreds of extremists, have things thrown at one by irate leftists, or be pursued over the roofs by a baying multitude of yobbos out for one's blood? Who would want to be called a 'racist', or a bought tool of the cigarette industry, or a believer in astrology and other absurdities?

Why then did I say what I had to say, write what I had to write? I did not go into exile idly as a protest (among other things) against censorship;

freedom of speech is for me a necessity without which I cannot live. It is easy to give in to pressures and not to say things which are unpopular, to keep silent when you know that orthodoxy is wrong, to keep your head down when others who dare to speak the truth are viciously attacked. But to do this is to sell out to enemies of freedom; it is to succumb to that 'civil cowardice' which toppled the Weimar Republic, and let in the Nazis. To give way is to sell the pass, and that I am not willing to do. I did not enter into these battles light-heartedly, and I emphatically do not enjoy this kind of confrontation. For me it is a duty that cannot be shunned, however much I might like to do just that. If I did I could no longer live with myself; that and that alone is the reason why I have battled so hard in the past, and go on battling. It does not make for popularity – but then there are more important things than popularity!

How does all this accord with my position on the various personality dimensions I have described in Chapter 6? Reasonably well, I should think. On questionnaires I come out as very stable, and I think I could not have done what I have done had it been otherwise. Of course all this carries a penalty; a lack of apparent warmth, an inability to be artistically creative, the absence of an elementary warning system modulated by incipient anxiety. On the second dimension I am somewhat introverted, but not extremely so. And what about P? Pretty near the average; I don't think I show too much of the paranoid, cold aggressiveness so characteristic of the high P scorer.

All this may be relevant to the quote at the beginning of this chapter. Introverts tend to be thinkers, extraverts doers. I have certainly been more of an observer than an actor. My inclination indubitably lies that way; perhaps that is the reason why I have never joined a political party, or engaged much in the political game. How about that other adage: 'Life is a comedy for those who think, and a tragedy for those who feel'? I think I do regard much of what happens as a comedy, and indeed without a robust sense of humour life would sometimes have seemed unbearable. But I cannot forget the savagery of the Hitler and Stalin regimes, the inhumanity of man to man (and particularly woman), and the general spectacle of nature red in tooth and claw. As a 'pure' thinker, I will never come up to the toast of the great mathematician, T. Hardy, who said of some works he had published: 'May it never be of any use to anybody!' I like to feel that much of what I have done may be of use to mankind in its eternal struggle against fate, against nature, against itself.

And how about the style? Was Buffon right when he said: *'Le style c'est l'homme même'*? I actually prefer Pascal's remarks: *'Quand on voit le style naturel, on est tout étonné et ravi, car on s'attendait de voir un auteur, et on trouve un homme.'* (When we come across a natural style, we are both astonished and delighted, for we expect to find an author, and we find a man.) I think I have a natural style, and I believe it is in line with my personality – clear, incisive, sardonic, factual, not given to meretricious sesquipedalianism, eminently suitable for scientific description, but not for literary excursions or philosophical confrontations. I like to think that a sense of humour is present in my writings – not in the form of jokes, but emerging from the very substance of the subject matter.

I once entitled a section of a paper on mental ability: 'Is intelligence?' avoiding the custom-ridden: 'Does intelligence exist?' The editor objected on what he said were grounds of syntax, and demanded the customary form of words. He did not realize, or didn't know that 'is' is an intransitive verb; he would no doubt have asked Shakespeare: 'To be or not to be what? You can't just say to be or not to be! You've got to be *something*.' Journal editors and the scientific societies that appoint them are getting more and more dictatorial, and the style and elegance of scientific writing worse and worse. My own views as editor are very simple – the writer, not I, is responsible for his article, and must be left to write it in his own way (unless he makes definite mistakes, leaves out important information, or violates important rules of grammar).

There are dangers in writing in a satirical, ironic or outright humorous vein – Sybil keeps warning me that many people will take everything seriously, however humorous the intention, and history has proved her right. I have found that my slightly ironic style infuriates politicians, psychoanalysts and philosophers more than outright, dead serious attacks – there is a suggestion that I do not take them seriously enough. I would take very seriously things said by a coalminer, or a taxi-driver, or even a prostitute – they live in the real world, and know what is happening to them. But treat as serious thinkers our politicians, psychoanalysts and philosophers, let alone most of our sociologists – the mind boggles. Grand generalizations far removed from fact, experiment or direct experience only serve to mislead the unwary, and to inflate the ego of the perpetrator. As Hume said: 'If we take in our hand any volume, let us ask, Does it contain any abstract reasoning concerning quantity or number? No! Does it contain any experimental reasoning concerning matter of fact and existence? No. Commit it to the flames; for it can contain nothing but sophistry and illusion.'

My feelings about modern art, particularly painting and sculpture, are not very different. I recall a visit to the Museum of Modern Art in New York (or was it the Guggenheim?) when I saw the prize exhibit on the ground floor. Placed on a pedestal, covered in glass, was this work of art: a toilet roll! My immediate reaction was that either the 'artist' was taking the Mickey, or else he was using the occasion to pass judgement on some forms of modern art – a lot of crap! Then I became aware of the opportunities this opened up for someone like myself. I too could become a famous artist! I thought of all the wonderful things I could put on a pedestal like that: a tube of toothpaste, or an old slipper, or a pair of knickers – there was no end to my genius. Alas, I had been anticipated in most of my bright ideas – what, then, about a stinking old sock, or a used condom, or soiled diapers? All had in fact been used in exhibitions of modern art in London; indeed, nothing filthy, disgusting, foul, loathsome, nauseous, offensive, revolting, vile, squalid, feculent, or obscene seems to have escaped the attention of those modern 'artists', hyped by critics and agents incapable of telling art from fraud.

Do all the different aspects of my personality hang together more or less harmoniously? Stendhal, my favourite writer, once said: 'I am nearly always mistaken when I think that a man has only a single character.' Genes pull us one way, environment another; we can discern the major directions, but it is hard to predict or explain each detail. No one is more aware of these limitations than the psychologist. My life might have been very different had I stayed in Germany, had I studied physics rather than psychology, had I gone to the USA rather than the UK, had I married someone other than Sybil – the list is endless.

What is clear is that it would be difficult to find much in the way of environmental determination in my life history; genetics occupies a much more important place. For intelligence and special abilities that goes without saying; interactions with my parents, supposedly aiding the growing child to acquire linguistic proficiency and other mental advantages, were largely absent for all practical purposes, and had little place in my relations with my grandmother who brought me up. In personality, those traits that may be thought to be characteristic of me – independence, dominance, non-conformism, emotional stability, assertiveness, rebelliousness, risk-taking, ego control, and (perhaps?) bloody-mindedness – are not those likely to be fostered in a child growing up virtually without parents, and in a fairly hostile environment. Sadly this is all psychology can say with respect to personality, intelligence and motivation – perhaps Allport was right after all when he said that writing my autobiography would teach me how little nomothetic personality study had to contribute!

One environmental factor may have been important, however. As an exile I ceased to identify with German culture, and became a true European, with firm roots in English and French culture as well as German. Indeed, through my work as Visiting Professor in the USA first in Philadelphia and then at Berkeley, and my numerous lecture tours to the States (to say nothing of my daughter's work for the World Bank in Washington, and my countless visits to her) I also became well acquainted with American history and culture, so that I feel at home in all four cultures, without feeling attached particularly to any one of them.

There is of course, as always, a negative as well as a positive side. He who has four mother countries has none; being fluent in three languages I had no true 'mother tongue'. We all long to have 'a local habitation and a name'; having more than one means we do not have a special one to call our own. To the English I will never be English; to the Germans I will never be German. In France and the USA I will always be a foreigner. Do I feel German, or English, or what? The answer is that I feel what I am: an exile with no true home. If I feel at home anywhere it is in London, having lived there for fifty-five years or more, but I do not feel a native – obviously because I am not. But neither do I have such a feeling in Berlin, although I was born there – too much has happened there to let me forget the Hitler years.

Language, too, is a problem. I have forgotten some of my native German, although I still speak it without an accent – many of the words are missing, particularly psychological and statistical terms. Thirty years of disuse have left their mark; during and after the war I refused to speak German, or visit Germany; memories were still too potent. It is only relatively recently that I have tried to get on speaking terms with the new generation and I am glad to say that I can again feel at home there when I pay my regular visits to Heidelberg to see Grossarth-Maticek, or give lectures in Munich, Hamburg, Berlin, or wherever. One cannot hate a whole country, and the sins of Hitler should not be visited on the innocent descendants of those who once supported him.

Einstein, too, fell between several stools as far as nationality is concerned, being born in Ulm (Germany), having worked during his genius period in Zurich (Switzerland) and Berlin (Germany), finishing his life in Princeton (USA). When asked what his true background was, he said: 'If I am right, the Germans will say I was German, the Swiss will say I was Swiss, and the French will say I was Jewish. If I am wrong, the Germans will say I was Jewish, the Swiss will say I was German, and the French will say I was Swiss.'

Do I have any regrets? I would like to answer with Edith Piaf's song: 'Non – je ne regrette rien!' But it would not be true. I dearly wish I had learned to put two fingers in my mouth and produce the shrill whistle that seems to come so effortlessly to the fans at Manchester United football games. I wish I had had brothers and sisters, and perhaps even a pair of loving parents; if I had, perhaps I would have been a nicer person! I would have liked to have developed an aggressive backhand at tennis – it was beginning to come when I left Germany. I still sometimes wish I could have gone into physics or astronomy; I find the recent developments in the hard sciences fascinating. And there is the scissors kick in soccer I never really mastered. But for someone who has been so lucky for so long, it would seem downright ungrateful to wish for more, and on the whole I really cannot complain. As they say in German: *'Denn wie man sich bettet so liegt man; s'deckt einen ja doch keiner zu!'* (As you go to bed, so you will lie; nobody is going to pull the covers over you!)

'How have you managed to write so much, and to become so influential a figure?' is a question I am often asked. Burt and others have pointed out that success in science, in art and in business depends in a multiplicative fashion on several factors, including intelligence, motivation, special abilities, persistence, personality, health, and so on. None by itself is sufficient; if even one is completely missing, the product is zero. I was blessed with a high IQ, strong scientific motivation, considerable persistence, good health, a stable, introverted personality which history has shown to be best fitted for scientific research, and special abilities of fast reading and writing which proved extremely important. I organized my life around research, putting almost everything else aside; this you must do if you want to get anywhere. The same is true in sport, in making money, or anything else; you must make sacrifices in order to get to the top in anything. I would like to have the time to go to more concerts and operas, to visit the theatre more frequently, to see more paintings and sculptures, read more books outside psychology, to play more tennis and squash, and to do a thousand and one things which make life pleasant. But science is a stern task master; you devote your life to it, or you will forever remain an amateur, perhaps gifted, but in the end ineffective.

I do not look upon all this as a sacrifice. My work has given me so much fun, so many rewards, such pleasure, that I would not hesitate to give up all these other things again had I to make the same choice once more. I often feel like a very ordinary person – perhaps with some gift for sport – into whose brain some celestial being has put a powerful computer. The computer does all the difficult work; my role is to furnish it with material – through extensive reading, data searches, experiments, listening to speakers at conferences, and talking things over with fellow-scientists.

It has often been suggested that there must be an awful lot of hard work at the back of such a large number of books and articles; this is only partly true. I usually start work around 8.30 a.m., having walked to my office from home through the beautiful Ruskin Park. I have coffee around 10.30, play tennis or squash for an hour or two at lunchtime (instead of eating lunch), return to work and finish around 4.00. This is not a 'hard day's work', particularly as Saturday and Sunday are free! It makes something like thirty hours' work a week – even though it is very concentrated work. I can dictate a 9,000-word article in a five-hour day, needing little if any corrections or amplification when typed. This needs total concentration; it also needs careful thinking out ahead of time. Much of my leisure time so-called is in fact occupied with thinking about work – articles and books are written in my mind long before I start dictation. For me the distinction between work and leisure is less clear than one might think – consciously and sub-consciously, the mind is always active, churning away madly, simmering like a witch's cauldron. Concentration on this internal activity is sometimes so intense that I fail to see and greet friends I meet in the street; no wonder professors have the reputation of being absent-minded!

Whatever I may be doing, the mind is bubbling away sub-consciously, trying to solve one or other of the problems thrown up by the research I am doing, or the writing I am busy with. I usually have the facts and figures in my head, so thinking can proceed unaided and unhindered. Occasionally an answer to a problem will burst into consciousness, making me aware of the fact that I was really thinking about it all the time. Such sub-conscious problem-solving takes its toll – when it is going on, my tennis is thirty per cent less effective than usual. I have come to rely on this process; I feel certain that whatever the problem, a solution will be generated in due time. Whether it is the right solution only time can tell – even wrong solutions can look very appetizing.

How do I write my articles and books? At first I used to type everything myself, not having a secretary. Then I took to dictating, at first to a secretary, then to a dictaphone. Of course you must have the ability to remember exactly what you have said already, what the general outline of your article or chapter may be, and where you are going – given that, the rest is easy. Or so it seems to me – I hate writing, or even typing – I can't keep up with my thinking, get impatient, and my writing becomes even more illegible, and my typing even more full of typos!

Speed of thinking, reading and writing also has another, less welcome side. Having finished something – an article, a book, a theory – I want to get on to something else, without carefully going over things again and again, making painstaking corrections, reading proofs conscientiously, and generally making sure that everything is ship-shape and Bristol fashion. Critics have sometimes complained about misprints, typos and other errors, and I must confess that as far as proof-reading is concerned I am just hopeless – I get caught up on the meaning, and forget the spelling! Sybil, on the other hand, is almost infallible in that respect; many contributors to *Personality and Individual Differences* have her to thank for innumerable corrections to their manuscripts, their bibliographies, and their presentation. Sybil of course is an extravert, and theoretically should be worse than an introvert like myself at such a task requiring constant detailed attention. Probably it is a question more of impulsivity, which is greater in people high on psychoticism, and Sybil is extremely low on that. What does that say about myself? Perish the thought!

Another aspect of my work is that it covers many diverse fields. I try to keep up with research and literature in many different areas, and while that was fairly easy thirty or even twenty years ago, it is now becoming impossible, due to a veritable flood of publications which is threatening to submerge us all. Even going through several journals and books a day does not enable me to keep really up-to-date in more than one or two areas. I try to compensate by working with experts in their various areas – people like Lindon Eaves and Nick Martin in genetics, Irene Martin in conditioning, Glenn Wilson in social attitudes, Jack Rachman in behaviour therapy, Ronald Grossarth-Maticek in the cancer and CHD field, the Hendricksons and Paul Barrett in the psychophysiology of intelligence and personality, David Nias on television and astrology, Gisli Gudjonsson on criminality, Sybil on personality, and so on. That method is working quite well, but whether it will continue to do so only the future will tell! In physics we now have papers written by over 150 collaborators; perhaps psychology is heading that way too. I hope not; ideas seldom originate in a whole committee, however high-powered. But as regards the 'Jack-of-all trades' method of working, I have no regrets. All these areas are related to some extent, and I have found interesting connections between all of them.

Did all this work achieve anything in the long run? Most of the things I have been identified with would no doubt have come about anyway, although perhaps a little later, and in a slightly different form. Psycho-analysis was obviously on the slide, incapable of fulfilling its promises; it would have sunk even without my feeble efforts to speed it on its way. The genetics of intelligence had already been firmly established in 1941, but the genetics of personality I think might not have been recognized so soon without my efforts.

The theory of personality I have advocated, with its firm biological basis, is perhaps my most personal achievement; some recognition of the physiological and hormonal basis of individual differences would presumably have occurred anyway, but not perhaps in this precise form, and not so soon. My theory of social attitudes and politics in general falls probably into the same general format, although its time may only now be coming.

Behaviour therapy, too, would undoubtedly have made its mark without me, but probably a good deal later. Just suppose that my predecessor at the Mill Hill Emergency Hospital, Eric Trist, had stayed on, and had been asked by Aubrey Lewis to get a profession of clinical psychology started in England! As a convinced psychoanalyst, he would have started it off on Freudian lines, and it would have taken generations to bring it back on to the right track. Even in the USA it might have taken much longer to establish behaviour therapy in the absence of the Maudsley example.

These are just subjective impressions, and they may be quite wrong. As I was a 'premature anti-Nazi' so I was premature in all these things, anticipating historical changes rather than causing them. But then historical changes are not pre-ordained; they come about because some people go out of their way to prepare them and see them on their way. These are questions and problems which historians have argued over endlessly, and without coming to any firm conclusion; I do not flatter myself that I am in any way nearer a solution.

I have mentioned the sacrifices one has to make if one wishes to pursue a successful scientific career, sacrifices which include relative poverty. But compared with the satisfaction to be derived from a good job well done, monetary rewards fade into nothingness. If someone offered me 100 million pounds to stop research, I wouldn't even have to think about it – work is more important than money any day.

And of course there are other satisfactions to be derived from a career in science. The first is meeting many friends who are working on the same problems, and become one's allies in the battle against nature's attempt to keep her secrets. There are all the wonderful places one is enabled to visit in the course of scientific congresses, or invited lectures, from Kyoto to the Isle of Capri, from San Francisco to Oslo, from Fez in Morocco to Cape Town, from Caracas to Buenos Aires, from Acapulco to Sydney, from Athens to Jamaica, from Syracuse to Hong Kong. The combination of far-away places and good scientific discussion is irresistible, and provides some of the high points of my life.

Have I, in writing this autobiography, over-emphasized my work, and said too little about myself? I have tended to follow George Eliot, when she said: 'It seems to me that just my works and the order in which they have appeared is what the part of the public which cares about me may most carefully know.' But of course that is a little too drastic; a list of my publications would not do instead of the eight chapters I have written. Havelock Ellis said that 'every artist writes his own autobiography', meaning that his artistic creations are a clue to his nature. For scientists this is less obviously true, and hence I had to say a little more about myself – not too little, not too much, I hope, but every reader will have his own opinion on that. After all, as Chesterton said: 'Our wisdom, whether expressed in private or public, belongs to the world, but our folly belongs to those we love.'

On the whole, looking back on my life, I think the account is in the black – more happiness, success and satisfaction than otherwise. Indeed, it is difficult to feel that it is all nearly over. Occasionally it has been brought home to me that my feeling of eternal youth is not shared by others; on several occasions recently I was told in so many words that I was regarded as 'part of history' rather than as an active participant!

Such an evaluation, however complimentary the intent, is rather upsetting. It seems so little time ago that I set out on my career in psychology, carried out my first experiment, wrote my first article and book – can it really be fifty years ago?

I have always been a fighter so I shall fight as hard as I can to stay in the race, continue my research, and try to resolve some of the problems that remain in my particular fields – personality, intelligence, behaviour therapy, smoking and disease, politics and social attitudes, and perhaps, if fate is kind, experimental aesthetics, the love of my life fifty years ago! This may be the end of my autobiography, but not, I hope and trust, of my scientific career – there is still a lot more to come!

Robert Browning said: 'Ah, but a man's reach should exceed his grasp, Or what's a heaven for?' I cannot speak for heaven, but anyone evaluating my work would have to say that I have lived up to Browning's injunction; my reach has certainly exceeded my grasp. I can only hope that my successors will be more successful in reaching for what we all want, and society needs more than anything else – a truly scientific psychology to deal properly with all the social evils that threaten us.

And now? I shall follow the advice of W. B. Yeats:

> Do not go gently into that good night,
> Old age should burn and rave at close of day;
> Rage, rage against the dying of the light . . .

Well, raging isn't really my scene, but I will do my best.

Currently listed members of British Psychology Departments with 60 or more citations in the 1985 Social Sciences Citation Index.

Psychologist	University	Citations
H. J. Eysenck	London, BPMF*	813
J. A. Gray	London, BPMF	251
D. Broadbent	London, MRC**	238
Elizabeth K. Warrington	London, BPMF	180
N. J. Mackintosh	Cambridge	176
J. M. Argyle	Oxford	170
M. Coltheart	London: Birkbeck College	164
P. B. Warr	Sheffield	120
D. A. Booth	Birmingham	101
M. R. Trimble	London, BPMF	97
J. Sandler	London: University College	97
Sybil B. G. Eysenck	London, BPMF	91
M. W. Eysenck	London: Birkbeck College	90
T. G. R. Bower	Edinburgh	85
O. J. Braddick	Cambridge	83
S. J. Cooper	Birmingham	82
D. N. Lee	Edinburgh	84
G. D. Wilson	London, BPMF	84
C. B. Trevarthan	Edinburgh	73
H. Giles	Bristol	70
H. R. Schaffer	Strathclyde	67
P. H. Venables	York	68
T. W. Robbins	Cambridge	69
L. Weiskranz	Oxford	64
A. F. Furnham	London: University College	62
E. T. Rolls	Oxford	61
W. Yule	London, BPMF	60

* British Postgraduate Medical Federation is part of the University of London; it contains institutes of various medical specialities associated with appropriate hospitals in these fields.

** Medical Research Council.

GLOSSARY OF TECHNICAL TERMS

Behaviourism:
A doctrine stating that as we can only observe behaviour in humans and animals, psychologists should concentrate on the analysis and explanation of behaviour. Introspection is often frowned upon, and even physiological explanations are not usually welcomed by fundamentalist behaviourists.

Behavioural genetics:
The study of heredity as far as it is involved in human and animal behaviour – e.g., intelligence, personality, criminality, etc.

Behaviour therapy:
A method of treating neurotic disorders by changing behaviour, and through it mental attitudes, rather than attempting, as psychoanalysis tries to do (unsuccessfully!) to cure neurotics by going back to early childhood events in the family. Cognitive behaviour therapy emphasizes rather more the cognitive elements always involved in behaviour therapy.

Biosocial:
Human behaviour is influenced by *both* biological factors (hunger, thirst, sex, etc.) and by social ones (laws, customs, etc.), and hence man is a biosocial animal.

Categorical classification:
Mental disorders are often diagnosed as if unitary diseases existed in this field – like hysteria, phobia, schizophrenia, etc. Unfortunately disease concepts are inappropriate in the mental field, and clear cases are the exception rather than the rule. A dimensional approach gives a much better picture of reality – i.e., a patient has such and such a score on a variety of personality dimensions, producing a unique profile.

Citation Index:
A listing of the number of times a given author has been quoted by other scientists in one of the major scientific journals, and by whom. Also listed are the occasions when a particular *journal* is quoted.

Client-centred therapy:
A special type of psychotherapy, introduced by Carl Rogers. Like most others, it does not work.

Clinical Psychology:
The application of psychological knowledge to psychiatric disorders, by way of diagnosis and treatment.

Correlations:
Correlation coefficients estimate the degree to which two traits, tests, or abilities are related in a given population. On a scale from 1.00 (perfect agreement) through 0.00 (complete lack of agreement) to 1.00 (complete disagreement) most IQ tests correlate around .60 to .80.

Cortical arousal:
A state of the brain in which the individual is highly alert, usually measured in terms of special EEG patterns (fast frequency, low amplitude of brainwaves).

Criterion analysis:
Special statistical technique to ascertain whether two groups (say schizophrenics and neurotics) differ categorically (i.e., suffer from different mental 'diseases'), or whether they merely differ along certain continua.

Dimensionality:
People differ in intelligence, personality, etc.; it is the task of psychology to ascertain the number of *dimensions* along which the differences could be measured. The usual method involved is factor analysis.

Epidemiology:
The study of the distribution of diseases, either by locality, or by personality characteristics and habits. Thus we may look at a regional map of cancer distribution, or look at the incidence of cancer in smokers and non-smokers, drinkers and non-drinkers, etc.

Factor analysis:
Factor analysis is a statistical technique to reduce a large number of correlations to a few factors which are indicative of the number of dimensions involved, and of their nature.

Group factors:
Factor analysis of mental tests usually results in one large 'intelligence' factor, and a number of group factors involving special abilities – e.g., verbal, numerical, spatial, memory, etc.

Neurosis:
Neurosis is a term applied to minor mental disorders involving anxiety, depression, and phobic fears. It is not very precisely defined, and does not constitute a 'categorical' but a 'dimensional' concept.

Physiology:
Physiology is the scientific discipline concerned with the physical properties of the various systems of the body – i.e., the central nervous system, the autonomic nervous system, the hormonal system, the muscular system, etc.

Proband:
A person taking part in a psychological, psychiatric or physiological experiment.

Projective test:
A projective test is based on the (largely erroneous) hypothesis that when faced with some unstructured stimulus (like an ink blot in the Rorschach test) the subject will *project* his own needs, wishes and complexes into the stimulus, and that the expert can deduce from the reply what motivated the subject. Unfortunately the evidence is clear that the 'expert' can't do anything of the kind.

Psychoanalysis:
Psychoanalysis is a theory about mental activity and mental disease which tried to explain human behaviour. It failed completely to live up to its major claim, namely, to be able to cure mental patients, and has now no scientific pretensions of any kind.

Psychology:
Psychology is the scientific study of human and animal behaviour.

Psychiatry:
Psychiatry is a medical speciality concerned with a wide variety of behaviour and mental disorders, ranging from neurosis to psychosis, from epilepsy to brain tumours. Psychiatrists have a medical training, but little by way of training in psychology. This can be a handicap when dealing with psychological disorders.

Psychometrics:
The application of statistical concepts and methods to solve psychological and sociological problems.

[287]

Psychosis:
This is an ill-understood term covering mainly the more serious mental disorders like schizophrenia and manic-depressive illness. Unlike neurotic disorders, psychotic disorders are probably due to physical causes, and best treated by drugs.

Psychotherapy:
This is a much abused and almost meaningless term referring to a wide range of methods used to treat neurotic and (sometimes) psychotic disorders. Methods used include psychoanalysis, hypnosis, suggestion, advice, religious confession, and almost anything you like to think of.

Psychophysiology:
The application of physiological concepts and methods to the study of psychological problems.

Relaxation treatment:
This involves the use of special exercises teaching patients to relax their musculature totally. Such relaxation is antagonistic to anxiety, and very useful in combating it.

Research:
See 'Projective tests'.

Social Psychology:
The application of psychological concepts and methods to social problems, like racial prejudice, criminality, or aggression. Social psychology is academically adjacent to Sociology, but has a much more scientific (rather than political) background.

Synergistic:
Different causal factors may be additive, but they may also multiply in their effects. Such multiplication, or mutual support and interaction, is called 'synergistic'.

TITLES IN THE INTERNATIONAL SERIES OF MONOGRAPHS IN EXPERIMENTAL PSYCHOLOGY

edited by the author (see page 150)

18. Claridge: *Personality Differences and Biological Variations: A Study of Twins*

19. Frank: *Psychiatric Diagnosis: A Review of Research*

20. Dutta & Kanungo: *Affect and Memory: A Reformulation*

BIBLIOGRAPHY

H. J. Eysenck

Many of my books are referred to in the body of this autobiography, and it seemed useful to provide readers with a list of them all. This is preceded by a diagram showing productivity over the years, with each article or book chapter counting one point, and each book ten points. The cumulative frequency is fairly linear after the first ten years, and seems to continue unabashed!

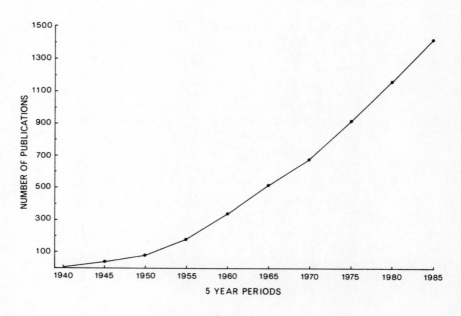

1.	1947	DIMENSIONS OF PERSONALITY	London: Routledge & Kegan Paul.
2.	1952	THE SCIENTIFIC STUDY OF PERSONALITY	London: Routledge & Kegan Paul.
3.	1952	THE STRUCTURE OF HUMAN PERSONALITY	London: Methuen. (1st Edition)
4.	1953	USES AND ABUSES OF PSYCHOLOGY	London: Penguin Books.
5.	1954	THE PSYCHOLOGY OF POLITICS	London: Routledge & Kegan Paul.
6.	1955	PSYCHOLOGY AND THE FOUNDATIONS OF PSYCHIATRY	London: H. K. Lewis.
7.	1956	SENSE AND NONSENSE IN PSYCHOLOGY	London: Penguin Books.
8.	1957	THE DYNAMICS OF ANXIETY AND HYSTERIA	London: Routledge & Kegan Paul.
9.	1957	PERCEPTUAL PROCESSES AND MENTAL ILLNESS (With Granger, G. & Brengelmann, J. C.)	London: Chapman & Hall. Maudsley Monograph.
10.	1959	MANUAL OF THE MAUDSLEY PERSONALITY INVENTORY	London: University of London Press.
11.	1960	(Ed.) HANDBOOK OF ABNORMAL PSYCHOLOGY	London: Pitman Books. (1st Edition)

12.	1960	(Ed.) EXPERIMENTS IN PERSONALITY (2 Vols.)	London: Routledge & Kegan Paul.
13.	1960	(Ed.) BEHAVIOUR THERAPY AND THE NEUROSES	Oxford: Pergamon Press.
14.	1960	THE STRUCTURE OF HUMAN PERSONALITY	London: Methuen. (2nd Edition)
15.	1962	KNOW YOUR OWN IQ	London: Penguin Books.
16.	1963	(Ed.) EXPERIMENTS WITH DRUGS	Oxford: Pergamon Press.
17.	1964	(Ed.) EXPERIMENTS IN MOTIVATION	Oxford: Pergamon Press.
18.	1964	(ED.) EXPERIMENTS IN BEHAVIOUR THERAPY	Oxford: Pergamon Press.
19.	1964	CRIME AND PERSONALITY (1st Edition)	London: Routledge & Kegan Paul. New York: Houghton Mifflin.
20.	1964	MANUAL OF THE EYSENCK PERSONALITY INVENTORY (with Eysenck, S. B. G.)	London: University of London Press.
21.	1965	THE CAUSES AND CURES OF NEUROSIS (with Rachman, S.)	London: Routledge & Kegan Paul. San Diego: R. R. Knapp, Educational and Industrial Training Service.
22.	1965	FACT AND FICTION IN PSYCHOLOGY	London: Penguin Books.
23.	1965	SMOKING, HEALTH AND PERSONALITY	London: Weidenfeld & Nicolson.
24.	1966	CHECK YOUR OWN IQ	London: Penguin Books.

25.	1966	THE EFFECTS OF PSYCHOTHERAPY	New York: International Science Press.
26.	1967	THE BIOLOGICAL BASIS OF PERSONALITY	Springfield: C. C. Thomas.
27.	1969	PERSONALITY STRUCTURE AND MEASUREMENT (with Eysenck, S. B. G.)	London: Routledge & Kegan Paul. San Diego: R. R. Knapps, EDITS.
28.	1970	THE STRUCTURE OF HUMAN PERSONALITY	London: Methuen. (3rd Edition)
29.	1971	READINGS IN EXTRAVERSION/ INTROVERSION (3 Vols.)	London: Staples Press.
30.	1971	RACE, INTELLIGENCE AND EDUCATION (Entitled in America: THE IQ ARGUMENT)	London: Maurice Temple Smith. New York: The Library Press.
31.	1972	PSYCHOLOGY IS ABOUT PEOPLE	London: Penguin Books.
32.	1972	(Ed.) LEXICON DE PSYCHOLOGIE (with Arnold, W. & Meili, R.) 3 Vols., in English	Freiburg: Verlag Herder.
33.	1973	(Ed.) HANDBOOK OF ABNORMAL PSYCHOLOGY	London: Pitman Books. (2nd Edition)
34.	1973	THE INEQUALITY OF MAN	London: Maurice Temple Smith.
35.	1973	(Ed.) EYSENCK ON EXTRAVERSION	London: Granada Publications.
36.	1973	(Ed.) THE MEASUREMENT OF INTELLIGENCE	Lancaster: Medical & Technical Publishers.

37.	1973	THE EXPERIMENTAL STUDY OF FREUDIAN THEORIES (with Wilson, G. D.)	London: Methuen.
38.	1974	(Ed.) CASE HISTORIES IN BEHAVIOUR THERAPY	London: Routledge & Kegan Paul.
39.	1975	KNOW YOUR OWN PERSONALITY (with Wilson, G. D.)	London: Maurice Temple Smith.
40.	1975	MANUAL OF THE EYSENCK PERSONALITY QUESTIONNAIRE (with Eysenck, S. B. G.)	London: Hodder & Stoughton.
41.	1976	A TEXTBOOK OF HUMAN PSYCHOLOGY (with Wilson, G. D.)	London: Medical and Technical Publishers. Baltimore: University Park Press.
42.	1976	SEX AND PERSONALITY	London: Open Books.
43.	1976	(Ed.) THE MEASUREMENT OF PERSONALITY	Lancaster: Medical and Technical Publishers.
44.	1976	PSYCHOTICISM AS A DIMENSION OF PERSONALITY (with Eysenck, S. B. G.)	London: Hodder & Stoughton. New York: Crane, Russak & Co.
45.	1977	REMINISCENCE, MOTIVATION AND PERSONALITY (with Frith, C. D.)	New York: Plenum Publishing Corporation.
46.	1977	YOU AND NEUROSIS	London: Maurice Temple Smith.
47.	1977	DIE ZUKUNFT DER PSYCHOLOGIE	Munchen: Paul List Verlag

[295]

48.	1977	CRIME AND PERSONALITY (2nd Edition)	London: Routledge & Kegan Paul. New York: Houghton Mifflin.
49.	1978	(Ed.) THE PSYCHOLOGICAL BASIS OF IDEOLOGY (with Wilson, G. D.)	Lancaster: MTP. Baltimore: University Park Press.
50.	1978	SEX VIOLENCE AND THE MEDIA (with Nias, D.)	London: Maurice Temple Smith. New York: St. Martin's Press.
51.	1979	THE STRUCTURE AND MEASUREMENT OF INTELLIGENCE	New York: Springer Verlag.
52.	1979	THE PSYCHOLOGY OF SEX (with Wilson, G. D.)	London: Dent.
53.	1980	THE CAUSES AND EFFECTS OF SMOKING	London: Maurice Temple Smith.
54.	1981	(Ed.) A MODEL FOR PERSONALITY	New York: Springer Verlag.
55.	1981	MINDWATCHING (with Eysenck, M. W.)	London: Michael Joseph.
56.	1981	THE BATTLE FOR THE MIND (with Kamin, L. J.) (American title: THE INTELLIGENCE CONTROVERSY)	London: Macmillan. Paperback – Pan Books. New York: John Wiley.
57.	1982	PERSONALITY, GENETICS AND BEHAVIOUR	New York: Praeger.
58.	1982	EXPLAINING THE UNEXPLAINED (Mysteries of the Paranormal) (with Sargent, Carl)	London: Weidenfeld & Nicolson.

59.	1982	ASTROLOGY – Science or Superstition? (with Nias, D.)	London: Maurice Temple Smith.
60.	1982	(Ed.) A MODEL FOR INTELLIGENCE	New York: Springer Verlag.
61.	1983	KNOW YOUR OWN PSI-Q. (with Sargent, Carl)	London: Multimedia Publications.
62.	1983	. . . 'I DO'. YOUR GUIDE TO A HAPPY MARRIAGE (with Kelly, B. N.)	London: Multimedia Publications.
63.	1985	PERSONALITY AND INDIVIDUAL DIFFERENCES: A NATURAL SCIENCE APPROACH (with Eysenck, M. W.)	New York: Plenum Press.
64.	1985	DECLINE AND FALL OF THE FREUDIAN EMPIRE	London: Viking.
65.	1987	RAUCHEN UND GESUNDHEIT	Dusseldorf: Walter Rau Verlag.
66.	1987	PERSONALITY DIMENSIONS AND AROUSAL (edited with Strelau, J.)	New York: Plenum Press.
67.	1988	THEORETICAL FOUNDATIONS OF BEHAVIOUR THERAPY (edited with Martin, I.)	New York: Plenum Press.
68.	1989	THE CAUSES AND CURES OF CRIMINALITY (with Gudjonsson, G. H.)	New York: Plenum Press.

69.	1989	GENES, CULTURE AND PERSONALITY: AN EMPIRICAL APPROACH (with Eaves, L. and Martin, N.)	New York: Academic Press.
70.	1989	MINDWATCHING (with Eysenck, M. W.)	London: Prion/ Multimedia. (2nd Edition)
71.	1989	SUGGESTION AND SUGGESTIBILITY (edited with Gheorghiu, V. A., Netter, P., and Rosenthal, R.	New York: Springer Verlag.

INDEX

Other than in the main entry under his name, the author is referred to as 'E' throughout the index

Index

Gray, Jeffrey, 194, 202–3, 262
Grossarth-Maticek, Ronald, 173,
 175–8, 181, 184, 281
Grundgens, 30
Guardian newspaper, 192–3
Gudjonsson, Gisli, 272, 281
Guilford, J. P., 47, 98, 124
Guthrie, E. R., 153
Guttman, Harry, 90

Haldane, J. B. S., 54
Hallam, R., 267
Halstead, H., 99
Hammon, E. C., 170
*Hans Eysenck: Consensus and
 Controversy* (Barbrack *et al*), 159
Harlow, H. F., 202
Hasenclever, E., 40
Hausmann, Hans, 48, 78
Hayek, F. A., 85
Hearnshaw, L. S. (*Cyril Burt,
 Psychologist*), 116
Hebb, Donald, 128, 230
Heidegger, M,. 3, 123
Heidelberg, Germany, 178–9, 180
Heine, Heinrich, 258
Hemsley, D., 262
Hendrickson, Alan *and* Elaine,
 214–15, 262, 281
Herbert, M., 261
heredity. *See also* genetics; and
 assortive mating, 87; as attitude
 determinant, 87; environment
 debate, 114; foundation of
 personality, 199–200; and
 intelligence, 191
Heron, A., 261
Herrnstein, R., 219, 266
Herzberg, Alexander, 132–6, 139
Heymans, G., 98
Himmelweit, Hilde, 100, 101, 109,
 112, 141, 259, 262
Heindenberg, Paul von, 36
Hitler, Adolf. *See also* Germany
 aggression, 58, 79; British failure to
 challenge, 46, 58; Chancellor, 39;
 Hitlermädchen, 36; Nazi party, 12,

13, 21, 26, 32, 50–51; opposition to,
 37; on psychology of politics, 85;
 rise of, 17, 32, 36–7, 38, 40
Hobbes, Thomas, 77
Hodgson, R., 262
Holland, H., 262
Hopkins, Pryns, 84, 133
Houdini (magician), 235
Hull, C., 150, 153
Humanist (periodical), 238
humour, 77–8
Humphrey, J., 261
Huxley, Sir Julian, 76, 164
hypnosis, 54, 233–4

Ilsemarie (childhood sweetheart), 14,
 21–2, 35–6, 37
incubation theory of fear/anxiety, 150
individual differences, 194–8; causes
 of, 195–6; model of, 194
Inglis, Brian, 139; *Science and
 Parascience*), 235
Inglis, Jimmy, 151, 154
Institute of Psychiatry, 87, 89. *See also*
 Maudsley Hospital; citations, 232;
 E's readership, 106; history and
 function, 107–9
intelligence. *See also* Burt, Sir Cyril;
 genetics; heredity; IQ tests;
 concept of, 207, 209; defined,
 207–9; E's work on, 101; gains in,
 211, 222, 272; measurement of
 212–15; mental speed, 212–15; and
 race, 215–17; regression to mean,
 222–3; and personality, 191
International Journal of Psychiatry, 113
International Society for the Study of
 Individual Differences (ISSID), 230
IQ Controversy (Snyderman *and*
 Rothman), 219–20, 266–8
IQ tests; Burt's methods, 116;
 invented, 206; marketing of, 166–7;
 motivation as factor, 102; other
 tests, 55: Binet, 67, 93; Raven's
 matrices, 92, 101; Thurstone, 95;
 theory of, 53, 70
Israel, M., 261